FOOD PROCESSING TECHNOLOGY
Principles and Practice

D1340335

FOOD PROCESSING TECHNOLOGY
Principles and Practice

P. FELLOWS
Department Catering Management, Oxford Polytechnic

ELLIS HORWOOD
NEW YORK   LONDON   TORONTO   SYDNEY   TOKYO   SINGAPORE

First published in 1988
Reprinted and issued in paperback
for the first time in 1990
Reprinted in 1992 and 1993 by
Ellis Horwood Limited
Market Cross House, Cooper Street
Chichester
West Sussex, PO19 1EB
A division of
Simon & Schuster International Group

Printed and bound in Great Britain by
Hartnolls, Bodmin

Library of Congress Cataloging-in-Publication Data

Available from the publisher

British Library Cataloguing in Publication Data

A catalogue record for this book is available from the British Library

ISBN   0-13-596354-0   (pbk)

1 2 3 4 5   97 96 95 94 93

Table of contents

To Denise

Acknowledgements

Permission to use material from the following sources is gratefully acknowledged:

Table 1.1, Inst. of Food Technologists, from Szczesniak (1963), Fig. 1.6, Van Nostrand Rheinhold Inc, from Henderson and Perry (1955), Table 1.8, CSIRO, from Kelford (1982), Figs 1.11, 12.5, Marcel Dekker Inc, from Karel (1975), Table 2.1, Figs 5.5, 5.10, 12.4, Table 24.2, Elsevier Applied Science from Brennan *et al.* (1976), Figs 3.1, 3., 3.6, Academic Press, from Loncin and Merson (1979), Figs 3.4, 5.4, 5.8, 12.8, 19.2 from Kluwer Academic Publishers, from Leuger and Beverloo (1975), Fig. 4.2 American Inst. Chemical Engineers, from Rushton *et al.* (1950), Fig. 4.3 the Editor, Food Processing, from Smith (1985), Figs 4.5, 4.6, Table 4.2, Inst. Chemical Engineers, from McDonagh (1987), Figs 4.10, 15.5, AVI, from Matz (1972), Figs 5.2, 5.3, Table 5.1, Westfalia Separators AG, W. Germany, from Hemfort (1983) (1984), Fig. 5.9, Dr R. P. Vine, Mississippi State University, from Vine (1987), Table 6.1, Elsevier Applied Science, from Madsden (1974), Figs 6.1, 6.2, Elsevier Applied Science, from Michaels (1974), Fig. 6.6, Society of Dairy Technology, from Pepper and Orchard (1982), Table 6.2, Cambridge University press, from Glover (1971), Fig. 7.4, Blackwell Scientific Publ., from Dawes and Large (1982), Fig. 8.1, Inst. Food Science and Technology, from Robinson (1986), Fig. 8.2, Science Reviews Ltd, from Hughes (1982), Fig. 8.3, AVI, from Farrall (1976), Fig. 8.4, Inst. Food Science and Technology, from Gould (1986), Fig. 9.1, from the editor J. Food Process Preservation, from Timbers (1984), Science Aliments, from Phillipon (1984), Food Processing USA from Wendl *et al.* (1983), Fig. 10.1, AVI, from Harper (1976), Fig. 10.2, Society Dairy Technology, from Ford *et al.* (1969), Fig. 10.2, AlFA Laval Spa, Monza, Italy, from Chiozzotto (1984), Figs 11.2, 23.4, 23.5, Churchill Livingstone from Hersom and Hulland (1980), Tables 11.2, 11.3, 11.4, Academic Press, from Stumbo (1973), Fig. 11.7, the Editor, Food Europe (UK edition) from Killeit (1986), Table 11.6, Inst. Food Technologists, from Everson (1964), Table 12.1, Fig. 12.7, Elsevier Applied Science, from Mannheim and Passy (1974), Tables 13.1, 13.2, CRC Press, from Harper (1979), Fig. 14.8, Elsevier Applied Science, from Masters (1983), Fig. 17.2, Ellis Horwood/VCH, from Lewis (1987), Table 18.1, Elsevier Applied Science, from Alvarez and Thorne (1981), Fig. 18.2, US Dept. Agriculture, from Patchen (1971). Table 19.2, Food and Agricultural Organisation of the United Nations, from Graham (1984), Fig. 19.7, the Editor, Food Processing USA, from Merryman (1963), Fig. 19.8, Academic Press, from Jul (1984), Table 19.5, Pergamon Books Ltd, from Guadagni (1968), Fig. 19.2, Academic Press, from Fennema and Powrie (1964), Table 20.2, Academic Press, from Bellows and King (1972), Figs 20.3, 20.4, Mr J. Rolfgaard, Atlass Industries A/S, Denmark, from Rolfgaard (1987), Figs 20.6, 20.7, Elsevier Applied Science, from Kessler (1986), Figs 20.8, Table 20.4, Elsevier Applied Science, from Thijssen (1974), Figs 22.1, 23.10, Elsevier Applied Science, from Briston (1980), Figs 22.6, 22.9, 23.7, Mr J. Briston, from Briston (1987), Fig. 22.3, Elsevier Applied Science, from Malin (1980), Fig. 22.4, Elsevier Applied Science, from Osborne (1980), Fig. 22.5, Elsevier Applied Science, from Goddard (1986), Fig. 23.6 Food Trade Press, from Briston and Katan (1974), Fig. 23.11, the Editor, Food Processing, from Guise (1987B).

I am indebted to my colleagues within the Food Science and Nutrition Group of the School of Biological and Molecular Sciences for their forbearance during the preparation of this book, and in particular to Dr Jeya Henry for his helpful advice and comments.

Special thanks are due to my wife, Denise, not only for her constant support, encouragement and constructive criticisms, but also for her tolerance of the shifting mounds of paperwork for so many months.

P. J. Fellows

Symbols

A	Area
a	Thermal diffusivity
a_w	Water activity
B	Time to sterilise food (canning)
Bi	Biot number
b	Permeability
c	Concentration
C_d	Drag coefficient (fluid dynamics)
c	Specific heat capacity
c_p	Specific heat at constant pressure
D	Diameter (pipe, vessel)
D	Dilution rate (fermentation)
D	Decimal reduction time (heat processing)
d	Diameter (sphere, size of sieve aperture)
d	Differential operator
E	Electrical field strength
E	Energy required for size reduction
F	Feed flow rate (sorting, fermentation)
F	F-value (canning)
Fr	Froude number
f	Slope of heat penetration curve (canning)
f	Frequency (microwaves)
G	Air velocity (dehydration)
g	Acceleration due to gravity ($9.81 \mathrm{\,m\,s^{-2}}$)
g	Retort temperature minus product temperature (canning)
H	Humidity
h	Heat transfer coefficient
h_c	Convective heat transfer coefficient
h_s	Surface heat transfer coefficient
I	Light intensity

I_h	Retort temperature minus initial product temperature (canning)
J	Flux (membrane concentration)
j	Heating/cooling factor (canning)
K	Mass transfer coefficient (dehydration, membrane concentration)
K	Constant
K_k	Kick's constant (size reduction)
K_r	Rittinger's constant (size reduction)
K_s	Substrate utilisation constant (fermentation)
k	Thermal conductivity
L	Length
L	Equivalent thickness of filter cake
l	Come-up time (canning)
M	Moisture content, dry-weight basis
M	Molar concentration
m	Mass
m	Mass flow rate
m	Moisture content (wet-weight basis)
N	Speed
Nu	Nusselt number
n	Number
P	Pressure
P	Product flow rate (sorting)
P	Power
P	Productivity (fermentation)
Po	Power number (mixing)
P_0	Vapour pressure of pure water
Q	Rate of heat transfer
Q	Volumeric flowrate
q_p	Specific rate of product formation (fermentation)
R	Universal gas constant
R	Reject flowrate (sorting)
R	Resistance to flow through a filter
R	Fraction of reflected light (packaging)
Re	Reynolds number
r	Radius
r	Specific resistance to flow through a filter
S	Substrate concentration (fermentation)
s	Compressibility of filter cake
T	Absolute temperature
T	Fractional transmission of light (packaging)
t	Time
U	Overall heat transfer coefficient
U	Thermal death time at retort temperature (canning)
V	Volume
V_c	Fractional volume of filter cake
v	Velocity
v_e	Air velocity needed to convey particles

v_f	Air velocity needed for fluidisation
W	Work index (size reduction)
x	Thickness, depth
x	Direction of heat flow
x	Mass fraction
$\bar{x}$	Average
Y	Yield (fermentation)
z	Height
z	z-value (canning)
α	Absorbance
β	Coefficient of thermal expansion
Δ	Difference, change
δ	Half dimension
$\tan \delta$	Loss tangent (microwaves)
ε	Porosity
ε	Voidage of fluidised bed
ε	Emmisivity (infrared radiation)
ε'	Dielectric constant (microwaves)
ε''	Loss factor (microwaves)
θ	Temperature
λ	Latent heat
λ	Wavelength
μ	Viscosity
μ	Specific growth rate (fermentation)
Π	Osmotic pressure
π	Constant $= 3.142$
ρ	Density
Σ	Sum
σ	Standard deviation
σ	Stefan–Boltzmann constant (infrared radiation)
ω	Angular velocity

Introduction

The present-day food industry has its origins in pre-history when the first food processing took place to preserve foods against famine, or to improve their eating quality. For example grain was sun dried to extend its storage life and meat was roasted to improve its flavour. Mechanical processing equipment was developed to reduce the time and labour involved in manual methods. For example, water, wind and animal power were harnessed to mill grains. The first biochemical processing began in Egypt with the development of fermented products, including cheeses and wines. For a long period such preservation and preparation methods were only used on a domestic scale to serve the needs of the family. However, as societies developed, specialisation took place and trades developed (for example bakers and brewers). These were the forerunners of current food industries.

In countries with a temperate climate, these processing techniques were developed over generations to allow food to be stored through the winter months and to increase the availability of foods out of season. The growth of towns and cities gave impetus to the development of preservation technologies and an extended storage life allowed foods to be transported from rural areas to meet the needs of urban populations. During the nineteenth century, larger scales of production were achieved in factories which were built to produce basic commodities, including starch, sugar, butter and baked goods. These batch processes were based on tradition and experience, and no detailed knowledge of the composition of foods or changes during processing existed. Towards the end of that century, an increase in scientific understanding started the change from craft-based industry to science-based industry that is continuing today. It was about this time that two distinct markets were defined. The first, which involved the bulk of the food that was processed, concerned cheaper foods, many of which were further prepared in the home or in catering establishments before consumption (for example flour, sugar, canned meats and vegetables). The second was a 'luxury' market, which included canned tropical fruits (for example pineapple and peaches) and coffee. The preparation of a wide range of 'ready to eat' meals, snackfoods and 'convenience' foods is a relatively recent development.

The aims of the food industry today, as in the past, are fourfold:

(1) to extend the period during which a food remains wholesome (the shelf life) by preservation techniques which inhibit microbiological or biochemical changes and thus allow time for distribution and home storage;
(2) to increase variety in the diet by providing a range of attractive flavours, colours, aromas and textures in food (collectively known as *eating quality*, *sensory quality* or *organoleptic quality*); a related aim is to change the form of the food to allow further processing (for example the milling of grains to flour);
(3) to provide the nutrients required for health (termed *nutritional quality* of a food);
(4) to generate income for the manufacturing company.

Each of these aims exists to a greater or lesser extent in all food production, but the processing of a given product may emphasise some more than others. For example, frozen vegetables are intended to have sensory and nutritional qualities that are as close as possible to the fresh product, but with a shelf life of several months instead of a few days or weeks. The main purpose of freezing is therefore to preserve the food. In contrast, sugar confectionery and snackfoods are intended to provide variety in the diet. A large number of shapes, flavours, colours and textures are produced from basic raw materials. The relative importance of preservative effect, modification of sensory properties and retention of nutritive value in different preparation procedures is shown in Fig. 1.

All food processing involves a combination of procedures to achieve the intended changes to the raw materials. These are conveniently categorised as *unit operations*, each of which has a specific, identifiable and predictable effect on a food. Unit operations are grouped together to form a process. The combination and sequence of operations determines the nature of the final product (for example Fig. 2).

In industrialised countries the market for processed foods is changing. Consumers no longer require a shelf life of several months at ambient temperature for the majority of their foods. Changes in family lifestyle, and increased ownership of freezers and microwave ovens, are reflected in demands for foods that are convenient to prepare, are suitable for frozen storage or have a moderate shelf life at ambient temperature. There is also an increasing demand by some consumers for foods that have undergone fewer changes during processing and thus either closely resemble the original material or have a 'healthy' image. Each of these is an important influence on changes that are taking place in the food-processing industry.

Changes in the technology used to prepare foods have been influenced by substantial increases in the cost of both energy and labour. Food processors have reconsidered the merits of investing relatively low amounts of capital in labour-intensive and energy-inefficient processes. Food processing equipment now allows increasingly sophisticated control of processing conditions to achieve the twin aims of reduced processing costs and reduced damage to the sensory and nutritional qualities of foods (particularly heat damage). Energy saving is also an important feature of most food-processing equipment. This requires a higher capital investment by manufacturers but reduces production costs, by using less energy and often

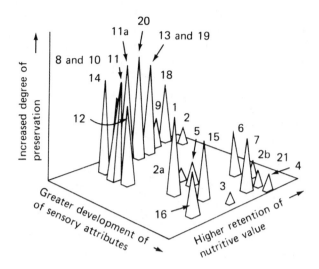

Fig. 1 — Relative effects of selected unit operations: 1, jam making; 2, cleaning; 2a, peeling; 2b, sorting; 3, milling; 4, mixing; 5, mechanical separations; 6, membrane separation; 7, fermentation; 8, irradiation; 9, blanching; 10, pasteurisation; 11, canning; 11a, ultrahigh-temperature sterilisation; 12, evaporation; 13, extrusion; 14, drying; 15, baking; 16, frying; 18, chilling; 19, freezing; 20, freeze-drying; 21, enrobing.

Fruit

Cleaning	Cleaning
Sorting	Sorting
Peeling	Peeling
Size reduction	Size reduction
(To slices)	(To pulp)
Sugar+water→Mixing	Mixing←Sugar
Filling	Heat treatment
Sealing	Filling (aseptic or non-aseptic)
Heat sterilisation (canning)	Sealing
Canned fruit slices	**Ultrahigh temperature fruit juice**

Fig. 2 — Linking unit operations.

fewer operators, and generates increased revenue from higher sales of the better-quality product. Microprocessors are now almost universally used to control food-processing equipment, and the automation of entire processes, from reception of materials, through processing and packaging to warehousing, is now a reality.

Heat has important influences on food processing in a number of respects: it is the most convenient way of extending the shelf life by destroying enzymic and microbiological activity in foods, or removing water to inhibit deterioration; it changes the nutritional and sensory qualities of foods; generation of heat is a major processing cost. The unit operations described in this book are therefore grouped according to the nature of heat transfer that takes place.

The book has an initial part, Part I, which describes some important basic concepts. Part II describes operations that operate at ambient temperature and involve minimum heating of foods; Part III includes those operations that heat foods to extend the shelf life or to alter the eating quality; Part IV describes operations that remove heat from foods to extend the shelf life or to operate at below ambient temperature to minimise changes in nutritional and sensory qualities; the final part, Part V, is concerned with operations that are integral parts of a food process but are supplementary to the main method of processing.

In each chapter, the theoretical basis of the unit operation is first described. Formulae required for calculation of processing parameters and sample problems are given where appropriate, and sources of more detailed information are indicated. Details of the equipment used for practical implementation of theoretical concepts are then given, and developments in technology that relate to savings in energy or labour or to improvement in product quality are noted. Finally the effect of the unit operation on sensory and nutritional properties of selected foods is examined.

This book therefore aims to show how a knowledge of the properties of foods is used to design processing equipment and to control processing conditions on an industrial scale, to achieve the desired aims of altering the eating quality or extending the shelf life with minimal changes to sensory and nutritional qualities. The book is intended to be an introductory text for students of food science and technology, or biotechnology. An advanced mathematical background is not assumed, and the book provides an additional perspective for students studying nutrition, catering or agriculture.

Part I
Basic principles

1

Basic principles

1.1 SENSORY CHARACTERISTICS AND NUTRITIONAL PROPERTIES OF FOOD

1.1.1 Sensory characteristics

To the consumer, the most important attributes of a food are its sensory characteristics (texture, flavour, aroma, shape and colour). These determine an individual's preference for specific products, and small differences between brands of similar products can have a substantial influence on acceptability. A continuing aim of the food manufacturer is to find improvements in processing technology which retain or create desirable sensory qualities or reduce the damage to food caused by processing. Examples of such improvements are described in subsequent chapters.

1.1.1.1 Texture

The textural attributes of foods are summarised in Table 1.1. The texture of foods is mostly determined by the moisture and fat contents, and the types and amounts of structural carbohydrates (cellulose, starches and pectic materials) and proteins. Changes in texture are caused by loss of moisture or fat, formation or breakdown of emulsions, hydrolysis of polymeric carbohydrates, and coagulation or hydrolysis of proteins. These changes are described in subsequent chapters. Detailed information on the textural characteristics of food is given by Mohsenin (1980) Lewis (1987) and Szczesniak (1983). The effect of food composition and structure on texture is described by Stanley and Tung (1976) and Sherman (1976).

1.1.1.2 Taste, flavour and aroma

Taste attributes consist of saltiness, sweetness, bitterness and acidity. These attributes are largely determined by the formulation used and are mostly unaffected by processing. Exceptions to this include respiratory changes to fresh foods (Chapter 18) and changes in acidity or sweetness during food fermentations (Chapter 7). Fresh foods contain complex mixtures of volatile compounds, which give characteristic

Table 1.1 — Textural characteristics of foods

Primary characteristic	Secondary characteristic	Popular terms
Mechanical characteristics		
Hardness		Soft → firm → hard
Cohesiveness	Brittleness	Crumbly, crunchy, brittle
	Chewiness	Tender, chewy, tough
	Gumminess	Short, mealy, pasty, gummy
Viscosity		Thin, viscous
Elasticity		Plastic, elastic
Adhesiveness		Sticky, tacky, gooey
Geometrical characteristics		
Particle size and shape		Gritty, grainy, coarse
Particle shape and orientation		Fibrous, cellular, crystalline
Other characteristics		
Moisture content		Dry → moist → wet → watery
Fat content	Oiliness	Oily
	Greasiness	Greasy

Adapted from Szczesniak (1963).

flavours and aromas. These compounds may be lost during processing, which reduces the intensity of flavour or reveals other flavour/aroma compounds. Volatile aroma compounds are also produced by the action of heat, ionising radiation, oxidation or enzyme activity on proteins, fats and carbohydrates. Examples include the Maillard reaction between amino acids and reducing sugars or carbonyl groups and the products of lipid degradation (Chapter 15), or hydrolysis of lipids to fatty acids and subsequent conversion to aldehydes, esters and alcohols. The perceived aroma of foods arises from complex combinations of many hundreds of compounds, some of which act synergistically. More detailed descriptions of the production of aroma compounds or loss of naturally occurring aroma compounds are given in subsequent chapters.

1.1.1.3 *Colour*
Many naturally occurring pigments are destroyed by heat processing, chemically altered by changes in pH or oxidised during storage (Table 1.2). As a result the processed food loses its characteristic colour and hence loses value. Synthetic pigments (Appendix B) are more stable to heat, light and changes in pH, and they are therefore added to retain the colour of some processed foods. Details of changes

Table 1.2 — Naturally occurring pigments in foods

Pigment	Typical source	Oil or water soluble	Stability to the following			
			Heat	Light	Oxygen	pH change
Anthocyanins	Fruits	Water soluble	High	High	High	Low
Betalaines	Beetroot	Water soluble	Moderate	High	High	High
Bixin	Seed coat of *Bixa orellana*	Oil soluble	Moderate to low	Low	High	—
Canxanthin		Oil soluble	Moderate	Moderate	Moderate	Moderate
Caramel	Heated sugar	Water soluble	High	High	High	High
Carotenes	Leaves	Oil soluble	Moderate to low	Low	Low	High
Chlorophylls	Leaves	Water soluble	High	High	High	Low
Cochineal[a]	Insect (*Dactylopius coccus*)	Water soluble	High	High	—	Moderate to high
Curcumin	Turmeric	Water soluble	Low	Low	Low	—
Norbixin	See Bixin	Water soluble	Moderate to low	Low	High	—
Oxymyoglobin	Animals	Water soluble	Low	—	High	Low
Polyphenols	Tea leaf	Water soluble	High	High	High	High
Quinones	Roots, bark	Water soluble	High	Moderate	—	Moderate
Xanthophylls	Fruits	Water soluble	Moderate	High	High	Low

[a] As aluminium lake.
From the data of Zapsalis and Beck (1985) and Coultate (1984).

to naturally occurring pigments are described in Chapters 9–14. Maillard browning is an important cause of both desirable changes in food colour (for example in baking or frying (Chapters 15 and 16), and in the development of off-colours (for example during canning and drying (Chapters 11 and 14)).

1.1.2 Nutritional properties

Many unit operations, especially those that do not involve heat, have little or no effect on the nutritional quality of foods. Examples include mixing, cleaning, sorting, freeze drying and pasteurisation. Unit operations that intentionally separate the components of foods (Chapters 2, 5 and 6) alter the nutritional quality of each fraction compared with the raw material. Unintentional separation of water-soluble nutrients (minerals, water-soluble vitamins and sugars) also occurs in some unit operations (for example blanching (Chapter 9), and in drip losses from roast or frozen foods (Chapters 15 and 19)).

Heat processing is a major cause of changes to nutritional properties of foods. For example gelatinisation of starches and coagulation of proteins improve their digestibility, and anti-nutritional compounds (for example a trypsin inhibitor in legumes) are destroyed. However, heat also destroys some types of heat-labile vitamin

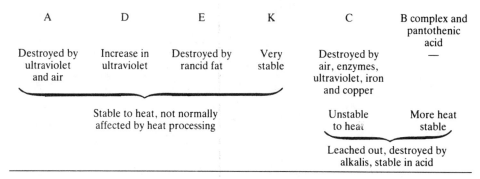

A	D	E	K	C	B complex and pantothenic acid
Destroyed by ultraviolet and air	Increase in ultraviolet	Destroyed by rancid fat	Very stable	Destroyed by air, enzymes, ultraviolet, iron and copper	—

Stable to heat, not normally affected by heat processing

Unstable to heat · More heat stable

Leached out, destroyed by alkalis, stable in acid

Fig. 1.1 — Stability of vitamins in food.

(Fig. 1.1), reduces the biological value of proteins (owing to destruction of amino acids or Maillard browning reactions) and promotes lipid oxidation. The effects of heat on proteins and lipids are described in detail by Mauron (1982) and Witting and Dimick (1982) respectively.

Oxidation is a second important cause of nutritional changes to foods. This occurs when food is exposed to air (for example in size reduction or hot-air drying (Chapters 3 and 14)) or as a result of the action of heat or oxidative enzymes (for example peroxidase or lipoxygenase). The main nutritional effects of oxidation are

(1) the degeneration of lipids to hydroperoxides and subsequent reactions to form a wide variety of carbonyl compounds, hydroxy compounds and short chain fatty acids, and in frying oils to toxic compounds (Chapter 16) and
(2) destruction of oxygen-sensitive vitamins (Fig. 1.1 and Appendix A).

Changes to lipids are discussed by Zapsalis and Beck (1985) and a discussion of the properties of vitamins and losses during processing is given by Bender (1978), Harris and Karmas (1975) and De Ritter (1982). Examples of vitamin losses caused by individual unit operations are described in subsequent chapters.

The importance of nutrient losses during processing depends on the nutritional value of a particular food in the diet. Some foods (for example bread and milk) are an important source of nutrients for large numbers of people. Vitamin losses are therefore more significant in these foods than in those which either are eaten in small quantities or have low concentrations of nutrients.

In industrialised countries, the majority of the population achieve an adequate supply of nutrients from the mixture of foods that is eaten. Losses due to processing of one component of the diet are therefore insignificant to the long-term health of an individual. In an example described by Bender (1987), complete meals which initially contained 16.5 μg of vitamin A lost 50% on canning and 100% after storage for 18 months. Although the losses appear to be significant, the original meal contained only 2% of the recommended daily intake (RDA), and the extent of loss is therefore of minor importance. The same meal contained 9 mg of thiamin and lost 75% after 18 months' storage. The thiamin content is ten times the RDA, and adequate quantities therefore remained. Possible exceptions are the special dietary needs of pre-term infants, pregnant women and the elderly. In these groups there may be either a special need for certain nutrients or a more restricted diet than normal. These special cases are discussed in detail by Watson (1986) and Francis (1986).

Reported vitamin losses during processing are included in subsequent chapters to give an indication of the severity of each unit operation. However, such data should be treated with caution. Variation in nutrient losses between cultivars or varieties can exceed differences caused by alternative methods of processing. Growth conditions, or handling and preparation procedures prior to processing, also cause substantial variation in nutrient loss. Data on nutritional changes cannot be directly applied to individual commercial operations, because of differences in ingredients, processing conditions and equipment used by different manufacturers.

1.2 MATERIAL AND ENERGY BALANCES

The law of conversion of mass states that the mass of material entering a process equals the mass of material leaving. This has applications in, for example, mixing (Chapter 4), fermentation (Chapter 7), evaporation (Chapter 12) and dehydration (Chapter 14). An example of a typical mass balance calculation is shown in Chapter 12. In general a mass balance for a process takes the following form:

$$\begin{array}{c}\text{mass of raw}\\\text{materials in}\end{array} = \begin{array}{c}\text{mass of products}\\\text{and wastes out}\end{array} + \begin{array}{c}\text{mass of stored}\\\text{materials}\end{array} + \text{losses}$$

Similarly an energy balance states that the amount of heat or mechanical energy entering a process = the total energy leaving with the products and wastes + stored energy + energy lost to the surroundings. If heat losses are minimised, energy losses to the surroundings may be ignored for approximate solutions to calculation of, for example, the quantity of steam, hot air or refrigerant required. For more accurate solutions a compensation should be made for heat losses.

1.3 FLUID FLOW

Many types of liquid food are transported during processing and powders and small-particulate foods are more easily handled as fluids (by fluidisation). Gases obey the same laws as liquids and, for the purposes of calculations, gases are treated as compressible fluids. The study of fluids is therefore of great importance in food processing. It is divided into fluid statics (stationary fluids) and fluid dynamics (moving fluids).

A property of static liquids is the pressure that they exert on the containing vessel. The pressure is related to the density of the liquid and the depth or the mass of liquid in the vessel. Liquids at the base of a vessel are at a higher pressure than at the surface, owing to the weight of liquid above (the *hydrostatic head*). This is important in the design of holding tanks and processing vessel, to ensure that the vessel is constructed using materials of adequate strength. A large hydrostatic head also affects the boiling point of liquids, which is important in the design of evaporation equipment (Chapter 12).

When a fluid flows through processing equipment (Fig. 1.2), there are friction

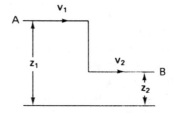

Fig. 1.2 — Application of Bernoulli's equation to frictionless fluid flow.

losses and changes in the potential energy, kinetic energy and pressure energy. Energy is also added by pumps, or by heating the fluid. To calculate the energy balance when a liquid flows through pipework, the effect of valves or bends on the flow rate, or the pressure developed by a pump, use is made of *Bernoulli's equation*

$$\frac{P_1}{\rho_1} + \frac{v_1^2}{2} + z_1 g = \frac{P_2}{\rho_2} + \frac{v_2^2}{2} + z_2 g \qquad (1.1)$$

where P (Pa) is the pressure, ρ (kg m^{-3}) the fluid density, g ($= 9.81$ m s^{-2}) the acceleration due to gravity, v (m s^{-1}) the velocity of the fluid and z (m) the height. The subscript 1 indicates the first position in the pipework, and the subscript 2 the second position in the pipework.

Properties of selected fluids are shown in Table 1.3.

Sample problem 1.1
A 20% sucrose solution flows from a mixing tank at 50 kPa through an horizontal pipe 5 cm in diameter at 25 m^3 h^{-1}. If the pipe diameter reduces to 3 cm, calculate the new pressure in the pipe. (The density of sucrose solution is 1070 kg m^{-3} (Table 1.3).)

Table 1.3 — Properties of fluids

	Thermal conductivity (W m^{-1} °K^{-1})	Specific heat (kJ kg^{-1} °K^{-1})	Density (kg m^{-3})	Dynamic viscosity (N s m^{-2})	Temperature (°C)
Air	0.024	1.005	1.29	1.73×10^{-5}	0
	0.031	1.005	0.94	2.21×10^{-5}	100
Carbon dioxide	0.015	0.80	1.98		0
Oxygen		0.92		1.48×10^{-5}	20
Nitrogen	0.024	1.05	1.3		0
Refrigerant 12	0.0083	0.92			
Water	0.57	4.21	1000	1.79×10^{-3}	0
	0.68	4.21	958	0.28×10^{-3}	100
Sucrose solution (60%)				6.02×10^{-2}	20
Sucrose solution (20%)	0.54	3.8	1070	1.92×10^{-3}	20
Sodium chloride solution (22%)	0.54	3.4	1240	2.7×10^{-3}	2
Acetic acid	0.17	2.2	1050	1.2×10^{-3}	20
Ethanol	0.18	2.3	790	1.2×10^{-3}	20
Rape-seed oil			900	1.18×10^{-1}	20
Maize oil		1.73			20
Olive oil	0.168			8.4×10^{-2}	29
Sunflower oil		1.93			20
Whole milk	0.56	3.9	1030	2.12×10^{-3}	20
				2.8×10^{-3}	10
Skim milk			1040	1.4×10^{-3}	25
Cream (20% fat)			1010	6.2×10^{-3}	3
Locust bean gum (1% solution)				1.5×10^{-2}	
Xanthan gum (1% solution)			100		

From Earle (1983), Lewis (1987) and Peleg and Bagley (1983).

Solution to sample problem 1.1

$$\text{Flow rate} = \frac{25}{3600} \text{ m}^3 \text{ s}^{-1}$$

$$= 6.94 \times 10^{-3} \text{ m}^3 \text{ s}^{-1}$$

$$\text{Area of pipe 5 cm in diameter} = \frac{\pi}{4} D^2$$

$$= \frac{3.142}{4} (0.05)^2$$

$$= 1.96 \times 10^{-3} \text{ m}^2$$

$$\text{Velocity of flow} = \frac{6.94 \times 10^{-3}}{1.96 \times 10^{-3}}$$

$$= 3.54 \text{ m s}^{-1}$$

Area of pipe 3 cm in diameter $= 7.07 \times 10^{-4} \text{ m}^2$

$$\text{Velocity of flow} = \frac{6.94 \times 10^{-3}}{7.07 \times 10^{-4}}$$

$$= 9.81 \text{ m s}^{-1}$$

Using equation (1.1),

$$\frac{P_1}{\rho_1} + \frac{v_1^2}{2} + z_1 = \frac{P_2}{\rho_2} + \frac{v_2^2}{2} + z_2$$

$$\frac{3.54^2}{2} + \frac{50 \times 10^3}{1070} + 0 = \frac{P_2}{1070} + \frac{9.81^2}{2} + 0$$

Therefore,

$$P_2 = 56656 \, Pa$$

$$= 56.7 \, kPa$$

In any system in which fluids flow, there exists a *boundary film* (or surface film) of fluid next to the surface over which the fluid flows (Fig. 1.3(a)). The thickness of the boundary film is influenced by a number of factors, including the velocity, viscosity, density and temperature of the fluid (Table 1.3). Fluids which have a low flow rate or high viscosity may be thought of as a series of layers which move over one another without mixing (Fig. 1.3(b)). This produces movement of the fluid in a single stream, which is termed *streamline* (or laminar) flow. In a pipe, the velocity of the fluid is highest at the centre and zero at the pipe wall. Above a certain flow rate, which is determined by the nature of fluid and the pipe, the layers of liquid mix together and *turbulent* flow is established (Fig. 1.3(c)) in the bulk of the fluid (the flow remains streamline in the boundary film).

Fluid flow is characterised by a dimensionless group (Appendix C) named the *Reynolds number* Re. This is calculated using

$$\text{Re} = \frac{Dv\rho}{\mu} \tag{1.2}$$

where D (m) is the diameter of the pipe, v (m s^{-1}) the average velocity, ρ (kg m^{-3}) the fluid density and μ (N sm^{-2}) the fluid viscosity.

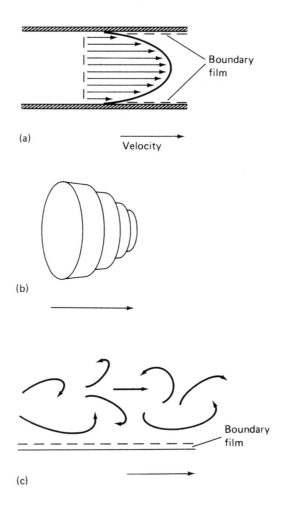

Fig. 1.3 — Fluid flow: (a) velocity distribution and boundary layers; (b) streamline flow; (c) turbulent flow.

Sample problem 1.2
Two fluids, milk and rape-seed oil, are flowing along pipes of the same diameter (5 cm) at 20°C and at the same flow velocity of $3 \, \text{m s}^{-1}$. Determine whether the flow is streamline or turbulent in each fluid. (Physical properties of milk and rape-seed oil are shown in Table 1.3).

Solution to sample problem 1.2
For milk from Table 1.3, $\mu = 2.10 \times 10^{-3} \, \text{N sm}^{-2}$ and $\rho = 1030 \, \text{kg m}^{-3}$. From equation (1.2),

$$\text{Re} = \frac{Dv\rho}{\mu}$$

Therefore,

$$Re = \frac{0.05 \times 3 \times 1030}{2.1 \times 10^{-3}}$$

$$= 73\,571$$

Thus the flow is turbulent (because Re is greater than 4000).
For rape-seed oil, from Table 1.3, $\mu = 118 \times 10^{-3}\,\mathrm{N\,s\,m^{-2}}$ and $\rho = 900\,\mathrm{kg\,m^{-3}}$. Therefore

$$Re = \frac{0.05 \times 3 \times 900}{118 \times 10^{-3}}$$

$$= 1144$$

Thus the flow is streamline (because Re is less than 2100).

A Reynolds number of less than 2100 describes streamline flow and a Reynolds number of more than 4000 describes turbulent flow. For Reynolds numbers between 2100 and 4000 *transitional* flow is present, which can be either laminar or turbulent at different times. These different flow characteristics have important implications for heat transfer and mixing operations; turbulent flow produces thinner boundary layers, which in turn permit higher rates of heat transfer. The implications of this for the design and performance of equipment are discussed in Chapters 10–12 and 16 (for liquids through pipes or over metal plates) and Chapters 14, 15 and 19 (for air moving over the surface of food or metal). The Reynolds number can be used to determine the power requirements for pumps and mixers used for blending and mixing operations (Chapter 4).

In turbulent flow, particles of fluid move in all directions and solids are retained in suspension more readily. This reduces the formulation of deposits on heat exchangers and prevents solids from settling out in pipework. Streamline flow produces a larger range of residence times for individual particles flowing in a tube. This is important when calculating the residence time required for heat treatment of liquid foods, as it is necessary to ensure that all parts of the food receive the required amount of heat.

Turbulent flow causes higher friction losses than streamline flow does and therefore requires higher energy imputs from pumps. Details of the calculation of friction losses in pipes and vessels are discussed by Lewis (1987) and Earle (1983). The loss of pressure in pipes is determined by a number of factors including the density and viscosity of the fluid, and the length and diameter of the pipe. Detailed descriptions and formulae are given by Earle (1983) and Loncin and Merson (1979).

1.3.1 Fluid flow through fluidised beds
When air passes upwards through a bed of food, the particles cause a resistance to air flow and the pressure falls. However, the area available for air flow is reduced and the velocity therefore increases. As the velocity increases, a point is reached where

the weight of the food is just balanced by the force of the air, and the bed becomes fluidised (for example fluidised-bed drying (Chapter 14) or fluidised-bed freezing (Chapter 19)). If the velocity is increased further, the bed becomes more open (the *voidage* is increased), until eventually the particles are conveyed in the fluid stream (for example pneumatic separation (Chapter 2), pneumatic drying (Chapter 14), or pneumatic conveying (Chapter 24)). The velocity of the air needed to achieve fluidisation of spherical particles is calculated using

$$v_f = \frac{(\rho_s - \rho)g}{\mu} \frac{d^2\varepsilon^3}{180(1 - \varepsilon)} \qquad (1.3)$$

where v_f (m s^{-1}) is the fluidisation velocity, ρ_s (kg m^{-3}) the density of the solid particles, ρ (kg m^{-3}) the density of the fluid, g (m s^{-2}) the acceleration due to gravity, μ (N s m^{-2}) the viscosity of the fluid, d (m) the diameter of the particles, ε the voidage of the bed.

Formulae for foods of other shapes are described by Kunii and Levenspiel (1969). The minimum air velocity needed to convey particles is found using

$$v_e = \sqrt{\left[\frac{4d(\rho_s - \rho)}{3C_d\rho} \right]} \qquad (1.4)$$

where v_e (m s^{-1}) is the minimum air velocity and C_d ($= 0.44$ for Re $= 500$–$200\,000$) the drag coefficient.

Sample problem 1.3
Peas which have an average diameter of 6 mm and a density of 880 kg m^{-3} are dried in a fluidised-bed drier (Chapter 14). The minimum voidage is 0.4 and the cross-sectional area of the bed is 0.25 m^2. Calculate the minimum air velocity needed to fluidise the bed if the air density is 0.96 kg m^{-3} and the air viscosity is 2.15×10^{-5} N s m^{-2}.

Solution to sample problem 1.3
From equation (1.3),

$$V_F = \frac{(880 - 0.96)9.81}{2.15 \times 10^{-5}} \frac{(0.006)^2(0.4)^3}{180(1 - 0.4)}$$

$$= 8.5 \, \text{m s}^{-1}$$

1.4 HEAT TRANSFER

Many unit operations in food processing involve the transfer of heat into or out of a food. There are three ways in which heat may be transferred: by radiation, by conduction and by convection. *Radiation* (Chapter 17) is the transfer of heat by electromagnetic waves (Fig. 17.1) (for example in an electric grill). *Conduction* is the movement of heat by direct transfer of molecular energy within solids (for example through metal containers or solid foods). *Convection* is the transfer of heat by groups of molecules that move as a result of differences in density (for example in heated air) or as a result of agitation (for example in stirred liquids). In the majority of applications all three types of heat transfer occur simultaneously but one type may be more important than others.

Steady-state heat transfer takes place when there is a constant temperature difference between two materials. The amount of heat entering a material equals the amount of heat leaving, and there is no change in temperature of the material. This occurs for example when heat is transferred through the wall of a cold store if the store temperature and ambient temperature are constant, and in continuous processes once operating conditions have stabilised. However, in the majority of food-processing applications the temperature of the food and/or the heating or cooling medium are constantly changing, and *unsteady-state* heat transfer is more commonly found. Calculations of heat transfer under these conditions are extremely complicated but are simplified by making a number of assumptions and in some cases using prepared charts to give approximate solutions.

1.4.1 Conduction

The rate at which heat is transferred by conduction is determined by the temperature difference between the food and the heating or cooling medium, and the total resistance to heat transfer. The resistance to heat transfer is expressed as the conductance of a material, or more usefully as the reciprocal which is termed the *thermal conductivity*. Under steady-state conditions the rate of heat transfer is calculated using

$$Q = \frac{kA(\theta_1 - \theta_2)}{x} \tag{1.5}$$

where Q ($\mathrm{J\,s^{-1}}$) is the rate of heat transfer, k ($\mathrm{J\,m^{-1}\,s^{-1}\,{}^{\circ}K}$ or $\mathrm{W\,m^{-1}\,{}^{\circ}K^{-1}}$) the thermal conductivity, A ($\mathrm{m^2}$) the surface area, $\theta_1 - \theta_2$ (°C) the temperature difference and x (m) the thickness of the material. $(\theta_1 - \theta_2)/x$ is also known as the temperature gradient.

Thermal conductivities of materials found in food processing are shown in Tables 1.3 and 1.4.

Although stainless steel conducts heat less well than aluminium and copper, the difference is small in relation to the low thermal conductivity of foods and does not limit the rate of heat transfer. Stainless steel is much less reactive than other metals, particularly with acidic foods, and is therefore used in most food-processing equipment that comes into contact with foods.

The thermal conductivity of foods is influenced by a number of factors concerned with the nature of the food (for example cell structure, the amount of air trapped between the cells, and the moisture content), and the temperature and pressure of the surroundings. A reduction in moisture content causes a substantial reduction in thermal conductivity. This has important implications in unit operations which

Table 1.4 — Thermal conductivity of selected foods and other materials

Type of material	Thermal conductivity ($W\ m^{-1}\ K^{-1}$)	Temperature of measurement (°C)
Construction materials		
Aluminium	220	0
Copper	388	0
Stainless steel	21	20
Other metals	45–400	0
Brick	0.69	20
Concrete	0.87	20
Foods		
Olive oil[a]	0.17	20
Whole milk[a]	0.56	20
Freeze-dried foods	0.01–0.04	0
Frozen beef[b]	1.30	− 10
Pork (lean)[b]	0.48	3.8
Frozen cod	1.66	− 10
Apple juice	0.56	20
Orange	0.41	0–15
Green beans	0.80	− 12.1
Cauliflower	0.80	− 6.6
Egg	0.96	− 8
Ice	2.25	0
Water[a]	0.57	0
Packaging materials		
Cardboard	0.07	20
Glass, soda	0.52	20
Polyethylene	0.55	20
Poly(vinyl chloride)	0.29	20
Insulating materials		
Polystyrene foam	0.036	0
Polyurethane foam	0.026	0
Other types	0.026–0.052	30

[a] Assuming convection currents are absent.
[b] Heat flow parallel to fibres.
From Earle (1983), Lewis (1987) and Woodams and Nowrey (1968).

involve conduction of heat through food to remove water (for example drying (Chapter 14), frying (Chapter 16) and freeze drying (Chapter 20)). In freeze drying the reduction in atmospheric pressure also influences the thermal conductivity of the food. Ice has a higher thermal conductivity than water and this is important in determining the rate of freezing and thawing (Chapter 19). A sample problem indicating the importance of thermal conductivity is shown in Chapter 16.

1.4.1.1 Unsteady-state conduction

The temperature at a given point within a food during processing depends on the time of heating or cooling and the position in the food. It therefore changes continuously. The factors that influence the temperature change are

(1) the temperature of the heating medium.
(2) the thermal conductivity of the food and
(3) the specific heat of the food.

Thermal diffusivity is related to the thermal conductivity, specific heat and density of a food by

$$a = \frac{k}{\rho c} \tag{1.6}$$

where a $(m^2 s^{-1})$ is the thermal diffusivity, ρ $(kg\,m^{-3})$ the density, c $(J\,kg^{-1}\,^\circ K^{-1})$ the specific heat capacity, and k $(Wm^{-1}\,K^{-1})$ the thermal conductivity.

The basic equation for unsteady state heat transfer in a single direction x is

$$\frac{d\theta}{dt} = \frac{k}{\rho c}\frac{d^2\theta}{dx^2} \tag{1.7}$$

where $d\theta/dt$ is the change in temperature with time.

Examples of solutions to this equation for simple shapes (for example a slab, cylinder or sphere) are described by Earle (1983), Jackson and Lamb (1981) and Loncin and Merson (1979).

1.4.2 Convection

When a fluid changes temperature, the resulting changes in density establish *natural-convection* currents. Examples include natural-circulation evaporators (Chapter 12), air movement in chest freezers (Chapter 19), and movement of liquids inside cans during sterilisation (Chapter 11). *Forced convection* takes place when a stirrer or fan is used to agitate the fluid. This produces higher rates of heat transfer and a more rapid temperature redistribution. Consequently, forced convection is more commonly used in food processing. Examples of forced convection include mixers (Chapter 4), fluidised-bed driers (Chapter 14), air blast freezers (Chapter 19) and liquids pumped through heat exchangers (Chapters 10–12).

The rate of heat transfer from a hot fluid to the surface of a food is found using

$$Q = h_s A(\theta_b - \theta_s) \tag{1.8}$$

where Q $(J\,s^{-1})$ is the rate of heat transfer, A (m^2) the surface area, θ_s the surface temperature, θ_b the bulk fluid temperature and h_s $(W\,m^{-2}\,K^{-1})$ the surface (or film) heat transfer coefficient.

The *surface heat transfer coefficient* is a measure of the resistance to heat flow, caused by the boundary film, and is therefore equivalent to the term k/x in the conduction equation. It is therefore higher in turbulent flow than in streamline flow. Typical values of h_s are given in Table 1.5.

Table 1.5 — Values of surface heat transfer coefficients

	Surface heat transfer coefficient h_s (W m^{-2} K^{-1})	Typical applications
Boiling liquids	2400–60000	Evaporation
Condensing saturated steam	12000	Canning, evaporation
Condensing steam		
With 3% air	3500	Canning
With 6% air	1200	
Condensing ammonia	6000	Freezing, chilling
Liquid flowing through pipes		
low viscosity	1200–6000	Pasteurisation
high viscosity	120–1200	Evaporation
Moving air (3 m s^{-1})	30	Freezing, baking
Still air	6	Cold stores

Adapted from Loncin and Merson (1979) and Earle (1983).

These data indicate that heat transfer through air is lower than through liquids. Larger heat exchangers are therefore necessary when air is used for heating (Chapters 14 and 15) or cooling (Chapters 18 and 19) and higher rates of heat transfer are obtained by moving air. Condensing steam produces higher rates of heat transfer than hot water at the same temperature (Chapters 10–12) and the presence of air in steam reduces the rate of heat transfer (Chapter 11).

The surface heat transfer coefficient is related to the physical properties of a fluid (for example density, viscosity, specific heat), gravity (which causes circulation due to changes in density), temperature difference and the length or diameter of the container under investigation. The formulae which relate these factors are expressed as dimensionless numbers (Appendix C) as follows:

$$\text{Nusselt number Nu} = \frac{h_c D}{k} \qquad (1.9)$$

$$\text{Prandtl number Pr} = \frac{c_p \mu}{k} \tag{1.10}$$

$$\text{Grashof number Gr} = \frac{D^3 \rho^2 g \beta \Delta\theta}{\mu^2} \tag{1.11}$$

where h_c $(\text{W m}^{-2}\text{K}^{-1})$ is the convection heat transfer coefficient at the solid–liquid interface, D (m) the characteristic dimension (diameter or length), k $(\text{W m}^{-1}\text{°K}^{-1})$ the thermal conductivity of the fluid, c_p $(\text{J kg}^{-1}\text{°K}^{-1})$ the specific heat at constant pressure, ρ (kg m^{-3}) the density, μ (N s m^{-2}) the viscosity, g (m s^{-2}) the acceleration due to gravity, β $(\text{m m}^{-1}\text{K}^{-1})$ the coefficient of thermal expansion, $\Delta\theta$ the temperature difference and v (m s^{-1}) the velocity.

For streamline flow through pipes,

$$\text{Nu} = 1.62(\text{Re Pr} \frac{D}{L})^{0.33} \tag{1.12}$$

where L (m) is the length of pipe, when Re Pr $D/L > 120$ and all physical properties are measured at the mean bulk temperature of the fluid.

For turbulent flow through pipes,

$$\text{Nu} = 0.023(\text{Re})^{0.8}(\text{Pr})^n \tag{1.13}$$

where $n = 0.4$ for heating or $n = 0.3$ for cooling, when Re $> 10\,000$, viscosity is measured at the mean *film* temperature and other physical properties are measured at the mean bulk temperature of the field.

The Grashof number is used for natural convection when there is no turbulence in the fluid. Formulae for other types of flow conditions and different vessels are described by Loncin and Merson (1979), Jackson and Lamb (1981) and Earle (1983).

Sample problem 1.4
Whole milk is cooled in the pipes of a tubular heat exchanger from 30°C to 10°C, by water at 1°C. The pipe diameter is 5 cm and the milk flow velocity is $1.0\,\text{m s}^{-1}$. Calculate the heat transfer coefficient for the milk using physical properties described in Table 1.3.

Solution to sample problem 1.4

$$\text{Mean bulk temperature} = \frac{30 + 10}{2}$$

$$= 20°C$$

From Table 1.3, $\rho = 1030\,\text{kg m}^{-3}$, $c = 3.9\,\text{kJ kg}^{-1}\text{°K}^{-1}$

and

$$k = 0.56\,\mathrm{W\,m^{-2}\,{}^{\circ}K^{-1}} .$$

If Re > 10 000 viscosity should be measured at the mean film temperature.

$$\text{Mean film temperature} = \frac{1 + \frac{1}{2}(30 + 10)}{2}$$

$$= 10.5{}^{\circ}\mathrm{C}$$

For milk at 10.5°C, $\mu = 2.8 \times 10^{-3}\,\mathrm{N\,s\,m^{-2}}$. From equation (1.2),

$$\mathrm{Re} = \frac{Dv\rho}{\mu}$$

$$= \frac{0.05 \times 1.0 \times 1030}{2.8 \times 10^{-3}}$$

$$= 18\,393$$

From equation (1.10)

$$\mathrm{Pr} = \frac{c_p\mu}{k}$$

$$= \frac{(3.9 \times 10^3)(2.8 \times 10^{-3})}{0.56}$$

$$= 19.5$$

From equations (1.9) and (1.13),

$$\mathrm{Nu} = \frac{h_c D}{k}$$

$$= 0.023(\mathrm{Re})^{0.8}(\mathrm{Pr})^{0.33}$$

Therefore,

$$h_c = 0.023\frac{k}{D}(\mathrm{Re})^{0.8}(\mathrm{Pr})^{0.33}$$

$$= 0.023\frac{0.56}{0.05}(18\,393)^{0.8}(19.5)^{0.33}$$

$$= 1768\,\mathrm{W\,m^{-2}\,{}^{\circ}K^{-1}}$$

Most cases of heat transfer in food processing involve heat transfer through a number of different materials. For example heat transfer from a hot fluid, though the wall of a vessel to a second fluid is shown in Fig. 1.4. The overall temperature

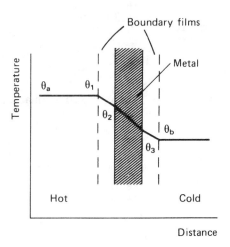

Fig. 1.4 — Temperature changes from a hot liquid through a vessel wall to a cold liquid.

difference is found using

$$\theta_a - \theta_b = \frac{Q}{A}\left(\frac{1}{h_a} + \frac{x}{k} + \frac{1}{h_b}\right) \qquad (1.14)$$

The unknown wall temperatures θ_2 and θ_3 are not required and all factors can be measured.

The sum of the resistances to heat flow is termed the *overall heat transfer coefficient* (OHTC) U and the rate of heat transfer may then be expressed as

$$Q = UA(\theta_a - \theta_b) \qquad (1.15)$$

The OHTC is an important term which is used for example to indicate the effectiveness of heating or cooling in different types of processing equipment. Examples are shown in Table 1.6.

Counter-current flow of fluids (Fig. 1.5) has a higher heat transfer efficiency than co-current flow and is therefore widely used in heat exchangers (Chapters 9–19). However, the temperature difference varies at different points in the heat exchanger and a logarithmic mean temperature difference is used in calculations:

$$\Delta\theta_m = \frac{\Delta\theta_1 - \Delta\theta_2}{\ln(\Delta\theta_1/\Delta\theta_2)} \qquad (1.16)$$

Table 1.6 — OHTCs in food processing

Heat transfer fluids	Example	OHTC $(W\,m^{-2}\,K^{-1})$
Hot water–air	Air heater	10–50
Viscous liquid–hot water	Jacketed vessel	100
Viscous liquid–hot water	Agitated jacketed vessel	500
Viscous liquid–steam	Evaporator	500
Non-viscous liquid–steam	Evaporator	1000–3000
Flue gas–water	Boiler	5–50
Evaporating ammonia–water	Chilled water plant	500

Adapted from Lewis (1987).

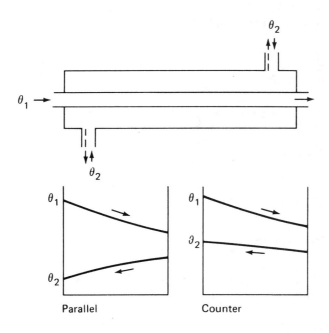

Fig. 1.5 — Parallel and counter-current flow through a heat exchanger.

where θ_1 is higher than θ_2.

Related sample problems are shown in Chapters 10, 12 and 14.

The heating time in batch processing is found using

$$t = \frac{mc}{UA} \ln\left(\frac{\theta_h - \theta_i}{\theta_h - \theta_f}\right) \tag{1.17}$$

where m (kg) is the mass, c $(J\,kg^{-1}K^{-1})$ the specific heat capacity, θ_h (°C) the temperature of the heating medium, θ_i (°C) the initial temperature, θ_f (°C) the final temperature, A (m^2) the surface area, U $(W\,m^{-2}K^{-1})$ OHTC.

Sample problem 1.5
In the counter-current heat exchanger shown in Fig. 1.5, milk is cooled from 73°C to 38°C at a rate of 2500 kg h^{-1}, using water at 15°C which leaves the heat exchanger at 40°C. The pipework 2.5 cm in diameter is constructed from stainless steel 3 mm thick; the surface film heat transfer coefficients are 1200 W m^{-2}K^{-1} on the milk side and 3000 W m^{-2}K^{-1} on the water side of the pipe. Calculate the OHTC and the length of pipe required.

Solution to sample problem 1.5
To find the OHTC, from equation (1.14),

$$\frac{1}{U} = \frac{1}{h_a} + \frac{x}{k} + \frac{1}{h_b}$$

$$= \frac{1}{1200} + \frac{3 \times 10^{-3}}{21} + \frac{1}{3000}$$

$$= 1.3 \times 10^{-3}$$

Therefore the OHTC is

$$U = 769.2\,W\,m^{-2}{}^{\circ}K^{-1}$$

To find the length of pipe required, we proceed as follows.
From equations (1.15) and (1.16),

$$Q = UA\,\Delta\theta_m$$

and

$$\Delta\theta_m = \frac{\Delta\theta_1 - \Delta\theta_2}{\ln(\Delta\theta_1/\Delta\theta_2)}$$

$$= \frac{(73 - 40) - (38 - 15)}{\ln[(73-40)/(38 - 15)]}$$

$$= 27.8°C$$

Now Q is the heat removed from the milk which equals $mc_P (\theta_a - \theta_b)$. From Table 1.3, $c_P = 3.9\,\text{kJ}\,\text{kg}^{-1}\,{}^\circ\text{K}^{-1}$. Therefore,

$$Q = \frac{2500}{3600}(3.9 \times 10^3)(73 - 38)$$

$$= 9.48 \times 10^4\,\text{J}$$

Now the area is

$$A = \frac{Q}{U\,\Delta\theta_m}$$

$$= \frac{9.48 \times 10^4}{769.2 \times 27.8}$$

$$= 4.4\,\text{m}^2$$

Also

$$A = \pi DL$$

Therefore the length of pipe is

$$L = \frac{A}{\pi D}$$

$$= \frac{4.4}{3.142 \times 0.025} = 56\,\text{m}$$

1.4.2.1 Unsteady-state heat transfer by conduction and convection

When a solid piece of food is heated or cooled by a fluid the resistances to heat transfer are the surface heat transfer coefficient and the thermal conductivity of the food. These two factors are related by the *Biot Number* Bi:

$$\text{Bi} = \frac{h\delta}{k} \tag{1.18}$$

where: h ($\text{W}\,\text{m}^{-2}\,\text{K}^{-1}$) is the heat transfer coefficient, δ the characteristic 'half dimension' (radius of cylinder or sphere; half-thickness of slab) and k ($\text{W}\,\text{m}^{-1}\,\text{K}^{-1}$) the thermal conductivity.

At small Bi values (less than 0.2) the surface film is the main resistance to heat flow and the time required to heat the solid food is found using equation (1.17), using the film heat transfer coefficient h_s instead of U. However, in most applications the thermal conductivity of the food limits the rate of heat transfer (Bi > 0.2). The calculations are complex, and a series of charts is available to solve the unsteady-state equations for simple shaped foods (Fig. 1.6). The charts relate the *temperature*

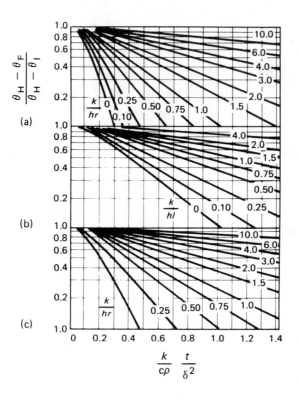

Fig. 1.6 — Chart for unsteady-state heat transfer: (a) sphere; (b) slab; (c) cylinder. (After Henderson and Perry (1955).)

factor (the fraction of the temperature change that remains to be accomplished (equation (1.19))), the *Fourier number* Fo (a dimensionless number which relates the thermal diffusivity, the size of the piece and the time of heating or cooling (equation (1.20))) and the Biot number Bi:

$$\frac{\theta_h - \theta_f}{\theta_h - \theta_i} \tag{1.19}$$

where the subscript h indicates the heating medium, the subscript f the final value and the subscript i the initial value.

$$\text{Fo} = \frac{k}{c\rho} \frac{t}{\delta^2} \tag{1.20}$$

Examples of unsteady-state calculations are shown below and in Chapter 18. More complex calculations are described by Lewis (1987), Earle (1983) and Jackson and Lamb (1981).

Sample problem 1.6
Peas which have an average diameter of 6 mm are blanched to give a temperature of 85°C at the centre. The initial temperature of the peas is 15°C and the temperature of the blancher water is 95°C. Calculate the time required, assuming that the heat transfer coefficient is 1200 W m^{-2} K^{-1} and, for peas, the thermal conductivity is 0.35 W m^{-1} K^{-1}, the specific heat is 3.3 kJ kg^{-1} K^{-1} and the density is 980 kg m^{-3}.

Solution to sample problem 1.6
From equation (1.18),

$$\text{Bi} = \frac{h\delta}{k}$$

$$= \frac{1200(3 \times 10^{-3})}{0.35}$$

$$= 10.3$$

Therefore,

$$\frac{k}{h\delta} = 0.097$$

From equation (1.19),

$$\frac{\theta_h - \theta_f}{\theta_h - \theta_i} = \frac{95 - 85}{95 - 15}$$

$$= 0.125$$

From the chart for a sphere (Fig. 1.6), Fo = 0.32. From equation (1.20),

$$\text{Fo} = \frac{k}{c\rho} \frac{t}{\delta^2}$$

$$= 0.32$$

Therefore,

$$\text{time } t = 0.32\frac{c\rho\delta^2}{k}$$

$$= \frac{0.32(3.3 \times 10^3)980(3 \times 10^{-3})^2}{0.35}$$

$$= 26.6\,\text{s}$$

1.4.3 Sources of heat and methods of application to foods

The cost of energy for food processing has become one of the major considerations in the selection of processing methods and ultimately the cost of the food and the profitability of the operation. Different fuels have specific advantages and limitations in terms of cost, safety, risk of contamination of the food, flexibility of use, and capital and operating costs for the heat transfer equipment. The following sources of energy are used in food processing:

(1) electricty;
(2) gas (natural and liquid petroleum gas);
(3) liquid fuel oil.

Solid fuels (anthracite, coal, wood and charcoal) are only used to a small extent. The advantages and limitations of each type of energy source are shown in Table 1.7. Direct or indirect methods may be used to heat foods but only indirect methods are used for cooling foods.

1.4.3.1 Direct methods

In direct methods the heat and products evolved from the burning fuel come directly into contact with the food. There is an obvious risk of contamination of the food by odours or incompletely burned fuel and, for this reason, only gas and, to a lesser extent, liquid fuels are used. Applications include baking ovens (Chapter 15) and kiln driers (Chapter 14). Direct methods should not be used confused with 'direct' steam injection where the steam is produced in a separate location from the processing plant.

Electricity is not a fuel in the same sense as the other types described above. It is generated by steam turbines heated by a primary fuel (for example coal or fuel oil) or by nuclear fission. However, electrical energy may be used directly by dielectric heating or microwave heating (Chapter 17).

1.4.3.2 Indirect methods

Indirect cooling of foods is described in Chapters 18 and 19. Indirect heating methods employ a heat exchanger to separate the food from the products of combustion. At its simplest an indirect system consists of burning fuel beneath a metal plate and heating by radiated energy from the plate. The most common type of indirect-heating system used in food processing is steam generated by a heat exchanger (a boiler) located away from the processing area. A second heat exchanger transfers the heat from the steam to the food under controlled conditions or the steam is injected into the food. A variation on this system involves an additional heat exchanger which

Table 1.7 — Advantages and limitations of different energy sources for food processing

	Electricity	Gas	Liquid fuel	Solid fuel
Energy per unit mass or volume	Not applicable	Low[a]	High[b]	Moderate to high[c]
Cost per kilojoule of energy	High	Low	Low	Low
Heat transfer equipment cost	Low	Low	High	High
Efficiency of heating[d]	High	Moderate to high	Moderate to low	Low
Flexibility of use	High	High	Low	Low
Fire or explosion hazard	Low	High	Low	Low
Risk of food contamination	Low	Low	High	High
Labour and handling costs	Low	Low	Low	High
Amount (%) used in Europe (1981 data)	9.60	38.20	30.44	21.76

[a] Heating value for gas is $1.17 \times 10^3 - 4.78 \times 10^3$ kJ kg^{-1}.
[b] Heating value for oil is $8.6 \times 10^3 - 9.3 \times 10^3$ kJ kg^{-1}.
[c] Heating value for coal is $5.26 \times 10^3 - 6.7 \times 10^3$ kJ kg^{-1} and for wood is $3.8 \times 10^3 - 5.26 \times 10^3$ kJ kg^{-1}.
[d] Efficiency defined as the amount of energy used to heat the product divided by the amount of energy supplied.
Data compiled from Farrall (1979) and Whitman *et al.* (1981).

transfers heat from the steam to air in order to dry foods or to heat them under dry conditions. The advantages of steam for process heating, and a description of equipment for producing and handling different types of steam, are given by Farrall (1979).

Indirect electrical heating uses resistance heaters or infrared heaters. Resistance heaters are nickel–chromium wires contained in solid plates, which are attached to the walls of vessels, in flexible jackets which wrap around vessels, or in immersion heaters which are submerged in the food. These types of heater are used for localised or intermittent heating. Infrared heaters are described in Chapter 17.

1.4.4 Energy conservation
A 1981 survey of food industries within the European Economic Community found large variations in energy consumption in different types of processing; flour milling has the lowest energy input (586 MJ per tonne of product) and cocoa and chocolate processing the highest (8335 MJ per tonne of product) (Whitman *et al.*, 1981). A comparison of energy inputs in different types of potato processing is shown in Table 1.8.

In all types of food processing, most of the energy (58%; range, 40–80%) is used for actual processing, but significant amounts are also used for packaging (11%; range, 15–40%), transport (12%; range, 0.56–30%), cleaning water (15%) and

Table 1.8 — Comparative energy inputs in potato processing

	Energy input (MJ t^{-1})				
	Hot air dried	Freeze dried	Canned	Retort pouched	Frozen
Processing	8	42	6	4	5
Packaging	1	2	14	7	7
Storage	0.1	0.1	0.1	0.1	32
(Home)	0	0	0	0	(24)
Transport	2	2	8	8	8
Total	11	46	28	19	52

From Olabode *et al.* (1977); reported in Kefford (1982).

storage (up to 85% of total energy input for deep-frozen foods). Boiler fuel accounts for 8.6–97.2% of the total energy input to a factory, but boiler utilisation averages only 45%, owing to the practice of keeping the boiler on low heat during periods of low production rates (for example evening and night shifts). In addition an average of only 58% of condensate is returned to the boiler and the heat contained in the condensate is therefore lost. On average 40% of the heat lost from factories is contained in vapours and steam and a further 10–20% is lost in hot water (Whitman *et al.*, 1981).

It is clear from this and other data (for example Kefford, 1982), that potentially the main energy savings in food processing are associated with boiler operation, the supply of steam or hot air, and re-use of waste heat. An *energy audit* is used to identify specific areas and equipment within a factory where energy savings can be made (Boardman, 1986). In summary, boiler operation is improved by

(1) returning condensate as feed water,
(2) pre-heating air for combustion of fuel,
(3) insulating the boiler and
(4) recovering heat from the flue.

Computer control of boiler operation is described by Wells and Swientek (1983). Energy savings in steam supply to processing areas are achieved by

(1) proper insulation of steam and hot-water pipes,
(2) minimising steam leaks and
(3) fitting steam traps.

Individual processing equipment is designed for energy saving. Examples include regeneration of heat in heat exchangers (Delashmit *et al.*, 1983) (examples in Chapters 9, 10, 15 and 16), multiple-effect or vapour recompression systems

(Chapter 12) and automatic defrosting and correct insulation of freezing equipment (Chapters 18–20). Microprocessor control of processing equipment (Chapter 24) is widely used to reduce energy consumption. Recovery of heat from drying air is more difficult than from steam or vapours because air is not recompressible. However, a number of heat exchanger designs are used to recover waste heat from air or gases (for example the *thermal wheel* in Fig. 1.7). Commercial applications of this equip-

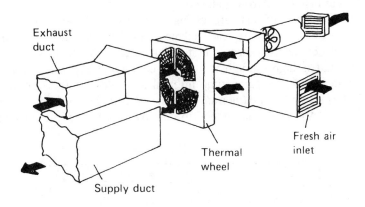

Fig. 1.7 — Thermal wheel. (Courtesy of the Electricity Council.)

ment are described in Chapter 15 (baking ovens) and Chapter 16 (deep-fat fryers). If the humidity of air is reduced, it is reheated more economically. The *rotaire wheel* (Fig. 1.8) and heat pump are examples of dehumidifying equipment. Heat pumps are

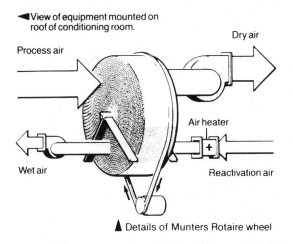

Fig. 1.8 — Rotaire wheel. (Courtesy of the Electricity Council.)

similar to refrigeration plant (Fig. 18.2) but operate by removing heat from a low-temperature source and using it to heat air or water. The application of heat pumps to low-temperature drying of confectionery is described by Anon. (1983a,b,c). The use of air knives for package drying is described by Anon. (1983d) and Beevers (1985). Other energy-saving techniques during dehydration are described by Senhaji and Bimbenet (1984), Flink (1977) and Green (1982).

1.4.5 Effect of heat on micro-organisms

The preservative effect of heat processing is due to the denaturation of proteins, which destroys enzyme activity and enzyme-controlled metabolism in micro-organisms. The rate of destruction is a first-order reaction; when food is heated to a temperature that is high enough to destroy contaminating micro-organisms, the same percentage die in a given time interval regardless of the numbers present initially. This is known as the *logarithmic order of death* and is described by a *death rate curve* (Fig. 1.9). The time needed to destroy 90% of the micro-organisms (to

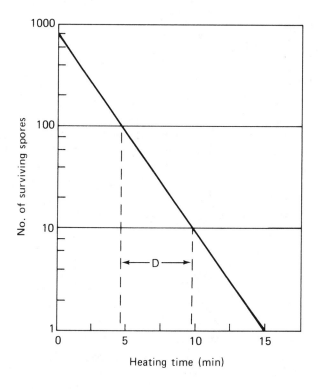

Fig. 1.9 — Death rate curve.

reduce their numbers by a factor of 10) is referred to as the *decimal reduction time* or *D* value (5 min in Fig. 1.9). *D* values differ for different microbial species (Table 1.9), and a higher *D* value indicates greater heat resistance.

There are two important implications arising from the logarithmic order of death. First, the higher the number of micro-organisms present in a raw material, the longer it takes to reduce the numbers to a specified level. In commercial operation the number of micro-organisms varies in each batch of raw material, but it is difficult to recalculate process times for each batch of food. A specific temperature–time combination is therefore used to process every batch of a particular product, and preparation procedures (Chapter 2) are used to ensure that the raw material has a satisfactory and uniform microbiological quality. Secondly, because microbial des-truction takes place logarithmically, it is theoretically possible to destroy all cells only after heating for an infinite time. Processing therefore aims to reduce the number of surviving micro-organisms by a pre-determined amount. This gives rise to the concept of *commercial sterility*, which is discussed further in Chapters 9-11.

The destruction of micro-organisms is temperature dependent; cells die more rapidly at higher temperatures. By collating D values at different temperatures, a *thermal death time* (TDT) curve is constructed (Fig. 1.10). The slope of the TDT

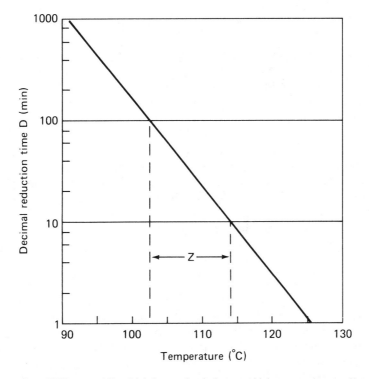

Fig. 1.10 — TDT curve. Microbial destruction is faster at higher temperatures (for example 100 min at 102.5 °C has the same lethal effect as 10 min at 113 °C).

curve is termed the *z value* and is defined as the number of degrees Celsius required to bring about a ten-fold change in decimal reduction time (10.5 °C in Fig. 1.10). The D value and z value are used to characterise the heat resistance of an enzyme, a micro-organism or a chemical component of a food (Table 1.9).

There are a large number of factors which determine the heat resistance of micro-organisms. General statements of the effect of a given variable on heat resistance are not always possible but the following factors are known to be important.

(1) *Type of micro-organism.* Different species and strains show wide variation in their heat resistance (Table. 1.9). Spores are much more heat resistant than vegetative cells.

(2) *Incubation conditions* during cell growth or spore formation. These include

  (a) temperature (spores produced at higher temperatures are more resistant than those produced at lower temperatures),
  (b) age of the culture (the stage of growth of vegetative cells affects their heat resistance) and
  (c) culture medium used (for example mineral salts and fatty acids influence the heat resistance of spores).

(3) *Conditions during heat treatment.* The important conditions are

  (a) pH of the food (pathogenic and spoilage bacteria are more heat resistant near to neutrality; yeasts and fungi are able to tolerate more acidic conditions but are less heat resistant than bacterial spores),
  (b) water activity of the food influences the heat resistance of vegetative cells (section 1.5); in addition moist heat is more effective than dry heat for spore destruction,
  (c) composition of the food (proteins, fats and high concentration of sucrose increase the heat resistance of micro-organisms; the low concentration of sodium chloride used in most foods does not have a significant effect; the physical state of the food, particularly the presence of colloids, affects the heat resistance of vegetative cells) and
  (d) the growth media and incubation conditions, used to assess recovery of micro-organisms in heat resistance studies, affect the number of survivors observed.

Most enzymes have D and z values within a similar range to micro-organisms, and, are therefore inactivated during normal heat processing. However, some enzymes are very heat resistant. These are particularly important in acidic foods, where they may be incompletely denaturated by the relatively short heat treatments and lower temperatures required for microbial destruction. The factors which influence heat resistance of enzymes are similar to those described for micro-organisms and are discussed in detail by Whitaker (1972).

A knowledge of the heat resistance of the enzymes and/or micro-organisms found in a specific food is used to calculate the heating conditions needed for their destruction. In practice the most heat resistant enzyme or micro-organism likely to be present in a given food is used as a basis for calculating process conditions. It is assumed that other less heat-resistant species are also destroyed. Methods for the calculation of processing time are described in Chapter 11.

Table 1.9 — Thermal properties of selected nutritional and sensory components of foods in relation to heat-resistant enzymes and bacteria

Component	Source	pH	z (°C)	D_{121} (min)	Temperature range (°C)
Thiamin	Carrot purée	5.9	25	158	109–149
Thiamin	Pea purée	Natural	27	247	121–138
Thiamin	Lamb purée	6.2	25	120	109–149
Lysine	Soya bean meal	—	21	786	100–127
Chlorophyll a	Spinach	6.5	51	13.0	127–149
a	Spinach	Natural	45	34.1	100–130
Chlorophyll b	Spinach	5.5	79	14.7	127–149
b	Spinach	Natural	59	48	100–130
Anthocyanin	Grape juice	Natural	23.2	17.8*	20–121
Betanin	Beetroot juice	5.0	58.9	46.6*	50–100
Carotenoids	Paprika	Natural	18.9	0.038*	52–65
Peroxidase	Peas	Natural	37.2	3.0	110–138
Peroxidase	Various	—	28–44	—	—
Clostridium botulinum spores type A + B	Various	> 4.5	5.5–10	0.1–0.3*	104
Bacillus stereothermophilus	Various	> 4.5	7–12	4.0–5.0	110 +

*D values at temperatures other than 121°C.
Adapted from Felliciotti and Esselen (1957), Taira *et al.* (1966), Gupta *et al.* (1964), Ponting *et al.* (1960), von Elbe *et al.* (1974), Adams and Yawger (1961), Esselen and Anderson (1956) and Stumbo (1973).

1.4.6 Effect of heat on nutritional and sensory properties

The destruction of many vitamins, aroma compounds and pigments (section 1.1) by heat follows a similar first-order reaction to microbial destruction. Examples of D and z values of selected vitamins and pigments are shown in Table 1.9. In general both values are higher than those of micro-organisms and enzymes. As a result, nutritional and sensory properties are better retained by the use of higher temperatures and shorter times during heat processing. It is therefore possible to select particular time–temperature combinations from a TDT curve (all of which achieve the same degree of enzyme or microbial destruction), to optimise a process for nutrient retention or preservation of desirable sensory qualities. This concept forms the basis of individual quick blanching (Chapter 9), high-temperature short-time (HTST) pasteurisation (Chapter 10), ultrahigh-temperature sterilisation (Chapter 11) and HTST extrusion (Chapter 13). The loss of nutrients and changes to sensory quality during heat processing are reported in Chapters 9–17.

1.5 WATER ACTIVITY

Deterioration of foods by micro-organisms can take place rapidly, whereas enzymic and chemical reactions take place more slowly during storage. In either case water is the single most important factor controlling the rate of deterioration. The moisture content of foods can be expressed either on a wet-weight basis:

$$m = \frac{\text{mass of water}}{\text{mass of sample}} \times 100 \tag{1.21}$$

$$m = \frac{\text{mass of water}}{\text{mass of water + solids}} \times 100 \tag{1.22}$$

or a dry-weight basis

$$M = \frac{\text{mass of water}}{\text{mass of solids}} \tag{1.23}$$

(Lewis, 1987).

The dry-weight basis is more commonly used for processing calculations, whereas the wet-weight basis is frequently quoted in food composition tables. It is important, however, to note which system is used when expressing a result. Dry-weight basis is used throughout this text unless otherwise stated.

A knowledge of the moisture content alone is not sufficient to predict the stability of foods. Some foods are unstable at a low moisture content (for example peanut oil deteriorates if the moisture content exceeds 0.6%), whereas other foods are stable at relatively high moisture contents (for example potato starch is stable at 20% moisture) (van den Berg, 1986). It is the *availability* of water for microbial, enzymic or chemical activity that determines the shelf life of a food, and this is measured by the water activity (a_w) of a food. Examples of unit operations that reduce the availability of water in foods include those that physically remove water (dehydration (Chapter 14), evaporation (Chapter 12) and freeze drying or freeze concentration (Chapter 20)) and those that immobilise water in the food (for example by the use of humectants in 'intermediate-moisture' foods and by formation of ice crystals in freezing (Chapter 19)). Examples of the moisture content and a_w of foods are shown in Table 1.10. The effect of reduced a_w on food stability is shown in Table 1.11.

Water in food exerts a vapour pressure. The size of the vapour pressure depends on

(1) the amount of water present,
(2) the temperature and
(3) the concentration of dissolved solutes (particularly salts and sugars) in the water.

Water activity is defined as the ratio of the vapour pressure of water in a food to the saturated vapour pressure of water at the same temperature:

Table 1.10 — Moisture content and water activity of foods

Food	Moisture content (%)	Water activity	Degree of protection required
Ice (0°C)	100	1.00[a]	
Fresh meat	70	0.985	
Bread	40	0.96	Package to prevent
Ice (− 10°C)	100	0.91[a]	moisture loss
Marmalade	35	0.86	
Ice (− 20°C)	100	0.82[a]	
Wheat flour	14.5	0.72	
Ice (− 50°C)	100	0.62[a]	Minimum protection or
Raisins	27	0.60	no packaging required
Macaroni	10	0.45	
Cocoa powder		0.40	
Boiled sweets	3.0	0.30	Package to prevent
Biscuits	5.0	0.20	moisture uptake
Dried milk	3.5	0.11	
Potato crisps	1.5	0.08	

[a] Vapour pressure of ice divided by vapour pressure of water.
Adapted from Troller and Christian (1978), van den Berg (1986) and Brenndorfer *et al*. (1985).

$$a_w = \frac{P}{P_0} \tag{1.24}$$

where P (Pa) is vapour pressure of the food and P_0 (Pa) the vapour pressure of pure water at the same temperature. a_w is related to the moisture content by the Brunauer–Emmett–Teller (BET) equation

$$\frac{a_w}{M(1-a_w)} = \frac{1}{M_1 C} + \frac{C-1}{M_1 C} a_w \tag{1.25}$$

where a_w is the water activity, M the moisture as percentage dry weight, M_1 the moisture (dry-weight basis) of a monomolecular layer and C a constant. A sample calculation is described by Karel (1975).

A proportion of the total water in a food is strongly bound to specific sites (for example hydroxyl groups of polysaccharides, carbonyl and amino groups of proteins, and hydrogen bonding). When all sites are (statistically) occupied by adsorbed water the moisture content is termed the *BET monolayer* value. Typical examples include gelatin (11%), starch (11%), amorphous lactose (6%) and whole spray-dried milk (3%). The BET monolayer value therefore represents the moisture content at which

Table 1.11 — The importance of water activity in foods

a_w	Phenomenon	Examples
1.00		Highly perishable fresh foods
0.95	*Pseudomonas*, *Bacillus*, *Clostridium perfringens* and some yeasts inhibited	Foods with 40% sucrose or 7% salt, cooked sausages, bread
0.90	Lower limit for bacterial growth (general), *Salmonella*, *Vibrio parahaemolyticus*, *Clostridium botulinum*, *Lactobacillus*, and some yeasts and fungi inhibited	Foods with 55% sucrose, 12% salt, cured ham, medium-age cheese. Intermediate-moisture foods (a_w = 0.90–0.55)
0.85	Many yeasts inhibited	Foods with 65% sucrose, 15% salt, salami, mature cheese, margarine
0.80	Lower limit for most enzyme activity and growth of most fungi; *Staphlococcus aureus* inhibited	Flour, rice (15–17% water) fruit cake, sweetened condensed milk, fruit syrups, fondant
0.75	Lower linmit for halophilic bacteria	Marzipan (15–17% water), jams
0.70	Lower limit for growth of most xerophilic fungi	
0.65	Maximum velocity of Maillard reactions	Rolled oats (10% water), fudge, molasses, nuts
0.60	Lower limit for growth of osmophilic or xerophilic yeasts and fungi	Dried fruits (15–20% water), toffees, caramels (8% water), honey
0.55	Deoxyribonucleic acid becomes disordered (lower limit for life to continue)	
0.50		Dried foods (a_w = 0–0.55), spices, noodles
0.40	Minimum oxidation velocity	Whole egg powder (5% water)
0.30		Crackers, bread crusts (3–5% water)
0.25	Maximum heat resistance of bacterial spores	
0.20		Whole milk powder (2–3% water), dried vegetables (5% water), cornflakes (5% water)

the food is most stable. At moisture contents below this level, there is a higher rate of lipid oxidation and, at higher moisture contents, Maillard browning and then enzymic and microbiological activies are promoted (Fig. 1.11 and Section 1.1).

The movement of water vapour from a food to the surrounding air depends upon both the moisture content and composition of the food and the temperature and humidity of the air. At a constant temperature the moisture content of food changes until it comes into equilibrium with water vapour in the surrounding air. The food then neither gains nor loses weight on storage under those conditions. This is called the *equilibrium moisture content* of the food and the relative humidity of the storage atmosphere is known as the *equilibrium relative humidity*. When different values of relative humidity versus equilibrium moisture content are plotted, a curve known as a *water sorption isotherm* is obtained (Fig. 1.12).

Each food has a unique set of sorption isotherms at different temperatures. The precise shape of the sorption isotherm is caused by differences in the physical structure, chemical composition and extent of water binding within the food, but all sorption isotherms have a characteristic shape, similar to that shown in Fig. 1.12. The first part of the curve, to point A, represents monolayer water, which is very stable, unfreezable and not removed by drying. The second, relatively straight part of the curve (AB) represents water adsorbed in multilayers within the food and solutions of soluble components. The third portion, (above point B) is 'free' water condensed within the capillary structure or in the cells of a food. It is mechanically trapped within the food and held by only weak forces. It is easily removed by drying and easily frozen, as indicated by the steepness of the curve. Free water is available for microbial growth and enzyme activity, and a food which has a moisture content above point B on the curve is likely to be susceptible to spoilage.

The sorption isotherm indicates the a_w at which a food is stable and allows predictions of the effect of changes in moisture content on a_w and hence on storage stability. It is used to determine the rate and extent of drying (Chapter 14), the optimum frozen storage temperatures (Chapter 19) and the moisture barrier properties required in packaging materials (Chapter 22).

The rate of change in a_w on a sorption isotherm differs according to whether moisture is removed from a food (*desorption*) or whether it is added to dry food (*absorption*) (Fig. 1.12). This is termed a *hysteresis loop*. The difference is large in some foods (for example rice) and is important for example in determining the protection required against moisture uptake.

1.5.1 Effect of a_w on foods

The effect of a_w on microbiological and selected biochemical reactions is shown in Fig. 1.11 and Table 1.11. Almost all microbial activity is inhibited below $a_w = 0.6$, most fungi are inhibited below $a_w = 0.7$, most yeasts are inhibited below $a_w = 0.8$ and most bacteria below $a_w = 0.9$. The interaction of a_w with temperature, pH, oxygen and carbon dioxide, or chemical preservatives has an important effect on the inhibition of microbial growth. When any one of the other environmental conditions is suboptimal for a given micro-organism, the effect of reduced a_w is enhanced. This permits the combination of several mild control mechanisms which result in the preservation of food without substantial loss of nutritional or sensory properties (Table 1.12).

Enzymic activity virtually ceases at a_w values below the BET monolayer value. This is due to the low substrate mobility and its inability to diffuse to the reactive site on the enzyme. Chemical changes are more complex. The two most important that

Table 1.12 — Interaction of a_w, pH and temperature in selected foods

Food	pH	a_w	Shelf life	Notes
Fesh meat	>4.5	>0.95	days	Preserve by chilling
Cooked meat	>4.5	0.95	weeks	Ambient storage when packaged
Dry sausage	>4.5	<0.90	months	Preserved by salt and low a_w
Fresh vegetables	>4.5	>0.95	weeks	'Stable' while respiring
Pickles	<4.5	0.90	months	Low pH maintained by packaging
Bread	>4.5	>0.95	days	
Fruit cake	>4.5	<0.90	weeks	Preserved by heat and low a_w
Milk	>4.5	>0.95	days	Preserved by chilling
Yoghurt	<4.5	<0.95	weeks	Preserved by low pH and chilling
Dried milk	>4.5	<0.90	months	Preserved by low a_w

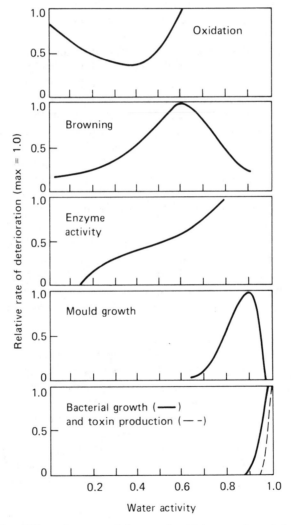

Fig. 1.11 — Effect of water activity on microbial, enzymic and chemical changes to foods. (After Karel (1975).)

occur in foods which have a low a_w are Maillard browning and oxidation of lipids. The a_w that causes the maximum rate of browning varies with different foods. However, in general, a low a_w restricts the mobility of reactants and browning is reduced. At a higher a_w, browning reaches a maximum. Water is a product of the condensation reaction in browning and, at higher moisture levels, browning is inhibited by 'end product inhibition'. At high moisture contents, water dilutes the reactants and the rate of browning falls.

Oxidation of lipids occurs at low a_w values owing to the action of free radicals. Above the BET monolayer value, anti-oxidants and chelating agents (which seques-

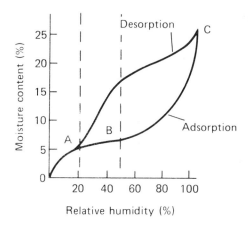

Fig. 1.12 — Water sorption isotherm.

ter trace metal catalysts) become soluble and reduce the rate of oxidation. At higher a_w values the catalytic activity of metals is reduced by hydration and the formation of insoluble hydroxides but, at high a_w values, metal catalysts become soluble, and the structure of the food swells to expose more reactive sites (Fig. 1.11).

1.6 BATCH AND CONTINUOUS PROCESSING

Food is processed either in discrete batches or in a continuous operation, and this is reflected in the design of processing equipment. Examples of batch and continuous equipment are described in each of the subsequent chapters for individual unit operations. In general the advantages of batch processing are as follows:

(1) greater flexibility in being able to change product types or production rates;
(2) lower capital costs for equipment;
(3) simpler operation and control.

The main disadvantages are:

(1) higher labour costs;
(2) higher operating costs for energy and water and less efficient use of materials and energy;
(3) higher floor space requirement;
(4) lower product uniformity.

Batch processing is used when regular changes in product formulation are required throughout the day or week, when small quantities of food are produced, or when production is intermittent throughout the year and the higher capital costs of continuous equipment cannot be justified.

Conversely, continuous operation has lower flexibility, although developments in automatic control (Chapter 24) have improved the ease and speed of changeover to different products or production rates. Capital costs are higher than batch equipment, but savings in energy, space and labour permit a rapid payback of the capital cost, provided high production rates can be maintained and plant utilisation is high. Processing is more easily controlled, and product quality and uniformity are therefore improved. Continuous processing is used when there is sufficient demand for a product to permit high production rates for a substantial part of the working day, throughout most of the year.

ACKNOWLEDGEMENT

Grateful acknowledgement is made for information supplied by the Electricity Council, London, SW1P 4RD.

REFERENCES

Adams, H. W., and Yawger, E. S. (1961) Enzyme inactivation and colour of processed peas. *Food. Technol.* **15** 314–317.

Anon. (1983a) *Electric heat pump drying* EC 4549/12.83. Electricity Council, London, SW1P 4RD.

Anon. (1983b) *Electric heat pumps for product drying*, Technical Information Ind 43. Electricity Council, London, SW1P 4RD.

Anon. (1983c) *Heat recovery for industry*, Technical Information Ind 18. Electricity Council, London SW1P 4RD.

Anon. (1983d) *Air knife drying*, Ec 4401/3.83. Electricity Council, London SW1P 4RD.

Beevers, A. (1985) How to save energy. *Food. Manuf.* **39** 41–43.

Bender, A. E. (1978) *Food processing and nutrition*. Academic Press, London, pp. 3–57.

Bender, A. E. (1987) The nutritional aspects of food processing. In: A. Turner (ed.), *Food technology international Europe*. Sterling, London, pp. 273–275.

van den Berg, C. (1986) Water activity. In: D. MacCarthy (ed.), *Concentration and drying of foods*. Elsevier Applied Science, Barking, Essex, pp. 11–36.

Boardman, J. (1986) Effecting efficient energy usage, *Food. Process.* May 29–31.

Brenndorfer, B., Kennedy, L., Oswin-Bateman, C. O., and Trim, D. S. (1985) *Solar Dryers*. Commonwealth Science Council, Commonwealth Secretariat, London, SW1Y 5HX.

Coultate, T. P. (1984) *Food, the chemistry of its components*. Royal Society of Chemistry, London, pp. 102–129.

Delashmit, R., Dougherty, M., and Robe, K. (1983) Spiral heat exchanger reuses 79% of 'lost' heat. *Food. Process. (USA)* October 106–107.

De Ritter, E. (1982) Effect of processing on nutrient content of food: vitamins. In: M,. Rechcigl (ed.), *Handbook of nutritive value of processed food*, Vol. 1. CRC Press, Boca Raton, Florida, pp. 473–510.

Earle, R. L. (1983) *Unit operations in food processing*, 2nd edn. Pergamon Press, Oxford, pp. 24–38, 46–63.

von Elbe, J. H., Maing, I. Y., and Amundson, C. H. (1974). Colour stability of betanin. *J. Food Sci.* **39** 334–337.

Esselen, W. B., and Anderson, A. A. (1956) *Food. Res.* **21** 322.

Farrall, A. W. (1979) *Food engineering systems*, Vol. 2. AVI, Westport, Connecticut, pp. 117–128.

Fellicotti, E., and Esselen, W. B. (1957) Thermal destruction rates of thiamine in puréed meats and vegetables. *Food Technol.* **11** 77–84.

Flink, J. M. (1977) Energy analysis in dehydration processes. *Food Technol.* **31** (3) 77.

Francis, D. (1986) *Nutrition for children*. Blackwell, Oxford.

Green, R. H. (1982) Energy performance of heat pumps and continuous dryers. In: J. Ashworth (ed.), *Proceedings of the Third International Drying Symposium*. Drying Research Ltd, Wolverhampton.

Gupte, S. M., El-Bisi, H. M., and Francis, F. J. (1964) Kinetics of the thermal degradation of chlorophyll in spinach purée. *J. Food. Sci.* **29** 379.

Harris, R. S., and Karmas, E. (1975) *Nutritional evaluation of food processing*, 2nd edn. AVI, Westport, Connecticut.

Henderson, S. M., and Perry, R. L. (1955) *Agricultural process engineering*. John Wiley, New York.

Jackson, A. T., and Lamb, J. (1981) *Calculations in food and chemical engineering*. Macmillan, London, pp. 1–57.

Karel, M. (1975) Water activity and food preservation. In: O. R. Fennema (ed.) *Principles of food science*, Part 2. Marcel Dekker, New York. pp. 237–263.

Kefford, J. F. (1982) Energy consumption in different food processing technologies. *CSIRO Food Res. Q.* **42** 60–64.

Kunii, D., and Levenspiel, O. (1969) *Fluidization engineering*. John Wiley, New York.

Leniger, H. A., and Beverloo, W. A. (1975) *Food process engineering*. D. Reidel, Dordrecht.

Lewis, M.J. (1987) *Physical properties of foods and food processing systems*. Ellis Horwood, Chichester, West Sussex; VCH, Weinheim.

Loncin, M., and Merson, R.L. (1979) *Food engineering — principles and selected applications*. Academic Press, New York.

Mauron, J. (1982) Effect of processing on nutritive value of food: protein. In: M. Rechcigl (ed.), *Handbook of nutritive value of processed foods*, Vol. 1. CRC Press, Boca Raton Florida, pp. 429–471.

Mohsenin, N. N. (1980) *Thermal properties of foods and agricultural materials.* Gordon and Breach, London.

Peleg, M., and Bagley, E. B. (1983) *Physical properties of foods*, AVI, Westport, Connecticut.

Ponting, J. D., Sanshuck, D. W., and Brekke, J. E. (1960) Color measurement and deterioration in grape and berry juices and concentrates. *J. Food. Sci.* **25** 471–478.

Senhaji, F. A., and Bimbenet, J. J. (1984) Energy saving in drying biological materials. In: B. M. McKenna (ed.), *Engineering and food.* Elsevier Applied Science, Barking, Essex, pp. 947–954.

Sherman, P. (1976) The textural characteristics of dairy products. In: J. M. De Man, P. W. Voisey, V. F. Rasper and D. W. Stanley (eds) *Rheology and texture in food quality.* AVI, Westport, Connecticut, pp. 382–404.

Stanley, D. W., and Tung, M. A. (1976) Microstructure of food and its relation to texture. In: J. M. De Man, P. W. Voisey, V. F. Rasper, and D. W. Stanley (eds), *Rheology and texture in food quality.* AVI, Westport, Connecticut, pp. 28–78.

Stumbo, C. R. (1973) *Thermobacteriology in food processing*, 2nd edn. Academic Press, New York.

Szczesniak, A. S. (1963) Classification of textural characteristics, *J. Food Sci.* **28** 385–389.

Szczesniak, A.S. (1983) Physical properties of foods: what they are and their relation to other food properties. In: M. Peleg, and E. B. Bagley (eds) *Physical properties of foods*, AVI, Westport, Connecticut, pp. 1-41.

Taira, H., Taira, H., and Sukurai, Y. (1966) Studies on amino acid contents of processed soybean, Part 8. *Jpn. J. Nutr. Food* **18** 359.

Troller, J. A., and Christian J. H. B. (1978) *Water activity and food.* Academic Press, London.

Watson, R. R. (1986) *Nutrition for the aged.* CRC Press, Boca Raton, Florida.

Wells, R. D., and Swientek, R. J. (1983) Computerized energy management saves $1.4 million/yr in fuel. *Food. Process.* (*USA*) January 96–98.

Whitaker, J. R. (1972) *Principles of enzymology for the food sciences.* Marcel Dekker, New York.

Whitman, W. E., Crawford, A. G., and Elsen, C. R. (1981) *Energy use in the food manufacturing industry*, Final Report to the Commission of the European Communities, No. EUR 7073 en. Commission of the European Communities, Brussels.

Witton, L. A., and Dimick, P. S. (1982) Effects of processing on food lipids. In: M. Rechcigl (ed.) *Handbook of nutritive value of processed food*, Vol. 1. CRC Press, Boca Raton, Florida, pp. 403–428.

Woodams, E. E., and Nowrey, J. E. (1968) Literature values of thermal conductivity of foods. *Food. Technol.* **22** (4), 150–158.

Zapsalis, C., and Beck, R. A. (1985) *Food chemistry and nutritional biochemistry.* John Wiley, New York, pp. 549–579, 415–504.

Part II
Ambient-temperature processing

In this part, methods used to prepare freshly harvested or slaughtered food, to alter the size of foods, to mix ingredients or to separate components of food are described. Each of these operations is used either to aid subsequent processing or to alter the eating quality of a food. The part concludes with methods of preserving foods that operate at ambient temperature: the long-established techniques of fermentation by micro-organisms and the more recent developments using ionising radiation. In each of these unit operations the sensory characteristics and nutritional properties of foods may be changed by removal of components or by the action of naturally occurring enzymes, but there is negligible damage to food quality due to heat.

2

Raw material preparation

At the time of harvest or slaughter, most foods are likely to contain contaminants, to have components which are inedible or to have variable physical characteristics (for example shape, size or colour). It is therefore necessary to perform one or more of the unit operations of cleaning, sorting, grading or peeling to ensure that foods with a uniformly high quality are prepared for subsequent processing. These are mechanical separation procedures which are applied near the beginning of a process to upgrade the quality of the raw material. They are a highly cost-effective method of improving the overall quality of batches of food. Other separation operations are described in Chapter 5. Further details are given by Leniger and Beverloo (1975) and applications of these techniques to fruit processing are described by Woodroof (1975).

2.1 CLEANING

Cleaning is the unit operation in which contaminating materials are removed from the food and separated to leave the surface of the food in a suitable condition for further processing. A classification of the type of contaminants found on raw foods is shown in Table 2.1.

Peeling fruits and vegetables (section 2.4), skinning meat or descaling fish may also be considered as cleaning operations. In vegetable processing, blanching (Chapter 9) also helps to clean the product.

Cleaning should take place at the earliest opportunity in a food process both to prevent damage to subsequent processing equipment by stones, bone or metals, and to prevent time and money from being spent on processing contaminants which are then discarded. In addition, the early removal of small quantities of food contaminated by micro-organisms prevents the subsequent loss of the remaining bulk by microbial growth during storage or delays prior to processing. Cleaning is thus an effective method of reducing food wastage, improving the economics of processing and protecting the consumer.

Equipment for cleaning is categorised into wet procedures (for example soaking,

Table 2.1 — Contaminants found on raw foods

Type of contaminant	Examples
Metals	Ferrous and non-ferrous metals, bolts, filings
Mineral	Soil, engine oil, grease, stones
Plant	Leaves, twigs, weed seeds, pods and skins
Animal	Hair, bone, excreta, blood, insects, larvae
Chemical[a]	Fertiliser, pesticides, herbicides
Microbial cells	Soft rots, fungal growth, yeasts
Microbial products	Colours, flavours, toxins

Adapted from Brennan et al. (1976).
[a] Not to be confused with adulterants (chemicals intentionally added to food which are forbidden by law) or additives (chemicals added to food to improve eating qualities or shelf life).

spraying, flotation washing and ultrasonic cleaning) and dry procedures (separation by air, magnetism or physical methods). The selection of a cleaning procedure is determined by the nature of the product to be cleaned and by the types of contaminant to be removed. In general, more than one type of cleaning procedure is required to remove the variety of contaminants found on most foods.

2.1.1 Wet cleaning
Wet cleaning is more effective than dry methods for removing soil from root crops or dust and pesticide residues from soft fruits or vegetables. It is also dustless and causes less damage to foods than dry methods. Different combinations of detergents and sterilants at different temperatures allow flexibility in operation. However, the use of warm cleaning water may accelerate chemical and microbiological spoilage unless careful control is exercised over washing times and subsequent delays before processing. Furthermore wet procedures produce large volumes of effluent, often with high concentrations of dissolved and suspended solids. There is then a requirement both to purchase clean water and to pay for high effluent disposal charges. To reduce costs, recirculated, filtered and chlorinated water is used whenever possible. Examples of wet-cleaning equipment include spray washers, brush washers, drum or rod washers and flotation tanks. They are described in detail by Brennan et al. (1976).

2.1.2 Dry cleaning
Dry cleaning procedures are used for products that are smaller, have greater mechanical strength and possess a lower moisture content (for example grains and nuts). After cleaning, the surfaces are dry, to aid preservation or further drying. Dry procedures generally involve smaller cheaper equipment than wet procedures do and produce a concentrated dry effluent which may be disposed of more cheaply. In

addition, plant cleaning is simpler and chemical and microbial deterioration of the food is reduced. However, additional capital expenditure may be necessary to prevent the creation of dust, which not only creates a health and explosion hazard but also recontaminates the product. The main groups of equipment used for dry cleaning are

(1) air classifiers,
(2) magnetic separators and
(3) separators based on screening of foods (section 2.2.1).

Classifiers (for example Fig. 2.1) use a moving stream of air to separate contami-

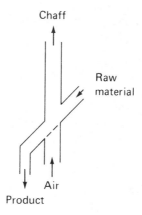

Fig. 2.1 — Separation of chaff by aspiration cleaning.

nants from foods by differences in their densities. The principle is similar to that of the cyclone separator which has found very wide application for removing solids from air or liquids from vapours. Classifiers are widely used in harvesting machines to separate heavy contaminants (for example stones) and light contaminants (for example leaves, stalks and husks) from grain or vegetables. Calculation of the air velocity required for separation is described in Chapter 1 (equations (1.3) and (1.4)).

Physical separation of contaminants from foods is possible when the food has a regular well-defined shape. For example round foods (peas, blackcurrants and rape-seed) are separated from contaminants by exploiting their ability to roll down an inclined conveyor belt. Contaminants (for example weed seeds in rape-seed or snails in blackcurrants) are carried up the conveyor and separated. A disc separator consists of a series of vertical metal discs with precisely engineered indentations in the sides. It is used to separate grain from weed seeds. The indentations match the shape of the grain and as the discs rotate, the grain is lifted out and removed. Discs may be changed to separate barley, oats, rice or wheat (Brennan *et al.*, 1976). Screens (section 2.2.1) are also used to remove contaminants from foods.

Contamination by metal fragments or bolts from machinery is a potential hazard in all processing, and most foods therefore pass through metal detectors before packaging. Ferrous metals are removed by either permanent magnets or electromagnets. Electromagnets are easier to clean (by switching off the power supply) but permanent magnets are cheaper. However, unless regularly inspected, permanent magnets may build up a mass of metal which is lost into the food all at once to cause gross recontamination. Non-ferrous metals, ferrous metal and metal-impregnated grease are identified by passing the food through a strong electromagnetic field. Distortion of the field by these materials causes activation of a warning light or siren. This equipment is described in detail by Mayo (1984). X-rays are used to detect metals and other types of solid contaminant inside packaged foods. The X-rays pass through the food as it passes on a conveyor and are converted to visible light by a phosphor strip. The light is magnified and transmitted by fibre optic cables to an image intensifier and video camera. The final image is displayed on a television monitor. The system activates a warning and may also automatically reject the contaminated item (Anon., 1984a; Williams *et al.*, 1983).

2.2 SORTING

Sorting is the separation of foods into categories on the basis of a measurable physical property. Like cleaning, sorting should be employed as early as possible to ensure a uniform product for subsequent processing. The four main physical properties used to sort foods are size, shape, weight and colour.

The effectiveness of a sorting procedure is calculated using

$$\text{effectiveness} = \frac{PX_p}{FX_f}\frac{R(1-X_r)}{F(1-X_f)} \tag{2.1}$$

where P (kg s^{-1}) is the product flow rate, F (kg s^{-1}) the feed flow rate, R (kg s^{-1}) the rejected food flow rate, X_p the mass fraction of desired material in product, X_f the mass fraction of desired material in the feed and X_r the mass fraction of desired material in the rejected food.

2.2.1 Shape and size sorting

The shape of some foods is important in determining their suitability for processing or their retail value. For example, for economical peeling, potatoes should have a uniform oval or round shape without protruberences. Cucumbers and gherkins are more easily packaged if they are straight, and foods with a characteristic shape (for example pears) have a higher retail value if the shape is uniform. Size sorting (termed *sieving* or *screening*) is the separation of solids into two or more fractions on the basis of differences in size. It is particularly important when the food is to be heated or cooled as the rate of heat transfer is in part determined by the size of the individual pieces and variation in size would cause over-processing or under-processing. Additionally, foods which have a uniform size are said to be preferred by consumers. The effect of screening on the nutritional value of milled grain is described in Chapter 3.

Shape sorting is accomplished manually or mechanically (for example the belt-and-roller sorter in Fig. 2.2, or the disc sorter (section 2.1.2)) or by image processing

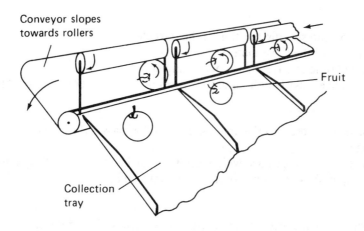

Fig. 2.2 — Belt-and-roller sorter.

(section 2.2.1.3). Screens with either fixed or variable apertures are used for size sorting. The screen may be stationary or, more commonly, rotating or vibrating.

2.2.1.1 Fixed aperture screens

Two common types of fixed aperture screen are the flat bed screen (or sieve) and the drum screen (rotary screen or reel). The multideck flat bed screen (Fig. 2.3) has a

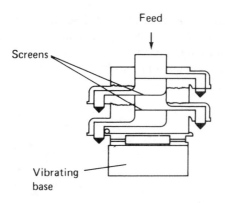

Fig. 2.3 — Multideck flat bed screen. (Courtesy of Gough Engineering Ltd.)

number of inclined or horizontal mesh screens, which have aperture sizes from $20\,\mu m$ to $125\,mm$, stacked inside a vibrating frame. Food particles that are smaller than the screen apertures pass through under gravity until they reach a screen with an aperture size that retains them. The smallest particles that are separated commercially are of the order of $50\,\mu m$. The rate of separation is controlled by

(1) the shape and size distribution of the particles,
(2) the nature of the sieve material,
(3) the amplitude and frequency of shaking and
(4) the effectiveness of methods used to prevent blocking (or blinding) of the sieves.

The *capacity* of a screen is the amount of food that passes through per square metre per second.

   These types of screen are widely used for sorting dry foods (for example flour, sugar and spices). The main problems encountered are

(1) blinding, particularly if the particle size is close to that of the screen aperture,
(2) high feed rates, which cause the screens to become overloaded and small particles are discharged with the oversized particles,
(3) large particles, which may block the screens and
(4) excessive moisture or high humidity, which causes small particles to stick to the screen or to agglomerate and form larger particles, which are then discharged as oversize.

   Vibration alone is often insufficient to separate particles adequately. A gyratory movement is necessary to spread the food over the entire sieve area, and a vertical jolting action breaks up agglomerates and dislodges particles that block sieve apertures.

   The particle size distribution of a material is expressed as either the mass fraction of material that is retained on each sieve or the cumulative percentage of material retained (Fig. 2.4) (data from sample problem 2.1). The mean overall diameter of particles (volume or mass mean diameter) is found using

$$d_V = \frac{\sum dx}{\sum x} \qquad (2.2)$$

where d_V (μm) is the volume or mass mean diameter, d (μm) the average diameter and x (g) the mass retained on a sieve.

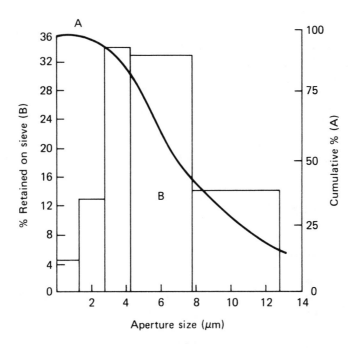

Fig. 2.4 — Retention of particles on sieves: (A) cumulative percentage, (B) mass fraction.

Sample problem 2.1

A sieve analysis of powdered sugar showed the following results. Calculate the mass mean diameter of the sample.

Sieve aperture (μm)	Mass retained (%)
12.50	13.8
7.50	33.6
4.00	35.2
2.50	12.8
0.75	4.6

Solution to problem 2.1

The cumulative percentages are as follows.

To find the mass mean diameter, find dx as follows.

Average diameter of particles d (μm)	x (%)	dx
0.375	4.6	1.725
1.625	12.8	20.8
3.25	35.2	114.4
5.75	33.6	193.2
10.0	13.8	138.0
Total	100.0	468.125

From equation (2.2),

$$\text{mass mean diameter} = \frac{468.125}{100} = 4.68 \ \mu\text{m}$$

Data plotted for cumulative % in Fig. 2.4

Aperture size (μm)	12.50	7.50	4.00	2.50	0.75
Cumulative percentage	13.8	47.4	82.6	95.4	100.0

Many types of drum screen are used for sorting small-particulate foods (for example peas or beans) that have sufficient mechanical strength to withstand the tumbling action inside the screen. Drum screens are almost horizontal (5–10° inclination), perforated metal or mesh cylinders. They may be *concentric* (one inside another), *parallel* (foods leave one screen and enter the next (Fig. 2.5)) or *series* (a single drum constructed from sections with different sized apertures). All types have a higher capacity than flat bed screens. The capacity of drum screens increases with their speed of rotation up to a critical point. Above this the food is held against the screen by centrifugal force and results in poor separation. Similarly there is an increase in capacity with the angle of the screen up to a critical angle. Above this the residence time is too short and products pass through without separation. Problems associated with blinding are less severe than with flat bed screens.

2.2.1.2 *Variable-aperture screens*
Variable-aperture screens have either a continuously diverging aperture or a stepwise increase in aperture. Both types handle foods more gently than drum screens and are therefore used to sort fruits and other foods that are easily damaged. Continuously variable screens employ pairs of diverging rollers, cables or felt-lined conveyor belts. These may be driven at different speeds to rotate the food and thus to align it, to present the smallest dimension to the aperture (Fig. 2.6).
    Stepwise increases in aperture are produced by adjusting the gap between driven

Fig. 2.5 — Parallel drum screen. (Courtesy of FlowMech Ltd.)

rollers and an inclined conveyor belt (Fig. 2.2). The food rotates and the same dimension is therefore used as the basis for sorting (for example the diameter along the core of a fruit). Details of sorting equipment are given by Brennan *et al.* (1976).

2.2.1.3 *Image processing*
Image processing is used to sort foods on the basis of length, diameter, number of surface defects and orientation of the food on a conveyor as well as colour (section 2.2.2). It has been used for example with maize cobs. The maize passes beneath three video cameras, placed 120° apart above a conveyor belt. The images of the surface of the cob are recorded and stored in the memory of a microprocessor. The information is then analysed and compared with pre-programmed specifications for the product, and the cob is either rejected or moved into a group with similar characteristics. In another system a video camera views foods and an operator compares the shapes with an electronic template overlaid on a monitor screen. The template reduces operator fatigue and allows greater concentration on the selection process.

2.2.2 Colour sorting
Small-particulate foods may be automatically sorted at very high rates using microprocessor controlled colour sorting equipment (Fig. 2.7). Particles are fed into the chute one at a time. The angle, shape and lining material of the chute are altered to control the velocity of the pieces as they pass a photodetector. The colour of the

Fig. 2.6 — Roller sorter. (Courtesy of Sunkist Growers).

background and the type and intensity of the light used for illuminating the food are closely controlled for each product. Photodetectors measure the reflected colour of each piece and compare it with pre-set standards. Defective foods are separated by a short blast of compressed air. Typical applications include peanuts, Michegan Navy beans (for baked beans), rice, diced carrot, maize kernels and small fruits. Coffee beans are viewed in ultraviolet light to cause bacterial contaminants to fluoresce, a separation that was not previously possible (Anon. 1982). Arrays of pulsed laser beams are used in another system (Gangi *et al.*, 1983) to illuminate tomatoes as they are discharged from a conveyor. Reflected light is measured by a microprocessor, which operates an automatic reject system.

A different type of equipment employs a sensor located above a conveyor belt, which views products as they pass beneath. The sensor detects up to eight colours and provides an alarm or control signal whenever a pre-selected colour passes the detector beam. It is also able to distinguish between different coloured foods which are to be processed separately. In a more sophisticated system, foods which have

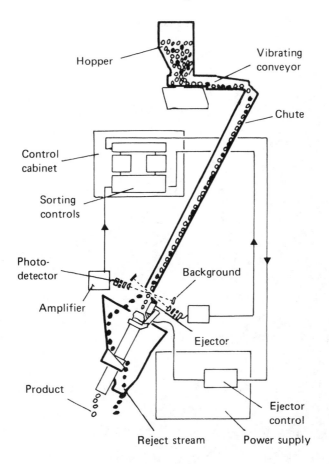

Fig. 2.7 — Colour sorter. (Courtesy of Sortex Ltd.)

variations in colour over their surface are colour sorted by image processing. The foods are fed in rows on a roller conveyor beneath a video camera. The relative intensities of reflected red, green and yellow light are transmitted to the microcomputer which constructs a composite image of each piece of food, showing both the spread of colour and the mean colour of inspected foods. The computer compares the constructed image with pre-set specifications and activates a compressed air ejector, a mechanical deflector or other mechanism to remove rejected food. When this type of system is used to sort baked goods, it is also used to control directly the gas or electricity supply to the ovens, which is reported to reduce energy consumption in ovens by 20% (Philpotts, 1983). The sorter can be adapted to different foods, by changing the microprocessor control (also Chapters 15 and 24).

2.2.3 Weight sorting
Weight sorting is more accurate than other methods and is therefore used for more valuable foods (for example eggs, cut meats and some tropical fruits). Eggs are

sorted at up to 12 000 h^{-1} into six to nine categories with a tolerance of 0.5 g. They are first visually inspected over tungsten lights (*candling*) to remove fertilised or malformed eggs. The weight sorter (Fig. 2.8) consists of a slatted conveyor which

Fig. 2.8 — Egg sorter. (Courtesy of Ben Nevis Packaging Ltd.)

transports the eggs above a series of counterbalanced arms. The conveyor operates intermittently and while stationary, the arms raise and weigh the eggs. Heavy eggs are discharged into a padded chute and light eggs are replaced on the conveyor to travel to the next weigher.

Aspiration and flotation sorting use differences in density to sort foods and are similar in principle and operation to aspiration and flotation cleaning. Grains, nuts and pulses are sorted by aspiration. Peas and lima beans are sorted by flotation in brine (specific gravity, 1.1162–1.1362). The denser starchy overmature pieces sink whereas the younger pieces float.

The collation of foods which have variable weight (for example frozen fish fillets) into bulk packs which have a uniform declared weight is time consuming and laborious. It is normally performed by operators who select items of food from a pool of materials and collate them by trial and error into a pack which is as close as possible to the required weight. There is frequently a large giveaway to ensure compliance with fill-weight legislation. A more recent method of collation sorting is performed automatically by a microcomputer. Items of food are weighed and placed in a magazine. Their weights are stored by a microcomputer which then selects the best combination of items to produce the desired number in a pack, with a minimum giveaway. The foods are packed and the next best combination is selected until the limit on allowable weight cannot be achieved. Other examples of microprocessor-controlled weighing are described in Chapter 24.

2.3 GRADING

This term is often used interchangeably with sorting but strictly means the assessment of a number of attributes to obtain an indication of overall quality of a food. Sorting (that is separation on the basis of one characteristic) may therefore be used as part of a grading operation but not vice versa.

Grading is carried out by trained operators. Meats, for example, are examined by inspectors for disease, fat distribution, carcass size and shape. Other graded foods include cheese and tea. In some cases the grade of food is determined from the results of laboratory analyses (for example wheat flour is assessed for protein content, dough extensibility, colour, moisture content and presence of insects). In general, grading is more expensive than sorting owing to the higher costs of skilled operators. However, many attributes that cannot be examined automatically can be simultaneously assessed, and this produces a more uniform high-quality product.

2.4 PEELING

Peeling is a necessary operation in the processing of many fruits and vegetables to remove unwanted or inedible material, and to improve the appearance of the final product. The main consideration is to minimise costs by removing as little of the underlying food as possible and reducing energy, labour and material costs to a minimum. The peeled surface should be clean and undamaged. There are five main methods of peeling:

(1) flash steam peeling;
(2) knife peeling;
(3) abrasion peeling;
(4) caustic peeling;
(5) flame peeling.

2.4.1 Flash steam peeling
Foods (for example root crops) are fed in batches into a pressure vessel which is rotated at 4–6 rev min^{-1}. High-pressure steam (1500 kPa) is introduced and all food surfaces are exposed to the steam by the rotation of the vessel for a pre-determined time, which differs according to the type of food. The high temperatures cause rapid heating of the surface layer (within 15–30 s) but the low thermal conductivity of the product (Chapter 1) prevents further heat penetration, and the product is not

cooked. Texture and colour are therefore preserved. The pressure is then instantly released which causes steam to form under the skin, and the surface of the food 'flashes off'. Most of the peeled material is discharged with the steam, and water sprays are needed only to remove any remaining traces. This type of peeler is gaining in popularity owing to the lower water consumption, minimum product loss, good appearance of the peeled surfaces, a high throughput (up to $4500 \, kg \, h^{-1}$) with automatic control of the peeling cycle, and the production of a more easily disposable concentrated waste (Anon., 1984b).

2.4.2 Knife peeling

Stationary blades are pressed against the surface of rotating fruits or vegetables to remove the skin. Alternatively the blades may rotate against stationary foods. This method is particularly suitable for citrus fruits where the skin is easily removed and there is little damage or loss of fruit.

2.4.3 Abrasion peeling

Food is fed onto carborundum rollers or placed into a rotating bowl which is lined with carborundum (an abrasive material made from silicon and carbon). The abrasive surface removes the skin and it is washed away by a copious supply of water. The advantages of the method include low energy costs as the process operates at room temperature, low capital costs and a good surface appearance of the food. Irregular product surfaces (for example 'eyes' on potatoes) may mar the appearance of the peeled product and require hand finishing. The limitations of the method are

(1) a higher product loss than flash peeling (25% compared with 8–18% losses, for vegetables),
(2) the production of large volumes of dilute waste which are difficult and expensive to dispose of and
(3) relatively low throughputs as all pieces of food need to contact the abrasive surfaces.

An exception is the peeling of onions where the skin is easily removed by abrasive rollers at production rates of up to $2500 \, kg \, h^{-1}$.

2.4.4 Caustic peeling

A dilute solution of sodium hydroxide (named *lye*) is heated to 100–120°C. In the older method of lye peeling, food is passed through a bath of 1–2% lye which softens the skin and the skin is then removed by high-pressure water sprays. Product losses are of the order of 17%. Although once popular for root crops, this method causes changes in the colour of some products and incurs higher costs. It is now largely replaced by steam or flash peeling. A development of lye peeling is named *dry caustic peeling*. Food is dipped in 10% sodium hydroxide and the softened skin is removed with rubber discs or rollers. This both reduces water consumption and product losses and gives a concentrated skin 'paste' which is more easily disposed of.

2.4.5 Flame peeling

This type of peeling is mostly used for onions. The peeler consists of a conveyor belt which carries and rotates the food through a furnace heated to higher than 1000°C. The outer 'paper shell' and root hairs are burned off, and the charred skin is removed by high-pressure water sprays. Average product losses are 9%.

ACKNOWLEDGEMENTS

Grateful acknowledgement is made for information supplied by the following: Gunson's Sortex Ltd, London E3 2QQ; Spectron Instruments Ltd, Abingdon, Oxfordshire UK; Gough and Co. Ltd., Hanley, Stoke on Trent, Staffordshire ST1 4AP UK; Backus Sormac BV, Venlo, Holland; Goring Kerr, Windsor, Berkshire, UK; Ben Nevis Packaging Ltd, Trowbridge, Wiltshire BA14 8AB, UK; Sunkist Growers Ltd, California, USA; Flo-Mech Ltd, Peterborough PE2 0YA, UK.

REFERENCES

Anon. (1982) It grades Japanese white rice at 800 million grains an hour. *Food Process Ind.* July 18–19.

Anon. (1984a) X(rays) mark the spot. *Food Manuf.* August 35.

Anon. (1984b) Veg peeled 'in a flash'. *Food Manuf.* September 35.

Brennan, J. G., Butters, J. R, Cowell, N. D., and Lilly, A. E. V. (1976) *Food engineering operations*, 2nd edn. Applied Science, London, pp. 3–57.

Gangi, A. R, Gangi, A. R., and Robe, K. (1983) Electronic scanner color-sorts tomatoes on all surfaces. *Food Process (USA)* April 106–107.

Leniger, H. A., and Beverloo, W. A. (1975) *Food process engineering*, D. Reidel, Dordrecht, pp. 236–268.

Mayo, G. (1984) Principles of metal detection. *Food Manuf.* August 27, 29, 31.

Philpotts, P. (1983) Eyes on the production line. *Food Process* **52** (6) 27–29.

Williams, D., Sawyer, C., Conklin, W. C., and Robe, K. (1983) X-ray scanner removes stones from almonds on conveyor belt. *Food. Process (USA)* October 56–57.

Woodroof, J. G. (1975) Fruit washing, peeling and preparation. In: *Commercial fruit processing*. J. G. Woodroof and B. S. Luh (eds), AVI, Westport, Connecticut, pp. 78–99.

3

Size reduction

Size reduction is the unit operation in which the average size of solid pieces of food is reduced by the application of grinding, compression or impact forces. The production of powders and fine particles is also known as *comminution*. When applied to the reduction in size of globules of immiscible liquids (for example oil globules in water) size reduction is more frequently referred to as *homogenisation* or *emulsification*. The size reduction of liquids to droplets (by atomisation) is described in Chapter 14. Size enlargement is achieved by extrusion (Chapter 13) or forming (Chapter 4).

Size reduction has the following benefits in food processing.

(1) There is an increase in the surface-area-to-volume ratio of the food which increases the rate of drying, heating or cooling and improves the efficiency and rate of extraction of soluble components (for example juice extraction from cut fruit (Chapter 5)).

(2) When combined with screening (Chapter 2), a pre-determined range of particle sizes is produced which is important for the correct functional or processing properties of some products (for example icing sugar, spices and cornstarch).

(3) A similar range of particle sizes allows more complete mixing of ingredients (Chapter 4) (for example dried soups and cake mixes).

Size reduction and emulsification have little or no preservative effect. They are used to improve the eating quality or suitability of foods for further processing and to increase the range of products available. In some foods they may promote degradation by the release of naturally occurring enzymes from damaged tissues, or by microbial activity and oxidation at the increased area of exposed surfaces, unless other preservative treatments are employed.

Different methods of size reduction are classified according to the particle size range produced, as follows:

(1) *chopping*, *cutting*, *slicing* and *dicing*:

(a) large to medium (stewing steak, cheese and sliced fruit for canning),

(b) medium to small (bacon, sliced beans and diced carrot), and

(c) small to granular (minced or shredded meat, flaked fish or nuts and shredded vegetables);

(2) *milling* to powders or pastes of increasing fineness (grated products > spices > flours > fruit nectars > powdered sugar, starches > smooth pastes);
(3) *emulsification* and *homogenisation* (mayonnaise, milk, essential oils, butter, ice cream and margarine).

3.1 SIZE REDUCTION OF SOLID FOODS

3.1.1 Theory
There are three types of force used to reduce the size of foods:

(1) *compression* forces;
(2) *impact* forces;
(3) *shearing* (or attrition) forces.

In most size reduction equipment, all three forces are present, but often one is more important than the others.

When stress (force) is applied to a food the resulting internal strains are first absorbed, to cause deformation of the tissues. On many occasions the strain does not exceed a certain critical level named the *elastic stress limit* (E). When the stress is removed, the tissues return to their original shape and release the stored energy as heat. As little as 1% of applied energy may actually be used for size reduction. However, when the strain within a localised area exceeds the elastic stress limit, the food is permanently deformed (Fig. 3.1). If the stress is continued, the strain reaches

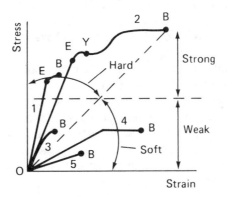

Fig. 3.1 — Stress–strain diagram for various foods: E, elastic limit; Y, yield point; B, breaking point; OE, elastic region; EY, inelastic deformation; YB, region of ductility. Material 1 (curve 1) is hard, strong and brittle, material 2 (curve 2) is hard, strong and ductile, material 3 (curve 3 is hard, weak and brittle, material 4 (curve 4) is soft, weak and ductile, material 5 (curve 5) is soft, weak and brittle. (After Loncin and Merson, (1979).)

a *yield point* (Y), above which the food begins to flow (known as the region of ductility (Y–B in Fig. 3.1)). Finally, the *breaking stress* is exceeded and the food fractures along a line of weakness. Part of the stored energy is then released as sound and heat. As the size of the piece is reduced, there are fewer lines of weakness available, and the breaking stress that must be exceeded increases. When no lines of weakness remain, new fissures must be created to reduce the particle size further, and this requires an additional input of energy. There is therefore a substantial increase in energy requirement as the size of the particles is reduced (see Sample problem 3.1). It is important to specify the required size distribution in the product to avoid unnecessary expenditure of time and energy in creating smaller particles than necessary.

The amount of energy that is absorbed by a food before it fractures is determined by its hardness and tendency to crack (*friability*) which in turn depends on the structure of the food. Harder foods absorb more energy and consequently require a greater energy input to create fractures. The more lines of weakness in a food, the lower is the energy input needed to cause fracturing. Compression forces are used to fracture friable or crystalline foods, combined impact and shearing forces are necessary for fibrous foods, and shearing forces are used for fine grinding of softer foods. It is thought that foods fracture at lower stress levels if force is applied for longer times. The extent of size reduction, the energy expended and the amount of heat generated in the food therefore depend on both the size of the forces and the time that food is subjected to the force.

Other factors which influence the energy input are the moisture content and heat sensitivity of the food. The moisture content significantly affects both the degree of size reduction and the mechanism of breakdown in some foods. Wheat for example is 'conditioned' to optimum moisture content before milling. Maize is thoroughly soaked and wet milled in order to obtain complete disintegration of the starchy material. Further details are given by Kent (1983). However, excess moisture in a 'dry' food can lead to agglomeration of particles which then block the mill. Very dry foods create excessive dust which causes a health hazard, and is extremely inflammable and potentially explosive.

Substantial amounts of heat are generated in high-speed mills. The heat sensitivity of the food determines the permissible temperature rise and the necessity to cool the mill. In *cryogenic grinding*, liquid nitrogen or solid carbon dioxide are mixed with foods (for example spices) before milling, to cool the product and to retain volatiles or other-heat sensitive components. Solid carbon dioxide is also used to cool meat during size reduction in the manufacture of sausagemeat.

The energy required to reduce the size of solid foods is calculated using one of three equations, as follows.

(1) *Kick's law* states that the energy required to reduce the size of particles is proportional to the ratio of the initial size of a typical dimension (for example the diameter of the pieces) to the final size of that dimension:

$$E = K_K \ln\left(\frac{d_1}{d_2}\right)$$
(3.1)

where E (J) is the energy required per unit mass of feed, K_K Kick's constant, d_1 (m) the average initial size of pieces and d_2 (m) the average size of ground particles. d_1/d_2 is known as the *size reduction ratio* which is used to evaluate the relative performance of different types of equipment.

(2) *Rittinger's law* states that the energy required for size reduction is proportional to the change in surface *area* of the pieces of food (instead of a change in dimension described in Kick's law):

$$E = K_R \left(\frac{1}{d_2} - \frac{1}{d_1} \right) \tag{3.2}$$

where K_R is Rittinger's constant.

(3) *Bond's law* is used to calculate the energy required for size reduction from

$$\frac{E}{W} = \sqrt{\left(\frac{100}{d_2}\right)} - \sqrt{\left(\frac{100}{d_1}\right)} \tag{3.3}$$

where W (40000–80000 J kg^{-1} for hard foods (sugar, grain) (Loncin and Merson, 1979)) is the Bond work index, d_1 the diameter of the sieve aperture that allows 80% of the mass of the feed to pass and d_2 the diameter of the sieve aperture that allows 80% of the mass of the ground material to pass.

In practice it has been found that Kick's law gives reasonably good results for coarse grinding in which there is a relatively small increase in surface area per unit mass. Rittinger's law gives better results with fine grinding where there is a much larger increase in surface area and Bond's law is intermediate between these two. However, equations (3.2) and (3.3) were developed from studies of hard materials (coal and limestone) and deviation from predicted results is likely with many foods.

Sample problem (3.1)
Food is milled from 6 mm to 0.0012 mm using a 10 hp motor. Would this motor be adequate to reduce the size of the particles to 0.0008 mm? Assume Rittinger's equation and that 1 hp = 745.7 W.
From equation (3.2),

Solution to sample problem 3.1

$$7457 = K_R \left(\frac{1}{0.0012 \times 10^{-3}} \right) - \left(\frac{1}{6 \times 10^{-3}} \right)$$

Therefore,

$$K_R = \frac{7457}{1/1.2 \times 10^{-6} - 1/6 \times 10^{-3}} = 0.0089$$

To produce particles of 0.0008mm

$$E = 0.0089 \frac{1}{0.0008 \times 10^{-3}} - \frac{1}{6 \times 10^{-3}} = 11\,123\,kW$$

$$= 15\,hp$$

Therefore the motor is unsuitable and an increase in power of 50% is required.

3.1.2 Equipment
This section describes selected equipment used to reduce the size of both fibrous foods to smaller pieces or pulps, and dry particulate foods to powders. A summary of the main applications is shown in Table 3.1 (also Table 3.2).

Table 3.1 — Applications of size reduction equipment

Equipment	Type of product[a]					Fineness[b]			
	1	2	3	4	5	a	b	c	d
Slicers			*	*	*	*			
Dicers			*	*	*	*			
Shredders			*	*	*		*		
Bowl choppers			*	*	*		*	*	
Pre-crushers	*			*	*		*		
Hammer mills	*	*		*	*		*	*	
Fine impact mills	*			*	*		*	*	*
Classifier mills	*				*				*
Air jet mills	*	*			*				*
Ball mills		*							*
Disc mills	*							*	*
Roller mills	*			*	*			*	*
Pulpers				*				*	*

[a] 1, soft, brittle, crystalline; 2, hard, abrasive; 3, elastic, tough, cuttable; 4, fibrous; 5, heat sensitive, greasy.
[b] a, coarse lumps; b, coarse grits; c, medium fine to fine; d, fine to ultrafine.
Adapted from Anon. (1986).

3.1.2.1 Size reduction of fibrous foods
Most meats, fruits and vegetables fall into the general category of 'fibrous' foods. Meats are frozen and 'tempered' to just below their freezing point (Chapters 17 and 19) to improve the efficiency of cutting. Fruits and vegetables have an inherently firmer texture and are cut at ambient or chill temperatures. There are five main types of size reduction equipment, classified in order of decreasing particle size as follows.
(1) *Slicing equipment* consists of rotating or reciprocating blades which cut the food as it passes beneath. In some designs (Fig. 3.2(a)) food is held against the blades

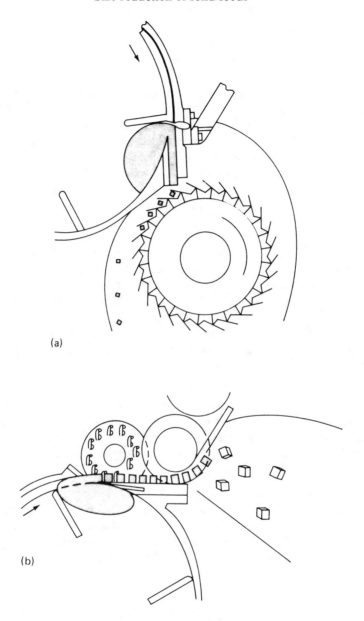

(a)

(b)

Fig. 3.2 — (a) Slicing equipment; (b) dicing equipment. (Courtesy of Urschel Ltd.)

by centrifugal force. In others (for slicing meats) the food is held on a carriage as it travels across the blade. Harder fruits such as apples are simultaneously sliced and de-cored as they are forced over stationary knives fitted inside a tube. In a similar design (the *hydrocutter*) foods are conveyed by water at high speed over fixed blades.

(2) *Dicing equipment* is for vegetables, fruits and meats. The food is first sliced and then cut into strips by rotating blades. The strips are fed to a second set of rotating knives which operate at right angles to the first set and cut the strips into cubes (Fig. 3.2(b)).

(3) *Flaking equipment* for flaked fish, nuts or meat is similar to slicing equipment. Adjustment of the blade type and spacing is used to produce the flakes.

(4) *Shredding equipment.* Typical equipment is a modified hammer mill (section 3.1.2.2.3) in which knives are used instead of hammers to produce a flailing or cutting action. A second type of shredder is known as the *squirrel cage disintegrator*. Here two concentric cylindrical cages inside a casing are fitted with knife blades along their length. The two cages rotate in opposite directions and food is subjected to powerful shearing and cutting forces as it passes between them.

(4) *Pulping equipment* is used for juice extraction from fruits or vegetables and for puréed and pulped meats. A combination of compression and shearing forces is used in each type of equipment. A rotary grape crusher consists of a cylindrical metal screen fitted internally with high-speed rotating brushes or paddles (Nelson and Tressler, 1980). Grapes are heated if necessary to soften the tissues, and pulp is forced through the perforations of the screen by the brushes. The size of the perforations determines the fineness of the pulp. Skins, stalks and seeds are discarded from the end of the screen. Other types of pulper, including roller presses and screw presses, are used for juice expression (Chapter 5).

A *bowl chopper* (Fig. 3.3) is used to chop meat and harder fruits and vegetables into a coarse pulp (for example for sausage meat or mincemeat preserve). A horizontal, slowly rotating bowl moves the ingredients beneath a set of high-speed rotating blades. Food may be passed several times beneath the knives until the required degree of size reduction and mixing has been achieved.

3.1.2.2 Size reduction of dry foods
There are a large number of mills available for application to specific types of food. In this section a selection of common types is described and a summary of their properties and applications is shown in Table 3.2. Other types of equipment are described by Loncin and Merson (1979) and Leniger and Beverloo (1975).

3.1.2.2.1 Ball mills
This type of mill consists of a slowly rotating, horizontal steel cylinder which is half filled with steel balls 2.5–15 cm in diameter. At low speeds or when small balls are used, shearing forces predominate. With larger balls or at higher speeds, impact forces become more important. A modification of the ball mill named the *rod mill* has rods instead of balls to overcome problems associated with the balls sticking in adhesive foods.

3.1.2.2.2 Disc mills
There are a large number of designs of disc mill. Each type employs shearing forces for fine grinding or shearing and impact forces for coarser grinding. For example,

Fig. 3.3 — Bowl chopper: 1, cutting blades; 2, cover; 3, rotating cutter bowl; 4, casing; 5, rotating unloader disc; 6, main motor drive. (Courtesy of Hoegger Alpina Ltd.)

(1) *single-disc mills* in which food passes through an adjustable gap between a stationary casing and a grooved disc which rotates at high speed,

(2) *double-disc mills* in which two discs rotate in opposite directions to produce greater shearing forces, and

(3) *pin-and-disc mills* which have intermeshing pins fixed either to the single disc and casing or to double discs (Fig. 3.4(a)).

These improve the effectiveness of milling by creating additional impact and shearing forces.

3.1.2.2.3 Hammer mills

A horizontal cylindrical chamber is lined with a toughened steel breaker plate. A high-speed rotor inside the chamber is fitted with hammers along its length (Fig. 3.4(b)). In operation, food is disintegrated mainly by impact forces as the hammers

Table 3.2 — Properties and applications of selected size reduction equipment

Type of equipment	Type(s) of force	Peripheral velocity ($m s^{-1}$)	Typical products
Pin-and-disc mill	Impact	80–160	Sugar, starch, cocoa powder, nutmeg, pepper, roasted nuts, cloves
Wing-beater mill	Impact and shear	50–70	Alginates, pepper, pectin, paprika, dried vegetables
Disc-beater mill	Impact and shear	70–90	Milk powder, lactose, cereals, dried whey
Vertical toothed disc mill	Shear	4–8 / 17	Frozen coffee extract, plastic materials / Coarse grinding of rye, maize, wheat, fennel, pepper, juniper berry
Cutting granulator	Impact (and shear)	5–18	Fish meal, pectin, dry fruit and vegetables
Hammer mill	Impact	40–50	Sugar, tapioca, dry vegetables, extracted bones, dried milk, spices, pepper
Ball mill	Impact and shear	—	Food colours
Roller mills	Compression and shear	—	Sugar cane, wheat (fluted rollers) / Chocolate refining (smooth rollers)

Source: Loncin and Merson (1979).

drive it against the breaker plate. In some designs the exit from the mill is restricted by a screen and food remains in the mill until the particles are sufficiently small to pass through the screen apertures. Under these 'choke' conditions, shearing forces play a larger part in the size reduction.

3.1.2.2.4   Roller mills

Two or more steel rollers revolve towards each other and pull particles of food through the 'nip' (the space between the rollers) (Fig. 3.4(c)). The main force is compression but, if the rollers are rotated at different speeds, or if the rollers are fluted (shallow ridges along the length of the roller), there is an additional shearing force exerted on the food. The size of the nip is adjustable for different foods and overload springs protect against accidental damage from metal or stones.

3.1.3   Effect on foods

Size reduction is a processing aid which permits control over the properties of foods, to improve the efficiency of mixing (Chapter 4) and heat transfer. The texture of many foods (for example bread, hamburgers and juices) is controlled by the conditions used during size reduction. There is also an indirect effect on the aroma and flavour of some foods. The disruption of cells and resulting increase in surface area promotes oxidative deterioration and higher rates of microbiological and enzymic activity. Size reduction therefore has little or no preservative effect. Dry foods (for example grains or nuts) have a sufficiently low a_w (Chapter 1) to permit storage for several months after milling without substantial changes in nutritive value or eating quality. However, moist foods deteriorate rapidly if additional preservative operations (for example chilling, freezing and heat processing) are not undertaken.

3.1.3.1 Sensory characteristics

There are small but largely unreported changes in the colour, flavour and aroma of dry foods during size reduction. Oxidation of carotenes bleaches flour and reduces the nutritive value. There is a loss of volatile constituents from spices and some nuts, which is accelerated if the temperature is allowed to rise during milling. In moist foods the disruption of cells allows enzymes and substrates to become more intimately mixed, which causes accelerated deterioration of flavour, aroma and colour. Additionally the release of cellular materials provides a suitable substrate for microbiological growth and this can also result in the development of off-flavours and aromas. The temperature therefore is maintained at 2–5°C (Chapter 18) to minimise microbial and enzymic activity.

The texture of foods is substantially altered by size reduction, both by the physical reduction in the size of tissues and also by the release of hydrolytic enzymes. The speed and duration of size reduction and the delay before subsequent preservation operations are closely controlled to achieve the desired texture. The relationship between the size of food particles and perceived texture is discussed by Stanley and Tung (1976) and Sherman (1976).

3.1.3.2 Nutritive value

The increase in surface area of foods causes small changes in nutritive value due to oxidation of fatty acids and vitamin A during size reduction. Losses of vitamin C and thiamin in chopped or sliced fruits and vegetables are substantial (for example 78% reduction in vitamin C during slicing of cucumber). These changes are reviewed by Erdman and Erdman (1982). Losses during storage depend on the temperature and moisture content of the food and on the concentration of oxygen in the storage atmosphere. In dry foods the main loss in nutritive value results from screening operations performed on the product after size reduction (for example the separation of bran from rice, wheat or maize in Table 3.3).

3.2 SIZE REDUCTION IN LIQUID FOODS (EMULSIFICATION AND HOMOGENISATION)

The terms *emulsifiers* and *homogenisers* are often used interchangeably for equipment used to produce emulsions. Emulsification is the formation of a stable emulsion by the intimate mixing of two or more immiscible liquids, so that one (the dispersed phase) is dispersed in the form of very small droplets within the second (the continuous phase). Homogenisation is the reduction in size (to 0.5–3μm) and increase in number of solid or liquid particles of the dispersed phase, by the application of intense shearing forces, to increase the intimacy and stability of the two substances. Homogenisation is therefore a more severe operation than emulsification. Both operations are used to change the functional properties or eating quality of foods. They have little or no effect on nutritional value or shelf life.

3.2.1 Theory

The two types of liquid–liquid emulsion are

(1) oil in water (o/w) (for example milk) and

(a)

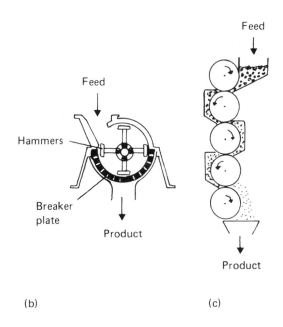

(b)   (c)

Fig. 3.4 — Mills: (a) pin and disc mill (courtesy of Alpine Process Technology); (b) hammer
mill; (c) roller mill. (After Leniger and Beverloo (1975).)

Table 3.3 — Effect of milling on vitamin content of selected grains

Product	Content per 100 g									
	Vitamin A (IU)	a-Tocopherol (mg)	Thiamin (mg)	Riboflavin (mg)	Niacin (mg)	Vitamin C (mg)	Pantothenic acid (mg)	Vitamin B$_6$ (mg)	Folic acid (μg)	Biotin (μg)
Maize										
Kernel	400	1.43	0.15	0.12	1.7	12	0.54	0.16	26.8	11.0
Flour	340	—	0.20	0.06	1.4	0	—	—	—	—
Rice										
Grain	0	0.68	0.34	0.05	4.7	0	1.10	0.55	20.2	12.0
White grain	0	0.10	0.07	0.03	1.6	0	0.55	0.17	14.1	5.0
Bran	0	—	2.26	0.25	29.8	0	2.8	2.5	150	60
Wheat										
Grain (hard)	0	1.35	0.57	0.12	4.3	0	1.5	0.4	14.4	12
80% extraction[a]	—	—	0.25	0.08	1.6	—	0.9	0.11	13	1.4
70% extraction[a]	—	—	0.08	0.05	1.1	—	0.7	0.06	10	1.1
bran	0	1.71	0.72	0.35	21.0	0	2.9	0.82	155	49

[a] Percentage extraction = weight of flour per 100 parts of flour milled.
Adapted from the data of Houston and Kohler (1970), Bauernfeind (1977), Toepfer et al. (1951) and Frigg (1976).

(2) water in oil (w/o) (for example margarine).

However, these are relatively simple systems and more complex emulsions are found in such products as ice cream, sausagemeat and cakes (section 3.2.3).
    The stability of emulsions is determined by

(1) the type and quantity of emulsifying agent (Appendix B, section B.2),
(2) the size of the globules in the dispersed phase,
(3) the interfacial forces acting at the surfaces of the globules,
(4) the viscosity of the continuous phase and
(5) the difference between the densities of the dispersed and continuous phases.

    The higher the interfacial tension between the continuous and dispersed phases, the more difficult it is to form and maintain a stable emulsion. Emulsifying agents present in, or added to, a food form micelles around each droplet of the dispersed phase to reduce the interfacial tension between the phases and prevent the droplets from coalescing. The energy input from the violent shearing action of homogenisers reduces the size of droplets. Emulsifying agents therefore lower the energy input needed to form an emulsion.
    Emulsifying agents are classified into polar and non-polar types. Those in which polar groups are dominant bind to water and therefore produce o/w emulsions. Non-polar agents are adsorbed to oils to produce w/o emulsions. They are characterised by the hydrophile–lipophile balance (HLB) value which is the ratio of hydrophilic to hydrophobic groups on the molecules of an emulsifier (Table 3.4). Polar emulsifying agents are also classified into ionic and non-ionic types. There are three ionic types (anionic, cationic and amphoteric) and one non-ionic type. Each has different

Table 3.4 — Selected emulsifying agents in food processing

Emulsifier	HLB value	Function and typical applications
Ionic		
Sodium stearyl-2-lactylates	—	Crumb softening (baked goods)
		Aid extrusion and reduce stickiness (pasta, snackfoods and chewing gum
		Improve whipping and aeration (instant potato, frozen cream and toppings)
		Dispersion (coffee whiteners)
Non-ionic		
Glyceryl monostearate	2.8	Anti-staling, crumb softening (bread, most baked goods)
		Fat crystal modification (peanut butter, coatings)
Sorbitol esters of fatty acids	4.7	Bloom retardation (chocolate, coatings)
		Overrun control (ice cream)

NB. All are used for combining oil and water to form stable emulsions.

surface activity over the pH range, owing to differences in their dissociation behaviour. Anionic types form negatively charged ions and are active in neutral to alkaline solutions. Cationic types form positively charged ions and are active in acidic solutions. Amphoteric emulsifiers have an isoelectric zone in which the charges on the molecule are balanced and there is no dissociation to ions. They are ineffective in the pH range of the isoelectric zone. However, when the pH is altered, the emulsifier develops a positive or negative charge (depending on whether acid or alkali is added) and assumes surface active-properties. Finally the activity of non-ionic emulsifiers is independant of pH. The type of emulsifying agent used is therefore carefully selected to create the emulsion required in a given food system. Commonly used emulsifying agents are described in Table 3.4 and Appendix B, section B.2.

Stabilisers (Appendix B, section B.2) are polysaccharide hydrocolloids which dissolve in water to form viscous solutions or gels. The increase in viscosity and the complex interactions with the globules of o/w emulsions form a three-dimensional network that stabilises the emulsion and prevents coalescence. Only microcrystalline cellulose and related cellulose powders are able to stabilise w/o emulsions.

The factors that influence the stability of an emulsion are related by *Stoke's Law*:

$$v = \frac{D^2 g(\rho_p - \rho_s)}{18\mu} \tag{3.4}$$

where v (m s^{-1}) is the velocity of separation of phases, D (m) the diameter of droplets in the dispersed phase, g (m s^{-2}) the acceleration due to gravity, ρ_p

$(kg\,m^{-3})$ the density of dispersed phase, ρ_s $(kg\,m^{-3})$ the density of continuous phase, and μ $(N\,s^{-1}\,m^{-1})$ the viscosity of continuous phase. The equation indicates that stable emulsions (that is a low separation velocity) are formed when droplet sizes are small (in practice between $1\,\mu m$ and $10\,\mu m$), the densities of the two phases are reasonably close and the viscosity of the continuous phase is high. Physical changes to droplets, and equations which relate droplet distortion to shear rate, are described by Loncin and Merson (1979).

3.2.2   Equipment
The four main types of homogeniser are as follows:
(1) high-speed mixers;
(2) pressure homogenisers;
(3) colloid mills;
(4) ultrasonic homogenisers.
They are described in more detail by Rees (1967).

3.2.2.1   High-speed mixers
Turbine or propeller-type high-speed mixers (Fig. 4.3) are used to pre-mix emulsions of low-viscosity liquids. They operate by a shearing action on the food at the edges and tips of the blades (Chapter 4).

3.2.2.2   Pressure homogenisers
These consist of a high-pressure pump, operating at 10 000–70 000 kPa, which is fitted with a homogenising valve on the discharge side. An example of one of the many different designs of valve is shown in Fig. 3.5. When liquid is pumped through the

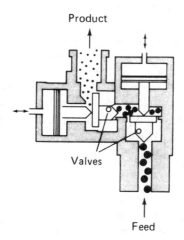

Fig. 3.5 — Hydraulic two-stage pressure homogenising valve. (Courtesy of APV Crepaco Inc.)

small, adjustable gap (300 μm) between the valve and the valve seat, the high pressure results in a high liquid velocity (8400 m s^{-1}). There is then an almost instantaneous drop in velocity as the liquid emerges from the valve. These extreme conditions of turbulence produce powerful shearing forces. The collapse of air bubbles (termed *cavitation*) and impact forces created in some valves by placing a hard surface (a *breaker ring*) in the path of the liquid further reduce the globule size. In some foods (for example milk products) there may be inadequate distribution of the emulsifying agent over the newly formed surfaces, which causes fat globules to clump together. A second similar valve is then used to break up the clusters of globules. Pressure homogenisers are widely used before pasteurisation (Chapter 10) and ultrahigh-temperature sterilisation (Chapter 11) of milk, and in the production of salad creams, ice cream and some sauces.

3.2.2.3 Colloid mills
These homogenisers are essentially disc mills (section 3.1.2.2.2). The small clearance (0.05–1.3 mm) between a vertical disc which rotates at 3000–15 000 rev min^{-1}, and a similar-sized stationary disc creates high shearing forces. They are more effective than pressure homogenisers for high-viscosity liquids, but with intermediate-viscosity liquids they tend to produce larger droplet sizes than pressure homogenisers do. Numerous designs of disc, including flat, corrugated and conical shapes, are available for different applications. Modifications of this design include the use of two counter-rotating discs or intermeshing pegs on the surface of the discs to increase the shearing action. For highly viscous foods (for example peanut butter, meat or fish pastes) the discs may be mounted horizontally (the *paste mill*). The greater friction created in viscous foods may require these mills to be cooled by recirculating water.

3.2.2.4 Ultrasonic homogenisers
High-frequency sound waves (18–30 kHz) cause alternate cycles of compression and tension in low-viscosity liquids and cavitation of air bubbles, to form an emulsion with droplet sizes of 1–2 μm. In operation, the dispersed phase of an emulsion is added to the continuous phase and both are pumped through the homogeniser at pressures of 340–1400 kPa. The ultrasonic energy is produced by a metal blade, which vibrates at its resonant frequency. Vibration is produced either electrically or by the liquid movement (Fig. 3.6). The frequency is controlled by adjusting the clamping position of the blade. This type of homogeniser is used for the production of salad creams, ice cream, synthetic creams and essential oil emulsions. It is also used for dispersing powders in liquids.

3.2.3 Effect on foods
3.2.3.1 Viscosity or texture
In many liquid and semi-liquid foods, the desired mouthfeel is achieved by careful selection of the type of emulsifying agent and stabiliser (Appendix B, section B.2) and control over homogenisation conditions. In milk, homogenisation reduces the average size of fat globules from 4 μm to less than 1 μm. The increase in viscosity is due to the higher number of globules and adsorption of casein onto the globule surface. These changes are discussed in detail by Harper (1979).

In solid food emulsions the texture is determined by the composition of the food,

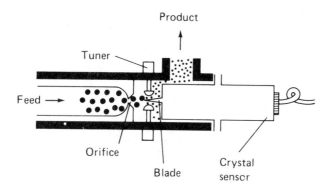

Fig. 3.6 — Ultrasonic homogeniser. (After Loncin and Merson (1979).)

the homogenisation conditions and post-processing operations (for example heating or freezing). Meat emulsions (for example sausage and paté) are o/w emulsions in which the continuous phase is a complex colloidal system of gelatin, proteins, minerals and vitamins, and the dispersed phase is fat globules. The stability of the continuous phase is determined in part by the water-holding capacity (WHC) and fat-holding capacity (FHC) of the meat proteins. The factors which affect WHC and FHC are described by Laurie (1985). The quality of the emulsion is influenced by

(1) the ratios of meat to ice to water to fat used,
(2) use of polyphosphates to bind water, and
(3) the time, temperature and speed of homogenisation.

The emulsion is set by heat during cooking.

Although butter is thought of as a w/o emulsion, the complete inversion of the o/w emulsion of cream does not take place. Cream is mechanically agitated (churned) to cause a partial breakdown of the emulsion. During this stage, air is incorporated to produce a foam (a colloidal system with a liquid continuous phase and a gaseous dispersed phase). Liquid fat is released from globules at the surfaces of air bubbles, and this binds together clumps of solid fat to form butter 'grains'. These are then agitated at low speed (working) to disperse water as fine droplets throughout the mass, and to rupture any fat globules remaining from the cream. The final product has a continuous phase of 85% fat which contains globules and crystals of solid fat and air bubbles. The dispersed phase (15%) consists of water droplets and buttermilk. The stability of butter is mostly due to its semi-solid nature which prevents migration of bacteria trapped in water droplets and not to the action of an emulsifying agent.

Margarine and low-fat spreads are w/o emulsions. They are produced from a blend of oils, which is heated with a solution of skim milk, salt, added vitamins and emulsifying agents. The mixture is emulsified and worked to the desired consistency in a continuous operation. Similar equipment is used for continuous butter-making (Fig.3.7). The fat content of margarine is similar to butter, but low-fat spreads have approximately 40% fat. The oils are chosen to have low melting points and these products are therefore spreadable at refrigeration temperatures.

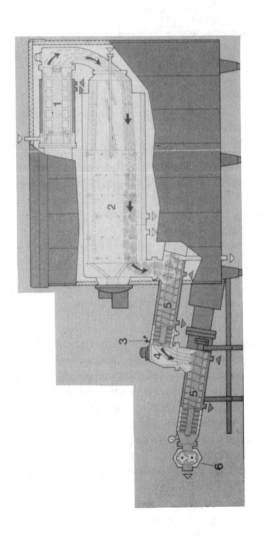

Fig. 3.7 — Continuous butter-making equipment: 1, churning section; 2, separation of buttermilk; 3, regulating gate; 4, vacuum chamber; 5, working-section; 6, butter pump. (Courtesy of Pasilac A/S.)

In other solid emulsions (for example ice cream and cake batters) the emulsion is formed as a liquid, and the texture of the final product is partly determined by subsequent unit operations (freezing and baking respectively). Ice cream is a thick o/w emulsion which has a complex continuous phase of ice crystals, colloidal milk solids, dissolved sugar, flavouring, colouring and stabilisers, and a solid–air foam. The dispersed phase is milk fat. Air is incorporated into the emulsion to create a foam during freezing. The amount of air is measured as the *overrun*:

$$\text{overrun} = \frac{m_1 - m_f}{m_f} \times 100 \qquad (3.5)$$

where m_1 (kg) is the mass of unit volume of liquid mix and m_f (kg) the mass of unit volume of finished product. Commercial ice creams have overruns of 60–100%.

Freezing partially destabilises the emulsion to produce a degree of clumping of fat globules, which improves the texture. Commercial ice creams usually have a softer texture than home-made products due to faster freezing, which produces smaller ice crystals (Chapter 19), and to emulsifiers and stabilisers, which permit a larger proportion of the aqueous phase to remain unfrozen. This prevents lactose crystallisation and reduces graininess. Less heat is needed to melt the ice cream and it does not therefore feel excessively cold when eaten. Cake batters are similarly o/w emulsions, in which the continuous phase is colloidal starch, a solution of sugar and flavours, and a foam produced during mixing. The dispersed phase is added fats or oils.

3.2.3.2   Colour, aroma, nutritional value and shelf life

Homogenisation has an effect on the colour of some foods. For example, in milk the larger number of globules causes greater reflectance and light scattering, and an increase in whiteness. *Flavour* and *aroma* are improved in many emulsified foods. Volatile components are dispersed finely throughout the food and hence have greater contact with taste buds when eaten.

The *nutritional value* of emulsified foods is changed if components are separated (for example in butter making) (Table 3.5), and there is improved digestibility of fats and proteins owing to the reduction in particle size (for example baby foods). The nutritional value of other foods is determined by the formulation used and is not affected by emulsification or homogenisation.

The action of homogenisers and emulsifying agents stabilises a product to give a uniform appearance and to prevent separation, but they do not in themselves preserve a food. Additional unit operations (for example chilling, freezing and baking) are necessary to extend the shelf life. In all food emulsions, such degradative changes as hydrolysis or oxidation of pigments, aroma compounds and vitamins, and microbial growth on the finely dispersed material, are minimised by careful control over the packaging and storage conditions. In many countries, special regulations are in force to control hygienic standards during preparation of food emulsions (particularly meat emulsions and ice cream) owing to the risk of dispersing pathogenic bacteria throughout the food.

Table 3.5 — Effect of emulsification on nutritional value

Nutrient (per 100g food)	Amount in the following	
	Cream (double)	Butter (salted)
Water (g)	48	15.4
Protein (g)	1.5	0.4
Fat (g)	48	82
Carbohydrate (g)	2.0	0
Energy (kJ)	1850	3040
Vitamin A (μg)	430	730
Vitamin D (μg)	0.28	0.50
Thiamin (μg)	20	0
Riboflavin (μg)	80	0

Adapted from Rolls (1982).

ACKNOWLEDGEMENTS

Grateful acknowledgement is made for information supplied by the following: Alpine Process Technology Ltd, Runcorn, Cheshire WA7 3DS, UK; Urschel International Ltd, Leicester LE6 0FH, UK; Peter Holland Ltd, Stamford, Lincolnshire PE9 2PE, UK; Hoegger Alpina Ltd, CH-9202 Gossau, Switzerland; Grindsted Products A/S, DK-8220 Brabrand, Denmark; Rannie, DK-2620 Albertslund, Denmark; Crepaco Inc., c/o Alfred & Co. Ltd; Wembley, Middlesex HAO 1WD, UK; Pasilac A/S, DK-8600 Silkeborg, Denmark; Soavi B and Figli, 43026 Parma, Italy.

REFERENCES

Anon. (1986) *Alpine process technology*, Technical literature 019/5e. Alpine Process Technology Ltd, Runcorn, Cheshire.

Bauernfeind, J. C. (1977) The tocopherol content of food and influencing factors. *Crit. Rev. Food Sci. Nutr.*, **8** 337–382.

Erdman, J. W., and Erdman, E. A. (1982) Effect of home preparation practices on nutritive value of food. In: M. Rechcigl (ed.) *Handbook of nutritive value of processed foods*, CRC Press, Boca Raton, Florida, pp. 237–263.

Frigg, M. (1976) Bioavailability of biotin in cereals. *Poult. Sci.* **55** 2310–2318.

Harper, W. J. (1979) Process induced changes. In: W. J. Harper and C. W. Hall (eds), *Dairy technology and engineering*. AVI, Westport, Connecticut, pp. 561–568.

Houston, D. F., and Kohler, G. O. (1970) *Nutritional properties of rice*. National Academy of Sciences, Washington, DC.

Kent, N. L. (1983). *Technology of cereals*, 3rd edn. Pergamon Press, Oxford, pp. 73–85.

Laurie, R. A. (1985) *Meat science*, 4th edn. Pergamon Press, Oxford, pp. 169–207.

Leniger, H. A., and Beverloo, W. A. (1975) *Food process engineering*. D. Reidel, Dordrecht, pp. 169–188.

Loncin, M., and Merson, R. L. (1979) *Food engineering*. Academic Press, New York, pp. 246–264.

Nelson, P. E., and Tressler, D. K. (1980) *Fruit and vegetable juice processing technology*, 3rd edn. AVI, Westport, Connecticut, pp. 268–309.

Rees, L. H. (1967) What to know about homogenizers. *Food. Engng* **39** (8) 69–71.

Rolls, B. A. (1982) Effect of processing on nutritive value of food: milk and milk products. In: M. Rechcigl (ed.), *Handbook of nutritive value of processed foods*. CRC Press, Boca Raton, Florida, pp. 383–399.

Sherman, P. (1976) The textural characteristics of dairy products. In: J. M. De Man, P. W. Voisey, V. F. Rasper and D. W. Stanley (eds), *Rheology and texture in food quality*. AVI, Westport, Connecticut, pp. 382–404.

Stanley, D. W., and Tung, M. A. (1976) Microstructure of food and its relation to texture. In: J. M. De Man, P. W. Voisey, V. F. Rasper and D. W. Stanley (eds), *Rheology and texture in food quality*. AVI, Westport, Connecticut, pp. 28–78.

Toepfer, E. W., Zook, E. G., Orr, M. L., and Richardson, L. R. (1951) *Folic acid content of foods*, Agriculture Handbook, No. 29, US Department of Agriculture, Washington, DC.

4

Mixing and forming

Mixing (or blending) is a unit operation in which a uniform mixture is obtained from two or more components, by dispersing one within the other(s). The larger component is sometimes called the continuous phase and the smaller component the dispersed phase by analogy with emulsions (Chapter 3), but these terms do not imply emulsification when used in this context. Mixing has no preservative effect and is intended solely as a processing aid or to alter the eating quality of foods. It has very wide applications in many food industries where it is used to combine ingredients to achieve different functional properties or sensory characteristics. Extruders (Chapter 13) and some types of size reduction equipment (Chapter 3) also serve a mixing function.

Forming is the unit operation in which foods that have a high viscosity or a dough-like texture are moulded into a variety of shapes and sizes, often immediately after a mixing operation. It is used as a processing aid to increase variety and convenience in baked goods, confectionery and snackfoods. It has no direct effect on the shelf life or nutritional value of foods. Close control over the size of formed pieces is critical (for example to control the rate of heat transfer to the centre of baked foods, to control the weight of larger items of food (for example loaves), and to increase the uniformity of smaller foods (for example biscuits, confectionery and snackfoods) and hence to control fill weights). Extrusion (Chapter 13) also incorporates a forming operation. These are examples of size enlargement operations.

4.1 MIXING

4.1.1 Theory of solids mixing
In contrast with liquids and viscous pastes (section 4.1.2) it is not possible to achieve a completely uniform mixture of dry powders or particulate solids. The degree of mixing that is achieved depends on

(1) the relative particle size, shape and density of each component,
(2) the efficiency of a particular mixer for those components,

(3) the tendency of the materials to aggregate and
(4) the moisture content, surface characteristics and flow characteristics of each
    components.

In general, materials that are similar in size, shape and density are able to form a
more uniform mixture than are dissimilar materials. During a mixing operation,
differences in these properties also cause 'unmixing' of the component parts. The
uniformity of the final product depends on the equilibrium achieved between the
mechanisms of mixing and unmixing, which in turn is related to the type of mixer, the
operating conditions and the component foods. In some mixtures, uniformity is
achieved after a given period and then unmixing begins. It is therefore important in
such cases to time the mixing operation accurately.

If a two-component mixture is sampled at the start of mixing (in the unmixed
state), most samples will consist entirely of one of the components. As mixing
proceeds, the composition of each sample becomes more uniform and approaches
the average composition of the mixture. One method of determining the changes in
composition is to calculate the standard deviation of each fraction in successive
samples:

$$\sigma_m = \sqrt{\left[\frac{1}{n-1} \sum (x - \bar{x})^2 \right]} \tag{4.1}$$

where: σ_m is the standard deviation, n the number of samples, x the concentration of
the component in each sample and $\bar{x}$ the mean concentration of samples. Lower
standard deviations are found as the uniformity of the mixture increases.

A number of mixing indices are available to monitor the extent of mixing and to
compare alternative types of equipment:

$$M_1 = \frac{\sigma_m - \sigma_\infty}{\sigma_0 - \sigma_\infty} \tag{4.2}$$

$$M_2 = \frac{\log\sigma_m - \log\sigma_\infty}{\log\sigma_0 - \log\sigma_\infty} \tag{4.3}$$

$$M_3 = \frac{\sigma_m^2 - \sigma_\infty^2}{\sigma_0^2 - \sigma_\infty^2} \tag{4.4}$$

where: σ_∞ is the standard deviation of a 'perfectly mixed' sample, σ_0 the standard
deviation of a sample at the start of mixing and σ_m the standard deviation of a sample
taken during mixing. σ_0 is found using

$$\sigma_0 = \sqrt{[V_1 (1 - V_1)]} \tag{4.5}$$

where V is the average fractional volume or mass of a component in the mixture.

In practice, perfect mixing (where $\sigma_\infty = 0$) cannot be achieved, but in efficient mixers the value becomes very low after a reasonable period. The mixing index M_1 is used when approximately equal masses of components are mixed and/or at relatively low mixing rates, M_2 is used when a small quantity of one component is incorporated into a larger bulk of material and/or at higher mixing rates, and M_3 is used for liquids or solids mixing in a similar way to M_1. In practice, all three are examined and the one that is most suitable for the particular ingredients and type of mixer is selected.

The mixing time is related to the mixing index using

$$\ln M = -Kt_{\mathrm{m}} \tag{4.6}$$

where: K is the mixing rate constant, which varies with the type of mixer and the nature of the components, and t_{m} (s) mixing time.

Sample problem 4.1
During preparation of a dough, 700 g of sugar are mixed with 100 kg of flour. Ten 100 g samples are taken after 1, 5 and 10 min and analysed for the percentage sugar. The results are as follows.

Percentage after										
Percentage after 1 min	0.21	0.32	0.46	0.17	0.89	1.00	0.98	0.23	0.10	0.14
Percentage after 5 min	0.85	0.80	0.62	0.78	0.75	0.39	0.84	0.96	0.58	0.47
Percentage after 10 min	0.72	0.69	0.71	0.70	0.68	0.71	0.70	0.72	0.70	0.70

Calculate the mixing index for each mixing time and draw conclusions regarding the efficiency of mixing. Assume that for 'perfect mixing' there is a probability that 99.7% of samples will fall within three standard deviations of the mean composition ($\sigma = 0.01\%$).

Solution to sample problem 4.1
Average fractional mass V_1 of sugar in the mix

$$= \frac{700}{100 \times 10^3}$$
$$= 7 \times 10^{-3}$$

From equation (4.5),

$$\sigma_0 = \sqrt{[7 \times 10^{-3}(1 - 7 \times 10^{-3})]}$$
$$= 0.08337$$
$$= 8.337\%$$

After 10 min

mean $\bar{x}$ of the samples $= 0.703$

using equation (4.1), after 1 min,

$$\sigma_m = \sqrt{\left[\frac{1}{10-1} \sum (x - 0.703)^2\right]}$$

(that is subtract 0.703 from x for each of the ten samples, square the result and sum the squares):

$$\sigma_m = \sqrt{(0.11 \times 1.837)}$$
$$= \sqrt{0.2020}$$
$$= 0.4495\%$$

After 5 min,

$$\sigma_m = 0.0772\%$$

and, after 10 min,

$$\sigma_m = 0.0125\%$$

Using equation (4.3), after 1 min,

$$M_2 = \frac{\log 0.4495 - \log 0.01}{\log 8.337 - \log 0.01}$$
$$= 0.566$$

After 5 min,

$$M_2 = 0.304$$

and, after 10 min,

$$M_2 = 0.0326$$

Interpretation: if the log M_2 is plotted against time, the linear relationship indicates that the mixing index gives a good description of the mixing process and that mixing takes place uniformly and efficiently.

Using equation (4.6), after 10 min,

$$\ln 0.0326 = -k \times 600$$

Therefore,

$$k = 0.0057$$

The time required for $\sigma_m = \sigma_\infty = 0.01\%$ is then found:

$$\ln 0.01 = -0.0057\ t_m$$

$$t_m = 808\ s$$

Therefore

remaining mixing time $= 808 - 600$
$= 208\ s$
$\approx 3.5\ min$

4.1.2 Theory of liquids mixing
The component velocities induced in liquids by a mixer are as follows (Fig. 4.1):

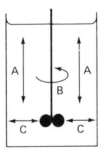

Fig. 4.1 — Component velocities in fluid mixing: A, longitudinal; B, rotational; C, radial.

(1) a radial velocity which acts in a direction perpendicular to the mixer shaft;
(2) a longitudinal velocity (parallel to the mixer shaft);
(3) a rotational velocity (tangential to the mixer shaft).

To achieve successful mixing, the radial and longitudinal velocities imparted to the liquid are maximised by baffles, off-centre or angled mixer shafts, or angled blades (section 4.1.3).
    To mix low-viscosity liquids adequately, turbulence must be induced throughout

the bulk of the liquid to entrain slow-moving parts within faster moving parts. A vortex should be avoided because adjoining layers of circulating liquid travel at a similar speed and entrainment does not take place. The liquids simply rotate around the mixer.

In high-viscosity liquids, pastes or doughs, a different action is needed. Mixing occurs by

(1) *kneading* the material against the vessel wall or into other material,
(2) *folding* unmixed food into the mixed part and
(3) *shearing* to stretch the material.

Efficient mixing is achieved by creating and recombining fresh surfaces in the food as often as possible. However, because the material does not easily flow, it is necessary either to move the mixer blades throughout the vessel or to move the food to the mixer blades.

Most liquid foods are non-Newtonian (their consistency changes with rate of shear). The most common types are *pseudoplastic* in which the consistency decreases with increasing shear rate, *dilatant* in which the consistency increases with shear rate and *viscoelastic* which exhibit viscous and elastic properties including stress relaxation, creep and recoil. These properties are described in detail by Lewis (1987). The rheological properties of many foods in this category change during mixing. The design of equipment should enable thorough mixing without overloading the motor or reducing the mixing efficiency.

Pseudoplastic foods (for example sauces) form a zone of thinned material around a small agitator as mixing proceeds, and the bulk of the food does not move. The higher the agitator speed, the more quickly the zone becomes apparent. Planetary or gate mixers, roller mills or multi-agitator systems (section 4.1.3.2) are used to ensure that all food is subjected to the mixing action. Dilatant foods (for example cornflour and chocolate) should be mixed with great care. If adequate power is not available in the mixer, the increase in consistency causes damage to drive mechanisms and shafts. A folding or cutting action, as for example in some planetary mixers or paddle mixers, is suitable for this type of food (section 4.1.3.2). Viscoelastic foods (for example bread dough) require a folding and stretching action to shear the material. Suitable equipment includes twin-shaft mixers and planetary mixers with intermeshing blades (section 4.1.3.2).

The rate of mixing is characterised by a mixing index (as described in section 4.1.1). The mixing rate constant (equation (4.6)) depends on the characteristics of both the mixer and the liquids. The effect of the mixer characteristics on K is given by

$$K \propto \frac{D^3 N}{D_t^2 z} \tag{4.7}$$

where D (m) is the agitator diameter, N (rev s^{-1}) the agitator speed D_t (m) the vessel diameter and z (m) the height of liquid.

The power requirements of a mixer vary according to the nature, amount and consistency of the foods in the mixer and the position, type, speed and size of the impeller. Liquid flow is defined by a series of dimensionless numbers: the Reynolds number Re (equation (4.8), also Chapter 1), the Froude number Fr (equation (4.9)) and the Power number Po (equation (4.10)):

$$Re = \frac{D^2 \, N \, \rho_m}{\mu_m} \tag{4.8}$$

$$Fr = \frac{D \, N^2}{g} \tag{4.9}$$

$$Po = \frac{P}{\rho_m N^3 D^5} \tag{4.10}$$

where P (kW) is the power transmitted via the agitator, ρ_m (kg m^{-3}) the density of the mixture and μ_m (Ns m^{-2}) the viscosity of the mixture . These are related as follows:

$$Po = K(Re)^n (Fr)^m \tag{4.11}$$

where K, n and m are factors related to the geometry of the agitator, which are found by experiment (for example Rushton et al., 1950). The Froude number is only important when a vortex is formed in unbaffled vessels and is therefore omitted from equation (4.11).

The density of a mixture is found by addition of component densities of the continuous and dispersed phases:

$$\rho_m = V_1 \rho_1 + V_2 \rho_2 \tag{4.12}$$

where V is the volume fraction. The subscripts 1 and 2 are the continuous phase and dispersed phase respectively.

The viscosity of a mixture is found using the following equations for baffled mixers and for unbaffled mixers:

$$\mu_m(\text{unbaffled}) = \mu_1^{V_1} \, \mu_2^{V_2} \tag{4.13}$$

$$\mu_m(\text{baffled}) = \frac{\mu_1}{V_1} \left(\frac{1 + 1.5 \, \mu_2 \, V_2}{\mu_1 + \mu_2} \right) \tag{4.14}$$

(Jackson and Lamb, 1981).

Characteristic changes in power consumption Po of propellers at different Reynolds numbers are shown in Fig. 4.2.

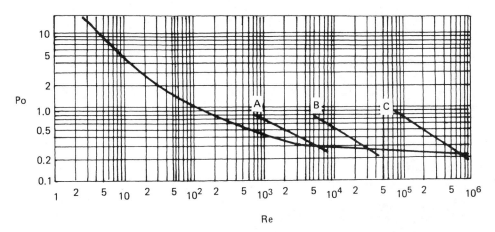

Fig. 4.2 — Changes in power number (Po = $P/\rho_m N^3 D^5$) versus Reynolds number (Re = D^2N ρ_m/μ_m) for propeller agitator. (30 cm propeller in 137 cm diameter tank, liquid depth 137 cm, propeller 30 cm above tank volume. (A) viscosity = 0.189 N s m^{-2}, (B) viscosity = 0.028 N s m^{-2}, (C) viscosity = 0.109 N s m^{-2}. (Propeller speed varied from 100 to 500 rpm). (After Rushton *et al.* 1950).

Sample problem 4.2
Olive oil and rape-seed oil are blended in a ratio of 1 to 5 by a propeller agitator 20 cm in diameter (section 4.1.3.1) operating at 750 rev min^{-1} in a cylindrical tank 1 m in diameter at 20°C. Calculate the size of the motor required.

Solution to sample problem 4.2
From Table 1.3, the viscosity of olive oil at 20°C is 0.084 N s m^{-2}, the density of olive oil 910 kg m^{-3}, the viscosity of rape-seed oil 0.118 N s m^{-2} and the density of rape-seed oil 900 kg m^{-3}. From equation (4.13),

$$\mu m = 0.084^{0.2}\ 0.118^{0.8}$$

$$= 0.110\ \text{N s m}^{-2}$$

From equation (4.12),

$$\rho_m = 0.2 \times 910 + 0.8 \times 900$$
$$= 902\ \text{kg m}^{-3}$$

From equation (4.8),

$$\text{Re} = (0.2)^2\ \frac{750}{60}\ \frac{902}{0.110}$$
$$= 4100$$

From Fig. 4.2, for Re = 4100, Po = 0.5. From equation (4.10),

$$P = 0.5 \times 902 \left(\frac{750}{60}\right)^3 (0.2)^5$$
$$= 281.9 \text{ J s}^{-1}$$
$$= 0.28 \text{ kW}$$

Since 1 Hp = 745.4 J s^{-1}, the size of the motor required is 281.9/745.4 = 38 hp = 0.28 kW.

Computer-aided systems are used to determine the optimum performance for a particular mixer in a given application or to select an appropriate mixer for a particular food. These systems take account of the type and size of the impeller, the shape of the vessel, the power input, the speed of mixing and limitations on temperature changes for a specific mix (also Chapter 24).

4.1.3 Equipment
The selection of a correct type and size of mixer depends on the type and amount of food being mixed and the speed of operation needed to achieve the required degree of mixing with minimum energy consumption. Mixers are classified into types that are suitable for

(1) low- or medium-viscosity liquids,
(2) high-viscosity liquids and pastes and
(3) dry powders or particulate solids.

Pownall (1986) has surveyed mixing equipment available for each category.

4.1.3.1 Mixers for low- or medium-viscosity liquids
A large number of designs of agitator are used to mix liquids in unbaffled or baffled vessels. The advantages and limitations of each vary according to the particular application but are summarised in Table 4.1.

4.1.3.1.1 Paddle agitators
The simplest of these are wide flat blades (Fig. 4.3(a)) which measure 50–75% of the vessel diameter and rotate at 20–150 rev min^{-1}. The blades are often pitched to promote longitudinal flow in unbaffled tanks.

4.1.3.1.2 Impeller agitators
These consist of two or more blades attached to a rotating shaft. The blades may be flat, angled (pitched) or curved. *Turbine agitators* are impeller agitators which have more than four blades mounted together. The size is 30–50% of the diameter of the vessel and they operate at 30–500 rev min^{-1}. The blades are flat, pitched or curved to increase radial and longitudinal flow. In addition blades may be mounted on a flat disc (the vaned disc impeller (Fig. 4.3(b))). These types of impeller are frequently mounted vertically in baffled tanks. High shearing forces are developed at the edges of the impeller blades and they are therefore used for pre-mixing emulsions (Chapter

Table 4.1 — Advantages and limitations of selected liquid mixers

Type of mixer	Advantages	Limitations
Paddle agitator	Good radial and rotational flow, cheap	Poor perpendicular flow, high vortex risk at higher speeds
Multiple-paddle agitator	Good flow in all three directions	More expensive, higher energy requirements
Propeller impeller	Good flow in all three directions	More expensive than paddle agitator
Turbine agitator	Very good mixing	Expensive and risk of blockage

3). Impellers which have short blades (less than a quarter of the diameter of the vessel) are known as *propeller agitators* (Fig. 4.3(c)). In each type the agitator is located in one of the positions shown in Fig. 4.4 to promote longitudinal and radial movement of the liquids and to prevent vortex formation. Alternatively, baffles are fitted to the vessel wall to increase shearing of the liquids and to interrupt rotational flow, but care is necessary in the design to ensure that the vessel may be adequately cleaned. Propeller agitators operate at 400–1500 rev min $^{-1}$ and are used for blending miscible liquids, diluting concentrated solutions, preparing syrups or brines and dissolving ingredients.

4.1.3.1.3 Powder–liquid contacting devices
A number of short-residence-time mixers are used to incorporate powders into liquids. In general, these operate by mixing a uniform stream of powder into sprays of liquid but may also involve subsequent mixing by blades or rotors. Typical examples are shown in Fig. 4.5. In addition, powders are mixed with liquids by pumping through pipes that are fitted internally with stationary mixing blades.

4.1.3.1.4 Other mixers
Pumps also ensure a degree of mixing by creating turbulent flow both in the pump itself and in the pipework (Chapter 1). There are a large variety of pumps available for handling different fluids and suspensions. The design and application of pumps are discussed by Leniger and Beverloo (1975).

4.1.3.2 Mixers for high-viscosity liquids and pastes
4.1.3.2.1 Slow-speed vertical-shaft impellers
More viscous liquids are mixed using multiple-paddle (gate) agitators or, more commonly, *counter-rotating agitators* to develop high shearing forces. The basic design in this group is the *anchor and gate agitator* (Fig. 4.6). It is often used with heated mixing vessels, when the anchor is fitted with scraper blades to prevent food

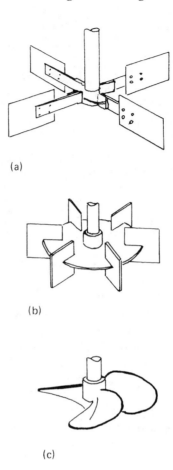

(a)

(b)

(c)

Fig. 4.3 — Agitators: (a) flat-blade agitator; (b) vaned disc impeller; (c) propeller agitator.
(After Smith (1985).)

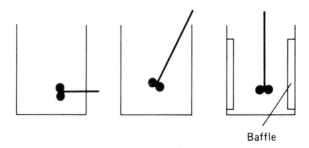

Baffle

Fig. 4.4 — Position of agitators for effective mixing of liquids.

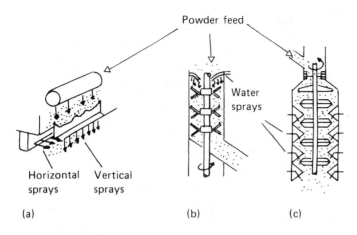

Fig. 4.5 — Powder–liquid contacting devices: (a) Neptune Chemix (part); (b) Schugi mixer; (c) Buss mixer. (After McDonagh (1987).)

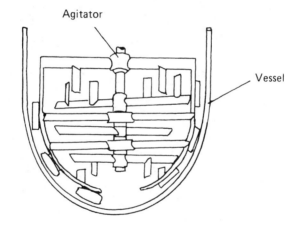

Fig. 4.6 — Anchor-and-gate agitator. (After McDonagh (1987).)

from burning onto the hot surface. Some complex designs have arms on the gate which intermesh with stationary arms on the anchor to increase the shearing action. Others have inclined vertical blades to promote radial movement in the food.

4.1.3.2.2   Twin-shaft horizontal blades

The most common design of this type is the *Z-blade* (or sigma-blade) mixer. This consists of two heavy-duty blades which are mounted horizontally in a metal trough. The trough tilts to discharge each batch of mixed product, or it may be fitted with a screw discharge in the base. The blades have a Z shape (Fig. 4.7) and intermesh as they rotate towards each other at similar or differential speeds (14–60 rev min^{-1}) to produce shearing forces between the two blades and between the blades and the

Fig. 4.7 — Z-blade mixer. (Courtesy of Winkworth Engineering Ltd.)

specially designed trough base. These mixers use a substantial amount of power which is dissipated in the product as heat. Mixing efficiency should therefore be high to reduce the mixing time. If necessary the walls of the trough are jacketed for temperature control. Special designs for shredding and mixing have serrated blades, and other blade configurations including the gridlap, double naben and double claw are available (McDonagh, 1987).

4.1.3.2.3 Planetary mixers
These types of mixer take their name from the path followed by rotating blades (40–370 rev min^{-1}), which include all parts of the vessel in the mixing action. An alternative design employs fixed rotating blades which are offset from the centre of a co-currently or counter-currently revolving vessel. In both types there is a small clearance between the blades and the vessel wall. For example gate blades are used for mixing pastes, blending ingredients and preparation of spreads. Hooks are used for dough mixing and whisks are used for batter preparation.

4.1.3.2.4 Continuous rotor–stator mixers
Screw conveyor mixers are typical of this group of mixers. A horizontal rotor fits closely into a slotted stationary casing (or 'barrel'). Single or twin screws are used to

convey viscous foods and pastes through the barrel and to force it through perforated plates or grids. The small clearance between the screw and the barrel wall causes a shearing and kneading action. This is supplemented by shearing and mixing as the food emerges from the end plate or grid. The screw may be interposed with pins to increase the shearing action. This type of equipment is also used for extrusion (Chapter 13) and butter or margarine manufacture (Chapter 3).

4.1.3.2.5   Multi-agitator systems
In this equipment, several types of blade serve different functions. One type is used to produce high rates of shear in the food but, because viscous material does not easily flow, a second (and sometimes third) type of mixer moves the bulk of the food to the region of the shearing action. A selection of the combinations of available blades is shown in Table 4.2.

4.1.3.2.6   Other mixers
A number of designs of mixer including butter churns, bowl choppers and rollers are each used in specific applications to mix foods, often with simultaneous homogenisation or size reduction. Roller mills and colloid mills are suitable for mixing high-viscosity materials in addition to their function as size reduction equipment (Chapter 3).

4.1.3.3   Mixers for dry powders and particulate solids
These mixers have two basic designs: the tumbling action of rotating vessels and the positive movement of materials in screw types. They are used for blending grains, flours and the preparation of powdered mixes (for example cake mixes and dried soups).

4.1.3.3.1   Tumbling mixers
These types of mixer include drum, double-cone, Y-cone and V-cone mixers (for example Fig. 4.8). They are filled approximately half full and rotate at speeds of 20–100 rev min^{-1}. Optimum mixing for a particular blend of ingredients depends on the shape and speed of the vessel. Speeds should be lower than the critical speed (when centrifugal force exceeds gravity). The efficiency of mixing is improved by internal baffles or counter-rotating arms. These mixers are also used for coating applications (Chapter 21).

4.1.3.3.2   Ribbon mixers
Two or more thin narrow metal blades (ribbons) are formed into helices which counter-rotate in a closed hemispherical trough (Fig. 4.9). The pitch of the ribbons is different so that one moves the material rapidly forwards through the trough, and the second moves the material slowly backwards. There is therefore a net forward movement of material and hence a continuous mixing and conveying action. This type of mixer is used for dry ingredients and small-particulate foods (for example as a pre-mixing stage prior to extrusion) (Chapter 13).

4.1.3.3.3   Vertical-screw mixers
A rotating vertical screw is contained within a conical vessel and orbits around a central axis to mix the contents thoroughly. This type of equipment is particularly

Table 4.2 — Multi-agitator systems

	Type of agitator								
	Anchor	Gate	Ribbon	Screw	Pitched blades	Marine propeller	Paddles	Rotor-stator	Colloid mill
Combination									
1	*								
2		*				*	*		
3			*					*	
4				*		*	*		
5							*		
6	*		*					*	
7	*			*			*	*	
8	*	*	*		*				
9									*
Purpose of agitator	Bulk movement	Bulk movement	Bulk movement	Shearing action	Shearing action	Shearing action	Shear/ bulk movement	Bulk movement/ shearing	Shearing action

Adapted from McDonagh (1987).

Fig. 4.8 — Double-cone mixer. (Courtesy of Winkworth Engineering Ltd.)

Fig. 4.9 — Ribbon mixer. (Courtesy of Winkworth Engineering Ltd.)

useful for the incorporation of small quantities of ingredients into a bulk of material. Other designs which have a fixed central screw are less effective but have a lower capital cost.

4.1.4 Effect on foods
The action of a mixer has no direct effect on either the nutritional quality or the shelf life of a food but may have an indirect effect by allowing components of the mixture

to react together. The nature and extent of the reaction depend on the components involved but may be accelerated if significant heat is generated in the mixer. For example, gluten development is promoted during dough making by the stretching and folding action which aligns, uncoils and extends protein molecules. This allows disulphide and hydrogen bonds to form and develop the strength of the gluten structure and hence to produce the desired texture in the bread.

In general, mixing has a substantial effect on sensory qualities and functional properties of foods. The main effects are to increase the uniformity of products by evenly distributing ingredients throughout the bulk. This increases consumer acceptability, increases the uniformity of foods which are further processed and reduces wastage during manufacture. In some foods, adequate mixing is necessary to ensure that the proportion of each component complies with legislative standards (for example mixed vegetables, sausages and other meat products).

4.2 FORMING

There are many designs of moulding and forming equipment made specifically for individual products. In this section the equipment used for bread, biscuits, pies and confectionery is described.

4.2.1 Bread moulders
This equipment (Fig. 4.10) shapes the dough into cylinders that will expand to the

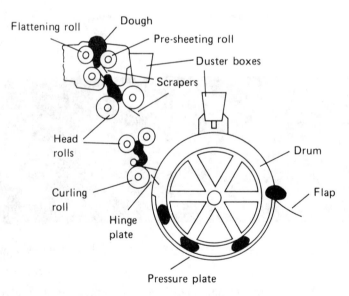

Fig. 4.10 — A drum moulder for bread doughs. (After Matz (1972).)

required loaf shape when proofed. The three stages are

(1) sheeting,
(2) curling and
(3) rolling–sealing.

The first three sets of rollers have successively smaller gaps (or 'nips') to roll the dough gently into sheets without tearing. The sheet is loosely curled, rolled into a cylinder and then sealed by a revolving drum, which presses the dough against a pressure plate. The pressure is gradually increased to expel trapped air. Compression of the dough structure causes the moisture content of the sheet to increase at the trailing end. It is preferable to have the moist part of the dough at the centre of the cylinder, and a variety of designs are used to change the direction of the sheet to roll the trailing edge first (for example *cross-grain* moulders and *reverse sheeting moulders*) (Matz, 1972).

4.2.2 Pie and biscuit formers

Pie casings are formed by depositing a piece of dough into aluminium foil containers or re-usable pie moulds and pressing it with a die. A filling is then deposited into the casing and a continuous sheet of dough is laid over the top. Finally the lids are cut by reciprocating blades (Fig. 4. 11). Biscuits are formed by one of four methods:

(1) the dough is pressed into shaped cavities in a *metal moulding roller* (die forming) (Fig. 4.12(a));
(2) shapes are cut from a sheet of dough using a *cutting roller*. Raised characters on a *printing roller* simultaneously imprint a design on the upper surface of the biscuit (Fig. 4.12(c));
(3) soft dough is extruded through a series of dies in a *wire-cut machine* (Fig. 4.12(c));
(4) a continuous ribbon of dough is extruded from a *rout press* (similar to a wirecut machine but without the cutting wires), and the ribbon is then cut to the required length using a reciprocating blade.

There are also numerous designs of equipment for laminating sheets of dough with fat (for croissants and pastries), folding doughs (to form pasties and rolls) and filling doughs (to form sausage rolls and cakes).

4.2.3 Confectionery moulders

Confectionery depositing–moulding equipment consists of individual moulds, which have the required size and shape for a specific product, attached to a continuous conveyor. They are carried below a depositor, which has a piston filler to deposit accurately the required volume of hot sugar mass into each mould. Depositors can place food of a single type, in layers, or centre filled (Fig. 4.13) (for example liquid centres or chocolate paste around hard-boiled sweets). The food is then cooled in a cooling tunnel. When it has hardened sufficiently, individual sweets are ejected and the moulds restart the cycle (Fig. 4.14).

The three main types of equipment differ in the method of ejection, and the material used for the mould:

(1) metal moulds fitted with ejector pins are used for hard confectionery (for example butterscotch);

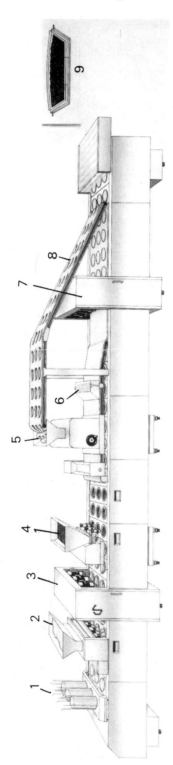

Fig. 4.11 — Pie manufacture: 1, foil dishes; 2, dough divider; 3, blocking unit; 4, filling depositor; 5, pastry lid sheeting machine; 6, rotary lattice cutter; 7, crimping/lidding unit; 8, scrap return conveyor; 9, pie cross section. (Courtesy of Machinefabriek C Rijkkaart BV.)

(a)

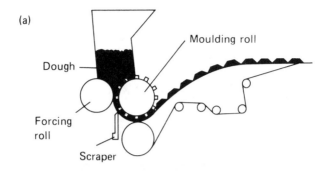

(b)

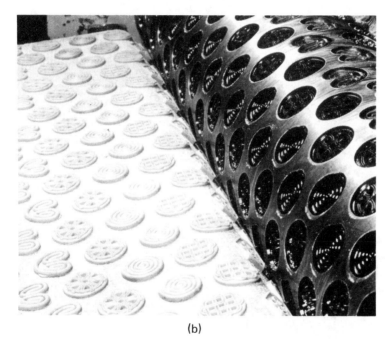

(c)

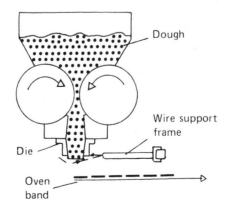

Fig. 4.12 — Biscuit formers: (a) rotary moulder; (b) moulding rollers; (c) wire-cut machine. (Courtesy of Baker Perkins Ltd.)

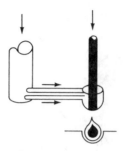

Fig. 4.13 — Depositing centre-filled confectionery. (Courtesy of Baker Perkins Ltd.)

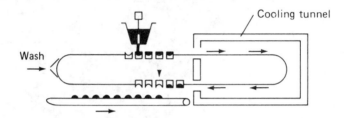

Fig. 4.14 — Confectionery moulding: an air demoulding depositor. (Courtesy of Baker Perkins Ltd.)

(2) flexible polyvinyl chloride moulds, which eject the food by mechanical deformation, are used for soft confectionery (for example toffee, fudge, fondant and chocolate);

(3) polytetrafluoroethylene-coated aluminium moulds, with compressed-air ejection, are used for jellies, gums, fondant and crèmes.

Each type of equipment is automatically controlled. Other types of forming equipment extrude sugar confectionery (Chapter 13) and shape it using a series of rollers, to produce a sugar 'rope'. Individual sweets are then cut from the rope and shaped by dies.

ACKNOWLEDGEMENTS

Grateful acknowledgement is made for information supplied by the following: Allen Machinery Systems, Stourbridge, West Midlands DY9 7NB, UK; Baker Perkins Ltd, Peterborough PE3 6TA, UK; Interfood Ltd, Hemel Hempstead, Hertfordshire HP2 7DU, UK; Robinson's of Derby, Derby DE2 6JL, UK; Machinefabriek C Rijkaart bv, Asperen, Holland; Sandvik Jahn, Huntingdon PE18 7EW, UK; Winkworth Machinery Ltd, Staines, Middlesex TW18 4PX, UK; Tweedy Ltd,

Burnley, Lancashire BB12 6JL, UK; Morton Machine Co. Ltd, Motherwell ML1 5SW, UK.

REFERENCES

Jackson, A.T., and Lamb, J., (1981) *Calculations in food and chemical engineering.* Macmillan, London, pp. 164–174.

Leniger, H.A., and Beverloo, W.A. (1975) *Food processing engineering*, D. Reidel, Dordrecht, pp. 129–137.

Lewis, M.J., (1987) *Physical properties of foods and food processing systems.* Ellis Horwood, Chichester, West Sussex; VCH, Weinheim, pp. 137–166.

Matz, S.A., (1972) *Bakery technology and engineering.* AVI, Westport, Connecticut, pp. 237–257.

McDonagh, M. (1987) Mixers for powder/liquid dispersions. *The Chem. Engr.*, March 29–32.

Pownall, S., (1986) The mixing link. *Food Manuf.* February 33, 35–36.

Rushton, J.N., Costich, E.W., and Everett, H.S., (1950) *Chem. Engng Prog.* **46**, 395.

Smith, T. (1985) Mixing heads. *Food Process.* February 39–40.

5

Mechanical separations

This chapter describes three unit operations for the mechanical (or physical) separation of food components:

(1) *centrifugation*, the separation of immiscible liquids, or solids from liquids by the application of centrifugal force,
(2) *filtration*, the separation of solids from liquids by passing the mixture through a bed of porous material;
(3) *expression*, the separation of liquids from solids by applied pressure.

Each finds widespread application in the food industry for the production, purification or concentration of foods or ingredients (for example juices, pectin, enzymes, cream and coffee solubles). Each is used as an aid to processing and is not intended to preserve food. Changes in nutritional and sensory qualities arise through intentional separation or concentration of food components, but the processing conditions do not involve heat and cause little damage to foods.

Gravity separation (sedimentation) has applications in cleaning raw materials (Chapter 2), in removing powders or dust from air, and in separating solids from effluents. Details of the theory and equipment used for sedimentation are described by Earle (1983). Sorting (Chapter 2) and membrane concentration (Chapter 6) are further examples of separation procedures applied to foods. Separation by fractional distillation and extraction by solvents are discussed by Leniger and Beverloo (1975).

5.1 CENTRIFUGATION

5.1.1 Theory
Centrifugal force is generated when materials are rotated; the size of the force depends on the radius and speed of rotation and the mass (or density) of the centrifuged material.

In the separation of immiscible liquids (for example emulsions (Chapter 3)), the denser liquid moves to the bowl wall and the lighter liquid is displaced to an inner annulus (Fig. 5.1). The thickness of the layers is determined by the density of the liquids, the pressure difference across the layers and the speed of rotation. The boundary region between the liquids at a given centrifuge speed forms at a radius r_n where the hydrostatic pressure of the two layers is equal. This is termed the *neutral zone* and is important in equipment design to determine the position of feed and discharge pipes. It is found using

$$r_n^2 = \frac{\rho_A r_A^2 - \rho_B r_B^2}{\rho_A - \rho_B} \tag{5.1}$$

where ρ (kg m^{-3}) is the density and r (m) the radius. The subscripts A and B refer to the dense and light liquid layers respectively.

If the purpose is to remove light liquid from a mass of heavier liquid (for example in cream separation from milk), the residence time in the outer layer exceeds that in the inner layer. This is achieved by reducing the radius of the outer layer (r_1 in Fig. 5.1) and hence by reducing the radius of the neutral zone. Conversely, if a dense liquid is to be separated from a mass of lighter liquid (for example the removal of water from oils), the radius of the outer layer (and the neutral zone) is increased.

Sample problem 5.1
A bowl centrifuge is used to break an oil-in-water emulsion (Chapter 3). Determine the radius of the neutral zone in order to position the feed pipe correctly. (Assume that the density of the continuous phase is 1000 kg m^{-3} and the density of the oil is 870 kg m^{-3}. The outlet radii from the centrifuge are 3 cm and 4.5 cm).

Solution to sample problem 5.1

$$r_n = \sum \left[\frac{1000(0.045)^2 - 870(0.03)^2}{1000 - 870} \right]$$
$$= \sqrt{\left(\frac{2.025 - 0.783}{130} \right)}$$
$$= 0.097 \, \text{m}$$

In centrifugal clarification, particles move to the bowl wall under centrifugal force. If liquid flow is streamline flow (Chapter 1), the rate of movement is determined by the densities of the particles and liquid, the viscosity of the liquid and the speed of rotation (equation (5.2)). Separation under turbulent flow conditions is described by Earle (1983).

$$Q = \frac{D^2 \omega^2 (\rho_s - \rho) V}{18 \mu \ln (r_2/r_1)} \tag{5.2}$$

where ω ($= 2\pi N/60$) is the angular velocity, $Q = $ (m^{3}s^{-1}) the volumetric flow rate, V (m^3) the operating volume of the centrifuge, D (m) the diameter of particle, ρ_s (kg m^{-3}) the density of particles, ρ (kg m^{-3}) the density of liquid, μ (N s m^{-2}) the

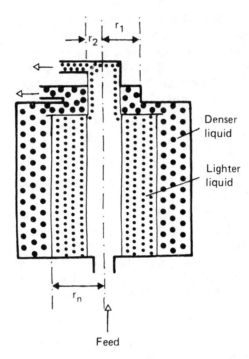

Fig. 5.1 — Separation of immiscible liquids: r_1, radius of dense phase outlet; r_2, radius of light phase outlet; r_n, radius of neutral zone.

viscosity of liquid, r_2 (m) the radius of centrifuge bowl, r_1 (m) the radius of liquid, N (rev s^{-1}) the speed of rotation.

For a given particle diameter, the average residence time of a suspension equals the time taken for the particle to travel through the liquid to the centrifuge wall:

$$t = \frac{V}{Q} \tag{5.3}$$

where t (s) is the residence time. The flow-rate can therefore be adjusted to retain a specific range of particle sizes.

Derivations and additional details of these equations are given by Brennan *et al.* (1976) and Earle (1983).

Sample problem 5.2
Beer with a specific gravity of 1.042 and a viscosity of 1.40×10^{-3} N s m^{-2} contains 1.5% solids which have a density of 1160 kg m^{-3}. It is clarified at a rate of 240 l h^{-1} in a bowl centrifuge which has an operating volume of 0.09 m^3 and a speed of 10000 rev min^{-1}. The bowl has a diameter of 5.5 cm and is fitted with a 4 cm outlet. Calculate the effect on feed rate of an increase in bowl speed to 15000 rev min^{-1} and the minimum particle size that can be removed at the higher speed.

Solution to sample problem 5.2
From equation (5.2),

$$\text{Initial flow rate } Q_1 = \frac{D^2(2\pi N_1/60)^2(\rho_s - \rho)V}{18\mu \ln(r_w/r)}$$

$$\text{New flow rate } Q_2 = \frac{D^2(2\pi N_2/60)^2(\rho_s - \rho)V}{18\mu \ln(r_w/r)}$$

As all conditions except the bowl speed remain the same,

$$\frac{Q_2}{Q_1} = \frac{(2\pi N_2/60)^2}{(2\pi N_1/60)^2}$$

$$\frac{Q_2}{(240/3600} = \frac{(2 \times 3.142 \times 15000/60)^2}{2 \times 3.142 \times 10000/60)^2}$$

Therefore,

$$Q_2 = 0.151 s^{-1}$$
$$= 5401 h^{-1}$$

To find the minimum particle size from equation (5.2),

$$D^2 = Q_2 = \frac{Q_2[18\mu \ln(r_w/r)]}{w^2(\rho_s - \rho)V}$$

$$= \frac{Q_2[18\mu \ln(r_w/r)]}{(2\pi N_2/60)^2(\rho_s - \rho)V}$$

$$= \frac{0.015(18 \times 1.40 \times 10^{-3} \times \ln(0.0275/0.02)}{(2 \times 3.142 \times (15000/60)^2(1160 - 1042)0.09}$$

$$D = \sqrt{\left(\frac{2.33 \times 10^{-4}}{2.62 \times 10^7}\right)}$$
$$= 6.8\,\mu m$$

5.1.2 Equipment
Centrifuges are classified into three groups for

(1) separation of immiscible liquids,

(2) clarification of liquids by removal of small amounts of solids (centrifugal clarifiers) and

(3) removal of solids (desludging or dewatering centrifuges).

Specific applications of centrifuges are described by Hemfort (1984) for the fermentation industries (Chapter 7) and by Hemfort (1983) for the food industry.

5.1.2.1 Liquid–liquid centrifuges

The simplest type of equipment is the *tubular bowl centrifuge*. It consists of a vertical cylinder (or bowl), typically 0.1 m in diameter and 0.75 m long, which rotates inside a stationary casing at between 15 000 rev min^{-1} and 50 000 rev min^{-1} depending on the diameter. Feed liquor (for example animal and vegetable oils and syrups) is introduced continuously at the base of the bowl and the two liquids are separated into annular layers, the denser liquid nearer to the bowl wall. The two liquids are discharged separately through a circular weir system into stationary outlets (Fig. 5.1).

However, the relatively thick annular layers cause some disruption to flow patterns and better separation is obtained by the thinner layers of liquid formed in the *disc bowl centrifuge* (Fig. 5.2). Here a cylindrical bowl, 0.2–1.2 m in diameter, contains inverted metal cones (or discs). The discs have a fixed clearance of 0.5–1.27 mm and rotate at 2000–7000 rev min^{-1}. They have matching holes which form flow channels for liquid movement. Feed is introduced at the base of the disc stack and the denser fraction moves towards the wall of the bowl, along the underside of the discs. The lighter fraction is displaced towards the centre along the upper surfaces (Fig. 5.2). The liquids therefore travel only a short distance, which results in better separation. The two liquid streams are removed continuously by a weir system at the top of the centrifuge in a similar way to the tubular bowl system. Disc bowl centrifuges are used to separate cream from milk and to clarify oils, coffee extracts and juices (Table 5.1). Disc bowl and tubular centrifuges have capacities of up to 150 000 l h^{-1}.

When tubular and disc bowl centrifuges are used for clarifying liquids with low solids concentrations (less than 5% w/w), the liquid exits via the centre weir. The outlet for the dense phase is closed. Solids therefore build up in the bowl and are periodically removed.

5.1.2.2 Centrifugal clarifiers

The simplest solid–liquid centrifuge is a *solid bowl clarifier*. This consists of a rotating cylidrical bowl, 0.6–1.0 m in diameter. Liquor, with a maximum of 3% w/w solids, is fed into the bowl and the solids form a cake on the bowl wall. When this has reached a pre-determined thickness the bowl is drained and the cake is removed automatically through an opening in the base of the bowl.

Feeds which contain a higher solids content (Table 5.1) are separated using *nozzle centrifuges* or *valve discharge centrifuges*. These centrifuges are similar to disc bowl types, but the bowls have a biconical shape (Fig. 5.3) and operate continuously. In the nozzle type, solids are continuously discharged through small holes at the periphery of the bowl and are collected in a containing vessel. In the valve type the

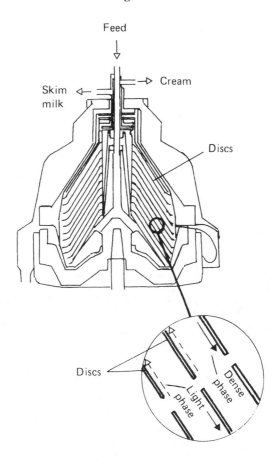

Fig. 5.2 — Disc bowl centrifuge. (Adapted from Hemfort (1983).

holes are fitted with valves that periodically open for a fraction of a second to discharge the accumulated solids. The advantages of the latter design include less wastage of liquor and the production of drier solids. Both types are able to separate feed liquor into three streams: a light phase, a dense phase and solids. Centrifugal clarifiers are used to treat oils, juices, beer and starches and to recover yeast cells (Chapter 7). They have capacities up to $300\,000\,l\,h^{-1}$.

5.1.2.3 Desludging, decanting or dewatering centrifuges
Feeds with high solids contents (Table 5.1) are separated using desludging centrifuges. There are a number of designs available including conveyor bowl, screen conveyor, basket and reciprocating conveyor centrifuges. In the *conveyor bowl centrifuge* the solid bowl rotates up to 25 rev min^{-1} faster than the screw conveyor (Fig. 5.4). This causes the solids to be conveyed to one end of the centrifuge, whereas the liquid fraction moves to the other larger-diameter end. The solids removed from this equipment are relatively dry compared with other types of equipment. The

Table 5.1 — Applications of centrifuges in food processing

Centrifuge type	Range of particle sizes (μm)	Solids content of feed (% w/w)	Applications							
			A	B	C	D	E	F	G	H
Disc bowl										
Clarifier	0.5–500	<5	★	★	★					
Self-cleaning	0.5–500	2–10	★	★	★	★	★			★
Nozzle bowl	0.5–500	5–25		★	★	★	★	★		★
Decanter	5–50 000	3–60		★	★	★	★	★	★	★
Basket	7.5–10 000	5–60							★	★
Reciprocating conveyor	100–80 000	20–75							★	★

A, liquid–liquid extraction; B, separation of liquid mixtures; C, clarification of liquids; D, concentration of slurries; E, liquid–solid–liquid extraction; F, dehydration of amorphous substances; G, dewatering of crystalline substances; H, wet classification.

Adapted from Hemfort (1983).

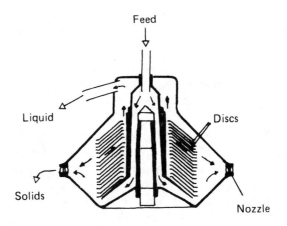

Fig. 5.3 — Nozzle centrifuge. (After Hemfort (1983).)

screen conveyor centrifuge has a similar design but the bowl is perforated to remove the liquid fraction. This type may have the bowl and screw assembly mounted vertically, with liquor fed from the top of the casing.

The *reciprocating conveyor centrifuge* (Fig. 5.5) is used to separate fragile solids (for example crystals from liquor) (also Chapter 20). Feed enters a rotating basket,

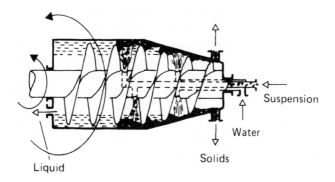

Fig. 5.4 — Conveyor bowl centrifuge. (After Leniger and Beverloo (1975).)

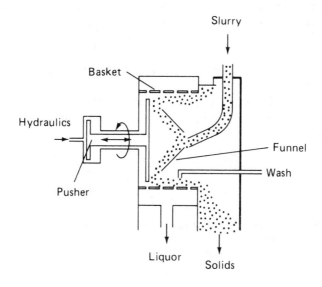

Fig. 5.5 — Reciprocating conveyor centrifuge. (After Brennan *et al*. (1976).)

0.3–1.2 m in diameter, through a funnel which rotates at the same speed. This gradually accelerates the liquid to the bowl speed and thus minimises shearing forces. Liquid passes through perforations in the bowl wall. When the layer of cake has built up to 5–7.5 cm, it is pushed forwards a few centimetres by a reciprocating arm. This exposes a fresh area of basket to the feed liquor. Problems caused by buckling of the cake are overcome in a modification of this design named the *multi-stage reciprocating conveyor centrifuge*. This equipment has a series of concentric reciprocating baskets. Each basket pushes the cake a few centimetres on to the next. Other advantages of this design include lower more uniform power consumption and improved separation.

The *basket centrifuge* has a perforated metal basket lined with a filtering medium, which rotates at up to 2000 rev min^{-1}. Separation occurs in automatically controlled cycles which last 5–30 min, depending on the feed material and the separation conditions. In the three stages of the cycle the feed liquor first enters the slowly rotating bowl; the speed is then increased and separation takes place; finally the bowl is slowed and the cake is discharged through the base by a blade. Capacities of dewatering centrifuges are up to 90 000 l h^{-1}. They are used for example to recover animal and vegetable proteins, to separate coffee, cocoa and tea slurries and to desludge oils.

5.2   FILTRATION

Filtration is used to clarify liquids by the removal of small amounts of solid particles (for example wine, beer, oils and syrups) or to separate liquids from the solid part of a food by cake filtration (for example fruit juices).

5.2.1   Theory

When a suspension of particles is passed through a filter, the first particles become trapped in the filter medium and, as a result, reduce the area through which liquid can flow. This increases the resistance to fluid flow and a higher pressure difference is therefore necessary to maintain the flow rate of filtrate. The rate of filtration is expressed as follows:

$$\frac{\text{Rate of}}{\text{filtration}} = \frac{\text{driving force (the pressure difference across the filter)}}{\text{resistance to flow}}$$

Assuming that the filter cake does not become compressed, the resistance to flow through the filter is found using

$$R = \mu r \left(\frac{V_c V}{A + L} \right) \qquad (5.4)$$

where R (m^{-2}) is the resistance to flow through the filter, μ ($N s m^{-2}$) the viscosity of the liquid, r (m^{-2}) the specific resistance of the filter cake, $V = $ (m^3) the volume of filtrate, V_c the fractional volume of filter cake in feed liquid volume V, A (m^2) the area of filter and L the equivalent thickness of the filter and initial cake layer.

For constant rate filtration the flow rate throught the filter is found using

$$Q = \frac{\mu r V V_c}{A^2 \Delta P} + \frac{\mu r L}{A \Delta P} \qquad (5.5)$$

where Q (V/t) (m^{3}s^{-1}) is the flow rate of the filtrate, ΔP (kPa) the pressure difference and t (s) the filtration time. This equation is used to calculate the pressure drop required to achieve a desired flow rate or to predict the performance of large scale filters on the basis of data from pilot-scale studies.

In constant-pressure filtration, the flow rate gradually decreases as the resistance to flow, caused by the accumulating cake, increases. Equation (5.5) is rewritten with ΔP constant as

$$\frac{tA}{V} = \frac{\mu r V_c V}{2\Delta P A} + \frac{\mu r L}{\Delta P} \tag{5.6}$$

If $t/(V/A)$ is plotted against V/A, a straight line is obtained (Fig. 5.6). The slope (equation (5.7)) and the intercept (equation (5.8)) are used to find the specific

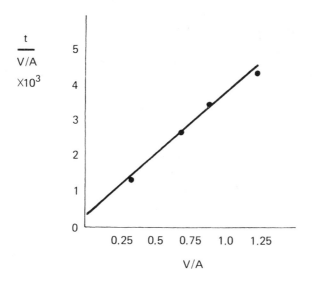

Fig. 5.6 — Graph of $t/(V/A)$ versus V/A.

resistance of the cake and the equivalent cake thickness of the filter medium:

$$\text{Slope} = \frac{\mu r V_c}{2\Delta P} \tag{5.7}$$

$$\text{Intercept} = \frac{\mu r L}{\Delta p} \tag{5.8}$$

If the filter cake is compressible (that is the specific resistance changes with applied pressure) the term r is modified as follows:

$$r = r'(\Delta P)^s \tag{5.9}$$

where r' is the specific resistance of cake under a pressure difference of 101 kPa and s is the compressibility of the cake. This is then used in equation (5.4).

Derivations of the above equations and further details are given by Earle (1983) and Jackson and Lamb (1981).

Sample problem 5.3
Pulp which contains 15% solids is filtered in a plate and frame filter press (section 5.2.2.1) with a pressure difference of 290 kPa. The masses of filtrate are shown below for a 1.5 h cycle. Calculate the specific resistance of the cake and the volume of filtrate that would be obtained if the cycle time were reduced to 45 min. (Assume that the cake is incompressible and the viscosity of the filtrate is $1.33 \times 10^{-3}\,\mathrm{N\,s\,m^{-2}}$.)

Time (min)	7.5	30.4	50	90
Mass of filtrate (kg)	1800	3800	4900	6800

Solution to sample problem 5.3

Time (s):	450	1825	3000	5400
V (m^3)	1.8	3.8	4.9	6.8
V/A	0.33	0.69	0.89	1.24
$t/(V/A)$	1364	2645	3371	4355

Plotting $t/(V/A)$ vs (V/A) (Fig. 5.6)

slope $= 2666.7$

intercept $= 300$

(1) From equation (5.7)

$$2666.7 = 1.33 \times 10^{-3} \times r \times 0.15/2 \times 290$$

$$r = 92\,273\,\mathrm{m^{-2}}$$

(2) From equation (5.6)

$$tA/V = 2666.7\,(V/A) + 300$$

For a 45 min (2700 s) cycle

$$2700 = 2666.7 \ (V/0.55)^2 + 300(V/0.55)$$

$$\frac{V}{0.55} = \frac{-300 \pm \sqrt{(90\,000 + 10\,800 \times 2666.7)}}{2 \times 2666.7}$$

$$= 0.52 \ \text{m}^3$$

5.2.2 Equipment

Gravity filtration is a slow process and finds little application in the food industry. Filtration equipment operates either by the application of pressure to the feed side of the filter bed (pressure filtration) or by the application of a partial vacuum to the opposite side of the filter bed (vacuum filtration). In addition the application of centrifugal force (centrifugal filtration) is described in section 5.1.2.3. Filter aids are usually applied to the filter or mixed with the food to improve the formation of filter cake.

5.2.2.1 *Pressure filters*

Two commonly used pressure filters are the batch *plate-and-frame filter press* (Fig. 5.7) and the *shell-and-leaf pressure filter*. In the plate-and-frame design, cloth or

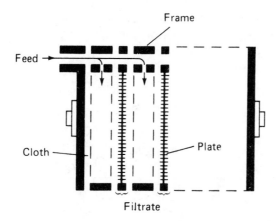

Fig. 5.7 — Plate-and-frame filter press.

paper filters are supported on vertical plates. Feed liquor is pumped into the press and liquid passes through the filter cloths. It flows down the grooved surfaces of the plates and is drained through an outlet channel in the base of each plate. A layer of cake builds up on the cloths until the space between the plates is filled. As filtration continues, a higher pressure is required to maintain the flow rate of filtrate. In practice the pressure is allowed to increase to a pre-determined value and the plates are backwashed with water. The press is then dismantled and the cake is removed ready to begin another cycle. The method has relatively low capital costs and high flexibility for different foods. The equipment is reliable and easily maintained. It is widely used, particularly for the production of apple juice and cider (for example Jones *et al.*, 1983). However, it is time consuming and highly labour intensive.

The *shell-and-leaf pressure filter* is used to overcome the problems of high labour costs and lack of convenience associated with plate and frame presses. It consists of mesh 'leaves', which are coated in filter medium and supported on a hollow frame which forms the outlet channel for the filtrate. The leaves are stacked horizontally or vertically inside a pressure vessel, and in some designs they rotate at 1–2 rev min^{-1} to improve the uniformity of cake buildup. Feed liquor is pumped into the shell at a pressure of approximately 400 kPa. When filtration is completed, the cake is blown or washed from the leaves. This equipment has a higher cost than plate filters and is best suited to routine filtration of liquors which have similar characteristics.

5.2.2.2   *Vacuum filters*
Vacuum filters operate at reduced pressure on the downstream side of the filter plate and are limited by the cost of vacuum generation to a pressure difference of 100 kPa. However, cake is removed at atmospheric pressure and these types of filter are therefore able to operate continuously. (Pressure filters have batch operation because the pressure must be reduced for cake removal.) Two common types of vacuum filter are the rotary drum filter and rotary disc filter.

Rotary drum filters consist of a slowly rotating horizontal cylinder which has the surface divided into a series of shallow compartments. Each compartment is covered in filter cloth and connected to a central vacuum pump (Fig. 5.8). As the drum

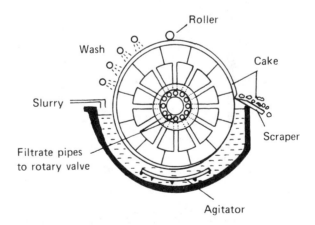

Fig. 5.8 — Rotary drum filter. (After Leniger and Beverloo (1975).)

rotates, it dips into a bath of liquor. Filtrate flows through the filter and out through channels in the drum. When the drum leaves the bath, the filter cake is sucked free of liquor and washed with sprays. Further round the drum, the vacuum is released and compressed air is blown from beneath the cloth to loosen the cake. The cake is then removed by a scraper and the individual compartment restarts the cycle. This type of filter is compact and has low labour costs and a high capacity. However, it has a high capital cost and produces cake which has a moderately high moisture content. It is best suited to materials that form a free-draining cake.

Rotary vacuum disc filters consist of a series of vertical discs which rotate slowly in a bath of liquor in a similar cycle to drum filters. Each disc is divided into portions and each portion has an outlet to a central shaft. The discs are fitted with scrapers to remove the cake continuously. This type of equipment has similar advantages to drum filters.

5.3 EXPRESSION

5.3.1 Theory

The main applications of expression are in the extraction of oils and juices. It is frequently combined with size reduction (Chapter 3) to maximise the yield of product. Components are extracted from plant materials either for direct consumption (for example, fruit juices) or for use in subsequent processing (for example sugar and vegetable oils). These materials are located within the cell structure of the plants and it is necessary to disrupt the cells in order to release them.

In oil-bearing seeds the oil is found inside cells in small droplets ($10–80 \mu$m in diameter). However, a single type of equipment is not suited to all oil-seeds, owing to variation in oil content, moisture content, porosity and solidity of the material, and the proportions of hulls in different oil-seeds. There are two methods of oil extraction: solvent extraction and expression. Solvent extraction is described by Davie and Vincent (1980). Expression is achieved either in two stages (size reduction to produce a pulp, followed by separation in a press) or in a single-stage, which both ruptures the cells and expresses the liquid. In general the single stage operation is more economical, permits higher throughputs and has lower capital and operating costs, but for some products that are especially hard (for example nuts) a two stage expression is more effective. Better extraction is achieved by heating, which reduces the oil viscosity, releases oil from intact cells and removes moisture. Moisture lubricates the pulp during pressing and causes a slower pressure increase and reduced oil yields. However, moisture also increases the flow of oil through the pores of the press cake, thus reducing the amount of oil entrained in the cake and increasing the oil yield. There is therefore an optimum pulp moisture content for each type of oil seed to obtain a maximum yield of oil.

In fruit processing (for example grape juice extraction for wine making, or apple or citrus juices), the press should remove the maximum quantity of juice, without substantial quantities of solids, or phenolic compounds from the skins which cause bitterness and browning. This is achieved by the use of lower pressures and fewer pressings. It is also necessary to increase the pressure slowly to avoid the formation of a dense impenetrable press cake, as the solid material is easily deformed.

The factors that influence the yield of liquid from a press include

(1) the maturity and growth conditions of the raw material,
(2) the extent of disruption of cell structure,
(3) the resistance of the solids to mechanical deformation,
(4) the rate of increase in pressure,
(5) the time of pressing,
(6) the maximum pressure applied,
(7) the thickness of the pressed solids,
(8) the temperatures of solids and liquid and
(9) the viscosity of the expressed liquid.

5.3.2 Equipment
5.3.2.1 Batch presses
Common types of equipment for fruit processing are the *plate-and-frame filter press* (section 5.2.2.1), the *tank press* and the *hydraulic ram press* (or *cage press*).

The *tank press* consists of a horizontal cylinder which is divided internally by a membrane. During an automatically controlled pressing cycle of 1.5 h, fruit pulp is fed into one side of the membrane through side openings and compressed air is applied to the opposite side of the membrane (Fig. 5.9). Juice flows out through

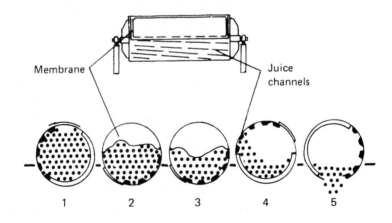

Fig. 5.9 — Tank press: 1, tank filled; 2, membrane partly inflated; 3, membrane inflated further; 4, loosening of residue; 5, discharge. (After Vine (1987).)

channels and, when pressing is completed, the tank is rotated to loosen and discharge the press residue. High yields of good-quality juice are obtained by the gentle increase in pressure and the sealed press reduces contamination of the juice. Capacities range from 3600 kg to 25 000 kg (Vine, 1987)

In the *hydraulic ram press*, up to 2 t of pulp are placed into a vertical heavy-duty perforated metal cylinder or slatted cage, either loose or in cloth bags depending on the nature of the pulp. In larger presses, ribbed layer plates are used to reduce the thickness of the pulp bed. A pressure plate is lowered onto the top of the stacked pulp and the pressure is gradually increased by an hydraulic system or motor-driven screw thread. Liquid flows through the perforated or slatted cage and is collected at the base of the press. This type of equipment is used for grape juice expression and for small-scale oil extraction. It has the advantage of close control over the pressure exerted on the pulp and may operate semi-automatically to reduce labour costs.

5.3.2.2 Continuous presses

There are several types of continuous press used commercially: the belt press is used in fruit processing, the screw press is used for both fruit processing and oil extraction (a similar design is used for extrusion (Chapter 13)), and the roller press is used for sugar cane processing. The advantages and limitations of continuous processing are described in Chapter 1.

Belt presses produce high yields of good-quality juice. They consist of a continuous belt, made from canvas–plastic composite material, which passes under tension over two hollow stainless steel cylinders, one of which is perforated. Pulped fruit is fed onto the inside of the belt and is pressed between the belt and the perforated cylinder. Juice flows through the perforations and the press cake continues around the belt and is removed by a scraper or auger. The main disadvantages of this equipment are the high capital costs and difficulty in maintenance and cleaning.

The *screw press* (or *screw expeller* in oil processing) consists of a robust horizontal metal cylinder (or 'barrel') containing a stainless steel helical screw (Fig. 5.10). The

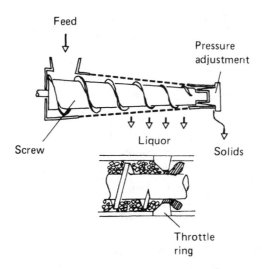

Fig. 5.10 — Screw press, showing throttle ring used for oil-seed pressing. (After Brennan *et al.* (1976) and Stein (1984).)

pitch of the screw flights gradually decreases towards the discharge end, to increase the pressure on the pulp as it is carried through the barrel. The final section of the barrel is perforated to allow expressed liquid to escape. The press cake passes through a discharge port in the barrel outlet. The pressure in the barrel is regulated by adjusting the diameter of the discharge port. In juice extraction the barrel is water cooled to reduce the effects of friction heat, generated by the movement of food, which may have an undesirable effect on flavour and aroma. This equipment produces a higher concentration of solids in the juice than the belt press does.

Screw presses are more commonly used in oil extraction where the heat reduces the viscosity of the oil. Some types of expeller have supplementary heaters fitted to the barrel to improve yields. Capacities range from $40 \, kg \, h^{-1}$ to $8000 \, kg \, h^{-1}$. The oil cake has 5–18% (w/w) residual oil, depending on the type of oil-seed and the operating conditions (Barker, 1987). A modified screw press is described by Stein (1984). In this equipment (Fig. 5.10), high shearing forces act on the seeds as they are forced through a series of throttle rings located in the barrel.

In the *Roller press*, pulp is fed between heavy fluted metal rollers. Pressure is applied to the pulp and liquid flows along the grooves and over the rollers to a collection pan. The solids are removed by a doctor blade. Modifications to this design include the use of a hollow perforated roller which is covered in filter cloth and maintained at a negative pressure. Liquid flows through the cloth into the roller and is discharged, and pulp is removed as before.

ACKNOWLEDGEMENTS

Grateful acknowledgement is made of information supplied by the following: Simon-Rosedowns Ltd, Hull HU2 0AD, UK; Westfalia Separator AG, D-4740 Oelde, West Germany.

REFERENCES

Barker, A. (1987). Private communication, Simon-Rosedowns Ltd, Hull, UK.

Brennan, J. G., Butters, J. R., Cowell, N. D., and Lilly, A. E. V. (1976) *Food engineering operations*. Applied Science, London, pp. 120–207.

Davie, J., and Vincent, L. (1980) Extraction of vegetable oils and fats. In: R. J. Hamilton and A. Bhati (eds.), *Fats and oils, chemistry and technology*. Applied Science, London, pp. 123–134.

Earle, R. L. (1983) *Unit operations in food processing*, 2nd edn. Pergamon Press, Oxford, pp 143–158.

Hemfort, H. (1983) *Centrifugal separators for the food industry*. Westfalia Separator AG, 4740 Oelde 1, West Germany.

Hemfort, H. (1984) *Centrifugal clarifiers and decanters for biotechnology*. Westfalia Separator AG, 4740 Oelde 1, West Germany.

Jackson, A. T. and Lamb, J. (1981) *Calculations in food and chemical engineering*, Macmillan, London, pp. 129–163.

Jones, H., Jones, N., and Swientek, R. J. (1983) Plate and frame filters clarify apple juice. *Food Process. (USA)* October, 104–105.

Leniger, H. A., and Beverloo, W. A. (1975) *Food process engineering*.D. Reidel, Dordrecht, pp. 498–531.

Loncin, M., and Merson, R. L. (1979) *Food engineering*. Academic Press, New York, p. 201.

Stein, W. (1984) New oil extraction process. *Food Enging. Int*. June 59, 61–63.

Vine, R. P. (1987) The use of new technology in commercial winemaking. In A. Turner (ed.), *Food technology international Europe*. Sterling. London, pp. 146–149.

6

Membrane concentration

Reverse osmosis (hyperfiltration) and ultrafiltration are both unit operations in which water and some solutes in a solution are selectively removed through a semi-permeable membrane. The two processes are similar in that the driving force for transport across the membrane is the pressure applied to the feed liquid. However, reverse osmosis is used to separate water from low-molecular-weight solutes (for example salts, monosaccharides and aroma compounds), which have a high osmotic pressure. A high pressure (4000–8000 kPa) is therefore necessary to overcome this (hence the term *reverse* osmosis). Ultrafiltration membranes have a higher porosity and retain only large molecules (for example proteins or colloids) which have a low osmotic pressure. Smaller solutes are transported across the membrane with the water. Ultrafiltration therefore operates at lower pressures (50–2000 kPa).

The main advantages of membrane concentration over concentration by evaporation (Chapter 12) are

(1) the food is not heated, and there is therefore negligible loss of nutritional or eating quality (section 6.4) and particularly less loss of volatiles, and
(2) in contrast with boiling, membrane concentration does not involve a change in phase and therefore uses energy more efficiently (Table 6.1).

Other advantages over evaporation include lower labour and operating costs, simple installation, operation with a single control valve, and no requirement for steam boilers.

The main limitations of membrane concentration are

(1) variation in the product flow rate when changes occur in the concentration of feed liquor,
(2) higher capital costs than evaporation
(3) a maximum concentration to 30% total solids and
(4) fouling of the membranes (deposition of polymers on the membrane), which reduces the operating time between periods of cleaning.

Table 6.1 — Comparison of reverse osmosis and evaporation of whey

Parameter	Reverse osmosis	Evaporation
Steam consumption	0	250–550 kg per 1000 l water removed
Electricity consumption	10 kW h per 1000 l water removed (continuous); 20 kW h per 1000 l water removed (batch)	Approximately 5 kW h per 1000 l water removed
Energy use (kW h)	3.6 (6–12% solids) 8.8 (6–18% solids) 9.6 (6–20% solids)	One effect 387 (6–50% solids) Two effects 90 (6–50% solids) Seven effects 60 (6–50% solids) MVR* 44
Labour	4 h day^{-1}	Normally two operators during whole operation (boiler house and evaporator)
Cooling-water consumption	0–29 300 kJ per 1000 l water removed (continuous); 0–58 600 kJ per 1000 l water removed (batch)	$(5.2–1.2) \times 10^6$ kJ per 1000 l water removed
Economical plant size	6000 l day^{-1} day or more, no upper limit	80 000–100 000 l day^{-1}
Concentration in final product	Maximum 30% total solids. Capacity varies with concentration	Up to 60% total solids

Adapted from Madsen(1974).
*MVR, Mechanical vapour recompression.

In both reverse osmosis and ultrafiltration the flow rates through the membrane depend on the resistance of the membrane material, the resistance of boundary layers of liquid on each side of the membrane (Chapter 1), and the extent of fouling.

6.1 THEORY

Movement of molecules through reverse osmosis membranes is by diffusion and not by liquid flow. The molecules dissolve at one face of the membrane are transported through the membrane and then removed from the other face. The flow rate of liquid (the *transport rate* or *flux*) is determined by the solubility and diffusivity of the molecules in the membrane material, and by the difference between the osmotic pressure of the liquid and the applied pressure. The pressure difference across the membrane (the transmembrane pressure) is found using

$$P = \frac{P_f + P_r}{2} - P_p \qquad (6.1)$$

where P (kPa) is the transmembrane pressure, P_f (kPa) the pressure of the feed, P_r (kPa) the pressure of the retentate (high-molecular weight fraction) and P_p (kPa) the pressure of the permeate (low-molecular-weight fraction).

Water flux increases with

(1) an increase in applied pressure,
(2) increased permeance of the membrane and
(3) lower solute concentration in the feed stream.

It is calculated using

$$J = kA(\Delta P - \Delta \Pi) \tag{6.2}$$

where J (kg h^{-1} is the flux, K (kg m^{-2} h^{-1} kPa^{-1}) the mass transfer coefficient, A (m^2) the area of the membrane, ΔP (kPa) the applied pressure and $\Delta \Pi$(kPa) the osmotic pressure

Osmotic pressure is found for dilute solutions using

$$\Pi = MRT \tag{6.3}$$

where T (°K) where °K $=$ °C $+ 273$) is the absolute temperature, R (kPa m^{-3} mol^{-1} K^{-1}) the universal gas constant, M(mol m^{-3}) the molar concentration and Π(kPa) the osmotic pressure.

Many foods have high osmotic pressures (for example (6–10) x 10^5 Pa for fresh fruit juice), and a high applied pressure is therefore needed. Solutes that are retained (or 'rejected') by the membrane either have a lower solubility than water in the membrane material or diffuse more slowly through the membrane. The rate of rejection is 100% (all solutes) for RO membranes, 95–100% of high molecular weight solutes for UF membranes and 0–10% of low molecular weight solutes in UF membranes (virally free passage). The important factors in determining the performance of a reverse osmosis membrane are its thickness, chemical composition and molecular structure. The selectivity of the process (that is the ability to remove water while retaining solutes) is a property of the membrane that increases with increasing applied pressure at lower pressures and then falls at higher pressures.

The pores of ultrafiltration membranes (section 6.1.2) are considerably larger (0.01–100 μm), and water and small solutes flow through the membrane under hydraulic (streamline, viscous) flow (Chapter 1). Larger solutes become concentrated at the membrane surface. The flux is therefore controlled by the applied pressure, and the solute concentrations in the bulk of the liquid and at the membrane surface

$$J = KA \ln \left(\frac{c_1}{c_2}\right) \tag{6.4}$$

where: c_1 is the concentration of solutes at the membrane and c_2 the concentration of solutes in the liquid.

Other factors that influence the flux include the liquid velocity, viscosity, temperature and presence of other components of higher or lower molecular weight. A high flow rate is necessary to reduce the formation of a layer of polymer gel at the membrane. In batch operation the liquid is recirculated until the desired concentration is achieved, whereas in continuous production an equilibrium is established, where the feed rate equals the sum of the permeate and concentrate flow rates. The ratio of this sum determines the degree of concentration achieved.

Sample problem 6.1
Fruit juice containing 9% w/w solids is pre-concentrated at 35 °C by reverse osmosis, prior to concentration in an evaporator. If the operating pressure is 4000 kPa and the mass transfer coefficient is 6.3×10^{-3} kg m^{-2} h^{-1} kPa^{-1}, calculate the area of membrane required to remove 5 t of permeate in an 8 h shift. (Assume that sucrose forms the majority of the solids in the juice and the universal gas constant is 8.314 kPa m^{-3} mol^{-1}K^{-1})

Solution to sample problem 6.1

$$\text{Molar concentration } (M) = \frac{\text{concentration (g l}^{-1})}{\text{molecular weight}}$$

$$\text{g l}^{-1} \equiv \text{kg m}^{-3} = 90/342 = 0.264 \text{ mol m}^{-3}$$

From equation (6.3),

$$\Pi = 0.264 \times 8.314 \,(35 + 273)$$
$$= 676 \text{ kPa}$$

Therefore,

$$\text{required flux} = \frac{5000}{8}$$
$$= 625 \text{ kg h}^{-1}$$

From equation (6.2)

$$6.25 = 6.3 \times 10^{-3} A(4000 - 676)$$

Thus,

$$A = 29.9 \text{ m}^2 = 30 \text{ m}^2$$

Different types of membrane reject solutes with specific ranges of molecular weight. These molecular weight 'cutoff' points are used to characterise membranes. For reverse osmosis membranes, the cutoff points range from molecular weights of 100 at 4000–7000 kPa to 500 at 2500–4000 kPa. Ultrafiltration membranes have cutoff points from a molecular weight of 7000 at 1000–2000 kPa to 25 000 at 300–1500 kPa.

6.1.1 Membranes

The chemical composition (or molecular structure) of reverse osmosis membranes is the main factor that controls the rate of diffusion of solutes. The materials used for reverse osmosis membranes should have a high water permeability, a high solute rejection and durability. The cost should be sufficently low for economical manufacture in relatively large quantities. 'Ultrathin' membranes (0.05–0.1 μm thick) are made from cellulose acetate, mixed cellulose esters (acetate–propionate–butyrate), polyacrylonitrile, polyamides or polyurethanes (Michaels 1974). They have a high stability and mechanical strength to resist the high operating pressures and the required permeability. *Loeb* membranes are heterogeneous membranes which consist of a thin layer of membrane (for example cellulose ester) on a thicker layer of porous support material (Fig. 6.1).

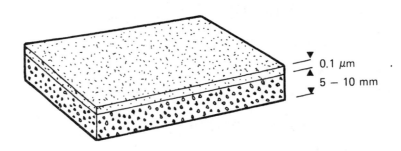

Fig. 6.1 — Asymmetric reverse osmosis membrane. (After Michaels (1974).)

The main requirement of an ultrafiltration membrane is the ability to form and retain a 'microporous' structure (Fig. 6.2) during manufacture and during operation under thermal and mechanical stress. The material and method used for the manufacture of the microporous structure are the most important factors in determining the properties of the membrane. Rigid or glassy polymers, which are thicker than reverse osmosis membranes (0.1–0.5 μm), are used. They are mechanically strong, durable and resistant to abrasion, heat and hydrolysis or oxidation in water. They do not creep, soften or collapse under pressure. For food applications, membranes should be capable of being cleaned and sanitised. Suitable materials include polysulphones, polyamides, poly(vinyl chloride), polystyrene, polycarbonates, polyethers and rigid cellulose esters. Hollow fibre membranes have a

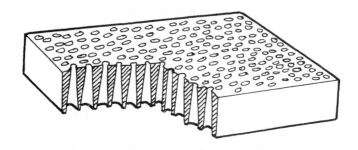

Fig. 6.2 — Microporous ultrafiltration membrane. (After Michaels (1974).)

microporous inner skin, which is surrounded by a layer of spongy support material (Fig. 6.3).

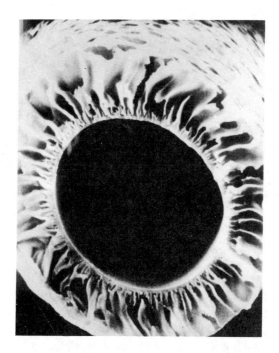

Fig. 6.3 — Hollow fibre membrane. (Courtesy of Patterson Candy International Ltd)

The inner skin is the separating membrane surface. The pore size in this skin determines the size of molecules which can pass through the membrane. Larger molecules are retained on the inside of the fibre. The hollow fibre is a coherent structure which can withstand pressures on either process or permeate side, without the need for a separate support. This unique feature allows a straightforward approach to process control by throttling permeate, makes cleaning in place more efficient and makes backflushing of the membrane possible as in the case of severe process disturbance.

6.2   EQUIPMENT

Membranes are held in cylindrical tubes in a number of different designs. Each consists of the membrane tubes mounted on a frame with associated pipework and controls. For example the spiral cartridge and tubular types are used for larger batches and continuous operation.

In a typical *spiral cartridge* system, alternating layers of polysulphone membranes and polyethylene supports are wrapped around a hollow central tube and are separated by channel spacers and drains (Fig. 6.4). Feed liquor enters the cartridge

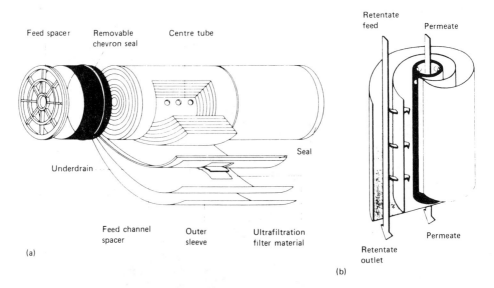

Fig. 6.4 — Spiral cartridge membrane: (a) components; (b) flow schematic diagram. (Courtesy of Millipore Ltd.)

and flows tangentially upwards through the membrane. Permeate flows into channels and then to the central tube, and the concentrate flows out of the other end of the cartridge. Separator screens cause turbulent flow (Chapter 1) to maximise the flux. The turbulent flow and the low volume of liquid in relation to the large membrane area reduce the need for large pumps.

In the *tubular* design a number of perforated stainless steel tubes are fabricated as a shell and tube heat exchanger and each tube is lined with a membrane. Special end caps connect up to 18 tubes in series or in parallel, depending on the application (Fig. 6.5).

6.3   APPLICATIONS

Reverse osmosis is most economical when treating dilute solutions. The largest commercial food application is the concentration of whey from cheese manufacture,

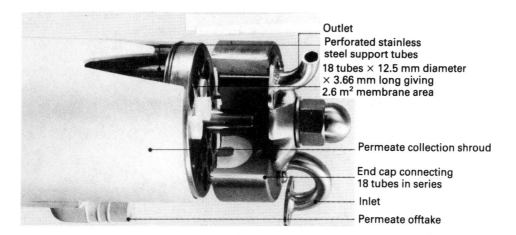

Outlet
Perforated stainless
steel support tubes
18 tubes × 12.5 mm diameter
× 3.66 mm long giving
2.6 m² membrane area

Permeate collection shroud

End cap connecting
18 tubes in series

Inlet

Permeate offtake

Fig. 6.5 — Tubular membrane. (Courtesy of Patterson Candy International Ltd.)

either as a pre-concentration stage prior to drying or for use in the manufacture of ice cream. Reverse osmosis is also used

(1) to concentrate and purify fruit juices prior to evaporation (for example Robe, 1983), and to concentrate enzymes (Chapter 7) and vegetable oils,
(2) to concentrate wheat starch, citric acid, egg white, milk, coffee, syrups, natural extracts and flavours,
(3) to clarify wine and beer,
(4) to fractionate fermentation liquors,
(5) to de-ash cheese whey but to retain lactose (Karel, 1975) and
(6) to demineralise and purify water.

In the last application, monovalent and polyvalent ions, particles, bacteria and organic materials with a molecular weight greater than 300 are all removed by up to 99.9% to give high-purity process water for beverage manufacture and similar applications.

A typical commercial reverse osmosis plant operates with a flux of $450 \, l \, h^{-1}$ at 4000 kPa up to a flux $1200–2400 \, l \, h^{-1}$ at 8000 kPa. A fourfold concentration of whey typically would have production rates of $80–90 \, t \, day^{-1}$. A comparison of 'once-through' and multi-stage recycling of liquid through banks of membranes is described by Pepper and Orchard (1982). Changes in pressure and flux in each system are shown in Fig. 6.6.

The most common commercial application of ultrafiltration is in the dairy industry. It is used to concentrate milk prior to the manufacture of dairy products, to concentrate whey to 30% solids (Fig. 6.7) or to remove lactose and salts selectively. In cheese manufacture, ultrafiltration has advantages in producing a higher product yield and nutritional value, simpler standardisation of the solids content, lower rennet consumption and easier processing. Other applications include

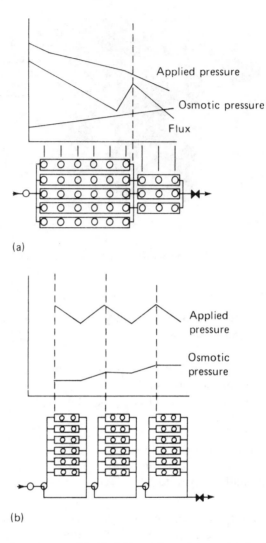

Fig. 6.6 — Changes in pressure and flux in (a) 'once-through tapered system' and (b) 'multi-stage' reverse osmosis. (After Pepper and Orchard (1982).)

(1) the concentration of sucrose and tomato paste,
(2) the treatment of still effluents in the brewing and distilling industries,
(3) separation and concentration of enzymes (Chapter 7), other proteins or pectin,
(4) treatment of process water to remove bacteria and contaminants (greater than 0.003 μm in diameter) (Mackintosh, 1983) and
(5) pre-treatment for reverse osmosis membranes to prevent fouling by suspended organic materials and colloidal materials.

Typical commercial operating pressures are 70–1000 kPa, at flux rates of up to 40 l min^{-1} per tube.

Fig. 6.7 — Whey ultrafiltration plant. (Courtesy of Patterson Candy International Ltd.)

6.4   EFFECT ON FOODS

Both reverse osmosis and ultrafiltration membranes concentrate foods without the application of heat, and this results in good retention of sensory and nutritional qualities. For example in whey the functional properties (emulsifying ability, foaming ability and solubility) of proteins are retained, and different products which have specified ranges of protein and lactose content (for example 35–80% protein and 47–4.7% lactose) are available for use in fortified jams, low-calorie mayonnaise, dips, sauces and skinless sausages, and as alternatives to egg albumin (Smallwood, 1986).

In a comparative assessment of concentrated orange juice prepared by reverse osmosis and vacuum-evaporation, taste panellists could not detect a difference between reverse osmosis juice and the control after 43 months, whereas vacuum evaporated juice was inferior to the control (Papanicolaou *et al.*, 1984).

The nutritional value of foods produced by membrane concentration is largely retained. Both types of membrane retain proteins, fats and larger carbohydrates, but the larger pore size of ultrafiltration membranes allows sugars, vitamins and amino acids to be lost (Table 6.2). The importance of nutritional changes to the diet is discussed in Chapter 1.

ACKNOWLEDGEMENTS

Grateful acknowledgement is made for information supplied by the following: Paterson Candy International Ltd, Whitchurch, Hampshire, UK; Millipore UK Ltd,

Table 6.2 — Loss of nutrients during membrane concentration of milk

Nutrient	Loss (%) Reverse osmosis	Ultrafiltration
Protein	0	5
Fat	0	0
Carbohydrate	0	43
Energy	0	13
Thiamin	0	38
Riboflavin	0	39
Nicotinic acid	8	41
Vitamin B_6	3	36
Vitamin B_{12}	0	2
Vitamin C	—	87
Folic acid	0	5
Pantothenic acid	0	32
Biotin	0	37

From Glover (1971).

Harrow, Middlesex., HA1 2YH, UK; Alfa Laval Co. Ltd, Brentford, Middlesex., TW8 9BT, UK.

REFERENCES

Glover, F. A. (1971) Concentration of milk by ultrafiltration and reverse osmosis. *J. Dairy Res.* **38** 373–379.

Karel, M. (1975) Concentration of foods. In: O. R. Fennema (ed.) *Principles of food science*, Part 2. Marcel Dekker, New York, pp. 295-308.

Mackintosh, B. (1983) Ultrafiltration for process waters. *Food Process.* September 29–31.

Madsen, R. F. (1974) Membrane concentration. In: A. Spicer (ed.), *Advances in preconcentration and dehydration of foods*. Applied Science, London, pp. 251–301.

Michaels, A. S. (1974). Tailored membranes. In: A. Spicer (ed.), *Advances in preconcentration and dehydration of foods*. Applied Science, London, pp. 213–250.

Papanicolaou, D., Katsaboxakis, K., and Codounis, M. (1984) *Rev. Gen. du Froid* **74** (4) 211–213.

Pepper, D., and Orchard, A. C. J. (1982) Improvements in the concentration of whey and milk by reverse osmosis. *J. Soc. Dairy Technol.* **35** (2) 49–53.

Robe, K. (1983) Hyperfiltration methods for preconcentrating juice saves evaporation energy. *Food Process.* (*USA*) 100–101.

Smallwood, M. (1986) Concentrating on natural proteins. *Food Process.* September 21–22.

7

Fermentation and enzyme technology

In food fermentations, the controlled action of selected micro-organisms is used to alter the texture of foods, preserve foods by production of acids or alcohol, or to produce subtle flavours and aromas, which increase the quality and value of raw materials. Today the preservative effect is supplemented by other unit operations (for example chilling or pasteurisation (Chapters 18 and 10) and more sophisticated packaging (Chapter 22)). The main advantages of fermentation as a method of food processing are

(1) the use of mild conditions of pH and temperature which maintain (and often improve) the nutritional properties and sensory characteristics of the food,
(2) the production of foods which have flavours or textures that cannot be achieved by other methods,
(3) low energy consumption due to the mild operating conditions,
(4) relatively low capital and operating costs and
(5) generally simple technology.

The separation of enzymes from microbial cells, or animal or plant sources for use *in vitro* in food processing is a more recent development. The separated and purified enzymes are termed 'technical' enzymes. They are added to foods as concentrated solutions or powders, to bring about specific reactions under mild conditions of temperature and pH. Enzymes can also be immobilised on support materials in a 'reactor' where they are re-used for extended periods. The main advantages of technical enzymes are

(1) highly specific changes to foods,
(2) minimum loss of nutritional quality at the moderate temperatures employed,
(3) lower energy consumption than corresponding chemical reactions and
(4) the production of new foods.

In this chapter, commercially important food fermentations and technical enzymes are described. The use of enzymes in food analysis is rapidly expanding and is discussed in detail by Guilbault (1984). The effects of naturally occurring enzymes on food quality are discussed in other chapters where their action relates specifically to the unit operation under consideration.

7.1 THEORY

The main factors that control the growth of micro-organisms in food fermentations are

(1) availability of carbon and nitrogen sources, and any specific nutrients required by individual micro-organisms,
(2) substrate pH,
(3) incubation temperature,
(4) moisture content,
(5) redox potential,
(6) stage of growth of micro-organisms and
(7) presence of other competing micro-organisms.

These factors are discussed in greater detail in microbiological texts (for example Jay, 1978) and in sections 7.1.1 and 7.1.2.

7.1.1 Batch culture
In batch culture the growth of micro-organisms can be described by a number of phases (Fig. 7.1). Cell growth during the logarithmic (or exponential) phase is at a

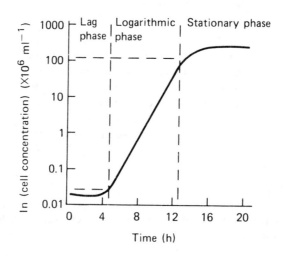

Fig. 7.1 — Phases in the growth of micro-organisms.

constant rate which is shown by

$$\ln C_b = \ln c_0 + \mu t \tag{7.1}$$

where c_0 is the original cell concentration, c_b the cell concentration after time t (biomass produced), μ (h^{-1} the specific growth rate and t (h) the time of fermentation. Graphically the natural logarithm (ln) of cell concentration versus time produces a straight line, the slope of which is the specific growth rate. The highest growth rate μ_{max} occurs in the logarithmic phase (Fig. 7.1).

The rate of cell growth eventually declines owing to exhaustion of nutrients and/ or accumulation of metabolic products in the growth medium. If different initial substrate concentrations are plotted against cell concentration in the stationary phase, it is found that an increase in substrate concentration results in a proportional increase in cell yield (AB in Fig.7.2). This indicates substrate limitation of cell

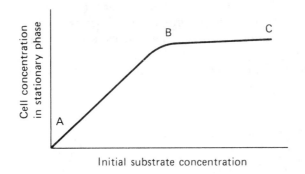

Fig. 7.2 — Effect of initial substrate concentration on cell concentration at the end of the logarithmic phase of growth. (After Stanbury and Whitaker (1984).)

growth, which is described by

$$c_b = Y(S_0 - S_r) \tag{7.2}$$

where c_b is the concentration of biomass, Y the yield factor (a dimensionless group; see Appendix C), S_0 the original substrate concentration and S_r the residual substrate concentration. The portion of the curve BC in Fig 7.2 shows inhibition of cell growth by products of metabolism.

The reduction in growth rate is related to the residual substrate concentration by Monod's equation

$$\mu = \frac{\mu_{max} S_r}{(K_s + S_r)} \tag{7.3}$$

where μ_{max} (h^{-1}) is the maximum specific growth rate, S_r $(mg^{-1} l)$ the residual substrate concentration and K_s $(mg^{-1} l)$ the substrate utilisation constant. K_s is a measure of the affinity of a micro-organism for a particular substrate (a high affinity produces a low value of K_s).

The rate of production of primary metabolic products (for example ethanol, amino acids and citric acid) is determined by the rate of cell growth, and is found using

$$q_p = Y_{p/s}\mu \tag{7.4}$$

where q_p is the specific rate of product formation and $Y_{p/s}$ is the yield of product related to the amount of substrate consumed.

The specific rate of product formation varies with the specific growth rate of cells for primary products. The rate of production of secondary products (those produced from primary products (for example aromatic compounds and fatty acids)), which are produced in the stationary growth phase, does not vary in this way and may remain constant or change in more complex ways.

The productivity of a culture is the amount of biomass produced in unit time (usually per hour) and is found using

$$P_b = \frac{(c_{max} - c_0)}{t_1 - t_2} \tag{7.5}$$

where P_b $(g\,l^{-1}\,h^{-1})$ is the productivity, c_{max} the maximum cell concentration during the fermentation, c_0 the initial cell concentration, t_1 (h) the duration of growth at the maximum specific growth rate, t_2 (h) the duration of the fermentation when cells are not growing at the maximum specific growth rate and including the time spent in culture preparation and harvesting.

Sample problem (7.1)
An inoculum containing 3.0×10^4 cells ml^{-1} of *Saccharomyces cerevisiae* is grown on glucose in a batch culture for 20 h. Cell concentrations are measured at 4 h intervals and the results are plotted in Fig. 7.1. The total time taken for culture preparation and harvest is 1.5 h. Calculate the maximum specific growth rate and the productivity of the culture.
Solution to sample problem 7.1

From equation (7.1) for the logarithmic phase,

$$\ln 2 \times 10^8 = \ln 3 \times 10^4 + \mu_{max}8.5$$

Therefore,

$$\mu_{max} = \frac{\ln 2 \times 10^8 - \ln 3 \times 10^4}{8 \cdot 5}$$

$$0.95 \ h^{-1}$$

From equation (7.5),

$$P_b = \frac{2 \times 10^8 - 3 \times 10^4}{8.5 + [(20 - 8.5) + 1.5]}$$

$$= 9.3 \times 10^6 \ cells \ h^{-1}$$

7.1.2 Continuous culture

Cultures in which cell growth is limited by the substrate in batch operation have a higher productivity if the substrate is added continuously to the fermenter, and biomass or products are continuously removed at the same rate. Under these conditions the cells remain in the logarithmic phase of growth. The rate at which substrate is added under such 'steady state' conditions is found using

$$D = \frac{F}{V} \tag{7.6}$$

where D (h^{-1}) is the dilution rate, F $(l \ h^{-1})$ the substrate flow rate and V (l) the volume of the fermenter.

The steady-state cell concentration and residual substrate concentration respectively are found using

$$\bar{c} = Y(S_0 - \bar{S}) \tag{7.7}$$

$$\bar{s} = \frac{K_s D}{\mu_{max} - d} \tag{7.8}$$

where $\bar{c}$ is the steady-state cell concentration, Y the yield factor, S_0 the original substrate concentration, $\bar{S}$ the steady state residual substrate concentration, K_s (mg l^{-1}) the substrate utilisation constant and μ_{max} (h^{-1}) the maximum specific growth rate.

The maximum dilution rate that can be used in a given culture is controlled by μ_{max} and is influenced by the substrate utilisation constant and yield factor (Fig. 7.3).

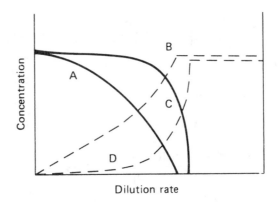

Fig. 7.3 — Effect of dilution rate in continuous culture on steady-state cell concentration
(————) and residual substrate concentration (– – –) for limiting substrate compared with
initial substrate concentration: curves A and B, micro-organism with a low K value; curves C
and D, micro-organism with a high K value.

The productivity of a continuous culture is found using

$$P_c = D\bar{c}\left(1 - \frac{t_3}{t_4}\right) \tag{7.9}$$

where P_c is the productivity (continuous culture), t_3 (h) the time period before steady
state conditions are established and t_4 (h) the duration of steady state conditions.

Further details of the above equations are given by Frazier and Westhoff (1978),
Stanbury and Whitaker (1984), Jay (1978) and other microbiological texts.

Sample problem (7.2)
Brewers' yeast is grown continuously in a fermenter with an operating volume of 12
m^3. The residence time is 20 h and the yeast has a doubling time of 3.2 h. A 2%
inoculum, which contains 5% yeast cells is mixed with the substrate. Calculate the
mass of yeast harvested from the fermenter per hour. (Assume that the density of the
broth is 1010 kg m^{-3}).

Solution to sample problem 7.2

$$\text{Flow-rate} = \frac{\text{volume of fermenter}}{\text{residence time}}$$

$$= \frac{12}{20}$$

$$= 0.6 \text{ m}^3 \text{ h}^{-1}$$

$$\text{Mass flow rate} = 0.6 \times 1010$$

$$= 606 \text{ kg h}^{-1}$$

$$\text{Initial yeast concentration} = \frac{\text{concentration in the inoculum}}{\text{dilution of inoculum}}$$

$$= \frac{5/100}{100/2}$$

$$= 0.001 \text{ kg kg}^{-1}$$

The doubling time is 3.2 h. Therefore in 20 h there are $20/3.2 = 6.25$ doubling times. As 1 kg of yeast grows to 2 kg in 3.2 h, 1 kg grows to $1 \times 2^{6.25} = 76$ kg in 20 h. Therefore,

$$\text{mass of product} = \text{initial concentration} \times \text{growth} \times \text{mass flow-rate}$$

$$= 0.001 \times 76 \times 606$$

$$= 46 \text{ kg h}^{-1}$$

7.2 FOOD FERMENTATIONS

The changes to the carbohydrates in a substrate by micro-organisms can be used to classify fermentations into those in which the main products are organic acids and those in which ethanol and carbon dioxide are the primary products. Micro-organisms that produce a single byproduct are named *homofermentative* whereas those that produce mixed products are *heterofermentative*. Lactic acid and ethanolic fermentations are the most important commercial fermentations. The Embden––Meyerhoff–Parnas metabolic pathway is common to both homolactic fermentations and the initial stages of ethanolic fermentations. The hexose monophosphate pathway is found in heterolactic fermentations. Details of these pathways are readily available (for example Stanier *et al.*, 1976), and the products of fermentation are described in Fig. 7.4. Many fermentations involve complex mixtures of micro-organisms or sequences of microbial populations which develop as changes take place in the pH, redox potential or substrate availability. Lactic acid fermentations are described in section 7.2.1, followed by ethanolic fermentations and those that produce both lactic acid and ethanol (sections 7.2.2 and 7.2.3).

7.2.1 Lactic acid fermentations

The sequence of lactic acid bacteria in a fermentation is determined mainly by their acid tolerance. For example in milk, *Streptococcus liquifaciens*, *Streptococcus lactis* or the closely related *Streptococcus cremoris* are inhibited when the lactic acid content reaches 0.7–1.0%. They are outgrown by more acid-tolerant species including *Lactobacillus casei* (1.5–2.0% acid) and *Lactobacillus bulgaricus* (2.5–3.0% acid). Similarly, in vegetable fermentations, *Lactobacilli* are stronger acid producers than *Streptococci*. Of the four main groups of lactic acid bacteria, *Streptococcus* and

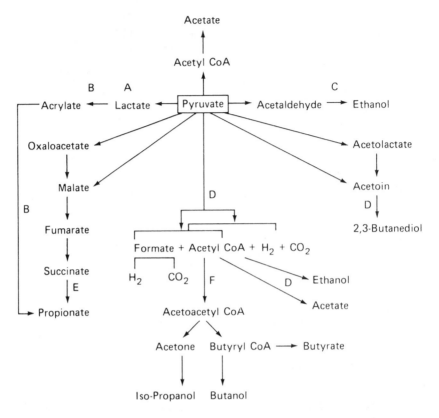

Fig. 7.4 — Fermentation products of pyruvate: A, lactic acid bacteria; B, *Clostridium propionicum*; C, yeast, *Acetobacter* species; D, yeast; E, propionic acid bacteria; F, *Clostridium* species (butyric and butylic organisms). (After Dawes and Large (1982).)

Pediococcus species are homolactic, *Leuconostoc* species are heterolactic and *Lactobacillus* species vary according to the strain.

In some fermentations, particularly those that involve low-acid substrates (for example milk and meat), a starter culture is added to generate large numbers of the desired micro-organism rapidly, and thus to reduce fermentation times and to inhibit growth of pathogens and spoilage bacteria. In other fermentations, the natural flora are sufficient to reduce the pH rapidly and to prevent the growth of undesirable micro-organisms. A selection of common lactic acid fermentations is shown in Table 7.1.

7.2.1.1 Meat and fish products
Fermented sausages (for example salami, pepperoni, medwurst and bologna) are produced from a mixture of finely chopped meats, spice mixtures, curing salts (sodium nitrite/nitrate), salt and sugar. The meat is filled into sausage casings, fermented and then pasteurised at 65–68 °C for 4–8 h, dried and stored at 4–7 °C.

Table 7.1 — Examples of lactic acid fermentations

| Food | Micro-organisms | Incubation conditions | | |
		Temperature (°C)	Time	Other
Cassava	*Corynebacterium* species *Geotrichum* species	Ambient	96 h	
Fish	*Bacillus pumilus*[a] *Bacillus licheniformis*[a]	Ambient	3–12 months	Fish to salt (between 3 to 1 and 5 to 1)
Maize	*Corynebacterium* species *Aerobacter* species *S. cerevisiae* *Lactobacillus* species *Candida mycoderma*	Ambient	24–72 h	
Meat	*Pediococcus cerevisiae*[a] *Lactobacillus plantarum* *Lactobacillus curvatus*	15–26	24 h	85–90% relative humidity
Milk (stirred yoghurt)	*Streptococcus thermophilus*[a] *L. bulgaricus*[a]	40–45	2–3 h	
Cheese Cottage	*Streptococcus diacetylactis*[a]	22	14–16	
Camembert and Brie	*S. cremoris*[a] *S. lactis*[a] *Penicilliumn caseicolum*[a]	32	[b]	
Cheddar	*S. cremoris*[a] *S. lactis*[a] *S. diactylactis*[a], *Lactobacilli*[a]	32	[b]	
Vegetables (cucumber and cabbage)	*Lactobacillus mesenteroides* *Lactobacillus brevis* *Penicillium cerevisiae* *L. plantarum*	Ambient	48–260 h	2.5–6% salt

[a]Prepared inocula used.
[b]Fermentation of cheeses continues for 1–12 months during ripening.

Preservation is due to

(1) the antimicrobial action of nitrite–spice mixtures and to a lesser extent from added salt,
(2) 0.8-1.2% lactic acid from the fermentation,
(3) heat (and antimicrobial components in smoke when the product is smoked),
(4) pasteurisation,
(5) reduction in water activity (Chapter 1) due to salt and drying and
(6) low storage temperature.

The technology of production is described in detail by Pederson (1971).

In southeast Asia, small fish, shrimp or waste fish are mixed with dry salt and fermented to produce a range of sauces and pastes (Table 7.1). Proteins in the fish are broken down by the combined action of bacterial enzymes, acidic conditions and autolytic action of the natural fish enzymes. Other bacteria including *L. mesenteroides*, *P. cerevisiae* and *L. plantarum* also play a role in acid production.

7.2.1.2   Vegetables

Cucumbers, olives and other vegetables are submerged in 2.5–6% w/w brine, which inhibits the growth of putrefactive spoilage bacteria. Air is excluded by plastic covers weighted down with water. A naturally occurring sequence of lactic acid bacteria predominate in the anaerobic conditions to produce approximately 1% w/w lactic acid. The relative importance of each species (Table 7.1) in the fermentation depends on the initial cell numbers on the vegetable, the salt content and the pH (Fleming, 1982). In some countries, inocula are used for the controlled fermentation of cucumbers. Here the brined vegetables are first acidified with acetic acid to prevent growth of spoilage micro-organisms. The pH is then adjusted and the brine is inoculated with either *L. plantarum* alone or a mixed culture with *P. cerevisiae*. Nitrogen gas is continuously purged through the vessel to remove carbon dioxide and to prevent splitting of the cucumbers (*bloating*).

Other methods of pickling involve different salt concentrations; for example 'salt-stock pickles' are preserved using 16% salt. They are then 'refreshed' by washing out the salt, packed in sweet vinegar and pasteurised. In 'dry salting' (for example sauerkraut from cabbage), alternate layers of vegetable and granular salt are packed into tanks. Juice is extracted from leaves by the salt to form a brine, and the fermentation follows a similar sequence to that described for cucumber pickles (Pederson, 1971). In each case preservation is achieved by the combination of acid, salt and in some cases a heat treatment.

7.2.1.3   Maize and cassava

In tropical countries, cereals and root crops are fermented to a range of beverages and staple foods. These are reviewed by Odunfa (1985) and Stanton (1985). Fermented maize flour is a staple food in many African countries. Maize kernels are soaked for 1–3 days, milled and formed into a dough. Initially *Corynebacterium* species hydrolyse starch and initiate lactic acid production. *Aerobacter* species increase the rate of acid production and *S. cerevisiae* contributes to the flavour of the product. As the acidity increases, *Lactobacillus* species predominate and continue acid production. Finally *Candida mycoderma* outgrows *S. cerevisiae* and contributes to the final flavour of the fermented dough. It is cooked to form a thick porridge within 1–2 days. The fermentation is therefore used to impart flavour and has only a minimal preservative effect.

Cassava is grated and the pressed pulp is fermented by *Corynebacterium* species, as for maize. The increased acidity promotes the growth of *Geotrichum* species, and releases gaseous hydrogen cyanide by hydrolysis of the cyanogenic glycosides in the cassava. Aldehydes and esters produced by *Geotrichum* species give the characteristic aroma and taste to the product. The fermented cassava is dried to a granular flour with a shelf life of several months. The fermentation therefore alters the eating quality, and preservation is achieved by drying.

7.2.1.4   Milk products
There are a large number of cultured milk products (for example yoghurt, cheese, Kefir, Koumiss, buttermilk, sour cream and Leben). Differences in flavour are due to the rate of production and concentration of lactic acid, volatile aldehydes, ketones, organic acids and diacetyl (acetyl methyl carbinol). The last is produced by fermentation of citrate in milk, and gives the characteristic 'buttery' aroma to dairy products. The change in texture is due to production of lactic acid from lactose, which causes a reduction in charge on the casein micelles. They coagulate at the isoelectric point to form characteristic flocs. These changes are described in detail by Fox (1987). Adjustment of the starter culture, incubation conditions and subsequent processing conditions alters the size and texture of the coagulated protein flocs and hence produces the many different textures encountered. Preservation is achieved by chilling (Chapter 18) and increased acidity (yoghurt) or reduced water activity (cheese) (Chapter 1).

7.2.1.4.1   Yoghurt
Skimmed milk is mixed with dried skimmed milk and heated at 82–93 °C for 30–60 min to destroy contaminating micro-organisms and to destabilise K-casein. It is inoculated with a mixed culture (Table 7.1) and initially *S. thermophilus* grows rapidly to produce diacetyl and lactic, acetic and formic acids. *L. bulgaricus* grows slowly but possesses weak protease activity which releases peptides from the milk proteins. These stimulate the growth of the *S. thermophilus*. The increased acidity slows the growth of *S. thermophilus* and promotes *L. bulgaricus*, which is stimulated by formate produced in the initial stage. *L. bulgaricus* produces most of the lactic acid and also acetaldehyde which, together with diacetyl, gives the characteristic flavour and aroma. Yoghurt production is described in detail by Davis (1975) and Robinson and Tamime (1975)

7.2.1.4.2   Cheese
More than 700 types of cheese are produced throughout the world, created by differences in fermentation, pressing and ripening condtions. The differences are described in detail by Kosikowski (1978). Most cheeses are allowed to ripen for several weeks or months but the fermentation of cottage cheese is stopped once casein precipitation has occurred and the flocs are removed along with some of the whey.

In the traditional manufacture of cheddar cheese, *S. lactis* is added to milk and fermented for 30 min. Rennet (section 7.5.4.4) is added and the culture is incubated for 1.5–2 h until it is firm enough to cut into small cubes. It is then heated to 38 °C to shrink the curd and to expel whey. The curd is recut and drained several times, milled, salted and placed in hoops (barrels). Pressure is applied to remove air and excess whey and the cheese is then ripened in a cool room for several months. Enzymes from both the micro-organisms and the cheese (including proteases, peptidases, lipase, decarboxylase and deaminases) produce compounds which give characteristic aroma and flavour. The time and temperature of ripening determine whether the cheddar has a mild, medium or sharp flavour.

7.2.2 Ethanolic fermentations

The initial stages of the Embden–Meyerhoff–Parnas pathway are common for ethanolic yeast fermentations and homolactic bacterial fermentations. In most products, ethanol is the main product, and this preserves the food, but in dough fermentation carbon dioxide is the main product which is required to produce the characteristic honeycomb texture in bread. Table 7.2 describes the conditions used in selected ethanolic and mixed acid–ethanol fermentations.

7.2.2.1 Bread

The fermentation and subsequent baking of wheat flour alter the texture and flavour of the flour and make it palatable as a staple food. Fermentation has no preservative effect and the main function is to produce carbon dioxide to leaven and condition the dough. Yeast and other micro-organisms present in the dough also contribute to the flavour of the bread. Yeast activity ceases when the internal temperature reaches 43 °C during baking (Chapter 15), and the yeast is finally killed at approximately 54 °C. Carbon dioxide is retained within the loaf when the gluten structure is set by heat above 74 °C. The heat treatment and reduction in water activity preserve the bread. The two main commercial methods of dough preparation are the *bulk fermentation* process and the *Chorleywood bread* process, which are described in detail by Chamberlain *et al*. (1965) and Oura *et al*. (1982). Details of production and different types of bread are described by Matz (1972).

7.2.2.2 Alcoholic beverages

Beer *wort* is produced by boiling malted grains (for example barley) to release maltose and other sugars and, in some beers, by adding hop flowers for bitterness. Developments in wort preparation, described by Atkinson (1987) and Hudson (1986), include

(1) the use of hop extracts and dextrose syrups to increase product uniformity,
(2) higher-temperature shorter-time boiling to reduce energy consumption.

In addition rectangular tanks are being replaced by cylindrical fermenters with conical bases; these have better control of temperature, easier cleaning, shorter fermentation times due to agitation of liquor by evolved carbon dioxide, and the formation of a yeast plug in the conical base which, when removed, reduces the load on filtration equipment (Chapter 5). Variation in the composition of the wort, the strain of yeast, and the fermentation time and conditions result in the wide range of beers produced. Other substrates including millet, sorghum and maize are also used where these are the staple crops. Sugars present in grape juice (or *must*) are fermented to produce 6–14% ethanol. Cells are removed by filtration or centrifugation (Chapter 5) and the wine is aged to reduce the acidity and to develop a

Table 7.2 — Alcoholic and mixed alcohol–acid fermentations

Food	Micro-organism	Temperature (°C)	Time	Other
		Incubation conditions		
Alcohol				
Beer				
Ale	*S. cerevisiae*[a] ('top yeast')	20	120–240 h	
Lager	*Saccharomyces carlesbergensis*[a] ('bottom yeast')	12–15	120–240 h	
Millet	*Saccharomycopsis fibuliger*	Ambient	120 h	
Bread	*S. cerevisiae*[a]	26	0.5–1 h	
Wine				
Agave (cactus)	*Saccharomyces carbajali*	30	200 h	
Bordeaux	*Saccharomyces oviformis*[a] *Saccharomyces chevalieri* *Kloeckera apiculata*	25	360 h	
Other grape	*S. cerevisiae* var. *ellipsoideus*[a]	25–30	100–360 h	
Palm	*Zymomonas* species	Ambient	4–12 h	
Rice	*Saccharomyces sake*	30	—	
Mixed alcohol–acid				
Coffee	*Leuconostoc* species *Lactobacillus* species *Bacillus* species *Erwinia* species *Aspergillus* species *Fusarium* species	Ambient	20–100 h	
Cocoa	Yeasts (see text) *L. plantarum* *Lactobacillus mali* *Lactobacillus fermentum* *Lactobacillus collinoides* *Acetobacter rancens* *Acetobacter aceti* *Acetobacter oxydans*	Ambient	144 h	
Soy sauce				
First stage	*Aspergillus soya*[e] *Mucor* species *Rhizopus* species	30	48–72 h	
Second stage	*Pediococcus soyae* *Saccharomyces rouxii*	15–25	3–6 months	15–20% brine
Tempeh	*Rhizopus oligosporus*[a]	30	24–48 h	
Vinegar	*S. cerevisiae*[a] *A. aceti*[a]	30 25	100–240 h 72–168 h 72–120 h	First stage Second stage
Citric acid	*Acetobacter niger*[a]	27	168 h	Substrate limited

[a]Inoculum used.

characteristic bouquet. The main acid in most wines is tartaric acid but, in some red wines, malic acid is present in a high concentration. In these, a secondary *malo-lactic* fermentation by lactic acid bacteria converts malic acid to lactic acid to reduce the acidity and to improve the flavour and aroma.

Other wines are produced throughout the world from many fruits, tree saps and vegetable pods. For example palm sap is fermented by naturally ocurring *Zymomonas* species to produce palm wine. Lactic acid bacteria produce small amounts of aldehydes and lactic and acetic acids, which give the product a characteristic aroma and flavour. Fermentation times in excess of 12 h produce an overacidified product and it is therefore consumed on the day of preparation.

7.2.3 Mixed alcoholic–acid fermentations

7.2.3.1 Vinegar and other food acids

Ethanolic fermentation by yeast is the first of a two part fermentation in the production of vinegar. In the second stage the ethanol is oxidised by *A. aceti* to acetic acid and a number of flavour compounds. This stage is extremely sensitive to the concentration of dissolved oxygen, and fermenters are carefully designed to ensure that an adequate supply of air is maintained (Beaman, 1967). The maturing of vinegar involves reactions between residual ethanol and acetic acid to form ethyl acetate, which imparts the characteristic flavour to the product.

Citric acid is widely used as an acidulant in foods. It is produced by fermentation of sugar by *A. niger*, in submerged culture, under conditions of substrate limitation. Details of commercial production are given by Kapoor *et al.* (1982). The production of other important food acids, including glutamic acid, gluconic acid, lactic acid, propionic acid and tartaric acid, is described by Pederson (1971).

7.2.3.2 Cocoa and coffee

Cocoa and coffee berries contain mucilaginous material which surrounds the beans. This is removed by fermentation to improve the rate of drying, the sensory quality and the appearance of the beans, each of which has an important influence on their economic value. Preservation is achieved by drying and sensory characteristics are developed by roasting. Cocoa beans are either heaped or placed in slatted fermentation bins (*sweat boxes*). Initial fermentation by yeasts, including *S. ellipsoideus*, *Saccharomyces apiculata* and *Hansenula*, *Kloeckera*, *Debaromyces*, *Schizosaccharomyces* and *Candida* species, produces ethanol from sugars in the pulp and raises the temperature in the box. Lactic acid bacteria then predominate in the anaerobic conditions. They reduce the pH and further raise the temperature. The loss of pulp during this period allows air to penetrate the bean mass. Ethanol is oxidised to acetic acid by acetic acid bacteria. This causes the temperature to rise to higher than 50 °C, and destroys the yeast population. The combination of heat and acetic acid (up to 2% w/w) kills the beans. The beans are then dried and roasted to produce the characteristic chocolate flavour and aroma (Carr, 1985). Stages in the manufacture of cocoa powder and chocolate are described by Meursing (1987). Coffee berries are soaked, pulped and fermented in slatted tanks (Table 7.2). Microbial pectic enzymes act with naturally occurring pectic enzymes to solubilise the mucilage. Details of chemical changes during the fermentation are described by Arunga (1982).

7.2.3.3 *Soy products*

Soy sauce and similar products are made by a two-stage fermentation in which one or more fungal species are grown on an equal mixture of ground cereals and soy beans. Fungal proteases, α-amylases and invertase (section 7.5.4.1) act on the soy beans to produce substrate for the second stage. The fermenting mixture is transferred to brine and the temperature is slowly increased. Acid production by *P. soyae* lowers the pH to 5.0, and an alcoholic fermentation by *S. rouxii* takes place. Finally the temperature is gradually returned to 15 °C and the characteristic flavour of soy sauce develops over a period of 6 months to 3 years. The liquid fraction is separated, clarified, pasteurised and bottled (Pederson, 1971). The final product contains 2.5% ethanol and 18% salt. Details of the biochemistry of flavour and aroma production are described by Yokotsuka (1960), Yong and Wood (1974) and (Wood 1982). The process is described in detail by Fukushima (1985).

In the production of tempeh, soy beans are soaked, deskinned, steamed for 30–120 min and fermented (Table 7.2). Fungal enzyme activity softens the beans, and mycelial growth binds the bean mass to form a solid cake. The fermentation changes the texture and flavour of soy beans but has no preservative effect.

7.3 EQUIPMENT

Solid substrates are incubated in trays or tanks, contained in rooms that have temperature and humidity control. Some meat products are filled into plastic or cellulose casings prior to fermentation. In tropical climates, fermentation often takes place at ambient temperature without special incubation facilities. Liquid substrates are incubated in either stainless steel tanks or in cylindrical stirred fermenters (Fig. 7.5). Fermenter design and operation is discussed in detail by Stanbury and Whitaker (1984) and in section 7.5.2.

7.4 EFFECT ON FOODS

The mild conditions used in food fermentations produce few of the deleterious changes to nutritional and sensory quality that are found with many other unit operations. Complex changes to proteins and carbohydrates soften the texture of fermented products. Changes in flavour and aroma are also complex and in general poorly documented. Flavour changes can be summarised as

(1) reduction in sweetness and increase in acidity due to fermentation of sugars to organic acids,
(2) an increase in saltiness in some foods (pickles, soy sauce, fish and meat products) due to salt addition and
(3) reduction in bitterness of some foods due to the action of debittering enzymes.

The aroma of fermented foods is due to a large number of volatile chemical components (for example amines, fatty acids, aldehydes, esters and ketones) and products from interactions of these compounds during fermentation and maturation. In bread and cocoa, the subsequent unit operations of baking and roasting produce

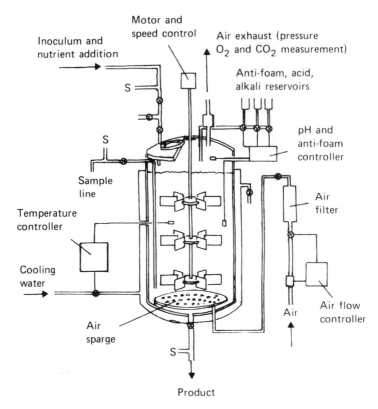

Fig. 7.5 — Batch fermenter showing controls and instrumentation: S, steam sterilisation points.

the characteristic aromas. The colour of many fermented foods is retained owing to the minimal heat treatment and/or a suitable pH range for pigment stability. Changes in colour may occur owing to

(1) added chemicals (for example nitrite and nitrate salts in fermented meat products),
(2) enzymic changes to pigments (for example degradation of chlorophyll and enzymic browning),
(3) formation of brown pigments by proteolytic activity and
(4) production of pigments by micro-organisms (for example the red colouration of fermented rice by *Monascus purpureus* (Nishikawa, 1932)).

Microbial growth causes complex changes to the nutritive value of fermented foods by changing the composition of proteins, fats and carbohydrates, and by the utilisation or secretion of vitamins. Micro-organisms absorb fatty acids, amino acids, sugars and vitamins from the food. However, in many fermentations (for example tempeh and cheese), micro-organisms secrete vitamins into the food and improve nutritive value (Table 7.3). Changes in nutritive value are discussed in detail by

Table 7.3 — Changes in vitamin content of selected foods during fermentation

Product	Content per 100g						
	Thiamin (mg)	Riboflavin (mg)	Niacin (mg)	Vitamin C (mg)	Pantothenic acid (mg)	Vitamin B_6 (mg)	Vitamin B_{12} (μg)
Whole milk	0.04	0.18	0.1	1	0.37	0.042	0.4
Yoghurt	0.04	0.18	0.1	1	—	0.040	—
Cheese (Cheddar)	0.03	0.46	0.1	0	0.50	0.08	1.0
Grapes	0.05	0.03	0.3	4	0.075	0.08	0
Wine (table)	Trace	0.01	0.1	—	—	—	—
Cabbage	0.05	0.07	0.3	51	0.21	0.16	0
Sauerkraut[a]	0.07	0.03	0.2	14	0.09	0.13	0
Cucumber	0.03	0.04	0.2	11	0.25	0.042	0
Dill pickle	Trace	0.02	Trace	6	—	—	—
Soy bean (unfermented)	0.22	0.06	0.90	—	—	0.08	—
Tempeh	0.13	0.49	4.39	—	—	0.35	—
Soy sauce	0.88	0.37	6.0	—	—	—	—

[a]Loss due to canning and storage.
Adapted from Murata *et al.* (1967), Watt and Merrill (1975) and Orr (1969).

Dworschak (1982) and the importance of these changes to the nutritive value of the diet is discussed in Chapter 1. Micro-organisms also hydrolyse polymeric compounds to produce substrates for cell growth. Hydrolysis may increase digestibility of proteins and polysaccharides. Changes in the structure and composition of fats and carbohydrates by hydrolytic enzyme activity does not affect their nutritional value, but the products of hydrolysis may be utilised by micro-organisms and are therefore removed from the food. In addition the nutritive value is altered by unit operations associated with fermentation (for example the physical separation of solid and liquid components, baking, roasting, pasteurisation or canning).

7.5 ENZYME TECHNOLOGY

Approximately 1% of the enzymes so far identified are used commercially as technical enzymes. The largest volume (35%) is proteases for use in detergent manufacture. In food processing, technical enzymes (Table 7.4) are used

(1) to reduce processing costs,
(2) to increase yields of extracts from raw materials or improve handling of materials, and
(3) to improve the shelf life and sensory characteristics of foods.

Enzymes are active at low concentrations and the rates of reaction are easily controlled by adjustment of incubation conditions. However, the cost of enzymes is high, and in some products enzymes must be inactivated or removed after processing, which adds to the cost of the product. Like other proteins, enzymes may cause allergic responses in some people, and they are usually coated or immobilised on carrier materials to reduce the risk of inhalation of enzyme dust by operators.

7.5.1 Theory

Microbial enzymes have optimum activity under similar conditions to the optimum growth conditions for the micro-organism concerned. Enzymes from closely related microbial species have optimum activity under similar conditions, whereas those from unrelated species have widely differing properties. Microbial enzymes are either *extracellular* (secreted by the cells into the surrounding medium) or *intracellular* (retained within the cell). Extracellular enzyme production occurs in either the logarithmic phase or the stationary phase of growth, whereas intracellular enzymes are produced during logarithmic growth but are only released into the medium when cells undergo lysis in the stationary or decline phase (Fig. 7.1).

7.5.2 Enzyme production from micro-organisms

The requirements of commercial enzyme production from micro-organisms are as follows.

(1) Micro-organisms must grow well on an inexpensive substrate,
(2) They should produce a constant high yield of enzyme in a short time,
(3) Methods for enzyme recovery should be simple and inexpensive and
(4) the enzyme preparation should be stable.

These requirements are met by constitutive mutant strains of micro-organisms, which permanently retain the required characteristics.

Enzymes are produced by either surface culture on solid substrates (for example rice hulls, fruit peels, soy bean meal, wheat flour and peanut meal) or by submerged culture using liquid substrates. Submerged cultures have lower handling costs and a lower risk of contamination and are more suited to automation than are solid substrates. The substrate should contain a carbon and energy source and a source of nitrogen for cell growth. In addition, specific nutrients may by required for cell growth and specific minerals may be necessary for enzyme production. In submerged cultures a *seed inoculum* is produced using similar incubation conditions to those used for production. The substrate (for example molasses, starch hydrolysate or corn steep liquor) is low cost and readily available in adequate quantities, with a uniform quality. In batch methods the inoculum is added to sterile substrate at 3–10% of the substrate volume. Fermenter capacities range from 1000 to 100 000 l. Cells are grown under controlled conditions for 30–150 h. Microprocessors are used to control pH, dissolved oxygen, carbon dioxide and temperature automatically (also Chapter 24). Computer control of fermenters is described by Armiger and Humphrey (1979).

7.5.2.1 Enzyme recovery

Extracellular enzymes are recovered from the fermentation medium by centrifugation, filtration (Chapter 5), fractional precipitation, chromatographic separation, electrophoresis, membrane separation (Chapter 6), freeze drying (Chapter 20) or a combination of these methods (Skinner, 1975). Intracellular enzymes are extracted by disruption of cells in a homogeniser or mill (Chapter 3). Recovery is more difficult and the yield is lower than for extracellular enzymes, because some enzymes are retained within the cell mass. If required, the specific activity of the enzyme is increased by precipitation using acetone, alcohols or ammonium sulphate or by ultrafiltration (Chapter 6). The success of commercial enzyme production depends on maximising the activity of the micro-organism and minimising the costs of the substrate and incubation and recovery procedures.

7.5.3 Application of enzymes to foods

Details of the factors that influence enzyme activity and kinetics are described by Whitaker (1972). In batch operation the enzyme is mixed with food and, after completion of activity, is either retained within the food or inactivated by heat. This method is widely used when the cost of the enzyme is low.

In continuous operation, enzymes are immobilised on support materials by

(1) micro-encapsulation in polymeric membranes which retain the enzyme but permit passage of substrates and products,
(2) attachment by electrostatic attraction to ion exchange resins,
(3) cross-linking with for example glutaraldehyde,
(4) adsorption onto colloidal silica and cross linking with glutaraldehyde,
(5) covalent bonding of non-essential residues on the enzyme to organic polymers (the most permanent form of attachment),
(6) entrapment in polymer fibres (for example cellulose triactetate and starches)
(7) copolymerisation with maleic anhydride and
(8) adsorption onto charcoal, polyacrylamide, or glass.

In (8) porous carriers have a high surface area and hence permit higher enzymic activities than non-porous carriers do. They also give protection to the enzyme against variations in the pH or temperature of the substrate but are more difficult to regenerate (Konecny, 1977).

The main advantages of enzyme immobilisation are

(1) enzymes are re-used without the cost of recovery from a food,
(2) continuous processing (Chapter 1), and
(3) closer control of pH and temperature to achieve optimum activity.

Immobilisation is at present used when an enzyme is difficult to isolate or expensive to prepare. However, because of these advantages, the technique is expanding into new areas of processing. The main limitations are

(1) the higher cost of carriers, equipment and process control,
(2) changes to the pH profiles and reaction kinetics of enzymes,
(3) loss of activity (25-60% loss) and
(4) risk of microbial contamination.

In operation, either immobilised enzymes are mixed with a liquid substrate and then removed by centrifugation or filtration and re-used, or the feed liquor is passed over an immobilised bed of enzyme fixed into a reactor. Immobilised enzymes should have the following characteristics:

(1) short residence times for a reaction;
(2) stability to variations in temperature and other operating conditions over a period of time (for example glucose isomerase is used for 1000 h at 60–65 °C),
(3) suitability for regeneration and
(4) high mass transfer rates between the carrier material and the substrate.
The most important enzymes used in food processing are shown in Table 7.4.

7.5.4 Applications of selected enzymes

7.5.4.1 Carbohydrases
This group of enzymes hydrolyse polysaccharides or oligosaccharides. The five commercially important types are

(1) α-amylase,
(2) glucoamylase,
(3) invertase,
(4) lactase, and
(5) glucose isomerase.

α-amylases randomly hydrolyse α-(1->4) linkages to liquefy starch and produce maltose. They do not hydrolyse α-(1->6) linkages and therefore leave low-molecular-weight dextrins and oligosaccharides unhydrolysed. *Glucoamylase* (or amyloglucosidase) is a saccharifying enzyme which removes successive glucose units from the non-reducing ends of starch molecules. Unlike α-amylases, it hydrolyses linear and branched chains to form glucose.

Commercial fungal amylase preparations, which contain smaller quantities of phosphatase, glucoamylase and protease, saccharify starch to a greater extent than a single amylase does. They produce substantial quantities of maltose without significant quantities of glucose. They are used in the following applications:

(1) to eliminate starch hazes and to reduce the viscosity of fruit juices;
(2) to convert cocoa starch to dextrins and thus to reduce viscosity and to improve the stability of chocolate syrups,
(3) to produce glucose syrups (Delrue, 1987);
(4) to reduce dough viscosity and to accelerate fermentation by yeast.

Bacterial amylases liquefy starch at higher temperatures (Table 7.4). They are used

Table 7.4 — Enzymes used in food processing

| Enzyme | Major source | Operating conditions | | Type of culture or application |
		pH range	Temperature (°C)	
α-amylases	*Aspergillus oryzae*	4.0–6.6	20–60	Surf., B, I
	Bacillus subtilis	5.0–7.5	20–90	Sub. B, I
Catalase	Beef liver	6.5–7.5	5–45	—
Cellulases	*A. niger*	3.0–5.0	20–60	Sub./surf., B
	Trichoderma viride			Surf./sub., B
	T. reesei			
Gluco-amylases	*A. niger*	3.5–5.0	30–60	Sub., B, I
	Rhizopus species			Surf., B, I
Glucose isomerase	*Aerobacter* species	7.0–7.5	60–70	Sub.
	Escherichia species			
	Lactobacillus species			
	Streptococcus species			
	Bacillus species			
Glucose oxidase	*A. niger*	4.5–7.0	30–60	Sub.Surf., B
Hemi-cellulases	Fungi	3.5–6.0	30–65	Sub.
Invertase	*Kluyveromyces fragilis*	4.5–5.5	55	Sub., B, I
	S. cerevisiae			
Lactase	*K. fragilis*	7	40	Sub., B, I
	Aspergillus species	4.0–5.0	50–60	Sub., B, I
	Chaetomium species			Sub., B, I
	Mucor pusillus			Surf., B, I
	Streptococcus lactis			Sub., B, I
	Candida pseudotropicalis			Sub., B, I
Lipases	Porcine pancreas	5.5–9.5	20–50	B
Pectic enzymes	*A. niger*	2.5–5.5	25–65	Surf./sub., B
Proteases	*B. subtilis*	6.0–8.5	20–55	Sub.
Acid	*A. oryzae*	4.0–7.5	20–50	Surf.
	Rhizopus species			
Neutral	*B. subtilis*	7.0–8.0	20–50	
	B. polymyxa			
Alkaline	*Bacillus* species	9.0–11.0	20–50	
Bromelain				
pineapple (*Ananas comosus*)		4.0–9.0	20–65	SA
Papain				
papaya (*Carica papaya*)		6.0–8.0	20–75	B, SA
Ficin				
fig (*Ficus carica*)		6.5–7.0	25–60	B, SA
Pepsin		1.5–4.0		B
Rennet (chymosin)		3.5–6.0	40	B
bovine				
M. pusillus				
M. miehei				

[a]B, batch application; I, immobilised; SA, surface application; surf., surface culture; sub., submerged culture.

to produce glucose and maltose syrups and to replace malted grain for brewing. In baking they are used to improve gas production, crust colour, shelf life and toasting characteristics of bread. Glucoamylase is used to increase the alcohol content and to reduce the carbohydrate content of beer, by converting dextrins to fermentable sugars during fermentation. It is also used in the production of vinegar and yeast from starch based products.

Invertase hydrolyses sucrose to glucose and fructose. It is used to remove sucrose from foods, to prevent crystallisation in molasses, and in the production of invert sugar, confectionery, liquers and frozen desserts. *Lactase* (β-D-galactosidase) hydrolyses lactose to D-glucose and D-galactose. It is used to prevent lactose crystallisation in ice cream and frozen milk concentrates, in starter cultures for cheese, and to prepare foods for those suffering from lactose intolerance (Bauer, 1986).

Glucose isomerase is used for the production of high-fructose corn syrup sweeteners from glucose. Different proportions of fructose and glucose are prepared by adjustment of the incubation time with the enzyme. Other applications include the production of dextrose from corn starch, clarification of fruit juice and wine, removal of glucose from egg white, inversion of sucrose and chillproofing of beer (Hultin, 1983)

7.5.4.2 Pectic enzymes
There are three types of pectic enzymes: pectinesterase, polygalacturonase and pectin lyase although the last is not used commercially. *Pectin esterase* hydrolyses the methoxyl group from pectin molecules to form low-methoxyl pectin and polygalacturonic (pectic) acid. *Polygalacturonase* hydrolyses α-(1- > 4) linkages of polygalacturonic acid to produce oligogalacturonans and galacturonic acid. Polygalacturonase has both endo and exo forms which respectively hydrolyse the polymer randomly and sequentially from the ends. Commercially the endo polygalacturonase is more useful as it produces more rapid depolymerisation. Fungal pectic enzyme preparations, consisting of polygalacturonase, pectin methylesterase, cellulase, hemicellulase and protease, are used

(1) to accelerate rates of filtration of fruit juices,
(2) to remove pectin from fruit base prior to gel standardisation in jam manufacture,
(3) to prevent undesirable gel formation in fruit and vegetable extracts and purees,
(4) to standardise the characteristics of pectin for the varied uses as a thickener,
(5) to recover citrus oils and
(6) to stabilise cloud in fruit juices (Rombouts and Pilnik, 1978).

7.5.4.3 Cellulases and hemicellulases
Fungal cellulase preparations, which contain smaller quantities of hemicellulase and pectinase, act on the α-(1- > 6) linkages of glucose units in soluble forms of cellulose. They are used

(1) to improve filtration of vanilla extracts,
(2) to tenderise vegetables prior to cooking,
(3) to degrade nut shells prior to oil extraction to save energy and

(4) to extract flavour compounds from vegetables which was previously difficult and expensive.

Hemicellulases reduce the viscosity of several plant gums by conversion of D-xylans to xylo-oligosaccharides, D-xylose and L-arabinose. They are used

(1) to reduce the viscosity of coffee concentrates,
(2) in the extraction and clarification of citrus juices,
(3) in the hydrolysis of apple and grape pomace to fermentable sugars and
(4) to increase the yield of essential oils, spices and other plant extracts.

7.5.4.4 *Proteases*

Proteases are classified according to their pH optima into acid, neutral and alkaline types. Acid proteases are produced mostly by fungi, and neutral and alkaline proteases are produced by both fungi and bacteria (Table 7.4). Neutral bacterial proteases, which have significant α-amylase and alkaline protease activity, are used to hydrolyse plant and animal proteins and to improve the flavour of crackers and the handling of pizza doughs. Acid fungal proteases which have significant α-amylase activity are used

(1) to hydrolyse gluten to reduce mixing times, to make dough more pliable and to improve the texture and loaf volume,
(2) in meat tenderisation,
(3) to prepare liquid meat products,
(4) to reduce the viscosity and to prevent gelation of concentrated soluble fish products and
(5) to reduce the setting time for gelatin without affecting the gel strength.

Bromelain is a mixture of proteases which hydrolyse plant and animal proteins to amino acids and peptides. It is used

(1) in meat tenderisers,
(2) to improve the handling of pizza doughs,
(3) to chillproof beer and
(4) in the production of waffles, pancakes and wafers.

Papain and *Ficin* have broad substrate specificities and stability at higher temperatures. They are used to chillproof beer and as meat tenderisers.

Rennet partially coagulates milk proteins to form casein curds in cheese production (section 7.2.1.4). A low proteolytic activity is required to prevent solubilisation of the casein and to achieve an adequate yield of correctly flavoured cheese. Calf rennet is expensive and the use of microbial proteases is therefore increasing. Fungal proteases have a lower activity than bacterial proteases and the protease from *M. meihei* or *M. pusillus* is used for short and medium fermentation times. The search for a improved microbial protease is continuing. Developments in recombinant deoxyribonucleic acid technology applied to cheese manufacture are described by Law (1986).

7.5.4.5 Oxidases

Glucose oxidase oxidises glucose in the presence of oxygen to form gluconic acid. It is used to desugar, and hence to stabilise, egg products, and to increase the shelf life of bottled beer, soft drinks and other oxygen sensitive foods. It has advantages over chemical anti-oxidants because it does not lose its activity over time as it is not itself oxidised. *Catalase* decomposes hydrogen peroxide to form water and oxygen. It is used to provide oxygen for desugaring egg products by glucose oxidase.

7.5.4.6 Lipases

Lipases hydrolyse fats and fatty acid esters to form diglycerides and monoglycerides. Preparations which contain smaller quantities of α-amylase and protease are used

(1) to improve whipping properties of egg albumin,
(2) to modify or solubilise fats, or to break down emulsions,
(3) to improve the flavour of dairy products,
(4) produce free fatty acids from butterfat.

The fatty acids are used in small amounts to enhance natural flavours, in larger amounts to give a buttery flavour and in large amounts to give a cheesy flavour. They are used in cheese dips, sauces, soups, baked products and chocolate confections.

7.5.4.7 Other enzymes in food processing

Diacetyl reductase converts the flavour compound diacetyl to flavourless acetoin to improve the flavour in beer (Eckett, 1985). Fungal *phosphodiesterases* can be used to make 5′-nucleotide flavour enhancers which accentuate 'meaty' flavours in soups, sauces and gravies. Enzymes are also used for debittering of fruit products; for example *limoninase* which hydrolyses the bitter component 'limonin' in orange juice or *nariniginase* which breaks down naringin in grapefruit juice. *Pentosanase* converts pentosans to D-xylose and L-arabinose to reduce bread staling, to reduce dough viscosity, to lighten the crumbs of rye bread and to prevent it from separating from the crust during baking. β-*glucanases* converts β-glucans to β-D-glucose to facilitate filtration of barley wort in brewing. *Stachyase* converts stachyose and rafinnose to monosaccharides to reduce flatulence produced by leguminous foods. The protease *trypsin* retards the development of oxidised flavours in milk and *collagenase* and *elastase* soften and tenderise connective tissues in meat.

ACKNOWLEDGEMENTS

Grateful acknowledgement is made for information supplied by the following: Novo Enzymes Division, Novo Alle, DK-2880 Bagsvaerd, Denmark; Rohm Enzyme, Rohm GmbH, D-6100 Darmstadt, West Germany

REFERENCES

Armiger, W. B., and Humphrey, A. E. (1979). Computer applications in fermentation technology. In: H. J. Peppler and D. Perlman (eds), *Microbial technology* 2nd edn, Vol. 2. Academic Press, New York, pp. 375–401.

Arunga, P. O. (1982) Coffee. In: A. H. Rose (ed.), *Fermented foods*, Vol. 7, *Economic microbiology*. Academic Press, London, pp. 259–274.

Atkinson, B. (1987) The recent advances in brewing technology. In A.Turner (ed.), *Food technology international Europe*, Sterling, London, pp. 142–145.

Bauer (1986) The use of enzymes in food processing. *Food Eur.*, October–November, 21–24.

Beaman, R. G. (1967) Vinegar fermentation, In: H. J. Peppler (ed.) *Microbial Technology*. Reinhold, New York, pp. 344–359.

Carr, J. G. (1985) Tea, coffee and cocoa, In: B. J. B. Wood (ed.), *Microbiology of fermented foods*, Vol. 2, Elsevier Applied Science, pp. 133–154.

Chamberlain, N., Collins, T. H. and Elton, G. A. H. (1965) *The Chorleywood bread process: the effect of flour strength compared with the bulk fermentation process*, Report, No. 82. British Baking Industries Research Association, Chorleywood, Hertfordshire.

Davis, J. G. (1975) Yoghourt: recent developments. *Proc. Inst. Food Sci. Technol.* **8** (1) pp. 50–66.

Dawes, I. and Large, P. J. (1982) Class 1 reactions: Supply of carbon skeletons. In: J. Mandelstam, K. McQuillen and I. Dawes (eds.), *Biochemistry of bacterial growth*. Blackwell, Oxford, pp. 125–158.

Delrue, R. M. (1987) A review of glucose and fructose syrups. In: A. Turner (ed.), *Food Technology International Europe*, Sterling, London, pp. 171–174.

Dworschak, E. (1982) In: M. Rechcigl (ed.), *Handbook of nutritive value of processed food*, Vol. 1. CRC Press, Boca Raton, Florida, pp. 63—76.

Eckett, A. (1985) Enzyme technology speeds processing. *Food Eur.* May 3.

Fleming, H. P. (1982) Fermented vegetables. In: A. H. Rose (ed.), *Fermented foods*,Vol. 7, *economic microbiology*. Academic Press, London, pp. 227–258.

Fox, P. F. (1987) New developments in cheese production, In: A. Turner (ed.), *Food technology international Europe*. Sterling, London, pp. 112–115.

Frazier, W. C. and Westhoff, D. C. (1978) *Food microbiology*, 3rd edn. McGraw-Hill, New York.

Fukushima, D. (1985) Fermented vegetable protein and related foods of Japan and China. *Food Rev. Int.* 1 (1) 149–209.

Guilbault, G. G. (1984) *Analytical uses of immobilised enzymes*. Marcel Dekker, New York.

Hudson, J. (1986) What's new in brewing technology. *Food Manuf.* **60**, 64–65.

Hultin, H. O. (1983) Current and potential uses of immobilised enzymes. *Food Technol.* **37** (10), 66, 68, 72, 74, 76–78, 80, 82, 176.

Jay, J. M. (1978) *Modern food microbiology*. D. van Nostrand, New York.

Kapoor, K. K., Chaudhury, K. and Tauro, P. (1982) Citric acid. In: G. Reed (ed.), *Prescott and Dunn's industrial microbiology*, 4th edn. AVI, Westport, Connecticut, pp. 709–747.

Konecny, J. (1977) Theoretical and practical aspects of immobilised enzymes. *Surv. Prog. Chem.* **8** 195–251.

Kosikowski, F. (1978) *Cheese and fermented milk products*, 2nd edn. PO Box 139, Brooktondale, New York 14817, USA.

Law, B. A. (1986). High tech cheese. *Food Manuf.* Sept. 42–44.

Matz, S. A. (1972) Bakery technology and engineering. AVI, Westport, Connecticut, pp. 165–236.

Meursing, E. H. (1987) Chocolate and cocoa powder manufacture. In: A. Turner (ed.), *Food technology international Europe*. Sterling, London, pp. 125, 127, 129.

Murata, K., Ikehata, H. and Miyamoto, T. (1967)Studies on the nutritional value of tempeh. *Food Technol. J. Food Sci.* **32**, 580–586.

Nishikawa, H. (1932) Biochemistry of filamentous fungi, I: Colouring matter of *M. purpureus* Went. *Agric. Chem. Soc. Jpn.* **8**, 1007–1015.

Odunfa, S. A. (1985) African fermented foods. In: B. J. B. Wood (ed.), *Microbiology of fermented foods*, Vol. 2. Elsevier Applied Science, Barking, Essex, pp. 155–192.

Orr, M. L. (1969) *Pantothenic acid, vitamin B6 and vitamin B12 in foods*, Home Economic Research Report No. 6. US Department of Agriculture, Washington, DC.

Oura, E., Suomalainen, H. and Viskari, R. (1982) Breadmaking. In: A. H. Rose (ed.), *Fermented foods* Vol. 7, *Economic Microbiology*. Academic Press, London. pp. 88–146.

Pederson, C. S. (1971) *Microbiology of food fermentations*. AVI, Westport, Connecticut, pp. 153–172, 260–268, 231–246.

Robinson, D. K. and Tamime, A. Y. (1975) Yoghurt: a review of the product and its manufacture. *J. Soc. Dairy Technol.* **28** (3), 149–163.

Rombouts, F. M. and Pilnik, W. (1978) Enzymes in fruit and vegetable juice technology. *Proc. Biochem.* **13** (8), 9–13.

Skinner, K. J. (1975) Enzymes technology. *Chem. Engng. News*, **53** (33), 22–29, 32–41.

Stanbury, P. F. and Whitaker, A. (1984) *Priciples of fermentation technology*. Pergamon Press, Oxford, pp. 11–25.

Stanier, R. Y., Adelberg, E. A. and Ingraham, J. L. (1976) *General Microbiology*, Macmillan, London.

Stanton, W. R. (1985) Food fermentation in the tropics. In: B. J. B. Wood (ed.), *Microbiology of fermented foods*, Vol. 2. Elsevier Applied Science, Barking, Essex, pp. 193–211.

Watt, B. K. and Merrill, A. L. (1975) Composition of foods, raw, processed, prepared. In: *Agricultural Handbook*, No. 8. US Department of Agriculture, Washington, DC.

Whitaker, J. R. (1972) *Principles of enzymology for the food sciences*. Marcel Dekker, New York, pp. 151–253, 287–348.

Wood, B. J. B. (1982). Soy sauce and miso. In: A. H. Rose (ed.), *Fermented foods* Vol. 7, *Economic microbiology*. Academic Press, London, pp. 39–86.

Yokotsuka, T. (1960) Aroma and flavour of Japanese soy sauce. *Adv. Food Res.* **10**, 75–134.

Yong, F. M. and Wood, B. J. B. (1974) Microbiology and biochemistry of soy sauce fermentation, Adv. Appl. Microbiol. **17**, 157–194.

8

Irradiation

Ionising radiation takes the form of γ-rays from isotopes or, commercially to a lesser extent, from X-rays and electrons. It is used at present (1987) in 20 countries to preserve foods by destruction of micro-organisms or inhibition of biochemical changes (Table 8.1).

Table 8.1 — Applications of food irradiation

Application	Dose range (kGy)	Examples of foods	Notes
Sterilisation	7–10	Herbs, spices	
	Up to 50	Long-term ambient storage of meat	Outside the permitted dose
Sterilisation of packaging materials	10–25		
Pathogen destruction	2.5–5		
Salmonella species *Shigella* species *Campylobacter* species	3–10	Frozen blocks, poultry, meat, frozen shrimps, spices	
Control of moulds	2–5	Extended storage of fresh fruit	
Extension of chill life from 5 days to 1 month	2–5	Soft fruit, fresh fish and meat at 0–4 °C	Experimental
Inactivation or control of parasites (*Trichinella* species *Taenia* species)	0.1–6	Pork	
Insect control, disinfestation	0.1–2	Fruit, grain, flour, cocoa beans, dry fruits	
Decontamination of food ingredients	7–10	Dry food mixes	
Inhibition of sprouting	0.1–0.2	Potatoes, onions, garlic	

Adapted from Ley (1987), Guise (1986), Goresline (1982) and Anon. (1985).

The main advantages of irradiation are as follows.

(1) There is little or no heating of the food and therefore negligible change to sensory characteristics.
(2) Packaged and frozen foods may be treated
(3) Fresh foods may be preserved in a single operation, and without the use of chemical preservatives.
(4) Energy requirements are very low.
(5) Changes in nutritional value of foods are comparable with other methods of food preservation.
(6) Processing is automatically controlled and has low labour costs.

The main disadvantage is the high capital cost of irradiation plant. Concern over the use of food irradiation has been expressed by some workers (for example Webb and Lang, undated). The main problems are

(1) loss of nutritional value,
(2) the possible development of resistance to radiation in micro-organisms,
(3) inadequate analytical procedures for detecting whether foods have been irradiated and
(4) public resistance due to fears of induced radioactivity.

Some of these aspects are discussed in detail by Welt (1985).

8.1 THEORY

The units used are given as a footnote to this page.† Details of the physical and chemical processes involved in the decay of radioactive materials to produce α-, β- and γ radiation, X-rays and free electrons are described by Desrosier and Rosenstock (1960).

γ-rays and electrons are distinguished from other forms of radiation by their ionising ability (that is they are able to break chemical bonds when absorbed by materials). The products of ionisation may be electrically charged (ions) or neutral (free radicals). These then further react to cause changes in an irradiated material known as *radiolysis*. These reactions are responsible for the destruction of micro-organisms, insects and parasites during food irradiation.

Water in fresh foods, or in other foods with a high moisture content, is ionised by radiation. Electrons are expelled from water molecules and break chemical bonds (Fig. 8.1). The products then recombine to form hydrogen, hydrogen peroxide, hydrogen radicals (H·), hydroxyl radicals (OH·) and hydroperoxy radicals (HO$_2$·) (Fig. 8.2).

† *Summary of units*:

Becqerel (Bq):	one unit of disintegration per second.
Half-life:	the time taken for the radioactivity of a sample to fall to half its initial value.
Electron volt (ev):	energy of radiation (usually as megaelectronvolts (MeV)).
Grays (Gy):	absorbed dose (where 1 Gy is the absorption of 1 J of energy per kilogram of food). Previously rads (radiological units) were used where 1 rad $= 10^{-2}$ J kg^{-1}. 1 Gy therefore equals 100 rads.

$$H_2O \rightarrow H_2O^+ + e^-$$
$$e^- + H_2O \rightarrow H_2O^-$$
$$H_2O^+ \rightarrow H^+ + OH\cdot$$
$$H_2O^- \rightarrow H\cdot + OH^-$$

Fig. 8.1 — Ionisation of water. (After Robinson (1986).)

$$H\cdot + H\cdot \rightarrow H_2$$
$$or \quad OH\cdot + OH\cdot \rightarrow H_2O_2$$
$$or \quad H\cdot + OH\cdot \rightarrow H_2O$$
$$or \quad H\cdot + H_2O \rightarrow H_2 + OH\cdot$$
$$or \quad OH\cdot + H_2O_2 \rightarrow H_2O + HO_2\cdot$$
$$H\cdot + O_2 \rightarrow HO_2$$

Fig. 8.2 — Formation of radicals by irradiation. (After Hughes (1982).)

The radicals are extremely short lived (less than 10^{-5} s) but are sufficient to destroy bacterial cells. Similar radicals are also present in non-irradiated foods owing to

(1) the action of enzymes (for example lipoxygenases and peroxidases),
(2) the oxidation of fats and fatty acids and
(3) the degradation of fat soluble vitamins and pigments.

In addition, reactive oxygen and its derivatives are produced in foods by peroxidases, xanthine oxidase and amino acid oxidase. Fat-soluble components and essential fatty acids are therefore lost during irradiation and some foods (for example dairy products) are unsuitable for irradiation owing to the development of rancid off-flavours. The presence of oxygen accelerates this process and meat is therefore irradiated in vacuum packs.

8.2 EQUIPMENT

Irradiation equipment consists of a high-energy isotope source to produce γ-rays or, less commonly, a machine source to produce a high-energy electron beam. γ-radiation from cobalt-60 (^{60}Co) or caesium-137 (^{137}Cs) is used in most commercial plants. ^{60}Co emits γ-rays at two wavelengths which have energies of 1.17 MeV and 1.33 MeV respectively. The activity of the ^{60}Co or ^{137}Cs sources is rated at $(222–370) \times 10^{10}$ Bq g^{-1}. This generates 15kW/M Ci (15 kw per/3.7 x 10^{16}Bq). An isotope source cannot be switched off and so is shielded within a pool of water below the process area, to allow personnel to enter. In operation the source is raised, and packaged food is loaded onto conveyors (or, in larger installations, onto trucks) and transported through the radiation field in a circular path. This makes maximum use of the emitted radiation and ensures a uniform dose. Isotope sources require a more complex materials-handling system (Chapter 24) than that used with machine sources (Fig.8.3).

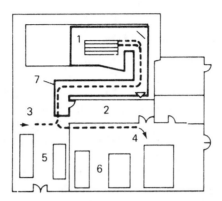

Fig. 8.3 — Isotope irradiation plant: 1, irradiation chamber; 2, control room; 3, infeed conveyor; 4, outlet conveyor; 5, raw food store; 6, irradiated product store; 7, concrete shielding wall. (After Farrall (1976).)

Machine sources are electron accelerators which consist of a heated cathode to supply electrons and an evacuated tube in which electrons are accelerated by a high-voltage electrostatic field. Either the electrons are used directly on the food, or a suitable target material is bombarded to produce X-rays. The main advantages of machine sources are

(1) they can be switched off and
(2) the electron beams can be directed over the packaged food to ensure an even dose distribution.

Handling equipment is therefore relatively simple. However, they are expensive and relatively inefficient in producing radiation.

Dosimeters are made from a number of materials, including polyvinylchloride (PVC), impregnated with a dye. Hydrogen chloride is released from the PVC by irradiation (Table 8.3) and produces a qualitative or quantitative change in colour to indicate the dose received. Other types of dosimeter, including photographic film, Perspex and cobalt glass, are described by McLaughlin *et al.* (1982). The residence time is determined by the dose required (Table 8.1) and the power output of the source. The source is then withdrawn and the food is removed for immediate distribution.

Radiation is contained within the processing area by the use of concrete walls and lead shielding. Openings in the shielding, for entry of products or personnel, must be carefully constructed to prevent leakage of radiation (for example around the edges of doors). Stringent safety procedures are required to prevent the source from being raised when personnel are present and to prevent entry to the building during processing. ^{60}Co has a half-life of 5.26 years and therefore requires the replacement of 12.3% of the activity each year to retain the rated output of the plant. Continuous processing is therefore desirable for economic operation of plant with a continuously decaying source (Wilkinson, 1986).

8.3   EFFECT ON MICRO-ORGANISMS

The reactive ions produced in foods by irradiation (Fig. 8.2) injure or destroy micro-organisms immediately, by changing the structure of cell membranes and affecting metabolic enzyme activity. However, a more important effect is on deoxyribonucleic acid (DNA) and ribonucleic acid molecules in cell nuclei, which are required for growth and replication. The effects of irradiation only become apparent after a period of time, when the DNA double-helix fails to unwind and the micro-organism cannot reproduce by cell division.

The rate of destruction of individual cells depends on the rate at which ions are produced and interreact with the DNA, whereas the reduction in cell numbers depends on the total dose of radiation received. Theoretically a logarithmic reduction in microbial numbers with increasing dose is expected. However, some bacterial species contain more than one molecule of DNA and others are capable of repairing damaged DNA. The rate of destruction is not therefore linear with received dose (Fig. 8.4). The sensitivity of micro-organisms to radiation is expressed as the D_{10}

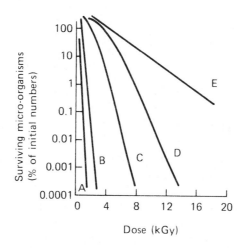

Fig. 8.4 — Microbial destruction by irradiation: curve A, *Psuedomonas*; curve B, *Salmonella*; curve C, *Bacillus cereus*; curve D, *Deinococcus radiodurans*; curve E, typical virus (After Gould (1986).)

value (the dose of radiation that reduces the microbial population to 10% of its initial value) by analogy with thermal destruction (Chapter 1). As in other food preservation methods the rate of destruction varies with microbial species. A simple guide is that, the smaller and simpler the organism, the higher the dose of radiation that is needed to destroy it. Viruses are very resistant to irradiation and are unlikely to be affected by the dose levels used in commercial processing. In general, vegetative cells are less resistant to radiation than are spores, and insects and parasites require the lowest dose used commercially.

Yeasts and moulds are readily destroyed and preventing their growth on fruits requires relatively low doses (Table 8.1). Spore forming species (for example *Clostridium botulinum* and *Bacillus cereus*), and those that are able to repair damaged DNA rapidly (for example *Deinococcus radiodurans*) are more resistant. Herbs and spices which are frequently contaminated by resistant spore-forming bacteria therefore require a dose of up to 10 kGy (Table 8.1). A dose of 48 kGy is needed for a 12 decimal reduction of *Cl. botulinum* (Lewis, 1987) but such a high dose would make products such as meat organoleptically unacceptable. Food-poisoning bacteria (for example *Salmonella typhimurium*) are less resistant to radiation, and doses of 3–10 kGy are sufficient for destruction (Guise, 1986). This is likely to become one of the most important applications of food irradiation as the incidence of food poisoning is steadily increasing in many countries (Guise 1986b).

Thus the dose administered to a food depends on the resistance of the organisms present and the objective of the treatment. Ripening and maturation of fruits and vegetables are arrested by inhibiting hormone production and interrupting the biochemical processes of cell division and growth. It should be noted, however, that enzymic spoilage of foods is not entirely prevented by irradiation and a separate heat treatment is required for prolonged storage. Bacteria which survive irradiation are more susceptible to heat treatment and the combination of irradiation with heating is therefore beneficial in causing a greater reduction in microbial numbers than would be achieved by either treatment alone (Gould, 1986).

Two potential problems of irradiation that are raised with respect to microbial destruction are

(1) that by destroying spoilage micro-organisms and not destroying pathogenic bacteria a valuable indicator of unwholesomeness is removed and
(2) that the destruction of toxin-producing bacteria after they have contaminated the food with toxins is a health hazard.

These are problems associated with poor manufacturing practice and occur in other types of food processing (for example aflatoxin production in nuts by *Aspergillus* species; cells are subsequently destroyed by drying, and evidence of the contamination is removed). It is therefore essential that codes of good manufacturing practice (for example Anon., 1987) are adhered to. These and other concerns (for example over operator safety) are discussed by Webb and Lang (1987).

8.4   EFFECT ON FOODS

8.4.1   Induced radioactivity

The maximum recommended dose for foods is 15 kGy, with the average dose not exceeding 10 kGy (World Health Organisation, 1977, 1981). At this dose, ^{60}Co and ^{137}Cs have insufficient emission energies to induce radioactivity in the food. Machine sources of electrons and X-rays do have sufficient energy, but the levels of induced radioactivity are insignificant (2% of the acceptable radiation dose in the worst case and 0.0001% under realistic processing and storage conditions) (Gaunt, 1986). The FAO–IAEA–WHO Expert Committee on Food Irradiation concluded that this dose 'presents no toxicological hazard and no special nutritional or microbiological problems in foods' (World Health Organisation, 1977, 1981). This was supported by the Advisory Committee on Irradiated and Novel Foodstuffs (Anon., 1986).

8.4.2 Radiolytic products
The ions and radicals produced during irradiation (section 8.1) are capable of reacting with components of the food to produce radiolytic products. However, the majority of the evidence from feeding experiments, in which animals were fed irradiated foods and high doses of radiolytic products, indicates that there are no adverse effects. Radiolytic type products can also arise from other methods of food processing (Gaunt, 1986) and as a result it is difficult to devise a test to determine whether foods have been irradiated. The extent of radiolysis depends on the type of food and the radiation dose employed. In commercial applications there is no detectable radiolysis because dose levels are low, and foods which are prone to production of radiolytic compounds (for example fatty foods) are not irradiated.

8.4.3 Nutritional and sensory value
At commercial dose levels, ionising radiation has little or no effect on the digestibility of proteins or the composition of essential amino acids (Josephson et al., 1975). At higher dose levels, cleavage of the sulphydryl group from sulphur amino acids in proteins causes changes in the aroma and taste of foods. Carbohydrates are hydrolysed and oxidised to simpler compounds and, depending on the dose received, may become depolymerised and more susceptible to enzymic hydrolysis. However, there is no change in the degree of utilisation of the carbohydrate and hence no reduction in nutritional value. The effect on lipids is similar to that of autoxidation, to produce hydroperoxides. The effect is reduced by irradiating foods while frozen, but foods that have high concentrations of lipid are generally unsuitable for irradiation.

There is conflicting evidence regarding the effect on vitamins as many studies have used vitamin solutions, which show greater losses than those found in the heterogeneous mixtures of compounds in foods. Water soluble vitamins vary in their sensitivity to irradiation. The extent of vitamin loss also depends on the dose received and the type and physical state of food under investigation. There is also conflicting evidence at low dose levels. For example, in grain disinfestation there are little or no vitamin losses, whereas inhibition of sprouting is variously reported to cause 0% and 28% loss of vitamin C at 0.1 kGy and 0.11 kGy respectively (Faizur Rahman, 1975; Gounelle et al., 1970). The effects on thiamine in meat and poultry are likewise inconsistent but other vitamins of the B group are largely unaffected (Table 8.2). Fat-soluble vitamins vary in their susceptibility to radiation. Vitamins D and K are largely unaffected whereas vitamins A and E undergo some losses, which vary according to the type of food examined. In summary, the consensus of opinion is that, at commercial dose levels, irradiation causes no greater damage to nutritional quality than other preservation operations used in food processing. Changes in

Table 8.2 — Effect of irradiation on water-soluble vitamins in selected foods

Food	Treatment (kGy)	Thiamin	Riboflavin	Niacin	Pyridoxine	Pantothenic a cid	Vitamin B_{12}
Beef	4.7–7.1	60	4	14	10	—	—
Pork	4.5	15	22	22	2	—	—
Haddock	1.5	22	0	0	+ 15	+ 78	10
Wheat	2.0	12	13	9	—	—	—
Flour	0.3–0.5	0	0	11	0	—	—

+ apparent increase. Adapted from Brooke *et al*. (1966) and Josephson *et al*. (1975).

nutritional quality are described in detail by Kraybill (1982). The importance of these changes to the nutritional value of a diet is discussed in Chapter 1.

8.5 EFFECT ON PACKAGING
Radiation is able to penetrate packaging materials and therefore reduces the risk of post-processing contamination and allows easier handling of products. However, packaging materials are themselves subject to changes induced by radiation (Table 8.3) and careful choice of materials is necessary to prevent contamination of the food

Table 8.3 — Changes to packaging materials caused by irradiation

Packaging material	Maximum dose (kGy)	Effect of radiation above maximum dose
Polystyrene	5000	—
Polyethylene	1000	—
PVC	100	Browning, evolution of hydrogen chloride
Paper and board	100	Loss of mechanical strength
Polypropylene	25	Becomes brittle
Glass	10	Browning

Adapted from the data of Guise (1986) and McLaughlin *et al*. (1982).

with radiolytic products from the packaging.

ACKNOWLEDGEMENT
Grateful acknowledgement is made for information supplied by Isotron plc, Swindon, Wiltshire, UK.

REFERENCES

Anon. (1985) Food irradiation processing. *Proceedings of IAEA–FAO Symppsium*, Washington, DC, 4–8 March 1985. IAEA, Wagramerstrasse, PO Box 100, A-1400 Vienna.

Anon. (1986) *The safety and wholesomeness of irradiated foods*, Report by the Advisory Committee on Irradiated and Novel Foods. HMSO, London.

Anon. (1987) *Good manufacturing practice, a guide to its responsible management.* Institute of Food Science and Technology, 20 Queensberry Place, London SW7 2DR, UK.

Brooke, R. O., Ravesi, E. M., Gadbois, D. F. and Steinberg, M. A. (1966) Preservation of fresh unfrozen fishery products by low level radiation. *Food Technol.* **20**, 1479–1482.

Desrosier, N. W. and Rosenstock, H. M. (1960) Radiation Technology, AVI, Westport, Conn., pp. 3–46.

Faizur Rahman, A. T. M. (1975) Radiation research in Bangladesh, *Food Irradiat. Inf.* **4**, 6.

Farrall, A. W. (1976) *Food engineering systems.* AVI, Westport, Connecticut.

Gaunt, I. F. (1986) Food irradiations — safety aspects. *Proc. Inst. Food Sci. Technol.* **19** (4), 171–174.

Goresline, H. (1982) Historical aspects of the radiation preservation of food. In: E. S. Josephson and M. S. Peterson (eds.), *Preservation of foods by ionizing radiation*, Vol.1. CRC Press, Boca Raton, Florida, pp. 1–46.

Gould, G. W. (1986) Food irradiation—microbiological aspects. *Proc. Inst. Food Sci. Technol.* **19** (4) 175–180.

Gounelle, H., Gulat-Marnay, C. and Fauchet, M. (1970) Effects of ionising irradiation on the vitamins B and C contents of food. *Ann. Nutr. Aliment.* **24** 41–49.

Guise, B. (1986) Irradiation waits in the wings. *Food Eur.* March–April 7–9.

Guise, B. (1986b) Food irradiation: the dream becomes a reality. *Food Process.* **4**, 27–29.

Hughes, D. (1982) *Notes on ionising radiation: quantities, units, biological effects and permissible doses*, Occupational Hygiene Monograph, No. 5. Science Reviews Ltd.

Josephson, E. S., Thomas, M. H. and Calhoun, W. K. (1975) Effects of treatment of foods with ionizing radiation. In: R. S. Harris and E. Karmas (eds.) *Nutritional evaluation of food processing.* AVI, Westport, Connecticut, pp. 393–411.

Kraybill, H. F. (1982) Effect of processing on nutritive value of food: irradiation, In: M. Rechcigl (ed.), *Handbook of nutritive value of processed food*, Vol. 1. CRC Press, Boca Raton, Florida, pp. 181–208.

Lewis, M. J. (1987) *Physical properties of foods and food processing systems.* Ellis Horwood, Chichester, West Sussex; VCH Weinheim, pp. 287–290.

Ley, F. J. (1987) Applying radiation technology to food. In: A. Turner (ed.), *Food technology international Europe.* Sterling, London, pp. 72–75.

McLaughlin, W. L., Jarrett, R. D. Snr. and Olejnik, T. A. (1982) Dosimetry. In: E. S. Josephson and M. S. Peterson (eds.), *Preservation of foods by ionizing radiation* Vol. 1, CRC Press, Boca Raton, Florida, pp. 189–245.

Robinson, D. S. (1986) Irradiation of foods. *Proc. Inst. Food Sci. Technol.* **19** (4), pp. 165–168.

Webb, T. and Lang, T. (1987) *Food irradiation, the facts.* Thorson, Wellingborough.

Webb, T. and Lang, T. (undated) *Food irradiation — issues of concern.* London Food Commission, PO Box 291, London N5 1DU.

Welt, M. A. (1985) Barriers to widespread approval of food irradiation. *J. Ind. Irradiat. Technol.* **3** (1), pp. 75–86.

World Health Organisation (1977) *Wholesomeness of irradiated food,* Report of the Joint FAO–IAEA–WHO Expert Committee, WHO Technical Report Series, No. 604. HMSO, London.

World Health Organisation (1981) *Wholesomeness of irradiated food,* Report of the Joint FAO–IAEA–WHO Expert Committee, WHO Technical Report Series, No. 659. HMSO, London.

Wilkinson, V. (1986) Food irradiation in practice. *Proc. Inst. Food Sci. Technol.* **19** (4), 169–170.

Part III
Processing by application of heat

Heat treatment is one of the most important methods used in food processing, not only because of the desirable effects on eating quality (many foods are consumed in a cooked form) but also because of the preservative effect on foods by the destruction of enzyme and microbiological activity, insects and parasites. The other main advantages of heat processing are

(1) destruction of anti-nutritional components of foods (for example trypsin inhibitor in legumes),
(2) improvement in availability of some nutrients (for example improved digestibility of proteins, gelatinisation of starches and release of bound niacin) and
(3) relatively simple control of processing conditions.

In general, higher temperatures and longer periods of heating produce greater destruction of micro-organisms and enzymes. High-temperature short-time processes achieve the same extension of shelf life as treatments at lower temperatures and longer times but permit greater retention of sensory and nutritive properties of foods (Chapter 1). The effect of this concept on design and operation of equipment used in heat processing is described in Chapters 9–17. Changes in sensory and nutritive value are reported where appropriate in these chapters, but caution is necessary in interpretation of such data (Chapter 1).

Mild processes (for example blanching (Chapter 9) and pasteurisation (Chapter 10)) cause fewer changes to the eating quality of foods and may be combined with other operations (for example freezing, or chilling (Chapters 18 and 19)) and correct packaging (Chapter 22) to achieve a longer shelf life. More severe heat treatments (for example baking, roasting or frying (Chapters 15 and 16)) are intended to alter the eating quality of foods, and preservation is not the main purpose. Shelf life is extended where necessary by chilling or freezing. To achieve a long shelf life by heating alone, it is necessary to apply a relatively severe treatment (for example heat sterilisation (Chapter 11)).

Another important effect of heating is the removal of water by evaporation. This is the basis of evaporation (concentration by boiling) (Chapter 12) and drying (Chapter 14). In these unit operations, heat is used to supply the latent heat of vaporisation of water (Chapter 1).

A. Heat processing using steam or water

9

Blanching

Blanching is used to destroy enzymic activity in vegetables and some fruits, prior to further processing. As such, it is not intended as a sole method of preservation but as a pre-treatment which is normally carried out between the preparation of the raw material (Chapter 2) and later operations (particularly heat sterilisation, dehydration and freezing (Chapters 11, 14 and 19)). Blanching is also combined with peeling and/or cleaning of food (Chapter 2), to achieve savings in energy consumption, space and equipment costs.

A few vegetables (for example onions and green peppers) do not require a blanching treatment to prevent enzyme activity during storage, but the majority suffer considerable deterioration if blanching is omitted or if they are under-blanched. To achieve adequate enzyme inactivation, food is heated rapidly to a pre-set temperature, held for a pre-set time and then cooled rapidly to near ambient temperatures. The factors which influence blanching time are

(1) the type of fruit or vegetable,
(2) the size of the pieces of food,
(3) the blanching temperature and
(4) the method of heating.

9.1 THEORY AND PURPOSES OF BLANCHING

The theory of unsteady-state heat transfer by conduction and convection, which is used to calculate blanching time, and a sample problem (Sample problem 1.6) are described in Chapter 1.

9.1.1 Enzyme inactivation

The maximum processing temperature in freezing and dehydration is insufficient to inactivate enzymes. If the food is not blanched, undesirable changes in sensory characteristics and nutritional properties take place during storage. In heat sterilisation, the time taken to reach sterilising temperatures, particularly in large cans, may be sufficient to allow enzyme activity to take place. It is therefore necessary to blanch foods prior to these preservation operations. Underblanching may cause more damage to food than the absence of blanching does. Heat, which is sufficient to disrupt tissues but not to inactivate enzymes, causes the mixing of enzymes and substrates. In addition, only some enzymes may be destroyed which causes increased activity of others and accelerated deterioration.

The heat resistance of enzymes is characterised by D and z values (Chapter 1). Enzymes which cause a loss of eating and nutritional qualities in vegetables and fruits include lipoxygenase, polyphenoloxidase, polygalacturonase and chlorophyllase. Two heat-resistant enzymes which are found in most vegetables are catalase and peroxidase. Although they are not implicated as a cause of deterioration during storage, they are used to determine the success of blanching. Peroxidase is the more heat resistant of the two and the absence of residual peroxidase activity indicates that other less heat-resistant enzymes are also destroyed.

9.1.2   Other functions of blanching

Blanching reduces the numbers of contaminating micro-organisms on the surface of foods and hence assists in subsequent preservation operations. This is particularly important in heat sterilisation (Chapter 11), as the time and temperature of processing are designed to achieve a specified reduction in cell numbers. If blanching is inadequate, a larger number of micro-organisms are present initially. This results in a larger number of spoiled containers after processing. Freezing does not substantially reduce the number of micro-organisms in unblanched foods and these are able to grow on thawing. A similar, although less severe problem occurs on rehydration of unblanched dried foods.

Blanching also softens vegetable tissues to facilitate filling into containers and removes air from intercellular spaces which assists in the formation of a head-space vacuum in cans (Chapters 11 and 23).

9.2   EQUIPMENT

The two most widespread commercial methods of blanching involve passing food through an atmosphere of saturated steam or a bath of hot water. Both types of equipment are relatively simple and inexpensive. There have been substantial developments to blanchers in recent years to reduce the energy consumption and to reduce the loss of soluble components of foods. The latter reduces the volume and polluting potential of effluents from the blancher and increases the yield of product.

The yield of food from the blanching operation is the most important factor in determining the commercial success of a particular method. In some methods the cooling stage may result in greater losses of product or nutrients than the blanching stage, and it is therefore important to consider both blanching and cooling when comparing different methods. Steam blanching results in higher nutrient retention provided that cooling is by cold-air or cold-water sprays. Cooling with running water (fluming) substantially increases leaching losses (washing of soluble components from the food), but the product may gain weight and the overall yield is therefore increased. Air cooling causes weight loss of the product due to evaporation, and this may outweigh any advantages gained by nutrient retention (Bomben et al., 1975).

There are also substantial differences in yield and nutrient retention due to differences in the type of food and differences in the method of preparation (for example slicing and peeling (Chapter 2)).

Recycling of water does not affect the product quality or yield but substantially reduces the volume of effluent produced. However it is necessary to ensure adequate hygienic standards for both the product and equipment, and this may result in additional costs which outweigh savings in energy and higher product yield. Microwave blanching is not yet used commercially on a large scale. It is discussed further in Chapter 17.

9.2.1 Steam blanchers

The advantages and limitations of conventional steam blanchers are described in Table 9.1. In general this is the preferred method for foods with a large area of cut

Table 9.1 — Advantages and limitations of different types of conventional blancher

Equipment	Advantages	Limitations
Conventional steam blanchers	Smaller loss of water-soluble components. Smaller volumes of waste and lower disposal charges than water blanchers, particularly with air cooling instead of water. Easy to clean and sterilise	Limited cleaning of the food, washers also required. Higher capital costs than water blanchers. Uneven blanching if the food is piled too high on the conveyor belt. Some mass loss in food Poorer energy efficiency than water blanchers
Conventional hot-water blanchers	Lower capital cost and better energy efficiency than steam blanchers	Large losses of water-soluble components, including vitamins, minerals and sugars. Higher costs in purchase of water; high charges for treatment of large volumes of dilute effluent. Risk of contamination by thermophilic bacteria

surfaces as leaching losses are much smaller than those found using hot-water blanchers.

At its simplest a steam blancher consists of a mesh conveyor belt that carries food through a steam atmosphere. The residence time of the food is controlled by the speed of the conveyor. Typically such equipment is 15 m long, 1–1.5 m wide and up to 2 m high. The efficiency of energy consumption is 19% when water sprays are used at the inlet and outlet to condense escaping steam. Alternatively, food may enter and leave the blancher through rotary valves or hydrostatic seals to reduce steam losses (efficiency, 27%), or steam may be re-used by passing through Venturi valves. Energy efficiency is improved to 31% using combined hydrostatic and Venturi devices (Scott *et al.*, 1981).

In conventional steam blanching, there is often poor uniformity of heating in the multiple layers of food. The time–temperature combination required to ensure enzyme inactivation at the centre of the bed results in overheating of food at the edges and a consequent loss of texture and other sensory characteristics. Individual quick blanching (IQB) which involves blanching in two stages, was developed to overcome this problem (Lazar *et al.*, 1971). In the first stage the food is heated in a single layer to a sufficiently high temperature to inactivate enzymes. In the second stage (termed *adiabatic holding*) a deep bed of food is held for sufficient time to allow the temperature at the centre of each piece to increase to that needed for enzyme inactivation. The reduced heating time (for example 25 s for heating and 50 s for holding 1 cm diced carrot compared with 3 min for conventional blanching), results in an improvement in the efficiency of energy consumption to 86–91% (Cumming *et al.*, 1984). The mass of product blanched per kilogram of steam increases from 0.5 kg per kilogram of steam in conventional steam blanchers to 6–7 kg per kilogram of steam, when small- particulate foods (for example peas, sliced or diced carrots) are blanched.

Nutrient losses during steam blanching are reduced by exposing the food to warm air (65°C) in a short preliminary drying operation (*pre-conditioning*). Surface moisture evaporates and the surfaces then absorb condensing steam during IQB. Losses are reduced to 5% of those found using conventional steam blanching (Lazar *et al.*, 1971). Pre-conditioning and individual quick blanching are reported to reduce nutrient losses by 81% for green beans, by 75% for Brussels sprouts, by 61% for peas and by 53% for lima beans and there is no reduction in the mass of blanched food (Bomben *et al.*, 1973). However, the cost of pre-conditioning must be balanced against the cost of effluent treatment to determine which method is more suitable.

The equipment for IQB steam blanching (Fig. 9.1(a)) consists of a bucket elevator (Chapter 24) which carries the food to a heating section. The elevator is located in a close fitting tunnel to reduce steam losses. A single layer of food is heated on a conveyor belt and then held on a holding elevator before cooling. The cooling section employs a fog spray to saturate the cold air with moisture. This reduces evaporative losses from the food and reduces the amount of effluent produced. Typically the equipment processes up to 4500 kg h^{-1} of food. The complete inactivation of peroxidase is achieved with a minimum loss in quality, indicated by the retention of 76–85% of ascorbic acid.

Batch fluidised-bed blanchers operate using a mixture of air and steam, moving at approximately 4.5 m s^{-1}, which fluidises and heats the product simultaneously. The design of the blanching chamber promotes continuous and uniform circulation of the food until it is adequately blanched. Although these blanchers are not yet developed to a commercial scale, they are reported to overcome many of the problems

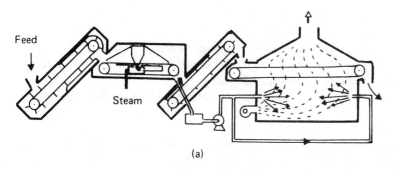

(a)

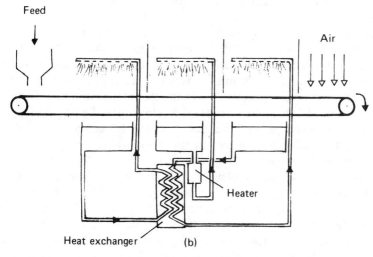

(b)

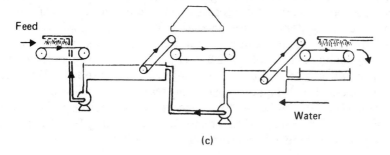

(c)

Fig. 9.1 — Blanchers: (a) IQB steam blancher (after Timbers *et al.* (1984)); (b) blancher–cooler
(after Philippon (1984)); (c) counter-current blancher (after Wendt *et al.* (1983)).

associated with both steam and hot-water methods (Gilbert *et al.*, 1980). The
advantages include

(1) faster, more uniform heating,
(2) good mixing of the product,
(3) a substantial reduction in the volume of effluent and
(4) shorter processing times and hence smaller losses of vitamins and other soluble
    heat sensitive components of food.

A continuous fluidised-bed blancher is described by Philippon (1984).

9.2.2 Hot-water blanchers

There are a number of different designs of blancher, each of which retains the food in hot water at 70–100°C for a specified time and then removes it to a dewatering–cooling section. The advantages and limitations of conventional hot-water blanchers are described in Table 9.1.

The *reel blancher* is a widely used method in which food enters a slowly rotating cylindrical mesh drum which is partly submerged in hot water. The food is moved through the drum by internal flights. The speed of rotation controls the heating time. *Pipe blanchers* consist of a continuous insulated metal pipe fitted with feed and discharge ports. Hot water is recirculated through the pipe and food is metered in. The residence time of food in the blancher is determined by the length of the pipe and the velocity of the water. These blanchers have the advantage of a large capacity while occupying a small floor space. In some applications they may be used to transport food simultaneously through a factory.

Developments in hot-water blanchers, based on the IQB principle, reduce energy consumption and minimise the production of effluent. For example the blancher–cooler, has three sections: a pre-heating stage, a blanching stage and a cooling stage (Fig. 9.1(b)). The food remains on a single conveyor belt throughout each stage and therefore does not suffer the physical damage associated with the turbulence of conventional hot-water blanchers. The food is pre-heated with water that is recirculated through a heat exchanger. After blanching, a second recirculation system cools the food. The two systems pass water through the heat exchanger, and this heats the pre-heat water and simultaneously cools the cooling water. Up to 70% of the heat is recovered. A recirculated water–steam mixture is used to blanch the food, and final cooling is by cold air. Effluent production is negligible and water consumption is reduced to approximately $1\,m^3$ per 10 t of product. The mass of product blanched is 16.7–20 kg per kilogram of steam, compared with 0.25–0.5 kg per kilogram in conventional hot-water blanchers. An alternative design, used for blanching broccoli, lima beans, spinach and peas, is described by Wendt *et al.* (1983) in which water and food move counter-currently (Fig. 9.1(c)).

9.3   EFFECT ON FOODS

The heat received by a food during blanching inevitably causes some changes to sensory and nutritional qualities. However, the heat treatment is less severe than for example in heat sterilisation (Chapter 11), and the resulting changes in food quality are less pronounced. In general, the time–temperature combination used for blanching is a compromise designed to ensure adequate enzyme inactivation but to prevent excessive softening and loss of flavour in the food (Fig. 9.2)).

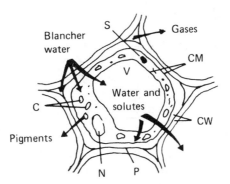

Fig. 9.2 — Effect of blanching on plant tissues: S, starch gelatinised; CM, cytoplasmic membranes altered; CW, cell walls little altered; P, pectins modified; N, nucleus and cytoplasmic proteins denatured; C, chloroplasts and chromoplasts distorted.

9.3.1 Nutrients
Minerals, water-soluble vitamins and other water-soluble components are lost during blanching. Losses of vitamins are mostly due to leaching, thermal destruction, and, to a lesser extent, oxidation. The extent of vitamin loss depends on a number of factors:

(1) the maturity of the food and variety;
(2) methods used in preparation of the food, particularly the extent of cutting, slicing or dicing;
(3) the surface-area-to-volume ratio of the pieces of food;
(4) method of blanching;
(5) time and temperature of blanching (lower vitamin losses at higher temperatures for shorter times);
(6) the method of cooling
(7) the ratio of water to food (in both water blanching and cooling).

Losses of ascorbic acid are used as an indicator of food quality, and therefore the severity of blanching (Table 9.2). The importance of these changes on the nutritional quality of diets is discussed in Chapter 1.

9.3.2 Colour and flavour
Blanching brightens the colour of some foods by removing air and dust on the surface and thus altering the wavelength of reflected light. The time and temperature of blanching also influence the change in food pigments according to their D value (Chapter 1). Sodium carbonate (0.125% w/w) or calcium oxide are often added to blancher water to protect chlorophyll and to retain the colour of green vegetables. Enzymic browning of cut apples and potatoes is prevented by holding the food in dilute (2% w/w) brine prior to blanching. When correctly blanched, most foods have

Table 9. 2 — Effect of blanching method on ascorbic acid losses in selected vegetables

Treatment	Loss (%) of ascorbic acid		
	Peas	Broccoli	Green beans
Water blanch–water cool	29.1	38.7	15.1
Water blanch–air cool	25.0	30.6	19.5
Steam blanch–water cool	24.2	22.2	17.7
Steam blanch–air cool	14.0	9.0	18.6

Differences in both steam versus water blanch and air versus water cooling are significant at the 5% level.
Adapted from Cumming *et al.* (1981).

no significant changes to flavour or aroma, but underblanching can lead to the development of off-flavours during storage of dried or frozen foods (Chapters 14 and 19). Changes in colour and flavour are described in more detail by Selman (1987).

9.3.3 Texture
One of the purposes of blanching is to soften the texture of vegetables to facilitate filling into containers prior to canning. However, when used for freezing or drying, the time–temperature conditions needed to achieve enzyme inactivation cause an excessive loss of texture in some types of food (for example certain varieties of potato) and in large pieces of food. Calcium chloride is therefore added to blancher water to form insoluble calcium pectate complexes and thus to maintain firmness in the tissues.

ACKNOWLEDGEMENT

Grateful acknowledgement is made for information supplied by Reekcroft Ltd, Epworth, South Yorkshire DN9 1EP, UK.

REFERENCES

Bomben, J. C., Dietrich, W. C., Farkas, D. F., Hudson, J. S., and de Marchena, E. S. (1973) Pilot plant evaluation of individual quick blanching for vegetables. *J. Food Sci.*, **38**, 590–594.

Bomben, J. C., Dietrich, W. C., Hudson, J. S., Hamilton, H. K., and Farkas, D. F. (1975) Yields and solids loss in steam blanching, cooling and freezing vegetables. *J. Food Sci.* **40**, 660–664.

Cumming, D. B., Stark, R., and Sanford, K. A. (1981) The effect of an individual quick blanching method on ascorbic acid retention in selected vegetables. J. Food Process Preserv., **5**, 31–37.

Cumming, D. B., Stark, R., Timbers, G. E., and Cowmeadow, R. (1984) A new blanching system for the food industry, II, Commercial design and testing. *J. Food Process Preserv.* **8**, 137–150.

Gilbert, H., Baxerres, J. L., and Kim, H. (1980). In: P. Linko, Y. Malkki, J. Olkku and J. Larinkan (ed), *Food process engineering*, Vol. 1, Applied Science, London, pp. 75–85.

Lazar, M. E., Lund, D. B., and Dietrich, W. C. (1971) IQB — a new concept in blanching. *Food Technol.* **25** 684–686.

Philippon, J. (1984) Methods de blanchiment–refroidissement des legumes destines a la congelation. *Sci. Aliments* **4**, 523–550.

Scott, E. P., Carroad, P. A., Rumsey, T. R., Horn, J., Buhlert, J., and Rose, W. W. (1981) Energy consumption in steam blanchers. *J. Food Process Engng* **5** 77–88.

Selman, J. D. (1987). The blanching process, In: S. Thorne (ed.), *Developments in food preservation*, Vol. 4. Elsevier Applied Science, Barking, Essex, pp. 205–249.

Timbers, G. E., Stark, R., and Cumming, D. B. (1984). A new blanching system for the food industry, I, Design, construction and testing of a pilot plant prototype. *J. Food Process Preserv.* **2**, 115–133.

Wendt, F. L., Laubacher, E. G., Wherry, R., Martin, P., and Robe, K., 1983. Blancher with heat recovery processes 6 lb of product per lb of steam. *Food Process USA.* **44** 62–63.

10

Pasteurisation

Pasteurisation is a relatively mild heat treatment, usually performed below 100°C, which is used to extend the shelf life of foods for several days (for example milk) or for several months (for example bottled fruit). It preserves foods by inactivation of enzymes and destruction of relatively heat-sensitive micro-organisms (for example non-sporing bacteria, yeasts and moulds) but causes minimal changes in the sensory characteristics or nutritive value of a food. The severity of the heat treatment and the resulting extension of shelf life are determined mostly by the pH of the food. In low-acid foods (pH > 4.5), the main purpose is destruction of pathogenic bacteria whereas, below pH 4.5, destruction of spoilage micro-organisms or enzyme inactivation is usually more important (Table 10.1).

Table 10.1 — Purpose of pasteurisation for different foods

Food	Main purpose	Subsidiary purpose	Minimum processing conditions[a]
pH < 4.5 Fruit juice	Enzyme inactivation (pectinesterase and polygalacturonase)	Destruction of spoilage microorganisms (yeasts, fungi)	65 °C for 30 min; 77 °C for 1 min; 88 °C for 15 s
Beer	Destruction of spoilage micro-organisms (wild yeasts, *Lactobacillus* species), and residual yeasts (*Saccharomyces* species)	—	65–68 °C for 20 min (in bottle); 72–75 °C for 1–4 min at 900–1000 kPa
pH > 4.5 Milk	Destruction of pathogens: *Brucella abortis*, *Mycobacterium tuberculosis*, (*Coxiella burnettii*[b])	Destruction of spoilage micro-organisms and enzymes	63 °C for 30 min; 71.5 °C for 15 s
Liquid egg	Destruction of pathogens *Salmonella seftenburg*	Destruction of spoilage micro-organisms	64.4 °C for 2.5 min 60°C for 3.5 min
Ice cream	Destruction of pathogens	Destruction of spoilage micro-organism	65 °C for 30 min; 71 °C for 10 min; 80 °C for 15 s

[a]Followed by rapid cooling to 3–7 °C.
[b]Rickettsia organism which causes Q fever.
Adapted from Fricker (1984), Wiggins and Barclay (1984), Lund (1975), and Hammid-Samimi and Swartzel (1984).

Processing containers of food, either which have a naturally low pH (for example fruit pieces) or in which the pH is artificially lowered (for example pickles) is similar to canning (Chapter 11). It is often termed *pasteurisation* to indicate the mild heat treatment employed. In this chapter the pasteurisation of liquid foods either packaged in containers or unpackaged, using heat exchangers is described.

10.1 THEORY

The sensible heat required to raise the temperature of a liquid during pasteurisation is found using

$$Q = mc \, (\theta_A - \theta_B) \tag{10.1}$$

Where: Q (W) is the rate of heat transfer, m (kg s^{-1}) the mass flow rate, c (kJ kg^{-1}°C^{-1}) the specific heat capacity and $\theta_A \rightarrow \theta_B$ the temperature change.

Sample problems of heat transfer during pasteurisation are given in Chapter 1 (Sample problems 1.4 and 1.5) and in section 10.2.2.

The extent of the heat treatment required to stabilise a food is determined by the D value of the most heat-resistant enzyme or micro-organism which may be present in the food (Chapter 1). For example milk pasteurisation is based on D_{60} and a 12 logarithmic cycle reduction in the numbers of *C. burnetii* (Harper, 1976), and liquid whole egg is treated to produce a $9D$ reduction in numbers of *S. seftenberg* (Hammid-Samimi and Swartzel, 1984). As flavours, colours and vitamins are also characterised by D values, pasteurisation conditions can be optimised for retention of nutritional and sensory quality by the use of high-temperature short-time (HTST) conditions. For example in milk processing the lower-temperature longer-time process (the *holder process*) caused a slightly greater loss of vitamins than HTST processing (Table 10.2) and it is less often used. Higher temperatures and shorter times (for example 88°C for 1 s, 94°C for 0.1 s or 100°C for 0.01 s for milk) are described as higher-heat shorter-time processing or flash pasteurisation.

Alkaline phosphatase is a naturally occurring enzyme in raw milk which has a similar D value to heat-resistant pathogens (Fig. 10.1). The direct estimation of pathogen numbers by microbiological methods is expensive and time consuming, and a simple test for phosphatase activity is therefore routinely used. If phosphatase activity is found, it is assumed that the heat treatment was inadequate to destroy the pathogenic bacteria or that unpasteurised milk has contaminated the pasteurised product. A similar test for the effectiveness of liquid-egg pasteurisation is based on residual α-amylase activity (Brooks, 1962).

10.2 EQUIPMENT

10.2.1 Pasteurisation of packaged foods

Some liquid foods (for example beers and fruit juices) are pasteurised after filling into containers. Hot water is normally used if the food is packaged in glass, to reduce the risk of thermal shock to the container (fracture caused by rapid changes in temperature). Maximum temperature differences between the container and water

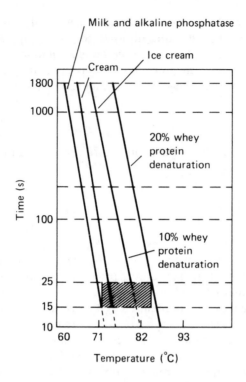

Fig. 10.1 — Time–temperature relationships for pasteurisation. The hatched area shows the range of times and temperatures used in commercial milk pasteurisation.(After Harper (1976)).

Table 10.2 — Vitamin losses during pasteurisation of milk

Vitamin	Method of pasteurisation	
	HTST	Holder
Vitamin A		
Vitamin D		
Riboflavin		
Vitamin B$_6$	0	0
Pantothenic acid		
Nicotinic acid		
Biotin		
Folic acid		
Thiamin	6.8	10
Vitamin C	10	20
Vitamin B$_{12}$	0	10

From Ford *et al.* (1969).

are 20°C for heating and 10°C for cooling. Metal or plastic containers are processed using steam–air mixtures or hot water as there is little risk of thermal shock. In all cases the food is cooled to approximately 40°C to evaporate surface water and therefore to minimise external corrosion to the container or cap, and to accelerate setting of label adhesives. Hot-water pasteurisers may be batch or continuous in operation. The simplest batch equipment consists of a water bath in which crates of packaged food are heated to a pre-set temperature and held for the required length of time. Cold water is then pumped in to cool the product. A continuous version consists of a long narrow trough fitted with a conveyor belt to carry containers through heating and cooling stages.

A second design consists of a tunnel divided into a number of heating zones (Fig. 10.2). Very fine (atomised) water sprays heat the containers as they pass through

Pre-heating | Pasteurisation | Cooling

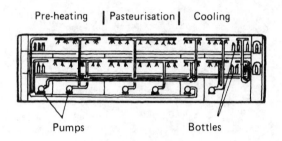

Pumps   Bottles

Fig. 10.2 — Tunnel pasteuriser. (After Chiozzotto (1984)).

each zone on a conveyor, to give incremental rises in temperature until pasteurisation is achieved. Water sprays then cool the containers as they continue through the tunnel. Savings in energy and water consumption are achieved by recirculation of water between pre-heat sprays, where it is cooled by the incoming food, and cooling zones where it is heated by the hot products (Anon., 1982).

Steam tunnels have the advantage of faster heating, giving shorter residence times, and smaller equipment. Temperatures in the heating zones are gradually increased by reducing the amount of air in the steam–air mixtures. Cooling takes place using fine sprays of water or by immersion in a water bath.

10.2.2 Pasteurisation of unpackaged liquids

Swept surface heat exchangers (Barclay *et al.*, 1984) or open boiling pans (Chapter 12) are used for small-scale batch pasteurisation of some liquid foods. However, the large-scale pasteurisation of unpackaged low viscosity liquids (for example milk, milk products, fruit juices, liquid egg, beers and wines) usually employs continuous equipment, and plate heat exchangers are widely used. Some products (for example fruit juices, wines) require de-aeration to prevent oxidative changes during storage. They are sprayed into a vacuum chamber and dissolved air is removed by a vacuum pump, prior to pasteurisation.

The *plate heat exchanger* (Fig. 10.3) consists of a series of thin vertical stainless

Fig. 10.3 — Plate heat exchanger. (Courtesy of Wincanton Engineering Ltd.).

steel plates, held tightly together in a metal frame. The plates form parallel channels, and liquid food and heating medium (hot water or steam) are pumped through alternate channels, usually in a counter-current flow pattern (Fig. 10.4). Each plate is

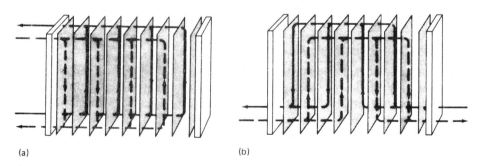

(a)   (b)

Fig. 10.4 — Counter-current flow through plate heat exchanger: (a) one pass with four channels per medium; (b) two passes with two channels per pass and medium. (Courtesy of HRS Heat Exchangers Ltd.).

fitted with a synthetic rubber gasket to produce a watertight seal and to prevent mixing of the product and the heating and cooling media. The plates are corrugated to induce turbulence in the liquids and this, together with the high velocity induced by pumping, reduces the thickness of boundary films (Chapter 1) to give high heat transfer coefficients (3000–11 500 W m^{-2}K^{-1}).

In operation (Fig. 10.5), food is pumped from a balance tank to a regeneration

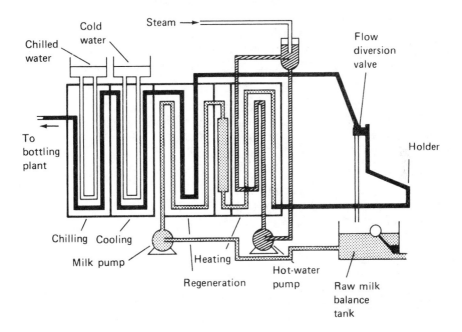

Fig. 10.5 — Pasteurisation using a plate heat exchanger. (Courtesy of APV Ltd.).

section, where it is pre-heated by food that has already been pasteurised. It is then heated to pasteurising temperature in a heating section and held for the time required to achieve pasteurisation in a holding tube. If the pasteurising temperature is not reached, a flow diversion valve automatically returns the food to the balance tank to be repasteurised. The pasteurised product is then cooled in the regeneration section (and simultaneously pre-heats incoming food) and then further cooled by cold water and, if necessary, chilled water in a cooling section. The regeneration of heat in this way leads to substantial savings in energy and up to 95% of the heat is recovered. Heat recovery is calculated using

$$\text{heat recovery } (\%) = \frac{\theta_2 - \theta_1}{\theta_3 - \theta_1} \times 100 \tag{10.2}$$

where θ_1 (°C) is the inlet temperature, θ_2 (°C) the pre-heating temperature, θ_3 (°C) the pasteurisation temperature.

Sample problem 10.1
Raw whole milk at 7°C is to be pasteurised at 72°C in a plate heat exchanger at a rate of 5000 l h⁻¹ and then cooled to 4.5°C. The hot water is supplied at 7500 l h⁻¹ at 85°C and chilled water has a temperature of 2°C. Each heat exchanger plate has an available area of 0.79 m². The overall heat transfer coefficients are calculated as 2890 $\mathrm{W\,m^{-2}\,K^{-1}}$ in the heating section, 2750 $\mathrm{W\,m^{-2}\,K^{-1}}$ in the cooling section and 2700 $\mathrm{W\,m^{-2}\,K^{-1}}$ in the regeneration section (Chapter 1, Sample problem 1.4). 75% of the heat exchange is required to take place in the regeneration section. Calculate the number of plates required in each section. (Assume that the density of milk is 1030 kg m⁻³, the density of water is 958 kg m⁻³ at 85°C and 1000 kg m⁻³ at 2°C, the specific heat of water is constant at 4.2 kJ kg⁻¹K⁻¹ and the specific heat of milk is constant at 3.9 kJ kg⁻¹K).

Solution to sample problem 10.1
To calculate the number of plates in each section, 1 litre = 0.001 m³; therefore the volumetric flow rate of milk is 5/3600 = 1.39 × 10⁻³ m³ s⁻¹ and the volumetric flow rate of hot water is 7.5/3600 = 2.08 × 10⁻³ m³ s⁻¹. From equation (10.1),

> heat required to heat milk to 72°C
> $$= 1.39 \times 10^{-3} \times 1030 \times 3900(72 - 7)$$
> $$= 3.63 \times 10^5 \text{ W}$$

For the regeneration stage,

> heat supplied = 75% of 3.63 × 10⁵
> $$= 2.72 \times 10^5 \text{ W}$$

and

> temperature change of the milk = 75% of (72 − 7)
> $$= 48.75°C$$

Therefore the cold milk leaves the regeneration section at 48.75 + 7 = 55.75°C and the hot milk is cooled in the regeneration section to 72 − 48.75 = 23.25 °C. The temperature difference across the heat exchanger plates is 72 − 55.75 = 16.25°C. From equation (1.15) ($Q = UA(\theta_A - \theta_B)$),

$$A = \frac{2.72 \times 10^5}{2700 \times 16.25} = 6.2 \text{ m}^2$$

As each plate area is 0.79 m²,

$$\text{number of plates} = \frac{6.2}{0.79}$$
$$= 7.8 \approx 8$$

In the heating stage,

$$Q = 25\% \text{ of total heat supplied } = 3.63 \times 10^5 \times 0.25$$
$$= 9.1 \times 10^4 \text{ W}$$

From equation (10.1), for hot water,

$$\theta_A - \theta_B = \frac{9.1 \times 10^4}{2.08 \times 10^{-3} \times 958 \times 4200}$$
$$= 10.85°C$$
$$\approx 11°C$$

The temperature of the hot water leaving the heating section is $85 - 11 = 74°C$. The temperature of the milk entering heating section is $55.75°C$ and the temperature of the milk after heating is $72°C$.

From equation (1.16) (log mean temperature difference),

$$\Delta\theta_m = \frac{(74 - 55.75) - (85 - 72)}{\ln[74 - 55.75)/(85 - 72)]}$$
$$= 15.44°C$$

From equation (1.15),

$$A = \frac{9.1 \times 10^4}{2890 \times 15.44}$$
$$= 2.04 \text{ m}^2$$

Therefore,

$$\text{number of plates} = \frac{2.04}{0.79}$$
$$= 3$$

For the cooling stage, for milk, from equation (10.1),

$$Q = 1.39 \times 10^{-3} \times 1030 \times 3900(23.25 - 4.5)$$
$$= 1.046 \times 10^5 \text{ W}$$

From equation (1.16),

$$\Delta\theta_m = \frac{(23.25 - 4.5) - (4.5 - 2)}{\ln[(23.25 - 4.5)/(4.5 - 2)]}$$
$$= 8.06°C$$

From equation (1.15)

$$A = \frac{1.046 \times 10^5}{2750 \times 8.06}$$
$$= 4.72 \text{ m}^2$$

Therefore,

$$\text{number of plates} = \frac{4.72}{0.79}$$
$$= 6$$

The advantages of heat exchangers over in-bottle processing include

(1) more uniform heat treatment,
(2) simpler equipment and lower maintenance costs,
(3) lower space requirements and labour costs,
(4) greater flexibility for different products and
(5) greater control over pasteurisation conditions.

The capacity of the equipment varies according to the size and number of plates, up to 80 000 l h^{-1}.

Other types of heat exchanger (described in Chapter 12 in their application to evaporation) are also used for pasteurisation. In particular, the concentric tube heat exchanger is suitable for more viscous foods and is used with dairy products, mayonnaise, tomato ketchup and baby foods. It consists of a number of concentric stainless steel coils, each made from double- or triple-walled tube. Food passes through the tube, and heating or cooling water is recirculated through the tube walls. Liquid food is passed from one coil to the next for heating and cooling, and heat is regenerated to reduce energy costs.

Pasteurised food is immediately filled into cartons or bottles (Chapters 22 and 23) and sealed to prevent recontamination. Significant levels of spoilage can arise from post-pasteurisation contamination (PPC). Care with cleaning and hygiene is therefore necessary.

10.3 EFFECT ON FOODS

Pasteurisation is a relatively mild heat treatment and even when combined with other unit operations (for example irradiation (Chapter 8) and chilling (Chapter 18)) there are only minor changes to the nutritional and sensory characteristics of most foods. However, the shelf life of pasteurised foods is usually only extended by a few days or weeks compared with several months with the more severe heat sterilisation (Chapter 11).

10.3.1 Colour, flavour and aroma
In fruit juices the main cause of colour deterioration is enzymic browning by polyphenoloxidase. This is promoted by the presence of oxygen, and fruit juices are therefore routinely deaerated prior to pasteurisation. The difference between the whiteness of raw and that of pasteurised milk is due to homogenisation, and pasteurisation has no measurable effect. Other pigments in plant and animal products are also unaffected by pasteurisation.

A small loss of volatile aroma compounds during pasteurisation of juices causes a reduction in quality and may also unmask other 'cooked' flavours. Volatile recovery (Chapter 12) may be used to produce high quality juices but this is not routinely used. Loss of volatiles from raw milk removes a hay-like aroma and produces a blander product.

10.3.2 Vitamin loss
Changes to the nutritional value of a diet, as a result of processing foods, are described further in Chapter 1. In fruit juices, losses of vitamin C and carotene are minimised by deaeration. Changes to milk are confined to a 5% loss of serum proteins and small changes to the vitamin content (Table 10.2).

Changes to nutritional quality during storage of pasteurised milk are discussed by Schroder *et al.* (1985), Allen and Joseph (1985) and Harper (1976).

ACKNOWLEDGEMENTS

Grateful acknowledgement is made for information supplied by the following: Wincanton Engineering Ltd, Sherborne, Dorset DT9 3ND, UK; HRS Heat Exchangers Ltd, Watford, Hertfordshire WD1 2DW, UK; APV International Ltd, Crawley, West Sussex RH10 2QB, UK.

REFERENCES

Allen, J. C. and Joseph, G. (1985) Deterioration of pasteurized milk on storage. *J. Dairy Res.* **52** 469–487.
Anon. (1982) *Food Process Ind.* February 29–30, 32–33, 35–36.
Barclay, N. I., Potter, T. D. and Wiggins, A. L. (1984) Batch pasteurisation of liquid whole egg. *J. Food Technol.* **19** 605–613.

Brooks, J. (1962) *J. Hygiene*, **60** 145–151.

Chiozzotto,P. (1984) La pastorizzazione della birra: l'impiego del 'flash pastorizzatore', *Ind. bevande* October 403–412.

Ford, J. E., Porter, J. W. G., Thompson, S. Y., Toothill, J. and Edwards-Webb, J. (1969) Effects of UHT processing and of subsequent storage on the vitamin content of milk. *J. Dairy Res.* **36** 447–454.

Fricker, R. (1984) The flash pasteurisation of beer. *J. Inst. Brew.* **90** May–June 146–152.

Hammid-Samimi, M. H. and Swartzel, K. R. (1984) Pasteurization design criteria for production of extended shelf-life refrigerated liquid whole egg. *J. Food Process Preserv.* **8** 219–224.

Harper, W. (1976) In: W. Harper and C. Hall (eds.), *Dairy technology and engineering*. AVI, Westport, Connecticut, pp. 141–169, 572.

Lund, D. B. (1975) Heat processing. In: M. Karel, O. R. Fennema and D. B. Lund (eds.), *Principles of food science*, Part 2. Marcel Dekker, New York, pp. 31–92.

Schroder, M. J. A, Scott, K. J., Bland, M. A. and Bishop, D. R. (1985) Flavour and vitamin stability in pasteurized milk in polyethylene-coated cartons and in polyethylene bottles. *J. Soc. Dairy Technol.* **38** 48–52.

Wiggins, A. L. and Barclay, M. N. I. (1984) Back to batch for liquid egg. *Food Manuf.* September 69, 71.

11

Heat sterilisation

Heat sterilisation is the unit operation in which foods are heated at a sufficiently high temperature and for a sufficiently long time to destroy microbial and enzyme activity. As a result, sterilised foods have a shelf life in excess of six months. The severe heat treatment during in-container sterilisation produces substantial changes in nutritional and sensory qualities of foods. Developments in processing technology therefore aim to reduce the damage to nutrients and sensory components, by either reducing the time of processing in containers or processing foods before packaging (aseptic processing). The theory of thermal destruction of micro-organisms and the effect of heat on nutrients and sensory components of foods is described in Chapter 1. In this chapter the effects of microbial heat resistance on the design of heat sterilisation procedures and equipment are described, first for in-container heat sterilisation and then for ultrahigh-temperature (UHT) processes.

11.1 IN-CONTAINER STERILISATION

11.1.1 Theory

The length of time required to sterilise a food is influenced by

(1) the heat resistance of micro-organisms or enzymes likely to be present in the food,
(2) the heating (retorting) conditions,
(3) the pH of the food,
(4) the size of the container and
(5) the physical state of the food.

In order to determine the process time for a given food, it is necessary to have information on both the heat resistance of micro-organisms or enzymes and the rate of heat penetration into the food. The factors that influence heat resistance of micro-organisms or enzymes and their characterisation by D and z values are described in Chapter 1.

11.1.1.1 Heat resistance of micro-organisms

In low-acid foods (pH>4.5), *Clostridium botulinum* is the most dangerous heat resistant, spore forming, pathogen likely to be present. Under anaerobic conditions inside a sealed container it can grow to produce a potent exotoxin, and its destruction is therefore a *minimum* requirement of heat sterilisation. Normally, foods receive more than this minimum treatment as other more heat-resistant spoilage bacteria may also be present (Table 11.1). In more acidic foods (pH 4.5–3.7), other micro-

Table 11.1 — Heat resistance of some spore-forming bacteria used as a basis for heat sterilisation processes for low-acid foods

Micro-organism	z value (°C)	D_{121} value (min)	Typical foods
Thermophilic (35–55°C)			
Bacillus			
stearothermophilus	10	4.0	Vegetables, milk
Clostridium			
thermosaccharolyticum	7.2–10	3.0–4.0	Vegetables
Mesophilic (10–40°C)			
Clostridium			
sporogenes	8.8–11.1	0.8–1.5	Meats
Bacillus subtilis	4.1–7.2	0.5–0.76	Milk products
C. botulinum toxins A and B	5.5	0.1–1.3	Low-acid foods
Psychrophilic (−5–1.5°C)			
C. botulinum toxin E	10	3.0 (60°C)	Low-acid foods

Adapted from Lund (1975), Brennan *et al.* (1976) and Licciardello *et al.* (1967).

organisms (for example yeasts and fungi) or heat-resistant enzymes are used to establish processing times and temperatures. In acidic foods (pH<3.7), enzyme inactivation is the main reason for processing and heating conditions are less severe (sometimes referred to as *pasteurisation*).

Thermal destruction of micro-organisms takes place logarithmically (Chapter 1) and a sterile product cannot therefore be produced with certainty no matter how long the process time. However, the *probability* of survival of a single micro-organism can be predicted using details of the heat resistance of the micro-organism and the temperature and time of heating. This gives rise to a concept known as *commercial sterility*. For example a process that reduces cell numbers by eight decimal reductions (an $8D$ process), applied to a raw material which contains 10^5 spores per container would reduce microbial numbers to 10^{-3} per container, or one micro-organism in every thousand containers. Commercial sterility therefore means that the vast majority of containers are sterile but there is a probability that non-pathogenic cells survive the heat treatment in a pre-determined number of containers.

The level of survival is determined by the type of micro-organism that is expected to contaminate the raw material. A 12D process is used when *C. botulinum* is likely to be present, but in foods that contain more heat-resistant spoilage micro-organisms (Table 11.1), the application of a 12D process would result in overprocessing and excessive loss of quality. In practice a 5D or 8D process is therefore used to give the most economical level of food spoilage consistent with adequate food quality and safety. However, because of the lower heat resistance of *C. botulinum*, the probability of survival remains similar to that obtained in a 12D process. For these processes to operate successfully, the microbial load on raw materials must be kept at a low level by hygienic handling and preparation procedures (Chapter 2), and in some foods by blanching (Chapter 9). Any failure in these procedures would increase the initial numbers of cells and, because of the logarithmic rate of destruction, would increase the incidence of spoilage after processing. In canning factories, accelerated storage trials on randomly selected cans of food ensure that these levels of commercial sterility are maintained before foods are released for retail sale.

In addition to information on heat resistance, it is necessary to collect data describing the rate of heat penetration into the food in order to calculate the processing time needed for commercial sterility.

11.1.1.2 Rate of heat penetration
Heat is transferred from steam or pressurised water through the container and into the food. Generally the surface heat transfer coefficient (Chapter 1) is very high and is not a limiting factor in heat transfer. The following factors are important influences on the rate of heat penetration into a food:.

(1) *Type of product.* Liquid or particulate foods (for example peas in brine) in which natural convection currents are established heat faster than solid foods (for example meat pastes and corned beef) in which heat is transferred by conduction (Fig. 11.1). The low thermal conductivity of foods (Chapter 1) is a major limitation to heat transfer in conduction heating foods.

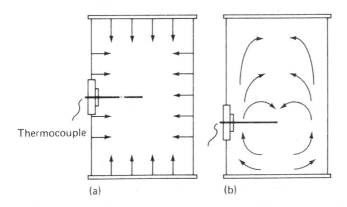

Fig. 11.1 — Heat transfer containers by (A) conduction and (B) convection.

(2) *Size of the container*. Heat penetration to the centre is faster in small containers than in large containers.
(3) *Agitation of the container*. End-over-end agitation (Fig. 11.2) and, to a lesser

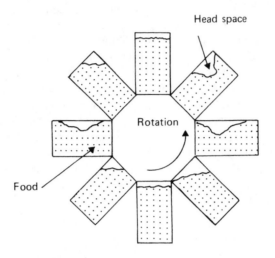

Fig. 11.2 — End-over-end agitation of containers. (After Hersom and Hulland (1980).)

extent, axial agitation increases the effectiveness of natural convection currents and thereby increases the rate of heat penetration in viscous or semi-solid foods (for example beans in tomato sauce).
(4) *Temperature of the retort*. A higher temperature difference between the food and the heating medium causes faster heat penetration.
(5) *Shape of the container*. Tall containers promote convection currents in convective heating foods.
(6) *Type of container*. Heat penetration is faster through metal than through glass or plastics owing to differences in thermal conductivity (Table 1.4).

The rate of heat penetration is measured by placing a thermocouple at the thermal centre of a container (the point of slowest heating) to record temperatures in the food during processing (it is assumed that all other points in the container receive more heat and are therefore adequately processed). In continuous sterilisers, self-contained miniature temperature recorders–transmitters are placed at the thermal centre of the container.

In cylindrical containers the thermal centre is at the geometric centre for conductive heating foods and approximately one third up from the base of the container for convective heating foods (Fig. 11.1). However, in convective heating, the exact position varies and should be found experimentally. A typical heat penetration curve is shown in Fig. 11.3. A broken heating curve occurs when a food is

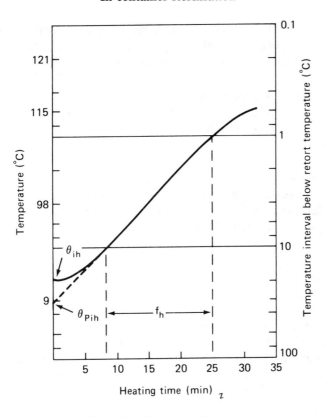

Fig. 11.3 — Heat penetration curve.

initially heated by convective heating but then undergoes a rapid transition to conductive heating (for example in foods which contain a high concentration of starch which undergoes a sol-to-gel transition).

The *F value* is used as a basis for comparing heat sterilisation procedures. It represents the total time–temperature combination received by a food and is quoted with suffixes indicating the retort temperature and the *z* value of the target micro-organism. For example, a process operating at 115°C based on a micro-organism with a *z* value of 10°C would be expressed as

$$F_{115}^{10}$$

The *F* value may also be thought of as the time needed to reduce microbial numbers by a multiple of the *D* value. It is found using

$$F = D(\log n_1 - \log n_2) \tag{11.1}$$

where n_1 is the initial number of micro-organisms and n_2 the final number of micro-organisms.

A reference F value F_0 is used to describe processes that operate at 121°C which are based on a micro-organism with a z value of 10°C. Typical F_0 values are 3–6 min for vegetables in brine, 4–5 min for cream soups and 12–15 min for meat in gravy.

11.1.1.3 Calculation of process times
Two methods are described in the following section. They are discussed in detail by Stumbo (1973) and Ball and Olson (1957) who also a describe a rapid method based on the use of nomograms.

11.1.1.3.1 Formula Method
This method enables rapid calculation of process times for different retort temperatures or container sizes, but is limited by the assumptions made about the nature of the heating process. The method is based on

$$B = f_h \log\left(\frac{j_h I_h}{g}\right) \tag{11.2}$$

where B (min) is the time of heating, f_h (min) is the time for the heat penetration curve to cover one logarithmic cycle and j_h is the thermal lag factor found by extrapolating the curve to find the pseudo-initial product temperature θ_{pih} (Fig. 11.3).

$$j_h = \frac{\theta_r - \theta_{pih}}{\theta_r - \theta_{ih}} \tag{11.3}$$

where I_h ($= \theta_r - \theta_{ih}$) (°C) is the difference between the retort temperature and the initial product temperature, g is the difference between the retort temperature and the final product temperature, θ_r is the retort temperature and θ_{ih} is the initial product temperature.

With the exception of g the above information can be found from a *heat penetration curve* (Fig. 11.3). The value of g is influenced by the following factors:

(1) the thermal death time of the micro-organism on which the process is based (Chapter 1),
(2) the slope f_h of the heating curve;
(3) the z value of the target micro-organism;
(4) the difference between the retort temperature and the temperature of the cooling water.

To take account of these variables, Ball (1923) developed the concept of comparing the F value at the retort temperature (denoted F_1) with a reference F value of 1 min at 121°C (denoted F). The thermal death time at the retort temperature is described by the symbol U and is related to the reference F value and F_1 using

$$U = FF_1 \tag{11.4}$$

If the reference F value is known, it is then possible to calculate U by consulting F_1 tables (Table 11.2). The value of g may then found from f_h/u and g tables (Table 11.3).

Table 11.2 – F_1 values for selected z values at retort temperatures below 121°C

121–θ_r	z value					
(°C)	4.4°C	6.7°C	8.9°C	10°C	11.1°C	12°C
5.6	17.78	6.813	4.217	3.594	3.162	2.848
6.1	23.71	8.254	4.870	4.084	3.548	3.162
6.7	31.62	10.00	5.623	4.642	3.981	3.511
7.2	42.17	12.12	6.494	5.275	4.467	3.899
7.8	56.23	14.68	7.499	5.995	5.012	4.329
8.3	74.99	17.78	8.660	6.813	5.623	4.806
8.9	100.0	21.54	10.00	7.743	6.310	5.337
9.4	133.4	26.10	11.55	8.799	7.079	5.926
10.0	177.8	31.62	13.34	10.00	7.943	6.579
10.6	237.1	38.31	15.40	11.36	8.913	7.305

Adapted from Stumbo (1973).

There is one further factor which influences the value of g: point 4 above (the difference between the retort temperature and the temperature of the cooling water). In conductive heating foods, there is a lag before cooling water begins to lower the product temperature, and this results in a significant amount of heating after the steam has been turned off. It is therefore necessary to include a cooling lag factor j_c. This is defined as the time taken for the cooling curve to cover one logarithmic cycle, and is analagous to j_h, the heating lag factor. The cooling portion of the heat penetration curve is extrapolated to find the pseudo-initial product temperature θ_{pic} at the start of cooling, in a similar way to θ_{pih}, and j_c is found using

$$j_c = \frac{\theta_c - \theta_{pic}}{\theta_c - \theta_{ic}} \tag{11.5}$$

where θ_c (°C) is the cooling-water temperature and θ_{ic} (°C) the actual initial product temperature at the start of cooling. When using Table 11.3 the appropriate value of j_c can then be used to find g.

Finally, in batch retorts, only 40% of the time taken for the retort to reach operating temperature (the come-up time l) is at a sufficiently high temperature to destroy micro-organisms. The calculated time B of heating is therefore adjusted to give the corrected processing time:

Table 11.3 — Selected f_h/U and g values when $z = 10$ and $j_c = 0.4$–2.0

	Values of g for the following j_c values					
f_h/U	0.40	0.80	1.00	1.40	1.80	2.00
0.50	0.0411	0.0474	0.0506	0.0570	0.0602	0.0665
0.60	0.0870	0.102	0.109	0.123	0.138	0.145
0.70	0.150	0.176	0.189	0.215	0.241	0.255
0.80	0.226	0.267	0.287	0.328	0.369	0.390
0.90	0.313	0.371	0.400	0.458	0.516	0.545
1.00	0.408	0.485	0.523	0.600	0.676	0.715
2.00	1.53	1.80	1.93	2.21	2.48	2.61
3.00	2.63	3.05	3.26	3.68	4.10	4.31
4.00	3.61	4.14	4.41	4.94	5.48	5.75
5.00	4.44	5.08	5.40	6.03	6.67	6.99
10.0	7.17	8.24	8.78	9.86	10.93	11.47
20.0	9.83	11.55	12.40	14.11	14.97	16.68
30.0	11.5	13.6	14.6	16.8	18.9	19.9
40.0	12.8	15.1	16.3	18.7	21.1	22.3
50.0	13.8	16.4	17.7	20.3	22.8	24.1
100.0	17.6	20.8	22.3	25.4	28.5	30.1
500.0	26.0	30.6	32.9	37.5	42.1	44.4

Adapted from Stumbo (1973).

$$\text{process time} = B - 0.4l \tag{11.6}$$

More complex formulae are necessary to calculate processing times where the product displays a broken heating curve.

Sample problem 11.1
A low-acid food is heated at 115°C using a process based on $F^{10}_{121.1} = 7\,\text{min}$. From heat penetration data the following information was obtained: $\theta_{ih} = 78°C$, $f_h = 20\,\text{min}$, $j_c = 1.80$ $f_c = 20\,\text{min}$, $\theta_{pih} = 41°C$ and $\theta_{ih} = 74°C$. The retort took 11 min to reach process temperature. Calculate the processing time.

Solution to sample problem 11.1

From equation (11.3),

$$j_h = \frac{115 - 41}{115 - 74}$$

$$= 2.00$$

and

$$I_h = 115 - 78$$

$$= 37°C$$

From Table 11.2 (for $121.1 - \theta_r = 6.1$ and $z = 10°C$),

$$F_1 = 4.084$$

From equation (11.4),

$$U = 7 \times 4.084$$
$$= 28.59,$$
$$\frac{f_h}{U} = \frac{20}{28.59}$$
$$= 0.7$$

From Table 11.3 (for $f_h/U = 0.7$, $j_c = 1.80$),

$$g = 0.241°C$$

(that is the thermal centre reaches 114.76°C). From equation (11.2),

$$B = 20 \log\left(\frac{2.00 \times 37}{0.241}\right)$$
$$= 49.7 \text{ min.}$$

From equation (11.6),

$$\text{process time} = 49.7 - (0.4 \times 11)$$
$$= 45.3 \text{ min}$$

This gives the process time for $F_0 = 7$ min. If the process time had been given, it would be possible to reverse the calculation to find F_0.

11.1.1.3.2   Improved general (graphical) method
Different combinations of temperature and time have the same lethal effect on micro-organisms (Chapter 1). The thermal death time (TDT) curve (Fig. 1.10) can be expressed by the following equation:

$$TDT = 10^{121 - \theta/z} \tag{11.7}$$

where $\theta(°C)$ is the temperature of heating. For example, if a product is processed at 115°C and the most heat-resistant micro-organism has a z value of 10°C,

$$TDT = 10^{(121 - 115/10)}$$
$$= 3.9 \text{ min}$$

3.9 min at 115°C therefore has an equivalent lethality to 1 min at 121°C.

The reciprocal of the TDT is known as the *lethal rate*. A process that is characterised by $F_0 = 1$ (that is 1 min at 121°C) is said to result in *unit sterility*. The lethal rate is therefore the fraction of unit sterility achieved in 1 min at the temperature of heating ($1/3.9 = 0.251$ in the above example). As the lethal rate depends on the z value of the micro-organism on which the process is based and the product temperature, tables of lethal rate values are available. Table 11.4 is for $z = 10$, the value for most heat-resistant spores. This method is preferable in practical situations for the determination of processing times.

Table 11.4 — Lethal rates for $z = 10°C$

Temperature (°C)	Lethal rate (min[a])	Temperature (°C)	Lethal rate (min)
90	0.001	108	0.049
92	0.001	110	0.077
94	0.002	112	0.123
96	0.003	114	0.195
98	0.005	116	0.308
100	0.008	118	0.489
102	0.012	120	0.774
104	0.019	122	1.227
106	0.031	124	1.945

[a] At 121°C per minute at θ_r.
Adapted from Stumbo (1973).

Sample problem 11.2
A convective heating food is sterilised at 115°C to give $F_0 = 7$ min. The come-up time of retort is 11 min. Calculate the processing time from the following heat penetration

data. Cooling started after 60 min.

Process time (min)	Temperature (°C)	Process time (min)	Temperature (°C)
0	95	35	115.5
5	101	40	115.5
10	108.5	45	115.5
15	111.5	50	115.6
20	113	55	115.6
25	115.5	60	115.6
30	115.5	65	100

Solution to sample problem 11.2
Lethal rates can be found at selected points on a heat penetration curve either by constructing a TDT curve and taking the reciprocal of TDTs (from Fig. 1.10) at the selected temperatures, or by consulting the appropriate lethal rate table (Table 11.4). Lethal rates are then plotted against processing time (Fig. 11.4) and the area

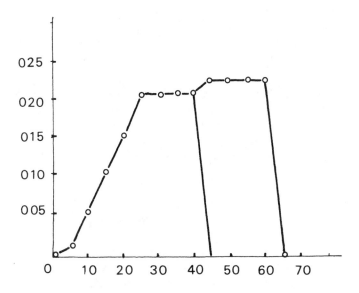

Fig. 11.4 — Lethal rate curve.

under the curve is measured by counting squares or using a planimeter.

Process time (min)	Lethal rate	Process time (min)	Lethal rate
0	0.002	35	0.218
5	0.01	40	0.218
10	0.055	45	0.224
15	0.109	50	0.224
20	0.155	55	0.224
25	0.218	60	0.224
30	0.218	65	0.005

For convection heating foods, the lethal rate curve is used to find the point in the process when heating should cease. A line is drawn parallel to the cooling part of the curve so that the total area enclosed by the curve is equal to the required lethality. The area under the curve ACE is $100.5 \, cm^2$. As $1 \, cm^2$ is 0.1 min at 121°C, the area ACE represents 10.05 min at 121°C. Therefore by reducing the area under the curve ABD to $70 \, cm^2$ ($F = 7 \, min$), the process time is 45 min. Thus the process time required for $F_0 = 7 \, min$ is 45 min.

With conduction heating foods the temperature at the centre of the container may continue to rise after cooling commences, because of the low rate of heat transfer. For these foods it is necessary to determine lethality after a number of trials in which heating is stopped at different times.

11.1.1.4　Exhausting
Exhausting removes air from containers before sealing. This reduces strain on the container which would otherwise result from expansion of the air during processing. The removal of oxygen in the air also prevents internal corrosion and oxidative changes in some foods. Steam is used to replace air and on cooling forms a partial vacuum in the head space. Containers are exhausted by

(1) hot filling the food into the container,
(2) cold filling the food and then heating the container and contents to 80–95°C with the lid partially sealed (clinched),
(3) mechanical removal of the air using a vacuum pump or
(4) steam flow closing, where a blast of steam (at 34–41.5 kPa) carries air away from the surface of the food immediately before the container is sealed.

The last method is best suited to liquid foods where there is little air trapped in the product and the surface is flat and does not interrupt the flow of steam. Hot filling is commonly used as it is also a useful pre-heating stage which reduces processing times.

11.1.1.5   Closing
The shelf life of sterilised foods depends in part on the ability of the container to isolate the food completely from the environment. The four major groups of heat-sterilisable containers are

(1) metal cans,
(2) glass jars or bottles,
(3) flexible pouches,
(4) rigid trays.

The materials are described in Chapter 22 and methods of filling and sealing are described in Chapter 23.

11.1.1.6   Retorting (heat processing)

11.1.1.6.1   By saturated steam
Latent heat is transferred to food when saturated steam condenses on the outside of the container. If air is trapped inside the retort, it forms an insulating boundary film (Chapter 1) around the cans which prevents the steam from condensing and causes underprocessing of the food. It also produces a lower temperature than that obtained with saturated steam (Appendix D). It is therefore important that all air is removed from the retort by the incoming steam using a procedure known as *venting*.

After sterilisation the containers are cooled with water. Steam is rapidly condensed in the retort, but the food cools more slowly and the pressure in the containers remains high. An overpressure of air is therefore used to prevent strain on the container seams (pressure cooling). When the food has cooled to below 100°C, the overpressure of air is removed and cooling continues to approximately 40°C. At this temperature, moisture on the container dries to prevent surface corrosion, and label adhesives set more rapidly.

Rigid polymer trays (Chapter 22) heat more rapidly than conventional containers owing to their thinner cross-section. Trays are processed in conventional equipment using saturated steam at 121°C.

11.1.1.6.2   By hot water
Foods are processed in glass containers or flexible pouches under hot water with an overpressure of air. Glass containers are thicker than metal cans to provide adequate strength, and this, together with lower thermal conductivity of glass (Table 1.4), results in slower heat penetration and longer processing times than for cans and there is a higher risk of thermal shock to the container. Foods in flexible pouches heat more rapidly owing to the thin cross-section of the container. This enables savings in energy and causes minimum overheating near the container wall. Liquid or semi-liquid foods are often processed horizontally to ensure that the thickness of food is constant across the pouch. Vertical packs promote better circulation of hot water in the retort, but special frames are necessary to prevent the pouches from bulging at the bottom, which would alter the rate of heat penetration and hence the degree of

sterilisation achieved. Although pouches are popular in the Far East and for containing military rations, they have yet to achieve large-scale commercial use in Europe and USA.

11.1.1.6.3 By flames
Sterilisation at atmospheric pressure using direct flame heating of spinning cans is described by Casimir (1975) and Beauvais *et al.* (1961). High rates of heat transfer are possible at flame temperatures of 1770°C. The consequent short processing times produce foods of high quality and reduce energy consumption by 20% compared with conventional canning. Each can is scanned by an infrared controller after processing, instead of the usual sampling procedures. The amount of heat given off from the can is a measure of heat received and, if the emitted heat is insufficient, the can is rejected. No brine or syrup is used in the can, and more product can therefore be packed into a given size of can, or smaller cans may be used. This reduces transport costs by 20–30%. In addition, any added salt or sugar goes directly into the product and therefore reduces the amount needed to achieve the desired sweetness or saltiness. However, high internal pressures (275 kPa at 130°C) limit the application of this method to small cans. It is used for example to process mushrooms, green beans, tomatoes, pears and cubed beef.

11.1.2 Equipment
Sterilising retorts may be batch or continuous in operation. The general advantages and limitations of batch and continuous equipment are described in Chapter 1. Batch retorts may be vertical or horizontal; the latter are easier to load and unload and have facilities for agitating containers, but require more floor space. Fig. 11.5 shows commercial vertical retorts in operation.

Continuous retorts (Fig. 11.6) permit close control over the processing conditions and hence produce more uniform products. They produce gradual changes in pressure inside cans, and therefore less strain on the can seams compared with batch equipment. The main disadvantages include a high in-process stock which would be lost if a breakdown occurred, and problems with metal corrosion and contamination by thermophilic bacteria if adequate preventative measures are not taken. Nair (1964) describes four types of hydrostatic steriliser in detail. In practice, large continuous sterilisers are used for the production of high-volume products where there is no requirement to change the container size or processing conditions regularly.

Computer control of retorts is described by Bown (1985, 1987), Hayakawa (1977) and Holdsworth (1983). Selected process variables including the temperature of the raw material, the temperature of the cooling water and the temperature of steam, the time of processing, and heating and cooling rates are monitored. This information is then processed by a computer to calculate the accumulated lethality, and to control air, steam and water flow rates, to produce the required degree of sterility in the product with minimum energy expenditure. Further details of automatic process control are given in Chapter 24.

Fig. 11.5 — Vertical retorts in operation. (Courtesy of Unilever Ltd)

11.2 ULTRAHIGH-TEMPERATURE PROCESSES

A major problem with in-container sterilisation of solid or viscous foods is the low rate of heat penetration to the thermal centre. This causes damage to nutritional and sensory characteristics of food near the walls of the container, and long processing times (hence low productivity). Methods of increasing the rate of heat transfer, including the use of thinner profile containers and agitation are described in section 11.1.1.2. An increase in retort temperature would also reduce processing times and protect nutritional and sensory qualities, but this is usually impractical; the higher pressures would require substantially stronger and hence more expensive containers and processing equipment.

Higher temperatures for a shorter time are possible if the product is sterilised before it is filled into pre-sterilised containers in a sterile atmosphere. This forms the basis of UHT processing (also termed *aseptic processing*). It is used to sterilise a wide range of liquid foods (for example milk, fruit juices and concentrates, cream, yoghurt, wine, salad dressing, egg and ice cream) and foods which contain small discrete particles (for example cottage cheese, babyfoods, tomato products, fruit and vegetables, soups and rice desserts). Processes for larger-particulate foods are currently under development (Manvell, 1987). The high quality of UHT foods competes with irradiated and chilled foods (Chapters 8 and 18), but UHT has an important additional advantage of a shelf life of at least six months without refrigeration.

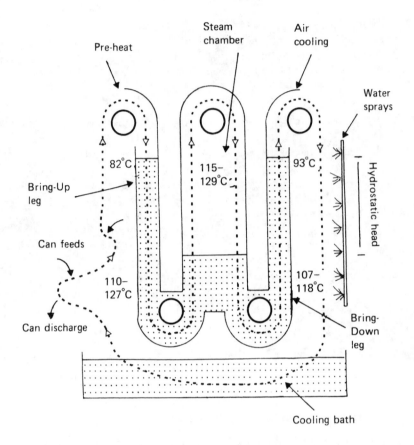

Fig. 11.6 — Continuous hydrostatic steriliser.

A second important advantage of UHT processing compared with canning, is that the processing conditions are independent of container size. For example, conventional retorting of A2 cans of vegetable soup requires 70 min at 121°C to achieve an F_0 value of 7 min, followed by 50 min cooling. Aseptic processing in a scraped-surface heat exchanger at 140°C for 5 s gives an F_0 value of 9 min. Increasing the can size to A10 increases the processing time to 218 min, whereas with aseptic processing the sterilisation time is the same. This permits the use of very large containers (for example 1 t aseptic bags of tomato purée, used as an ingredient for other manufacturing processes). Other advantages include cheaper packaging, high productivity as a result of automation, and energy efficiency. UHT is an economical method of milk processing because in contrast with pasteurised milk, distribution does not require a highly developed refrigerated transport network and there is therefore a larger distribution radius.

The main limitations of UHT processing are the cost and complexity of the plant, which arises from the necessity to sterilise packaging materials, associated pipework and tanks, the maintenance of sterile air and surfaces in filling machines, and the higher skill levels required by operators and maintenance staff (Rose, 1986).

11.2.1 Theory

For a given increase in temperature, the rate of destruction of micro-organisms increases faster than the rate of destruction of nutrients and sensory components (Fig. 11.7 and Chapter 1). Calculation of processing times is sometimes based on enzyme denaturation because at temperatures above 132–143°C some enzymes have higher heat resistance than contaminating micro-organisms. In contrast with in-container sterilisation where the most lethal effect frequently occurs at the end of the heating stage and the beginning of the cooling stage, UHT processes heat the food rapidly to a holding temperature and the major part of the lethality accumulates at a constant temperature. The sterilising value is calculated by multiplying the lethal rate at the holding temperature by the holding time. The come-up time and cooling periods are very short and in most cases are treated as a safety factor. The criteria for UHT processing are however the same as for canning, that is the attainment of commercial sterility.

11.2.2 Processing

Food is heated in relatively thin layers in a continuous heat exchanger with close control over the sterilisation temperature and holding time. The sterilised product is cooled in a second heat exchanger, or in a vacuum chamber if deaeration is also required. Containers are not required to withstand sterilisation conditions, and laminated cartons (Chapter 22) are therefore widely used. They have considerable economic advantages compared with cans and bottles, in both the cost of the pack and the transport and storage costs. Cartons are pre-sterilised with hydrogen peroxide, and filling machines are enclosed and maintained in a sterile condition by ultraviolet light and filtered air. A positive air pressure is maintained in the filling machine to prevent entry of contaminants (Chapter 23).

The process is successfully applied to liquid and small-particulate foods but problems remain with larger pieces of solid food. The major difficulties are

(1) enzyme inactivation at the centre of the pieces of food causes overcooking of the surfaces, thus limiting particle sizes,
(2) agitation is necessary to improve the rate of heat transfer and to aid temperature distribution, but this causes damage to the product,
(3) until recently there was a lack of suitable equipment for processing and filling,
(4) settling of solids is a problem if the equipment has a holding tube.

In (4) this causes uncontrolled and overlong holding times and variable proportions of solids in the filled product, (Hersom, 1984).

11.2.3 Equipment

A theoretically ideal UHT process would heat the product instantly to the required temperature, hold it at that temperature to achieve sterility and cool it instantly to filling temperature. In practice the degree to which this is achieved depends in part on the sophistication of control and hence the cost of equipment, and secondly on the properties of the food (for example viscosity, presence of particles, heat sensitivity and tendency to form deposits on hot surfaces). The equipment used for UHT processing has the following characteristics:

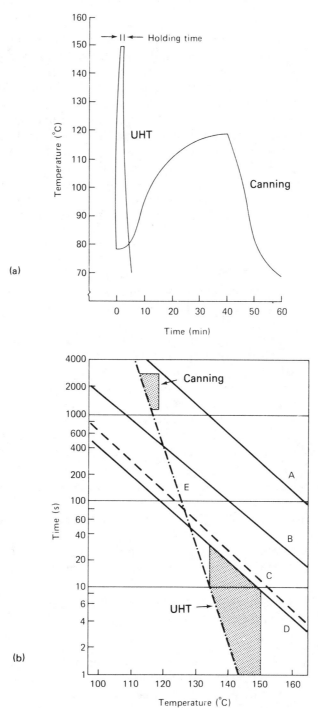

Fig. 11.7 — (a) Time–temperature conditions for UHT and canning; (b) rates of microbial and nutrient destruction in UHT processing: line a, 40% thiamin; line b, 10% thiamin; line c, 1% lysine; line d, 3% thiamin; line e, microbial. (After Killeit (1986).)

(1) operation above 132°C;
(2) exposure of a relatively small volume of product to a large surface area for heat transfer;
(3) maintenance of turbulence in the product as it passes over the heating surface;
(4) use of pumps to give a constant delivery of product against the pressure in the heat exchanger;
(5) constant cleaning of the heating surfaces to maintain high rates of heat transfer and to reduce burning-on of the product.

Equipment is classified according to the method of heating into

(1) direct systems (steam injection and steam infusion),
(2) indirect systems (plate heat exchangers, tubular heat exchangers and scraped-surface heat exchangers),
(3) other systems (microwave, dielectric and induction heating).

Indirect systems are automatically cleaned in place after 3–4 h of operation to remove accumulated deposits. The cleaning programme does not involve loss of sterile conditions, and processing resumes immediately afterwards. The chemical composition and formation of deposits during UHT treatment of milk are described by Lalande *et al.* (1984).

11.2.3.1 *Steam injection (uperisation) and steam infusion*
Each of these methods is used to intimately combine the product with potable steam. In steam injection potable (culinary) steam at a pressure of 965 kPa is introduced into a pre-heated liquid product (76°C) in a finely divided form by a steam injector, to heat the product to 150°C rapidly. After a suitable holding period (for example 2.5 s) the product is flash cooled in a vacuum chamber to 70°C, and condensed steam and volatiles in the product are removed. The moisture content of the product therefore returns to approximately the same level as the raw material. The main advantages of this system are as follows.

(1) It is one of the fastest methods of heating and the fastest method of cooling and is therefore suitable for more heat-sensitive foods.
(2) Volatile removal is an advantage with some foods (for example milk).

However

(1) The method is only suitable for low-viscosity products.
(2) There is relatively poor control over processing conditions.
(3) There may be difficulty in maintaining sterility in low-pressure parts of the equipment.
(4) There is a requirement for potable steam which is more expensive to produce.
(5) Regeneration of energy is less than 50% compared with more than 90% in indirect systems.

(6) Flexibility for changing to different types of product is low.

Further details are described by Burton and Perkins (1970) and Zadow (1975).
In steam infusion the food is sprayed in a free-falling film into high-pressure
(450 kPa) steam in a pressurised vessel (Fig. 11.8). It is heated to 142–146°C in 0.3 s,

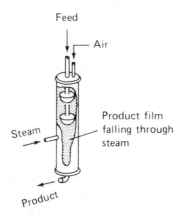

Fig. 11.8 — UHT sterilisation by steam infusion. (Courtesy of Crepaco Inc.)

and is held for 3 s in a holding tube before flash cooling in a vacuum chamber to
65–70°C. Heat from the flash cooling is used to pre-heat the feed material. A
microcomputer is used to control temperature, pressure, level, flow rate, valve
operation and the cleaning sequence, at production rates of up to 9000 kg h^{-1}
(Swientek, 1983). It has advantages over injection methods because the liquid does
not contact hotter surfaces and burning-on is therefore eliminated. Other advantages
include

(1) almost instantaneous heating of the food to the temperature of the steam, and
    very rapid cooling which results in high retention of sensory characteristics and
    nutritional properties,
(2) greater control over processing conditions than steam injection,
(3) lower risk of localised overheating of the product and
(4) the method is more suitable for higher viscosity foods than steam injection is.

The main disadvantages, in addition to the disadvantages of steam injection, are
blockage of the spray nozzles and separation of components in some foods.

11.2.3.2 *Plate heat exchangers*
The application of this type of equipment is described in detail for pasteurisation
(Chapter 10). In UHT sterilisation, it has a number of limitations which are due to
the higher temperatures and pressures involved. For example

(1) operating pressures are limited by the plate gaskets to approximately 700 kPa,
(2) liquid velocities at this relatively low available pressure drops are low $(1.5\text{--}2\,\mathrm{m\,s}^{-1})$,
(3) the low flow rates cause uneven heating and solids deposits on the plates with some foods, and this requires more frequent cleaning,
(4) gaskets are susceptible to damage by high temperatures and caustic cleaning fluids, and are therefore replaced more regularly than in pasteurising applications,
(5) the equipment is limited to low viscosity liquids and
(6) careful initial sterilisation of the large mass of metal in the plate stack is necessary to allow uniform expansion of the metal, and prevent distortion and damage to the plates or seals.

However, plate heat exchangers also have a number of advantages: they are

(1) relatively inexpensive,
(2) economical in floor space and water consumption,
(3) efficient in energy use (more than 90% energy regeneration),
(4) flexible in production rate, by varying the number of plates and
(5) easily inspected by opening the plate stack.

11.2.3.3 Tubular heat exchangers
Shell-and-tube heat exchangers are described in Chapter 12, in their application to evaporation by boiling. The advantages of this type of equipment for UHT processing include

(1) few seals, which permit easier cleaning and maintenance of aseptic conditions,
(2) operation at higher pressures (7000–10000 kPa) and hence higher liquid flow rates $(6\,\mathrm{m\,s}^{-1})$ than plate heat exchangers and
(3) turbulent flow at the walls of the tubes due to the higher flow rates, and hence more uniform heat transfer and less product deposition.

The main disadvantages are as follows.

(1) It is difficult to inspect heat transfer surfaces for food deposits.
(2) It is limited to relatively low-viscosity foods (up to $1.5\,\mathrm{N\,s\,m}^{-2}$),
(3) A complete shutdown is needed when any one component of the system fails, unlike plate heat exchangers where plates can be replaced,
(4) Low flexibility to changes in production capacity; larger-diameter tubes cannot be used because higher pressures are needed to maintain the liquid velocity, and large-diameter pipes have a lower resistance to pressure. An increase in production rate therefore requires duplication of the equipment.

The concentric tube heat exchanger is a combination of both plate and tubular designs (Fig. 11.9(a)). Counter-current flow and helical corrugations are used to

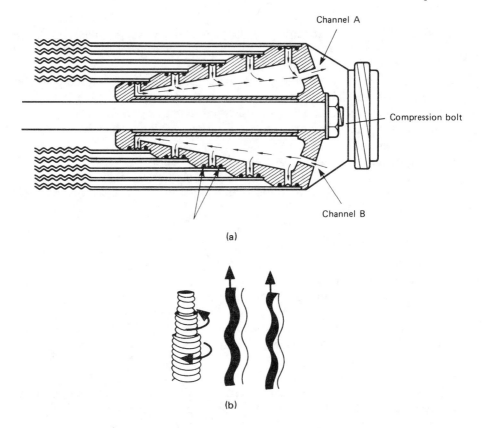

Fig. 11.9 — Concentric tube heat exchanger: (a) cross-section; (b) effect of rotation of tubes.
(Courtesy of HRS Heat Exchangers Ltd.)

generate turbulence and hence to increase the rate of heat transfer. This equipment is able to operate at high pressures (up to 2000 kPa) with viscous liquids. Turbulence can be further increased at the expense of throughput or maximum particle size, by altering the relative positions of tubes (Fig. 11.9(b)).

11.2.3.4   *Scraped-surface heat exchangers*
The main advantages of this equipment for UHT processing are its suitability for viscous foods and particulates (less than 1 cm), and its flexibility for different products by changing the geometry of the rotor assembly. However, it has a very high capital cost and heat recovery is not possible. It is used in the preparation of fruit sauces and fruit bases for yoghurts and pies. Similar types of equipment are also used for freezing (Chapter 19), for evaporation by boiling (Chapter 12, Fig. 12.8) and for the continuous production of margarines and butter (Chapter 3).

11.2.3.5   *Jupiter double-cone heat exchanger*
This equipment combines indirect heating in a jacketed double cone, with direct heating by steam or superheated liquor. It is the most advanced system yet developed

for processing large (2–2.5 cm) particles of food. In a sequence of microprocessor-controlled operations, solid pieces of food are fed into the double-cone vessel, which is then rotated slowly (4–12 rev min^{-1}) on a horizontal axis (Fig. 11.10). Steam at

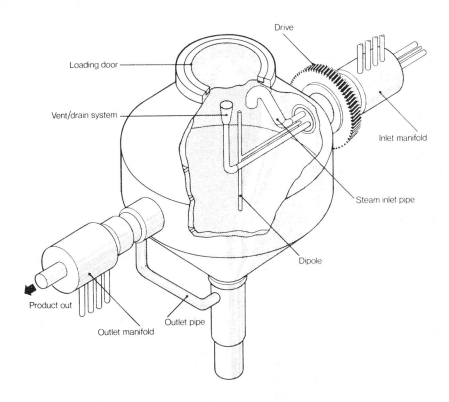

Fig. 11.10 — Double-cone heat exchanger for UHT sterilization of particulate foods.
(Courtesy of APV Ltd.)

206 kPa is introduced and the product is tumbled through the steam. Steam in the jacket is at the same temperature to prevent the food from burning onto the cone. Liquor is added during sterilisation to prevent damage to the solids by the tumbling action. Sterilisation times are for example 2–4 min to achieve $F_0 = 10$ for carrot cubes, depending on their size. After sterilisation the product is rapidly cooled with cold water and sterile air, and the condensate–water–stock is removed. The liquid portion of the product is sterilised separately in a plate or tubular system and added to the solids. The cone then acts as a mixer. The blended solids–liquids are discharged to an aseptic filler using an overpressure of sterile air. This avoids pumping the softened product and further reduces damage to the food. Cooking liquor from the solids is used to make sauce, to top up containers or to inject into solids during subsequent processing.

Other sterilising systems which are undergoing development (but are not necessarily aseptic systems) are Multi-therm, Achilles, and ohmic heating. In the former two the food is heated by a combination of hot liquid and microwave energy. Further details are given in Chapter 17. In ohmic heating a conducting fluid is heated directly by electrical energy. An alternating current is passed from electrodes, through the fluid which is contained in a non-conducting pipe. There is sufficient resistance in the fluid for energy losses to occur, and the fluid heats evenly. Conversion efficiencies from electrical energy to heat of greater than 90% are claimed, and particulate feeds may be processed without shearing forces associated with some other types of heat exchangers.

11.3   EFFECT ON FOODS

The purpose of heat sterilisation is to extend the shelf life of foods while minimising the changes in nutritive value and eating quality. Differences between the D and z values of micro-organisms, enzymes and sensory or nutritional components of foods are exploited to optimise processes for the retention of nutritional and sensory qualities (Chapter 1). Preceding sections describe how this is achieved in practice by a reduction in size or cross-sectional area of containers, by agitation during processing or by aseptic processing. In this section the changes to foods caused by traditional canning techniques are compared with those caused by UHT processing.

11.3.1   Colour

The time–temperature combinations used in canning have a substantial effect on most naturally occurring pigments in foods. For example in meats the red oxymyoglobin pigment is converted to brown metmyoglobin, and purplish myoglobin is converted to red–brown myohaemichromogen. Maillard browning and caramelisation also contribute to the colour of sterilised meats. However, this is an acceptable change in cooked meats. Sodium nitrite and sodium nitrate are added to some meat products to reduce the risk of growth of *C. botulinum*. The resulting red–pink coloration is due to nitric oxide myoglobin and metmyoglobin nitrite.

In fruits and vegetables, chlorophyll is converted to pheophytin, carotenoids are isomerised from 5,6-epoxides to less intensely coloured 5,8-epoxides, and anthocyanins are degraded to brown pigments. The changes to natural pigments are described further in Chapter 1. Loss of colour is often corrected using permitted synthetic colours (section B.1). Discolouration of canned foods during storage occurs for example when iron or tin react with anthocyanins to form a purple pigment, or when colourless leucoanthocyanins form pink anthocyanin complexes in some varieties of pears and quinces. In sterilised milk slight colour changes are due to caramelisation, Maillard browning and changes in the reflectivity of casein micelles.

In UHT processing, meat pigments change colour, but there is little caramelisation or Maillard browning. Carotenes and betanin are virtually unaffected, and chlorophyll and anthocyanins are better retained. There are no such readily detectable changes to the colour of milk.

11.3.2   Flavour and aroma

In canned meats there are complex changes (for example pyrolysis, deamination and decarboxylation of amino acids, degradation, Maillard reactions and caramelisation of carbohydrates to furfural and hydroxymethylfurfural, and oxidation and decarboxylation of lipids). Interactions between these components produce more than 600 flavour compounds in ten chemical classes. In fruits and vegetables, changes are due to complex reactions which involve the degradation, recombination and volatilisation of aldehydes, ketones, sugars, lactones, amino acids and organic acids. In milk the development of a cooked flavour is due to denaturation of whey proteins to form hydrogen sulphide and the formation of lactones and methyl ketones from lipids. In aseptically sterilised foods the changes are again less severe, and the natural flavours of milk, fruit juices and vegetables are better retained. Changes to milk are discussed in detail by Burton, (1984).

11.3.3 Texture or viscosity

In canned meats, changes in texture are caused by coagulation and a loss of water-holding capacity of proteins, which produces shrinkage and stiffening of muscle tissues. Softening is caused by hydrolysis of collagen, solubilisation of the resulting gelatin, and melting and dispersion of fats through the product. Polyphosphates (section B.2) are added to some products to bind water. This increases the tenderness of the product and reduces shrinkage. In fruits and vegetables, softening is caused by hydrolysis of pectic materials, gelatinisation of starches and partial solubilisation of hemicelluloses, combined with a loss of cell turgor. Calcium salts may be added to blancher water (Chapter 9), or to brine or syrup, to form insoluble calcium pectate and thus to increase the firmness of the canned product. Different salts are needed for different types of fruit (for example calcium hydroxide for cherries, calcium chloride for tomatoes and calcium lactate for apples) owing to differences in the proportion of demethylated pectin in each product. Small changes in the viscosity of milk are caused by modification of K-casein, leading to an increased sensitivity to calcium precipitation and coagulation.

In aseptically processed milk and fruit juices the viscosity is unchanged. The texture of solid fruit and vegetable pieces is softer than the unprocessed food due to solubilisation of pectic materials and a loss of cell turgor but is considerably firmer than canned products. Meat pieces are yet to be processed commercially. The relatively long time required for collagen hydrolysis and the relatively low temperature needed to prevent toughening of meat fibres are conditions found in canning but not in UHT processing. Toughening of meat is therefore likely under UHT conditions. The texture of meat purées is determined by size reduction and blending operations (Chapters 3 and 4) and is not substantially affected by aseptic processing.

11.3.4 Nutritive value

The importance of changes caused by processing on the nutritional value of a diet are discussed in Chapter 1. Canning causes the hydrolysis of carbohydrates and lipids, but these nutrients remain available and the nutritive value of the food is not affected. Proteins are coagulated and, in canned meats, losses of amino acids are 10–20%. Reductions in lysine content are proportional to the severity of heating but rarely exceed 25%. The loss of tryptophan and, to a lesser extent, methionine, reduces the biological value of the proteins by 6–9%. Vitamin losses (Table 11.5) are mostly confined to thiamin (50–75%) and pantothenic acid (20–35%). In canned fruits and vegetables, significant losses may occur in all water-soluble vitamins,

Table 11.5 — Loss of vitamins in canned and bottled foods
(including losses due to preparation and blanching)

Food	Carotene		Thiamin		Riboflavin		Niacin		Vitamin C		Panto-thenic acid	Vitamin B₆	Folacin	Biotin
Low-acid foods														
Carrots	0–9	(6)	67		38–60		32		75		54	80	59	40
Beef	—		67		100		100		—		—	—	—	—
Green beans	22–52		62		54–63		40		79		61	50	57	—
Mackerel	4		60		39		29		—		—	46	—	—
Milk	0		35		0		0		50–90		0	50	10–20	—
Mushrooms	—		80		46		52		33		54	—	84	54
Peas	0–30	(3)	75	(84)	47	(67)	71	(91)	67	(80)	80	69	59	78
Potatoes	—		56		44		56		28		—	59	—	—
Salmon	9		73		0		0		—		58	57	—	—
Spinach	0–32	(9)	80	(84)	45	(47)	50	(50)	72	(79)	78	75	35	67
Tomatoes	0	(2)	17	(22)	25	(59)	0	(1)	26	(26)	30	10	54	55
Acid foods														
Apple	0–4		31		48		—		74		15	0		
Cherries (sweet)	41		57		64		46		68		—	6		
Peaches	65	(70)	49	(57)	39		39	(38)	56	(58)	71	21		
Pears	—		45		45		0		73		69	18		
Pineapple	25		7	(10)	30		0		57	(57)	12	—		

The values in parentheses indicate the vitamin loss after storage for 12 months at 10–15°C.
Adapted from De Ritter (1982), Rolls (1982), Burger (1982) and March (1982).

particularly ascorbic acid. However, there are large variations owing to differences in the types of food, the presence of residual oxygen in the container, and methods of preparation (peeling and slicing) or blanching (Chapters 2 and 9). In some foods, vitamins are transfered into the brine or syrup, which is also consumed. There is thus a smaller nutritional loss.

Sterilised soya–meat products may show an increase in nutritional value owing to an unidentified factor that decreases the stability of the trypsin inhibitor in soy beans. Aseptically processed meat and vegetable products lose thiamin and pyridoxine (Table 11.6) but other vitamins are largely unaffected. There are negligible vitamin losses in aseptically processed milk (Table 11.7) and lipids, carbohydrates and minerals are virtually unaffected. Riboflavin, pantothenic acid, biotin, nicotinic acid, vitamin B₆ are unaffected. The effect of processing conditions on vitamin content of canned foods are discussed in detail by Lamb *et al.* (1982), and changes in sterilised milk are discussed by Burton (1984). Nutrient losses also occur during periods of prolonged storage, and these should also be considered when assessing the importance of sterilised foods in the diet.

ACKNOWLEDGEMENTS

Grateful acknowledgement is made for information supplied by the following: HRS Heat Exchangers Ltd, Watford, Hertfordshire WD1 2DW, UK; APV International

Table 11.6 — Effect of aseptic and conventional sterilisation on losses of thiamin and pyridoxine

	Thiamin loss (%)		Pyridoxine loss (%)	
Product	UHT	Conventional	UHT	Conventional
Strained lima beans	15.8	40.3	9.5	10.1
Strained beef	9.2	21.6	4.1	2.9
Concentrated tomato juice	0	2.8	0	0

From Everson *et al*. (1964).

Table 11.7 — Changes in nutritive value of milk after UHT and in-bottle sterilisation

	Loss (%) on processing	
Nutrient	UHT	In-bottle
Thiamin	10	35
Ascorbic acid	25	90
Vitamin B_{12}	10	90
Folic acid	10	50
Pantothenic acid	0	0
Biotin	0	0
β-carotene	0	0
Pyridoxine	10	50
Vitamin D	0	0
Whey proteins (denaturation)	12–40[a]	87
Lysine	—	10
Cystine	—	13
Biological value	—	6

[a] Direct UHT at 135°C for 2 s (12.3%), indirect UHT at 135°C for 2 s (40.3%).
Adapted from Rolls (1982), Kieseker (1972) and Ford *et al*. (1969).

Ltd, Crawley, West Sussex RH10 2QB, UK; Unilever Ltd, London EC4P 4BQ, UK; Crepaco International, 1040 Brussels, Belgium; A Johnson and Co. Ltd, Wokingham, Berkshire RG11 2PU, UK.

REFERENCES

Ball, C. O. (1923) Thermal process time for canned food. *Bull. Natl Res. Council* **7** No. 37.

Ball, C. O., and Olson, F. C. W. (1957) *Sterilisation in food technology*. McGraw-Hill, New York.

Beauvais, J., Thomas, G., and Cheftel, H. (1961) *Food Technol.* **15** 5–9.

Bown, G. (1985) *Retort control — the application of a microcomputer based control system*, Technical Memorandum, No. 391. Campden Food Preservation Research Association, Chipping Campden, Gloucestershire GL55 6LD, UK.

Bown, G. (1987) Process control microcomputers in the food industry. In: S. Thorne (ed.), *Developments in food preservation*, Vol. 4. Elsevier Applied Science, Barking, Essex, pp. 35–85.

Brennan, J. G., Butters, J. R., Cowell, N. D., and Lilly, A.E.V. (1976) *Food engineering operations*, 2nd edn, Applied Science, London. pp. 251–285.

Burger, I. H. (1982) Effect of processing on nutritive value of food: meat and meat products. In: M. Rechcigl (ed.), *Handbook on the nutritive value of processed foods*, Vol. 1. CRC Press, Boca Raton, Florida, pp. 323–336.

Burton, H. (1984) Reviews of the progress of dairy science: the bacteriological, chemical, biochemical and physical changes that occur in milk at temperatures of 100–150 °C. *J. Dairy Res.* **51** 341–363.

Burton, H., and Perkins, A. G. (1970) Comparison of milks processed by the direct and indirect methods of UHT sterilization, Part 1. *J. Dairy Res.* **37** 209–218.

Casimir, D. J. (1975) Flame sterilisation. *CSIRO Food Res. Q.* **35** 34–39.

De Ritter, E. (1982) Effect of processing on nutritive content of food: vitamins. In: M. Rechcigl (ed.), *Handbook on the nutritive value of processed foods*, Vol. 1, CRC Press, Boca Raton, Florida. pp. 473-510.

Everson, G. J., *et al.* (1964) Aseptic canning of foods, Part II, Thiamine retention as influenced by processing method, storage time and temperature, and type of container; Part III, Pyridoxine retention, as influenced by processing method, storage time and temperature, and type of container. *Food Technol.* **18** 84–88.

Feliciotti, E., and Esselen, W. B. (1957) *Food Technol.* **11** 77–84.

Ford, J. E., Porter, J. W. G., Thompson, S. Y., Toothill, J., and Edwards-Webb, J. (1969) Effects of UHT processing and of subsequent storage on the vitamin content of milk. *J. Dairy Res.* **36** 447–454.

Hayakawa, K.-I. (1977) Mathematical methods for estimating proper thermal processes and their computer implementation. *Adv. Food Res.* **23** 76–141.

Hersom, A., and Hulland, E. (1980) *Canned Foods*, 7th edn. Churchill Livingstone, Edinburgh, pp. 122-258.

Hersom, A. C. (1984) Problems and possible solutions to aseptic processing of low acid particulate food products. *Proceedings of the Second International Conference and Exhibition on Aseptic Packaging* (*Aseptipak'84*), 4–6 April 1984, *Princeton, New Jersey*. Schotland Business Research Inc.

Holdsworth, S. D. (1983) Developments in the control of sterilising retorts. *Proc. Biochem*. October, 24–28.

Killeit, U. (1986) The stability of vitamins. *Food Eur.* March–April 21–24.

Kieseker, F. G. (1972) *Specialist courses for the food industry, AIFST–CSIRO* **2** 54.

Lalande, M., Tissier, J., and Corrieu, G. (1984) Fouling of a plate heat exchanger used in ultra-high-temperature sterilisation of milk. *J. Dairy Res.* **51** 557–568.

Lamb, F. C., Farrow, R. P., and Elkins, E. R. (1982) Effect of processing on nutritive value of food: canning. In: M. Rechcigl (ed.), *Handbook on the nutritive value of processed foods* Vol. 1. CRC Press, Boca Raton, Florida. pp. 11–30.

Licciardello, J. J., Ribich, C. A., Nickerson, J. T. R., and Goldblith, S. A. (1967) *Appl. Microbiol.* **15** 344.

Lund, D. B. (1975) Heat processing. In: M. Karel, O. Fennema and D. Lund (eds), *Principles of food science* Vol. 2, *Principles of food preservation*. Marcel Dekker, New York. pp. 32–86.

Manvell, C. (1987) Sterilisation of food particulates — an investigation of the APV Jupiter system. *Food Sci. Technol. Today* **1** 106–109.

March, B. E. (1982) Effect of processing on nutritive value of food: fish. In: M. Rechcigl (ed.), *Handbook on the nutritive value of processed foods*, Vol. 1. CRC Press, Boca Raton, Florida. pp. 363-381.

Nair, J. H. (1964) Hydrostatic sterilizers. *Food Engng.* December 37–42.

Rolls, B. A. (1982) Effect of processing on nutritive value of food: milk and milk products. In: M. Rechcigl (ed.), *Handbook on the nutritive value of processed foods*, Vol. 1. CRC Press, Boca Raton, Florida. pp. 383–399.

Rose, D. (1986) Aseptics: the problems with 'low acids'. *Food Manuf.* October 61–62, 64.

Stumbo, C. R. (1973) *Thermobacteriology in food processing*, 2nd edn. Academic Press, New York.

Swientek, R. J. (1983) Free falling film UHT system 'sterilises' milk products with minimal flavour change. *Food Process* **44** 114–116.

Zadow, J. G. (1975) Ultra heat treatment of dairy products. *CSIRO Food Res. Q.* **35** 41–47.

12

Evaporation

Evaporation is the partial removal of water from liquid foods by boiling. Separation is achieved by exploiting the difference in volatility between water and solutes. It contrasts with other methods of concentration (for example membrane concentration (Chapter 6)), in which water is removed by exploiting a difference in rate of diffusion at room temperature, and freeze concentration (Chapter 20) in which a difference in freezing point is employed. Most concentrated foods are further processed before consumption.

The main functions of evaporation are as follows:

(1) It is used to pre-concentrate foods (for example fruit juice, milk and coffee) prior to drying, freezing or sterilisation and hence to reduce their weight and volume. This saves energy in subsequent operations and reduces storage, transport and distribution costs.
(2) Evaporation increases the solids content of a food (for example jam and molasses) and hence preserves it by a reduction in water activity (Chapter 1).
(3) There is greater convenience for the consumer (for example fruit drinks for dilution, soups, tomato or garlic pastes) or for the manufacturer (for example liquid pectin, fruit concentrates for use in ice cream or baked goods).
(4) Evaporation changes the flavour and/or colour of a food (for example caramelised syrups for use in baked goods and sugar confectionery).

12.1 THEORY

During evaporation, latent heat is transferred from the heating medium (steam) to the food, to raise the temperature to its boiling point (sensible heat). The vapour pressure rises and latent heat of vaporisation is supplied by the steam to form bubbles of vapour in the liquid. The vapour is then removed from the surface of the boiling liquid. The rate of evaporation is determined by both the rate of heat transfer into the food and the rate of mass transfer of vapour from the food (Chapter 1). These processes are represented schematically in Fig. 12.1.

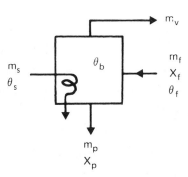

Fig. 12.1 — Steady-state operation of an evaporator: m_f (kg s^{-1}), mass transfer rate of feed liquor; m_p (kg s^{-1}), mass transfer rate of product; X_f, solids fraction of feed; X_p, solids fractions of product, m_v (kg s^{-1}), mass transfer rate of vapour produced; m_s (kg s^{-1}), mass transfer rate of steam used; θ_f (°C), initial feed temperature; θ_b (°C), boiling temperature of food; θ_s (°C), temperature of steam.

12.1.1 Heat and mass transfer

Mass and heat balances (Chapter 1) for the evaporator are used to calculate the degree of concentration, energy usage and processing times. The mass balance states that the mass of feed entering the evaporator equals the mass of product and vapour removed from the evaporator; for the water component, this is given by

$$m_f(1 - X_f) = m_p(1 - X_p) + m_v \tag{12.1}$$

For solutes, the mass of solids entering the evaporator equals the mass of solids leaving the evaporator:

$$m_f X_f = m_p X_p \tag{12.2}$$

The total mass balance is $m_f = m_p + m_v$ \hfill (12.3)

Assuming that there are negligible heat losses from the evaporator, the heat balance states that the amount of heat given up by the condensing steam equals the amount of heat used to raise the feed temperature to boiling point and then to boil off the vapour:

$$\begin{aligned} Q &= m_s \lambda_s \\ &= m_f c_p(\theta_b - \theta_f) + m_v \lambda_v \end{aligned} \tag{12.4}$$

c (J kg^{-1}°C^{-1}), specific heat capacity of feed liquor; λ_s (J kg^{-1}), latent heat of condensing steam, λ_v (J kg^{-1}), latent heat of vaporisation of water that is

$$\begin{matrix} \text{Heat supplied} \\ \text{by steam} \end{matrix} = \text{Sensible heat} + \begin{matrix} \text{Latent heat} \\ \text{of vaporisation} \end{matrix}$$

The rate of heat transfer across evaporator walls and boundary films (Chapter 1) is found using equation (1.15). ($Q = UA(\theta_s - \theta_b)$).

Sample Problem 12.1
A single-effect, vertical short-tube evaporator (section 12.2.1.2) is to be used to concentrate syrup from 10% solids to 40% solids at a rate of 100 kg h^{-1}. The feed enters at 15°C and is evaporated under a reduced pressure of 47.4 kPa (at 80°C). Steam is supplied at 169 kPa (115°C). Assuming that the boiling point remains constant and that there are no heat losses, calculate the quantity of steam used per hour and the number of tubes required. (Additional data: the specific heat of syrup is constant at 3.960 kJ kg^{-1}K^{-1}, the specific heat of water is 4.186 kJ kg^{-1}K^{-1}, the latent heat of vaporisation of the syrup is 2309 kJ kg^{-1}, the overall heat transfer coefficient is 2600 W m^{-2}K^{-1} and the latent heat of steam is 2217 kJ kg^{-1} at 115°C.)

Solution to sample problem 12.1

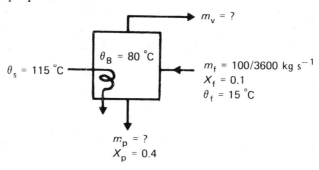

To find the quantity of steam used per hour, we find that, from equation (12.2),

$$\frac{100}{3600} \times 0.1 = m_p \times 0.4$$
$$m_p = 0.0069 \text{ kg s}^{-1}$$

From equation (12.1),

$$\frac{100}{3600} (1 - 0.1) = 0.0069 \, (1 - 0.4) + m_v$$
$$m_v = 0.0209 \text{ kg s}^{-1}$$

From a mass balance, we find the following table.

	mass (kg s^{-1})		
	Solids	Liquid	Total
Feed	0.00278	0.025	0.0278
Product	0.00276	0.00414	0.0069
Vapour			0.0209

From equation (12.4), the heat required for evaporation is

$$Q = 0.0278 \times 3960 \ (80 - 15) + 0.0209 \times 2309 \times 10^3$$
$$= 5.54 \times 10^4 \text{ J s}^{-1}$$

Now $\dfrac{\text{heat supplied by 1 kg}}{\text{of steam per second}}$ = latent heat + $\dfrac{\text{sensible heat}}{\text{on cooling to 80°C}}$

$$= 2217 \times 10^3 + 1 \times 4186 \times (115 - 80)$$
$$= 2.36 \times 10^6 \text{ J s}^{-1}$$

On the assumption of a heat balance in which the heat supplied by the steam equals the heat required for evaporation,

mass of steam $= \dfrac{5.54 \times 10^4}{2.36 \times 10^6}$
$$= 0.023 \text{ kg s}^{-1}$$
$$= 84.5 \text{ kg h}^{-1}$$

To find the number of tubes, we have from equation (1.15), ($Q = UA\Delta t$) that

$$5.54 \times 10^4 = 2600 \times A \ (115 - 80)$$

Therefore

$$A = 0.61 \text{ m}^2$$

Now

area of one tube $= 0.025 \times 1.55 \times 3.142$
$$= 0.122 \text{ m}^2$$

Thus,

$$\text{number of tubes} = \frac{0.61}{0.122}$$
$$= 5$$

Related problems are given in Chapter 1 (Sample problems 1.4 and 1.5).

12.1.2 Factors influencing the rate of heat transfer
The following factors influence the rate of heat transfer and hence determine processing times and the quality of concentrated products:

(1) *Temperature difference between the steam and boiling liquid.* A higher temperature difference is obtained by evaporation under reduced pressure (which lowers the boiling point of the food). In commercial evaporators the boiling point is not reduced below 40°C, because of the high costs of vacuum generation and the extra strength required in the processing equipment. The temperature difference becomes smaller as foods become more concentrated, owing to elevation of the boiling point. The rate of heat transfer therefore falls as evaporation proceeds. The boiling points of a solution at different pressures can be found using a *Duhring plot* (Fig. 12.2). In large evaporators, the boiling point of liquid

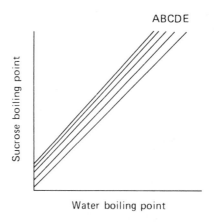

Fig. 12.2 — Duhring plot for sucrose for various sucrose concentrations per 100 g of water; line A, 1000 g; line B, 800 g; C, 600 g; line D, 400 g; line E, 200 g.

at the base may be slightly raised as a result of increased pressure from the weight of liquid above (the hydrostatic head). In such cases the boiling point is measured half-way up the evaporator for use in processing calculations.

(2) *Deposits on heat transfer surfaces.* The 'fouling' of evaporator surfaces reduces the rate of heat transfer. It is related to the temperature difference between the food and the heated surface and to the consistency and chemical composition of

the food. For example, denaturation of proteins or deposition of polysaccharides causes the food to burn onto hot surfaces. It is reduced in some types of equipment by continuously removing food from the evaporator walls. Metal corrosion may occur on the steam side of evaporation equipment, but the effects are reduced in commercial operation by anti-corrosion chemicals, treatments or surfaces. Both types of deposit are described in detail by Pulido (1984).

(3) *Boundary films* (Chapter 1). A film of stationary liquid at the evaporator wall is often the main resistance to heat transfer. The thickness of the boundary film is reduced by promoting convection currents within the food or by mechanically induced turbulence (section 12.2.2). The viscosity of many foods increases as concentration proceeds. This reduces the Reynolds number (Chapter 1) and hence reduces the rate of heat transfer. In addition, more viscous foods are in contact with hot surfaces for longer periods and, as a result, suffer greater heat damage.

12.1.3 Factors influencing the economics of evaporation

The main factors that influence the economics of evaporation are loss of concentrate and energy expenditure. Product losses are caused by

(1) *foaming*, due to proteins and carbohydrates in the food, which reduce the rate of heat transfer and cause inefficient separation of vapour and concentrate, and
(2) *entrainment*, in which a fine mist of concentrate is produced during the violent boiling, and is carried over in the vapour.

Most designs of equipment include *disengagement spaces* or separators to minimise entrainment.

A substantial amount of energy is needed to remove water from foods by boiling (2257 kJ per kilogram of water evaporated at 100°C). The economics of evaporation are therefore substantially improved by correct design and operation of equipment to minimise the various resistances to heat transfer (Chapter 1). Three methods are used to reduce energy consumption; each re-uses the heat contained in vapours produced from the boiling food. They are as follows.

(1) *Vapour recompression*, in which the pressure (and therefore the temperature) of vapour is increased, using a mechanical compressor or Venturi-type steam jet. The resulting high pressure steam is re-used as a heating medium.
(2) *preheating*, in which either vapour is used to heat the incoming feed liquor or the water used to raise steam in a boiler.
(3) *multiple effect evaporation* in which several evaporators (or 'effects') are connected together. Vapour from one effect is used directly as the heating medium in the next. However, the vapour can only be used to boil liquids at a lower boiling temperature. The effects must therefore have progressively lower pressures in order to maintain the temperature difference between the feed and the heating medium.

The number of effects used in a multiple effect system is determined by the savings in energy consumption (Table 12.1) compared with the higher capital investment required, and the provision of increasingly higher vacua in successive effects (Rumsey *et al*, 1984). In the majority of applications, three to six effects are used (Fig. 12.3) but up to nine effects have been reported (Anon, 1981).

Fig. 12.3 — Commercial falling-film evaporators. (Courtesy of APV Ltd.).

Table 12.1 — Steam consumption with vapour recompression and multiple-effect evaporation

| Number of effects | Steam consumption (kg per kg of water evaporated) | |
	Without vapour recompression	With vapour recompression
1	1.1	0.6
2	0.6	0.4
3	0.4	0.3

From Mannheim and Passy (1974).

Different arrangements of multiple effect evaporators are shown in Fig. 12.4 using triple-effect evaporation as an example. The relative advantages and limitations of each arrangement are described in Table 12.2.

Table 12.2 — Advantages and limitations of various methods of multiple-effect evaporation

Arrangement of effects	Advantages	Limitations
Forward feed	Least expensive, simple to operate, no feed pumps required between effects, lower temperatures with subsequent effects and therefore less risk of heat damage to more viscous product.	Reduced heat transfer rate as the feed becomes more viscous, rate of evaporation falls with each effect, best quality steam used on initial feed which is easiest to evaporate. Feed must be introduced at boiling point to prevent loss of economy (if steam supplies sensible heat, less vapour is available for subsequent effects).
Reverse feed	No feed pump initially, best-quality steam used on the most difficult material to concentrate, better economy and heat transfer rate as effects are not subject to variation in feed temperature and feed meets hotter surfaces as it becomes more concentrated thus partly offsetting increase in viscosity	Interstage pumps necessary, higher risk of heat damage to viscous products as liquor moves more slowly over hotter surfaces, risk of fouling.
Mixed feed	Simplicity of forward feed and economy of backward feed, useful for very viscous foods	More complex and expensive
Parallel	For crystal production, allows greater control over crystallisation and prevents the need to pump crystal slurries	Most complex and expensive of the arrangements, extraction pumps required for each effect

Adapted from Brennan *et al.* (1976).

12.2 EQUIPMENT

Evaporators consist of

(1) a heat exchanger (termed a *calandria*) which transfers heat from steam to the food,
(2) a means of separating the vapours produced and
(3) a mechanical or steam ejector vacuum pump.

Mechanical pumps have lower operating costs but higher capital costs than steam ejector pumps. The selection of an evaporator should include the following considerations:

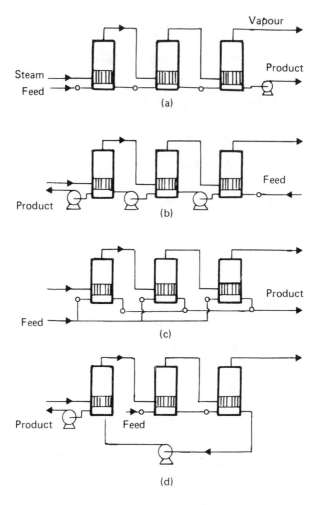

Fig. 12.4 — Arrangement of effects in multiple-effect evaporation: (a) forward; (b) reverse; (c) parallel; (d) mixed. (After Brennan *et al.* (1976).)

(1) operating capacity (as kilograms of water removed per hour),
(2) degree of concentration required (as percentage of dry solids in the product),
(3) heat sensitivity of the product in relation to the residence time and temperature of evaporation,
(4) the requirement for volatile recovery facilities,
(5) ease of cleaning,
(6) reliability and simplicity of operation,
(7) size of the evaporator in relation to its capacity and
(8) capital and operating costs in relation to capacity and product quality (Mannheim and Passy, 1974).

Ideally an evaporator should selectively remove water without changing the solute composition, so that the original product is obtained on dilution. This is approached in some equipment but, the closer to the ideal that is achieved, the higher the cost. As with other unit operations the selection of a particular method is therefore a compromise between the cost of production and the quality required in the product. Sophisticated computer-controlled evaporators (for example Anon. (1986) and the thermally accelerated short-time evaporator (TASTE) (Kennedy *et al*, 1983)) are used if an adequate return on investment is possible owing to the higher product quality. In some applications it may be more cost effective to combine two types of evaporator, for example initial concentration in an external calandria evaporator followed by a falling-film evaporator as the second effect. The majority of evaporator designs operate continuously but batch boiling pans are used for the preparation of small quantities of materials, or in applications where flexibility is required for frequent changes of product. The advantages and limitations of batch and continuous operation are described in Chapter 1.

12.2.1 Natural circulation evaporators
12.2.1.1   Open- or closed-pan evaporators
These consist of a hemispherical pan heated directly by gas or electrical resistance wires or heated indirectly by steam passed through internal tubes or an external jacket. They are fitted with a lid for vacuum operation and a stirrer or paddle (Chapter 3) to increase the rate of heat transfer and to prevent food from burning onto the pan. They have relatively low rates of heat transfer (Table 12.3) and low energy efficiencies, and they cause damage to heat-sensitive foods. However, they have low capital costs, are easy to construct and maintain and are flexible for applications where frequent changes of product are likely, or when used for relatively low or variable production rates. They have therefore found wide application in the preparation of ingredients such as sauces and gravies or in the manufacture of jam and other preserves (for example Darrington, 1982).

12.2.1.2   Short-tube evaporators
This type of equipment is an example of a *tube-and-shell heat exchanger*. It is also used in pasteurisation (Chapter 10), heat sterilisation (Chapter 11) and freezing (Chapter 19). It consists of a vessel (or *shell*) which contains a (vertical, or less commonly horizontal) bundle of tubes. The feed liquor is heated by steam condensing on the outside of the tubes. Liquor rises through the tubes, boils and recirculates through a central *downcomer*. The vertical arrangement of tubes promotes natural convection currents and therefore higher rates of heat transfer (Fig. 12.5). In some designs the tubes are fitted as a 'basket' which is easily removed for cleaning. These evaporators have low construction and maintenance costs, high flexibility and higher rates of heat transfer than open or closed pans, when used with relatively low-viscosity liquids (Table 12.3). They are generally unsuited to high-viscosity liquors as there is poor circulation of liquor and a high risk that the food burns onto the tube walls, with consequent problems of heat damage, low rates of heat transfer and difficulty in cleaning. They are widely used for concentrating syrups, salt and fruit juices.

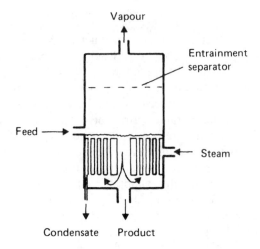

Fig. 12.5 — Vertical short-tube evaporator. (After Karel (1975).)

12.2.1.3 Long-tube evaporators

These evaporators consist of a vertical bundle of tubes, each up to 5 cm in diameter, contained within a steam shell 3–15 m high. Liquor is heated almost to boiling point before entering the evaporator. It is then further heated inside the tubes and boiling commences. The expansion of steam forces a thin film of rapidly concentrating liquor up the walls of each tube (Fig. 12.6). The concentrate is separated from the vapour

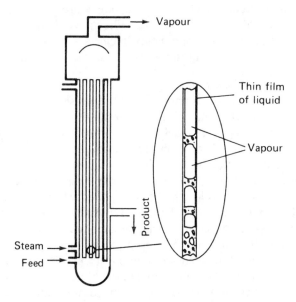

Fig. 12.6 — Climbing-film evaporator.

and removed from the evaporator, passed to subsequent effects in a multiple-effect system, or recirculated. Vapour is re-used in multiple-effect or vapour recompression systems (section 12.1.3).

For low-viscosity (up to approximately 0.1 N s m^{-2}) foods (for example milk), the thin film of liquor is forced up the evaporator tubes and this arrangement is therefore known as a *climbing-film evaporator*. For more viscous foods, or those that are very heat sensitive, the feed is introduced at the top of the tube bundle. The force of gravity supplements the forces arising from expansion of the steam, to produce very high liquor flow rates (up to 200 m s^{-1} at the end of 12 m tubes). This type of equipment is known as a *falling-film evaporator* and has found widespread use for a variety of products (for example yeast extracts, fruit juices (Anon., 1981) and starch processing). Forward-feed, multiple-effect systems, capable of evaporating 45 000 l of milk per hour, have been described (Anon., 1986). Both types of long-tube evaporator are characterised by

(1) short residence times,
(2) high heat transfer coefficients (Table 12.3) and
(3) efficient energy use (0.3–0.4 kg of steam per kilogram of water evaporated in multiple-effect systems).

12.2.1.4   External calandria evaporators
These are tube-and-shell heat exchangers which are, fitted with an external pipe for recirculation of the product. In this way, convection currents are established to produce relatively high rates of heat transfer. The calandria is easily accessible for cleaning. They are suitable for concentrating heat-sensitive foods, including dairy products and meat extracts, when operated under partial vacuum.

12.2.2   Forced circulation evaporators
In forced-circulation evaporators a pump or scraper assembly moves the liquor, usually in thin layers, and thus maintains high heat transfer rates and short residence times (Table 12.3). This also results in more compact equipment and higher production rates but increases both the capital and the operating costs of the equipment.

12.2.2.1   Plate evaporators
Plate evaporators are similar in construction to the heat exchangers used for pasteurisation and ultrahigh-temperature (UHT) sterilisation (Chapters 10 and 11). However, in this case the heating medium is steam and the climbing- and falling-film principle is used to concentrate liquids in the spaces between plates (section 12.2.1.3). Feed liquor enters at the base of each climbing film section, boils and rises to the top of the plates. It then enters a falling-film section where boiling continues. The number of climbing- or falling-film sections fitted within a single machine depends on the production rate and degree of concentration required. The mixture of vapour and concentrate is separated outside the evaporator, and the vapour may be re-used in vapour recompression or multiple-effect systems.

Despite the high capital investment, these types of evaporator have high rates of heat transfer, short residence times and high energy efficiencies (Table 12.3). They are compact, capable of high throughputs and easily dismantled for maintenance and inspection. They are more suitable for liquors of higher viscosity (0.3–0.4 N s m^{-2}) than long-tube evaporators are, because the food is pumped through the plate stack. They are widely used for concentrating heat-sensitive foods, including yeast extracts, dairy products and meat extracts.

12.2.2.2 Expanding-flow evaporator

This evaporator uses similar principles to the plate evaporator but has a stack of inverted cones instead of a series of plates. It is similar in appearance to the Centri-therm evaporator (Fig. 12.7). Feed liquor flows to alternate spaces between the

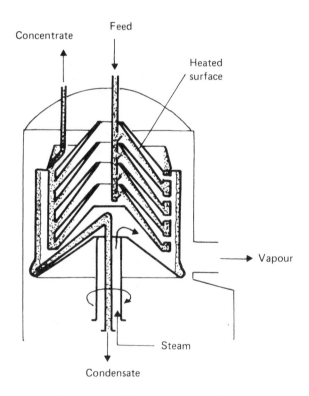

Fig. 12.7 — Centri-term evaporator. (After Mannheim and Passy (1974).)

cones from a central shaft and evaporates as it passes up through channels of increasing flow area (hence the name of the equipment). The vapour–concentrate mixture leaves the cone assembly tangentially and is separated by a special design of shell which induces a cyclone effect. Steam is fed down alternate channels. The reduction in flow area along each channel maintains a high film coefficient for the condensing steam. This evaporator has a number of advantages including compactness, short residence times and a high degree of flexibility achieved by changing the number of cones.

12.2.2.3 Mechanical (or agitated) thin-film evaporators

Scraped- or wiped-surface evaporators are characterised by differences in the thickness of the film of food being processed. Wiped-film evaporators have a film thickness of approximately 0.25 mm whereas in thin-film evaporators it is up to 1.25 mm. Both types consist of a steam jacket surrounding a high-speed rotor, fitted with short blades along its length (Fig 12.8). The design is similar to a scraped-surface

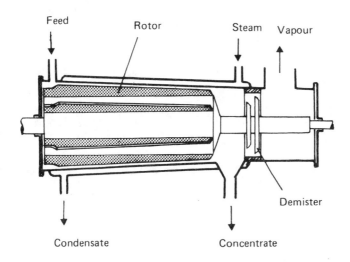

Fig. 12.8 — Mechanical thin film evaporator. (After Leniger and Beverloo (1975).)

aseptic steriliser (Chapter 11). Feed liquor is introduced between the rotor and the heated surface. Evaporation takes place rapidly as a thin film of liquor is swept through the machine by the rotor blades. The blades keep the film violently agitated and thus promote high rates of heat transfer and prevent the product from burning onto the hot surface (Anon., 1981). The residence time of the liquor is adjusted between 0.5 s and 100 s depending on the type of food and the degree of concentration required.

This type of equipment is highly suited to viscous (up to 20 N s m^{-2}) heat-sensitive foods or to those that are liable to foam or foul evaporator surfaces (for example fruit pulps and juices, tomato paste, meat extracts, honey, cocoa mass, coffee and dairy products). However, the capital costs are high owing to the precise alignment required between the rotor and wall. Operating costs are also high as only single effects are possible, which reduces the throughput and gives poor steam economy. It is therefore used for 'finishing' highly viscous products after concentration in other equipment. In this case the volume of food is smaller, there is less water to be removed and benefits of economy are fewer, but the product is valuable and there is a substantial risk of heat damage.

A second design of mechanical thin film evaporator is the *Centri-therm evaporator* (Fig. 12.7) which, although similar in appearance to the expanding flow evaporator (section 12.2.2.2), operates using a different principle. Here, liquor is fed from a central pipe to the undersides of rotating hollow cones. It immediately spreads out to form a layer approximately 0.1 mm thick. Steam condenses on the inside of each cone, and heat is conducted rapidly through the thin metal to evaporate the liquor. In contrast with the expanding-flow evaporator, in which liquid is moved by pressure of vapour, the Centri-therm employs a centrifugal force (750–3010 N) to move the liquor rapidly across the heated surface of the cone. Residence times are 0.6–1.6 s (Lewicki and Kowalczyk, 1980), even with concentrated liquors (up to 20 N s m^{-2}). Very high overall heat transfer coefficients (OHTCs) and short residence times are possible (Table 12.3). This is due in part to the thin layers of liquor but also to the droplets of condensed steam which are flung from the rotating cones as fast as they are formed. There is therefore no boundary film of condensate to impede heat transfer. The equipment produces a concentrate which, when rediluted, has sensory and nutritional qualities that are virtually unchanged from those of the feed material. It is used for coffee and tea extracts, meat extract, fruit juices (Fischer *et al.*, 1983) and enzymes for use in food processing.

Table 12.3 — Comparison of residence times and heat transfer coefficients in selected evaporators

Type of evaporator	Number of stages	Residence time (approximate)	OHTC (W m^{-2} K^{-1})	
			Low viscosity	High viscosity
Open or vacuum pan	Single	30 min to several hours	500–1000	<500
Vertical short tube	Single	—	570–2800	—
Climbing film	Single	10–60 sec	2250–6000	<300
Falling film	Single	5–30 sec	2000–3000	—
Plate	Three	2–30 sec	2000–3000	—
Expanding flow	Two	0.5–30 sec	2500	—
Agitated film	Single	20–30 sec	2000–3000	1700
Centri-Therm	Single	1–10 sec	8000	—

Adapted from Mannheim and Passy (1974) and Earle (1983).

12.3 EFFECT ON FOODS

Many aroma compounds are more volatile than water and are thus lost during evaporation. This reduces the sensory quality of most concentrates, although in some foods the loss of unpleasant volatiles improves the product quality (for example in cocoa (Anon., 1981) and milk). Some volatiles are retained in the product by

(1) mixing the concentrate with a portion of dilute feed, to achieve the required solids concentration,

(2) volatile recovery by vapour condensation and fractional distillation or
(3) by stripping volatiles from the feed liquor with inert gas and adding them back
    after evaporation.

The advantages and limitations of each procedure have been reviewed by Mannheim
and Passy (1972) and Thijssen (1970). Flash coolers, in which the food is sprayed into
a vacuum chamber, are used to cool a viscous product rapidly and hence to reduce
heat damage.

Evaporation darkens the colour of foods, partly because of the increase in
concentration of solids, but also because the reduction in water activity promotes
chemical changes (for example Maillard browning (Chapter 1 and Fig. 1.11)). As
these changes are time and temperature dependent, short residence times and low
boiling temperatures produce concentrates which have a good retention of sensory
and nutritional qualities. A comparison of nutrient losses in milk preserved by
evaporation and UHT sterilisation is shown in Table 12.4. Vitamins A and D and
niacin are unaffected. Additional vitamin losses occur during storage (for example
50% loss of vitamin C in marmalade over 12 months at 18°C (Lincoln and McCay,
1945) and 10% loss of thiamin over 24 months in peanut butter at 18°C). The effect of
changes due to processing on the nutritive value of a diet are discussed in Chapter 1.

Table 12.4 — Vitamin losses in concentrated and UHT sterilised milk

Product	loss (%)				
	Thiamin	Vitamin B_6	Vitamin B_{12}	Folic acid	Ascorbic acid
Evaporated milk	20	40	80	25	60
Sweetened condensed milk	10	< 10	30	25	25
UHT sterilised milk	< 10	< 10	< 10	< 10	< 25

From Porter and Thompson (1976).

ACKNOWLEDGEMENT

Grateful acknowledgement is made for information supplied by APV International
Ltd, Crawley, West Sussex RH10 2QB, UK.

REFERENCES

Anon. (1981) Special feature: evaporation plant. *Food Process Ind.*, February
    25–29.
Anon. (1986) Computer controls evaporation. *Food Process.* May 17–18.

Brennan, J. G., Butters, J. R., Cowell, N. D., and Lilly, A. E. V. (1976) *Food engineering operations*. Applied Science, London, pp. 286–312.

Darrington, H. (1982) Profile of a jammy business., *Food. Manuf.* December, 33, 37.

Earle, R. L. (1983) *Unit operations in food processing*, 2nd edn. Pergamon Press, Oxford, pp. 105–115.

Fischer, M., Jacobsen, J. F., and Robe, K. (1983) Evaporator concentrates juices to 700 Brix in single pass vs 2 to 3 passes before. *Food Process. (USA)* January 92–94.

Karel, M. (1975) Concentration of foods. In: O. R. Fennema (ed.), *Principles of food science*, Part 2, *Physical principles of food preservation*. Marcel Dekker, New York, pp. 266–308.

Kennedy, D., Viera, J., and Swientek, R. J., (1983) TASTE evaporator control saves $70,000/yr. *Food Process. (USA)* October 60–61.

Leniger, H. A., and Beverloo, W. A. (1975) *Food process engineering*. D. Reidel, Dordrecht, pp. 467–489.

Lewicki, P. P., and Kowalczyk, R. (1980) In: P. Linko, Y. Malkki, J. Olkku and J. Larinkari (eds), *engineering*, Vol. 1, *Food processing systems*. Applied Science, London, pp. 501–505.

Lincoln, R., and McCay, C. M. (1945) Retention of ascorbic acid in marmalade during preparation and storage, *Food. Res.* **10** 357–359.

Mannheim, C. H., and Passy, N. (1972) Aroma retention and recovery during concentration of liquid foods. *Proceedings of the Third Nordic Aroma Symposium Hemeelinna*.

Mannheim, C. H., and Passy, N. (1974) In: A. Spicer (ed.), *Advances in preconcentration and dehydration of foods*. Applied Science, London, pp. 151–194.

Porter, J. W. G., and Thompson, S. Y. (1976). *Effects of processing on the nutritive value of milk*, Vol.1, *Proceedings of the Fourth International Conference on Food Science and Technology, Madrid*.

Pulido, M. L. (1984) Deposits and their control in multiple effect evaporators. *Sugar Azucar* **79** 13, 16, 17, 19.

Rumsey, T. R., Conant, T. T., Fortis, T., Scott, E. P., Pedersen, L. D., and Rose, W. W. (1984) Energy use in tomato paste evaporation. *J. Food. Process Engng.* **7** 111–121.

Thijssen, H. A. C., (1970) Concentration processes for liquid foods containing volatile flavours and aromas. *J. Food. Technol.* **5** 211–229.

13

Extrusion

Extrusion is a process which combines several unit operations including mixing, cooking, kneading, shearing, shaping and forming. In essence an extruder consists of a screw pump (similar to a screw press or screw conveyor (Chapters 5 and 24)) in which food is compressed and worked to form a semi-solid mass. This is forced through a restricted opening (the die) at the discharge end of the screw. If the food is heated the process is known as *extrusion cooking* (or *hot extrusion*).

The main purpose of extrusion is to increase the variety of foods in the diet, by producing a range of products with different shapes, textures, colours and flavours from basic ingredients. Extrusion cooking is a high-temperature short-time (HTST) process which reduces microbial contamination and inactivates enzymes. However, the main method of preservation of both hot- and cold-extruded foods is by the low water activity of the product. Extrusion is gaining in popularity for the following reasons.

(1) *Versatility.* A wide variety of products are possible by changing the minor ingredients and the operating conditions of the extruder. The process is extremely flexible in being able to accommodate the demand by consumers for new products. Extruded foods cannot be easily produced by other methods.
(2) *Reduced costs.* Extrusion has lower processing costs and higher productivity than other cooking or forming processes. Savings in raw materials (19%), energy (100%), labour (14%) and capital investment (44%) are reported when extrusion of breakfast cereals is compared with traditional methods (Darrington 1987).
(3) *High production rates and automated production.* For example production rates of up to $315\,kg\,h^{-1}$ for snackfoods, $1200\,kg\,h^{-1}$ for low-density cereals and $9000\,kg\,h^{-1}$ for dry expanded petfoods are possible (Mans, 1982). Details of automatic control of extruders are described by Olkku *et al.* (1980).
(4) *No process effluents* are produced.

Extrusion is an example of a *size enlargement process*, in which small granular foods or powdered particles are re-formed into larger pieces. Other examples of size enlargement include agglomeration of powders (Chapter 14) and forming or moulding equipment (Chapter 4).

13.1 THEORY

The two factors that most influence the nature of the extruded product are the operating conditions of the extruder and the rheological properties of the food. The most important operating parameters are the temperature, pressure, diameter of the die apertures and shear rate. The shear rate is influenced by the internal design of the barrel and the speed and geometry of the screw(s). The properties of the feed material are an important influence on the texture and colour of the extrudate; the most important factors are the moisture content, the physical state of the materials, and their chemical composition, particularly the amounts and types of starches, proteins, fats and sugars.

During extrusion cooking of starch-based foods (for example maize grits and wheat flours), the moisture content is increased by added water and the starch is subjected to intense shearing forces at an elevated temperature. The starch granules swell, absorb water and become gelatinised. The macromolecular structure of the starch molecules opens up and a viscous plasticised mass is produced (Mercier, 1980). Starch is solubilised but not substantially degraded. The changes in solubility under different conditions of temperature and shear rate are monitored by measuring the *Water Absorption Index* (WAI) and the *Water Solubility Characteristic* (WSC). The WAI of cereal products generally increases with the severity of processing, reaching a maximum at 180–200°C. The WSC decreases as the WAI increases. In cereal processing, the viscosity of the paste is also monitored *in situ* to assess the severity of processing and, in pilot scale work, to establish suitable processing conditions.

During extrusion cooking of protein based-foods (for example soy meal and defatted oil-seed flours) the quaternary structure of the proteins opens in the hot moist conditions, to produce a viscous plasticised mass. The proteins are then polymerised, cross-linked and re-oriented to form the fibrous structure of texturised vegetable protein (TVP). The *nitrogen solubility index* is a measure of the extent of protein denaturation. It decreases during extrusion cooking, and feed materials should therefore have largely undenatured proteins.

The rate of heat transfer between the barrel jacket and food during extrusion cooking is found using equation (1.15) (Chapter 1). Related sample problems are found in Chapter 1 (Sample problems 1.4 and 1.5).

13.2 EQUIPMENT

Extruders are classified according to the method of operation (cold extruders or extruder–cookers) and the method of construction (single- or twin-screw extruders). The principles of operation are similar in all types, however; feed materials in granular form are fed into the extruder barrel. The screw(s) then convey the material and compress and 'work' (shear or knead) it to transform the granular feed material into a semi-solid plasticised mass. The food is then extruded through an interchangeable die and cut at the die either by rotating knives or subsequently by a guillotine, to form a variety of shapes, including rods, spheres, doughnuts, tubes, strips, squirls or shells. Many extruded foods are suitable for coating or enrobing (Chapter 21).

13.2.1 Extrusion cookers

Food is heated in an extrusion cooker by a steam-jacketed barrel and/or by a steam-heated screw. In some designs, electric induction heating elements are used to heat the barrel directly. Heat is also generated in the product by friction, caused by the action of the screw and internal ribs on the barrel. Compression is achieved in the extruder barrel by

(1) increasing the diameter of the screw and decreasing the screw pitch,
(2) using a tapered barrel with a constant or decreasing screw pitch, or
(3) placing restrictions in the screw flights.

Additional back pressure is created by the die. A high pressure and small die are used to form expanded products. The rapid release of pressure as the food emerges from the die causes instantaneous expansion of steam and gas in the material, to form a low-density product. Moisture is lost by evaporation. The extent of expansion is controlled by the pressure and temperature generated in the extruder and the rheological properties of the food. These profiles are shown in Fig. 13.1. The moisture content of some products (for example snackfoods, crispbread and breakfast cereals (Table 13.1)) is further reduced by subsequent drying.

A low pressure and/or large die aperture are used to produce high density products. For example, *preforms* or *half-products* are made by extruding and drying pre-gelatinised cereal doughs to form small hard pellets. They are suitable for extended storage and transport to other processors, where the final product is produced by frying, toasting or puffing. When the half-products are heated in air or oil, they are softened and develop the correct physical properties for expansion. The residual moisture in the pellets then turns to steam, to expand the product rapidly. Other types of hot-extruded products are shown in Table 13.2.

Both types of hot extrusion are HTST processes, which minimises the loss of nutrients from foods and reduces microbial contamination. The long shelf life is due to the low water activity (0.1–0.4) (Chapter 1).

13.2.2 Cold extrusion

Here the product is extruded into strips without cooking or distortion of the food caused by expansion. The extruder has a deep-flighted screw, which operates at a low speed in a smooth barrel, to work and extrude the material with little friction. It is used to produce pasta, hot dogs, pastry doughs and certain types of confectionery (Table 13.2).

Both hot and cold extruders may be fitted with a special die to inject a filling into an outer shell continuously. This is known as *coextrusion* and is used for example to produce filled confectionery.

Process parameters for extrusion cooking

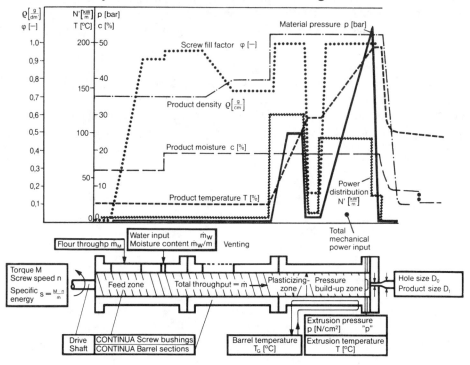

Fig. 13.1 — Operating parameters of an extruder for expanded food products. (Courtesy of Werner and Pfeiderer Ltd.).

13.2.3 Single screw extruders

These extruders are classified according to the extent of shearing action on the food into

(1) high shear (breakfast cereals and snackfoods),
(2) medium shear (breadings and semi-moist petfoods) and
(3) low shear (pasta and meat products).

The screw has a number of sections, including a feed section to compress particles into a homogeneous mass, a kneading section to compress, mix and shear the plasticised food and, in high shear screws, a cooking section (Fig. 13.2). Transport of material through single-screw extruders depends largely on friction at the barrel surface. Material flows forwards (drag flow), owing to the action of the screw and, to a lesser extent, backwards along the barrel (pressure flow and leakage flow). Pressure flow is caused by the buildup of pressure behind the die and by material movement between the screw and the barrel. Slipping can be minimised by special grooves on the inside of the barrel. Single-screw extruders have lower capital and operating costs and require less skill to operate and maintain than twin-screw machines.

Table 13.1 — Typical operating data for five type of extruder

Measured parameter	Pasta extruder	High-pressure forming extruder	Low-shear cooking extruder	Collet extruder	High-shear cooking extruder
Feed moisture (%)	22	25	28	11	15
Product moisture (%)	22	25	25	2	4
Maximum product temperature (°C)	52	79	149	199	149
Maximum pressure (kPa)	—	1500–7000	—	70 000	17 000
Residence time (s)	—	15–45	—	—	30–90
Screw speed (rev min^{-1})	30	40	60	300	450
Net energy input to product (kW h kg^{-1})	0.02	0.03	0.07	0.10	0.07

Adapted from Harper (1979).

13.2.4 Twin-screw extruders

The screws in twin-screw extruders rotate within a 'figure of 8' shaped bore in the barrel. Extruders are classified according to the direction of rotation and the way in which the screws intermesh. Co-rotating intermeshing screws are most commonly found in food-processing applications (Figs 13.3 and 13.4); the rotation moves material through the extruder, and intermeshing improves mixing and prevents rotation of the material in the barrel.

Twin screw extruders have the following advantages:

(1) The throughput is independent of feedrate, and fluctuations in production rate can be accommodated by the positive displacement action of the screws. In contrast a single screw must be full of material to operate effectively. The positive displacement also produces higher rates of heat transfer and better control of heat transfer than a single screw does.
(2) Twin-screw machines handle oily, sticky or very wet materials or other products that slip in a single screw. The limitations for single- and twin-screw machines are respectively 4% and 20% fat, 10% and 40% sugar, and 30% and 65% moisture. There is therefore greater flexibility in operation.
(3) Forward or reverse conveying is used to control the pressure in the barrel. For example, in the production of liquorice and fruit gums, the food is heated and

Table 13.2 — Applications of five types of extruder.

Product	Pasta extruder	High-pressure forming extruder	Low-shear cooking extruder	Collet extruder	High-shear cooking extruder
Flour-based products					
Snacks			★	★	★
Crispbread and croutons			★	★	★
Cereals				★	★
Pasta products	★				
Confectionery					
Chewing gum, liquorice, wine gums		★	★		★
Protein-based foods					
Petfoods and animal feeds			★	★	★
Sausage products			★		
Meat analogues and protein supplements				★	★

Adapted from Harper (1979).

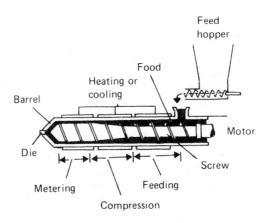

Fig. 13.2 — Single-screw extruder. (Courtesy of Werner and Pfeiderer Ltd.)

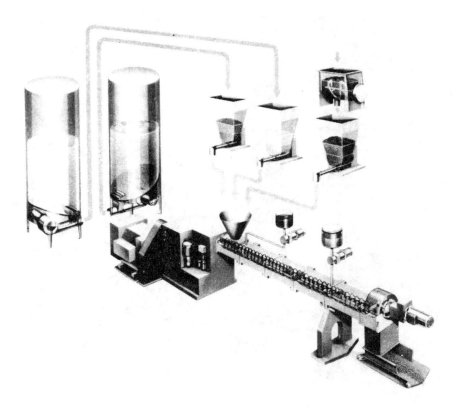

Fig. 13.3 — Twin-screw extruder. (Courtesy of Werner and Pfeiderer Ltd.)

compressed by forward conveying, the pressure is released to vent excess moisture or to add additional ingredients by reverse conveying, and the food is then recompressed for extrusion.

(4) A short discharge section develops the pressure required for extrusion and thus subjects a smaller part of the machine to wear than in single-screw extruders.

(5) A mixture of particle sizes, from fine powders to grains, may be used, whereas a single screw is limited to a specific range of granular particle sizes.

13.3 APPLICATIONS

Typical operating conditions and applications of different types of extruder are shown in Tables 13.1 and 13.2.

13.3.1 Cereal products
13.3.1.1 *Crispbread*
Wheat flour, milk powder, corn starch and sugar are mixed (for example in a ribbon blade mixer (Chapter 4)), water is added and the product is extruded under a high temperature and pressure. The crispbread is toasted to reduce the moisture content

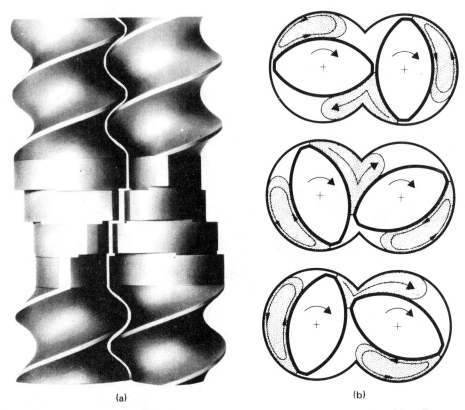

Fig. 13.4 — Kneading elements in a twin-screw extruder showing dough mixing: (a) sealing
profile; (b) movement of material. (Courtesy of Werner and Pfeiderer Ltd.)

futher and to brown the surface. Savings compared with oven baking are up to 66%
in energy consumption, as less moisture is removed, and up to 60% in capital costs
and floor space, as large ovens are unnecessary (Vincent, 1984).

13.3.1.2 Cornflakes

Traditional manufacture required large maize kernels (grits), as the size of the
individual grit determined the size of the final cornflake. Grits were then pressure
cooked for 3 h, dried to 21% moisture, tempered for 2 h to ensure an even moisture
distribution, flaked, toasted and sprayed with a vitamin solution. The total processing time exceeded 5 h. Dough pellets are now produced in a low-pressure extruder.
The size of the pellets determines the size of the cornflakes. They are then flaked,
toasted and sprayed as before. The advantages of extrusion cooking are

(1) a reduction in raw material costs (19.4%) as maize grits of any size may be used, a
reduction in energy consumption (100%), capital expenditure (44%) and labour
costs (13.8%) (Darrington, 1987),

(2) rapid processing to produce cornflakes within minutes of startup,
(3) close control over the size and quality of the final product and
(4) flexibility to change the product specification easily (Slater, 1984).

13.3.2 Protein-based foods
13.3.2.1 *Texturised vegetable protein*
Extrusion cooking of soya beans destroys enzymes (for example a urease which reduces the shelf life, and a lipoxidase which causes off flavours by oxidation of soya oil) and a trypsin inhibitor which reduces protein digestibility. This improves the acceptability, digestibility and shelf life of the product. Defatted soya flour, concentrate or isolate are moistened and the pH is adjusted. A lower pH (5.5) increases chewiness in the final product, whereas a higher pH (8.5) produces a tender product and more rapid rehydration. Colours, flavours and calcium chloride firming agent are added, and the material is plasticised in a cooker extruder at 60–104°C. It is then extruded to form expanded texturised strands, which are cooled and dried to 6–8% moisture content. Details of the production of texturised soya products are given by Smith and Ben-Gera (1980).

13.3.3 Confectionery products
HTST extrusion cooking is used to produce a gelatinised chewy product (for example fruit gums and liquorice) from a mixture of sugar, glucose and starch. The heat gelatinises the starch, dissolves the sugar and vaporises excess water which is vented from the machine under vacuum. Colourings and flavours are added to the plasticised material and, after mixing, it is cooled and extruded. The product texture is adjusted from soft to elastic by control over the formulation and processing conditions. The shape is changed by changing the die, and a variety of flavours and colours may be added. These different combinations permit a very large range of potential products, each produced by the same equipment. Product uniformity is high, no afterdrying is required, and there is a rapid startup and shutdown.

Hard-boiled sweets are produced from granulated sugar and corn syrup. The temperature in the extruder is raised to 165°C to produce a homogeneous, decrystallised mass. Acids, flavours and colour are added to the sugar mass in a forming extruder, and the moisture content is reduced to 2% as the product emerges from the die into a vacuum chamber. It is then fed to stamping or forming machines to produce the required shape. Compared with traditional methods which use boiling pans (Chapter 12), energy consumption in an extruder operating at $1000 \, kg \, h^{-1}$ is reduced from 971 to 551 kJ per kilogram of sugar mass, and steam consumption is reduced from 0.485 to 0.193 kg per kilogram of sugar mass (Huber, 1984).

13.4 EFFECT ON FOODS

13.4.1 Sensory characteristics
The HTST conditions in extrusion cooking have only minor effects on the natural colour and flavour of foods. However, in many foods the colour of the product is determined by the synthetic pigments (section B.1) added to the feed material as water- or oil-soluble powders, emulsions or lakes. Fading of colour due to product expansion, excessive heat or reactions with proteins, reducing sugars or metal ions

may be a problem in some extruded foods. Added flavours are mixed with ingredients before cold extrusion, but this is largely unsuccessful in extrusion cooking as the flavours are volatilised when the food emerges from the die. Micro-encapsulated flavours are suitable but expensive. Flavours are therefore applied to the surface of extruded foods in the form of emulsions or viscous slurries (Chapter 21). However, this may cause stickiness in some products and hence require additional drying. Production of characteristic textures is one of the main features of extrusion technology. Details of changes to carbohydrates and proteins are des-cribed in section 13.1.

13.4.2 Nutritional value

Vitamin losses in extruded foods vary according to the type of food, the moisture content, the temperature of processing and the holding time. However, in general, losses are minimal in cold extrusion. The HTST conditions in extrusion cooking, and the rapid cooling as the product emerges from the die, cause relatively small losses of vitamins and essential amino acids. For example at an extruder temperature of 154°C there is a 95% retention of thiamin and little loss of riboflavin, pyridoxine, niacin or folic acid in cereals. Losses of ascorbic acid and vitamin A are up to 50%, depending on the time that the food is held at the elevated temperatures (Harper, 1979). Loss of lysine, cystine and methionine in rice products varies between 50 and 90% depending on processing conditions (Seiler, 1984). In soy flour the changes to proteins depend on the formulation and processing conditions. High temperatures and the presence of sugars cause Maillard browning and a reduction in protein quality. Lower temperatures and low concentrations of sugars result in an increase in protein digestibility, owing to rearrangement of the protein structure. Destruction of anti-nutritional components in soya products improves the nutritive value of TVP. The effect of losses due to processing on nutritional value of foods in the diet is discussed further in Chapter 1.

ACKNOWLEDGEMENTS

Grateful acknowledgement is made for information supplied by the following:
Werner and Pfeiderer (UK) Ltd, Stockport SK66AG, UK, Vincent Processes Ltd, Shaw, Newbury, Berkshire RG132NT, UK; Baker Perkins Ltd, Peterborough PE6TA, UK.

REFERENCES

Darrington, H. (1987) A long-running cereal. *Food Manuf.*, **3**, 47–48.
Harper, J. M. (1979) Food extrusion. *CRC Crit. Rev. Food. Sci. Nur.*, February 155–215.
Harper, J. M. (1987) High-temperature short-time extrusion cooking, In: A. Turner (ed.), *Food technology international,Europe*, Sterling, London, pp. 51, 53, 55.
Huber, G. R. (1984) New extrusion technology for confectionery products. *Manuf. Confect.*, May, 51–52, 54.
Mans, J. (1982) Extruders. *Prep. Foods*, **11**, 60–63.
Mercier, C. (1980) Structure and digestibility alterations of cereal starches by twin-

screw extrusion-cooking. In: P. Linko, Y. Malkki, J. Olkku and J. Larinkari (eds), *Food process engineering*, Vol. 1. Applied Science, London, pp. 795–807.

Olkku, J., Hassinen, H., Antila, J., Pohjanpalo, H., and Linko, P. (1980) Automation of HTST-extrusion cooker. In: P. Linko, Y. Malkki, J. Olkku and J. Larinkari (eds), *Food process engineering*, Vol. 1. Applied Science, London, pp. 777–790.

Seiler, K. (1984) Extrusion cooking and food processing. *Food Trade Rev.* March 124–125, 127.

Slater, G. (1984) Application of extrusion to the production of breakfast cereals. *Food. Trade Rev.* March 127–128, 131–132.

Smith, O. B., and Ben-Gera, I. (1980) The application of high temperature short time extrusion cooking in the food industry. In: P. Linko, Y. Malkki, J. Olkku and J. Larinkari (eds), *Food process engineering*, Vol. 1, Applied Science, London, pp. 726–744.

Vincent, M. W. (1984) *Extruded confectionery—equipment and process*. Vincent Processes Ltd, Shaw, Newbury, Berkshire, RG13 2NT, UK.

B. Heat processing using hot air

14

Dehydration

Dehydration (or drying) is defined as the application of heat under controlled conditions to remove the majority of the water normally present in a food by evaporation (or in the case of freeze drying (Chapter 20) by sublimation). This definition excludes other unit operations which remove water from foods (for example mechanical separations (Chapter 5), membrane concentration (Chapter 6), evaporation (Chapter 12) and baking (Chapter 15)) as these normally remove much less water than dehydration. The main purpose of dehydration is to extend the shelf life of foods by a reduction in water activity (Chapter 1). This inhibits microbial growth and enzyme activity, but the product temperature is usually insufficient to cause inactivation. The reduction in weight and bulk of food reduces transport and storage costs and, for some types of food, provides greater variety and convenience for the consumer. Drying causes deterioration of both the eating quality and the nutritive value of the food. The design and operation of dehydration equipment aim to minimise these changes by selection of appropriate drying conditions for individual foods. Examples of commercially important dried foods are sugar, coffee, milk, potato, flour (including bakery mixes), beans, pulses, nuts, breakfast cereals, tea and spices.

14.1 THEORY

Dehydration involves the simultaneous application of heat and removal of moisture from foods. Factors that control the rates of heat and mass transfer are described in Chapter 1. Dehydration by heated air or heated surfaces is described in this chapter. Microwave, dielectric and radiant driers are described in Chapter 17 and freeze drying is described in Chapter 20.

14.1.1 Drying using heated air

14.1.1.1 Psychrometrics

The capacity of air to remove moisture from a food depends on the temperature and the amount of water vapour already carried by the air. The content of water vapour in air is expressed as either *absolute humidity* (the mass of water vapour per unit mass of dry air (in kilograms per kilogram) termed *moisture content* in Fig. 14.1) or *relative humidity* (RH) (in per cent) (the ratio of the partial pressure of water vapour in the air to the pressure of saturated water vapour at the same temperature, multiplied by 100). Psychrometry is the study of the interrelationships of the temperature and humidity of air. These properties are most conveniently represented on a *psychrometric chart* (Fig. 14.1).

The temperature of the air, measured by a thermometer bulb, is termed the *dry-bulb* temperature. If the thermometer bulb is surrounded by a wet cloth, heat is removed by evaporation of the water from the cloth and the temperature falls. This lower temperature is called the *wet-bulb temperature*. The difference between the two temperatures is used to find the relative humidity of air on the psychrometric chart. An increase in air temperature, or reduction in RH, causes water to evaporate from a wet surface more rapidly and therefore produces a greater fall in temperature. The *dew point* is the temperature at which air becomes saturated with moisture (100% RH) and any further cooling from this point results in condensation of the water from the air. Adiabatic cooling lines are the parallel straight lines sloping across the chart, which show how absolute humidity decreases as the air temperature increases.

Sample problems 14.1
Using the psychrometric chart (Fig 14.1), calculate the following

(1) the absolute humidity of air which has 50% RH and a dry-bulb temperature of 60°C;
(2) the wet-bulb temperature under these conditions;
(3) the RH of air having a wet-bulb temperature of 45°C and a dry-bulb temperature of 75°C;
(4) the dew point of air cooled adiabatically from a dry-bulb temperature of 55°C and 30% RH;
(5) the change in RH of air with a wet-bulb temperature of 39°C, heated from a dry-bulb temperature of 50°C to a dry-bulb temperature of 86°C;
(6) the change in RH of air with a wet-bulb temperature of 35°C, cooled adiabatically from a dry-bulb temperature of 70°C to 40°C.

Solutions to sample problems 14.1

(1) 0.068 kg per kilogram of dry air (find the intersection of the 60°C and 50% RH lines, and then follow the chart horizontally right to read off the absolute humidity);
(2) 47.5°C (from the intersection of the 60°C and 50% RH lines, extrapolate left parallel to the wet-bulb lines to read off the wet-bulb temperature);
(3) 20% (find the intersection of the 45°C and 75°C lines and follow the sloping RH line upwards to read off the % RH);
(4) 36°C (find the intersection of the 55°C and 30% RH lines and follow the wet-bulb line left until the RH reaches 100%);
(5) 50–10% (find the intersection of the 39°C wet-bulb and the 50°C dry-bulb

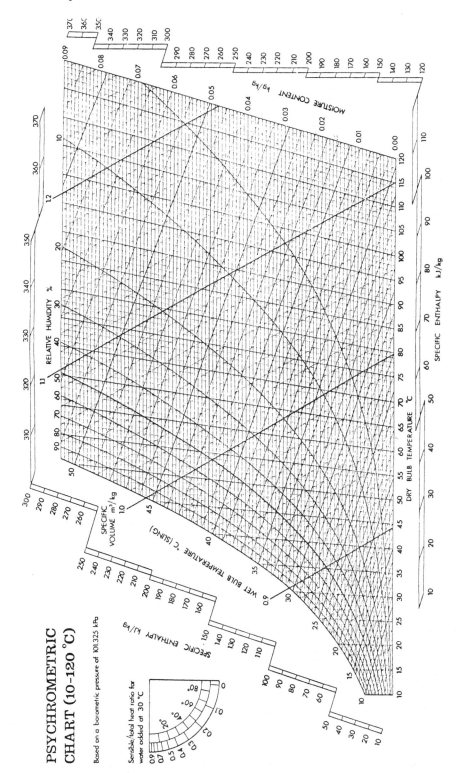

Fig. 14.1 — Psychrometric chart (10–120 °C based on barometric pressure of 101.325 kPa.
(Courtesy of Chartered Institution of Building Services Engineers.)

temperatures, and follow the horizontal line to the intersection with the 86°C dry-bulb line; read the sloping RH line at each intersection (this represents the changes that take place when air is heated prior to being blown over food));
(6) 10–70% (find the intersection of the 35°C wet-bulb and 70°C dry bulb temperatures, and follow the wet-bulb line left until the intersection with the 40°C dry-bulb line; read sloping RH line at each intersection (this represents the changes taking place as the air is used to dry food; the air is cooled and becomes more humid as it picks up moisture from the food)).

14.1.1.2 Mechanism of drying
When hot air is blown over a wet food, heat is transferred to the surface, and latent heat of vaporisation causes water to evaporate. Water vapour diffuses through a boundary film of air (Chapter 1) and is carried away by the moving air (Fig. 14.2).

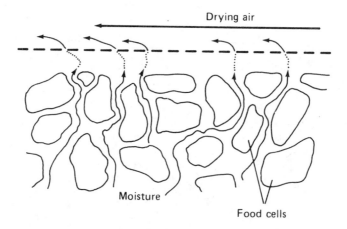

Fig. 14. 2 — Movement of moisture during drying.

This creates a region of lower water vapour pressure at the surface of the food, and a water vapour pressure gradient is established from the moist interior of the food to the dry air. This gradient provides the 'driving force' for water removal from the food. Water moves to the surface by the following mechanisms:

(1) liquid movement by capillary forces;
(2) diffusion of liquids, caused by differences in the concentration of solutes in different regions of the food;
(3) diffusion of liquids which are adsorbed in layers at the surfaces of solid components of the food;
(4) water vapour diffusion in air spaces within the food caused by vapour pressure gradients.

Foods are characterised as *hygroscopic* and *non-hygroscopic*. Hygroscopic foods are those in which the the partial pressure of water vapour varies with the moisture content. Non-hygroscopic foods have a constant water vapour pressure at different moisture contents. The difference is found by using sorption isotherms (Chapter 1).

When food is placed into a drier, there is a short initial settling down period as the surface heats up to the wet-bulb temperature (AB in Figs 14.3(a) and (b)). Drying

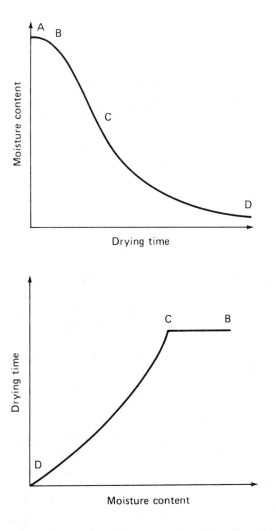

Fig. 14.3 (a) and (b) — Drying curves. The temperature and humidity of the drying air are constant and all heat is supplied to the surface by convection.

then commences and, provided that water moves from the interior of the food at the same rate as it evaporates from the surface, the surface remains wet. This is known as the *constant-rate period* and continues until a certain *critical moisture content* is reached (AB in Fig. 14.3(a)). In practice, however, different areas of the surface of the food dry out at different rates and, overall, the rate of drying declines gradually during the 'constant'-rate period. Thus the critical point is not fixed for a given food and depends on the amount of food in the drier and the rate of drying. The three characteristics of air that are necessary for successful drying in the constant rate period are

(1) a moderately high dry-bulb temperature,
(2) a low RH and
(3) a high air velocity.

The boundary film of air surrounding the food acts as a barrier to the transfer of both heat and water vapour during drying (Chapter 1). The thickness of the film is determined primarily by the air velocity. If this is too low, water vapour leaves the surface of the food and increases the humidity of the surrounding air, to cause a reduction in the water vapour pressure gradient and the rate of drying. (Similarly, if the temperature of the drying air falls or the humidity rises, the rate of evaporation falls and drying slows.)

When the moisture content of the food falls below the critical moisture content, the rate of drying slowly decreases until it approaches zero at the *equilibrium moisture content* (that is the food comes into equilibrium with the drying air). This is known as the *falling-rate period*. Non-hygroscopic foods have a single falling-rate period (CD in Figs 14.3(a) and (b)), whereas hygroscopic foods have two periods. In the first period, the plane of evaporation moves inside the food, and water diffuses through the dry solids to the drying air. It ends when the plane of evaporation reaches the centre of the food and the partial pressure of water falls below the saturated water vapour pressure. The second period occurs when the partial pressure of water is below the saturated vapour pressure, and drying is by desorption (Chapter 1).

During the falling-rate period, the rate of water movement from the interior of the food to the surface falls below the rate at which water evaporates to the surrounding air. The surface therefore dries out. This is usually the longest period of a drying operation and, in some foods (for example grain drying) where the initial moisture content is below the critical moisture content, the falling-rate period is the only part of the drying curve to be observed. During the falling-rate period, the factors that control the rate of drying change. Initially the important factors are similar to those in the constant-rate period, but gradually the rate of mass transfer becomes the controlling factor. This depends mostly on the temperature of the air and the thickness of the food. It is unaffected by both the RH of the air (except in determining the equilibrium moisture content) and the velocity of the air. The air temperature is therefore controlled during the falling rate period, whereas the air velocity and temperature are more important during the constant-rate period. In practice, foods may differ from these idealised drying curves owing to shrinkage, changes in the temperature and rate of moisture diffusion in different parts of the food, and changes in the temperature and humidity of the drying air.

The surface temperature of the food remains close to the wet-bulb temperature of the drying air until the end of the constant-rate period, due to the cooling effect of the evaporating water. During the falling-rate period the amount of water evaporating from the surface gradually decreases but, as the same amount of heat is being supplied by the air, the surface temperature rises until it reaches the dry-bulb temperature of the drying air. Most heat damage to food therefore occurs in the falling rate period.

14.1.1.3 Calculation of drying rate

The rate of drying depends on the properties of the drier (the dry-bulb temperature, RH and velocity of the air, and the surface heat transfer coefficient (Chapter 1)), the properties of the food (the moisture content, surface-to-volume ratio and the surface temperature and rate of moisture loss. The size of food pieces has an important effect on the drying rate in both the constant- and the falling-rate periods. In the constant-rate period, smaller pieces have a larger surface area available for evaporation whereas, in the falling-rate period, smaller pieces have a shorter distance for moisture to travel through the food. Other factors which influence the rate of drying include

(1) the fat content of the food (higher fat contents generally result in slower drying, as water is trapped within the food),
(2) the method of preparation of the food (cut surfaces lose moisture more quickly than losses through skin (Chapters 2 and 3)) and
(3) the amount of food placed into a drier in relation to its size (in a given drier, faster drying is achieved with smaller quantities of food).

The rate of heat transfer is found using

$$Q = h_S A\ (\theta_a - \theta_s) \tag{14.1}$$

The rate of mass transfer is found using

$$-m_c = K_g A (H_s - H_a) \tag{14.2}$$

Since, during the constant-rate period, an equilibrium exists between the rate of heat transfer to the food and the rate of mass transfer in the form of moisture loss from the food, these rates are related by

$$-m_c = \frac{h_c A}{\lambda}\ (\theta_a - \theta_s) \tag{14.3}$$

where Q ($J\,s^{-1}$) is the rate of heat transfer, h_c ($W\,m^{-2\circ}K^{-1}$) the surface heat transfer coefficient for convective heating, A (m^2) the surface area available for drying, θ_a (°C) the average dry-bulb temperature of drying air, θ_s (°C) the average wet-bulb temperature of drying air, m_c ($kg\,s^{-1}$) the change in mass with time (drying rate), K_g

(kg m^{-2} s^{-1}) the mass transfer coefficient, H_s (kilograms of moisture per kilogram dry air) the humidity at the surface of the food (saturation humidity), H_a (kilograms of moisture per kilogram dry air) the humidity of air, and λ (J kg^{-1}) the latent heat of evaporation at the wet-bulb temperature.

The surface heat transfer coefficient (h_c) is related to the mass flow rate of air using the following equations: for parallel air flow,

$$h_c = 14.3G^{0.8} \tag{14.4}$$

and for perpendicular air flow,

$$h_c = 24.2G^{0.37} \tag{14.5}$$

where G (kg m^{-2} s^{-1}) is the mass flow rate of air.

For a tray of food, in which water evaporates only from the upper surface, the drying time is found using

$$-m_c = \frac{h_c}{\rho\lambda x}(\theta_a - \theta_s) \tag{14.6}$$

where ρ (kg m^{-3}) is the bulk density of food and x (m) the thickness of the bed of food.

The drying time in the constant rate period is found using

$$t = \frac{\rho\lambda x(M_i - M_c)}{h_c(\theta_a - \theta_s)} \tag{14.7}$$

where t (s) is the drying time, M_i (kg per kilogram of dry solids) the initial moisture content and M_c (kg per kilogram of dry solids) the critical moisture content.

For water evaporating from a spherical droplet in a spray drier (Section 14.2.1.8), the drying time is found using

$$t = \frac{r^2\rho_l\lambda}{3h_c(\theta_A - \theta_S)} \frac{M_i - M_f}{1 + M_i} \tag{14.8}$$

where ρ_l (kg m^{-3}) is the density of the liquid r (m) the radius of the droplet, M_f (kg per kilogram of dry solids) the final moisture content.

In the falling-rate period, moisture gradients change throughout the food and the temperature slowly increases from the wet-bulb temperature to the dry-bulb temperature as the food dries. The following equation is used to calculate the drying time from the start of the falling-rate period to the equilibrium moisture content using a number of assumptions concerning for example the nature of moisture movement and the absence of shrinkage of the food:

$$t = \frac{\rho x (M_c - M_e)}{K_g (P_s - P_a)} \ln \left(\frac{M_c - M_e}{M - M_e} \right). \tag{14.9}$$

where M_e (kg per kilogram of dry solids) is the equilibrium moisture content, M (per kilogram of dry solids) the moisture content at time t from the start of the falling-rate period, P_s (Torr) the saturated water vapour pressure at the wet-bulb temperature and P_a (Torr) the partial water vapour pressure.

Calculation of moisture content is described in Chapter 1. Derivations of the above equations are described by Tomkins *et al.* (1973), Karel (1975) and Hall (1979).

Sample problem 14.2
A conveyor drier (section 14.2.1.3) is required to dry peas from an initial moisture content of 78% to 16% moisture (wet-weight basis), in a bed 10 cm deep which has a voidage of 0.4. Air at 85°C with a relative humidity of 10% is blown perpendicularly through the bed at 0.9 m s^{-1}. The drier belt measures 0.75 m wide and 4 m long. Assuming that drying takes place from the entire surface of the peas and there is no shrinkage, calculate the drying time and energy consumption in both the constant- and the falling-rate periods. (Additional data: the equilibrium moisture content of the peas is 9%, the critical moisture content 300% (dry-weight basis), the average diameter 6 mm, the bulk density 610 kg m^{-3}, the latent heat of evaporation 2300 kJ kg^{-1}, the saturated water vapour pressure at wet-bulb temperature 61.5 Torr and the mass transfer coefficient 0.015 kg m^{-2} s^{-1}.)

Solution to sample problem 14.2
In the constant-rate period, from equation (14.5),

$$h_c = 24.2(0.9)^{0.37}$$
$$= 23.3 \text{ W m}^{-2°}\text{K}^{-1}$$

From Fig. 14.1 for $\theta_a = 85°\text{C}$ and RH $= 10\%$,

$$\theta_s = 42°\text{C}$$

To find the area of the peas,

$$\text{volume of a sphere} = \frac{4}{3} \pi r^3$$

$$= 4/3 \times 3.142(0.003)^3$$
$$= 339 \times 10^{-9} \text{ m}^3$$

$$\text{volume of the bed} = 0.75 \times 4 \times 0.1$$
$$= 0.3 \text{ m}^3$$

$$\text{volume of peas in the bed} = 0.3(1 - 0.4)$$
$$= 0.18 \text{ m}^3$$

$$\text{number of peas} = \frac{\text{volume of peas in bed}}{\text{volume each pea}}$$
$$\equiv \frac{0.18}{339 \times 10^{-9}}$$
$$\equiv 5.31 \times 10^5$$

$$\text{area of sphere} = 4\pi r^2$$
$$= 4 \times 3.142(0.003)^2$$
$$= 113 \times 10^{-6} \text{ m}^2$$

and

$$\text{total area of peas} = 5.31 \times 10^5 \times 113 \times 10^{-6}$$
$$= 60 \text{ m}^2$$

From equation (14.3),

$$\text{drying rate} = \frac{23.3 \times 60}{2.3 \times 10^6} (85 - 42)$$
$$= 0.026 \text{ kg s}^{-1}$$

From a mass balance,

$$\text{volume of bed} \qquad = 0.03 \text{ m}^3$$
$$\text{bulk density} \qquad = 610 \text{ kg m}^{-3}$$

Therefore,

$$\text{mass of peas} = 0.3 \times 610$$
$$= 183 \text{ kg}$$

$$\text{initial solids content} = 183 \times 0.22$$
$$= 40.26 \text{ kg}$$

Therefore

$$\text{initial mass water} = 183 - 24.15$$
$$= 158.85 \text{ kg}$$

After constant-rate period, solids remain constant and

$$\text{mass of water} = 96.6 - 24.15$$
$$= 72.45 \text{ kg.}$$

Therefore

$$(158.85 - 72.45) = 86.4 \text{ kg water lost}$$

at a rate of 0.026 kg 5^{-1}

$$\text{Drying time} = \frac{86.4}{0.026} = 3323 = 55.4 \text{ min}$$

Therefore

$$\text{energy required} = 0.026 \times 2.3 \times 10^6$$
$$= 6 \times 10^4 \text{ J s}^{-1}$$
$$= 60 \text{ kW}$$

In the falling-rate period, from section 14.1.1.1,

$$\text{RH} = \frac{P_A}{P_0} \times 100$$

$$10 = \frac{P}{61.5} \times 100$$

Therefore,
$$P = 6.15 \text{ Torr}$$

The moisture values are

$$M_c \quad = \frac{75}{25} = 3$$

$$M_f \quad = \frac{16}{84} = 0.19$$

$$M_e \quad = \frac{9}{91} = 0.099$$

From equation (14.9),

$$t = \frac{(3 - 0.099)610 \times 0.1}{0.015 \, (61.5 - 6.15)} \ln \left(\frac{3 - 0.099}{0.19 - 0.099} \right)$$
$$= 737.7 \text{ s}$$
$$= 12.3 \text{ min}$$

From a mass balance, at the critical moisture content, 96.6 kg contains 25% solids = 24.16 kg. After drying in the falling-rate period, 84% solids = 24.16 kg. Therefore,

$$\text{total mass} = \frac{100}{84} \times 24.16$$
$$= 28.8 \text{ kg}$$

and

$$\text{mass loss} = 96.6 - 28.8$$
$$= 67.8 \text{ kg}$$

Thus,

$$\text{average drying rate} = \frac{67.8}{737.7}$$
$$= 0.092 \text{ kg s}^{-1}$$

and

$$\text{average energy required} = 0.092 \times 2.3 \times 10^6$$
$$= 2.1 \times 10^5 \text{ J s}^{-1}$$
$$= 210 \text{ kW}$$

14.1.2 Drying using heated surfaces

Heat is conducted from a hot surface, through a thin layer of food, and moisture is evaporated from the exposed surface. The main resistance to heat transfer is the thermal conductivity of the food (Table 1.4). Knowledge of the rheological properties of the food is necessary to determine the thickness of the layer of food and the way in which it should be applied to the heated surface. Additional resistances to heat transfer arise if the partly dried food lifts off the hot surface. Equation (1.15) is used in the calculation of drying rates (Chapter 1).

Sample problem 14.3
A single-drum drier (section 14.2.2.1) 0.7 m in diameter and 0.85 m long operates at 150°C and is fitted with a doctor blade to remove food after $\frac{3}{4}$ rev. It is used to dry a 0.6 mm layer of 20% w/w solution of gelatin, pre-heated to 100°C, at atmospheric pressure. Calculate the speed of the drum required to produce a product with a moisture content of 4 kg of solids per kilogram of water. (Additional data: the density of gelatin feed is 1020 kg m^{-3} and the overall heat transfer coefficient 1200 W m^{-2}K^{-1}; assume that the critical moisture content of the gelatin is 450% (dry weight basis).)

Solution to sample problem 14.3
First,

$$\begin{aligned} \text{drum area} &= \pi DL \\ &= 3.142 \times 0.7 \times 0.85 \\ &= 1.87 \text{ m}^2 \end{aligned}$$

Therefore

$$\begin{aligned} \text{mass of food on the drum} &= (1.87 \times 0.75)\, 0.0006 \times 1020 \\ &= 0.86 \text{ kg} \end{aligned}$$

From a mass balance (initially the food contains 80% moisture and 20% solids),

$$\begin{aligned} \text{mass of solids} &= 0.86 \times 0.2 \\ &= 0.172 \text{ kg} \end{aligned}$$

After drying, 80% solids $= 0.172$ kg. Therefore

$$\begin{aligned} \text{mass of dried food} &= \frac{100}{80} \times 0.172 \\ &= 0.215 \text{ kg} \end{aligned}$$

$$\begin{aligned} \text{mass loss} &= 0.86 - 0.215 \\ &= 0.645 \text{ kg} \end{aligned}$$

From equation (14.1)

$$\begin{aligned} Q &= 1200 \times 1.87 \,(150 - 100) \\ &= 1.12 \times 10^5 \text{ J s}^{-1} \end{aligned}$$

$$\text{drying rate} = \frac{1.12 \times 10^5}{2.257 \times 10^6} \text{ kg s}^{-1}$$

$$= 0.05 \text{ kg s}^{-1}$$

and

$$\text{residence time required} = \frac{0.645}{0.05}$$
$$= 13 \text{ s.}$$

As only three-quarters of the drum surface is used. 1 rev should take $(100/75) \times 13 = 17.3$ s. Therefore speed $= 3.5$ rev min^{-1}.

14.2 EQUIPMENT

Most commercial driers are insulated to reduce heat losses, and they recirculate hot air to save energy. Many designs have energy-saving devices which recover heat from the exhaust air (Chapter 1) or automatically control the air humidity (Zagorzycki, 1983; Masters, 1972). Computer control of driers is increasingly sophisticated (Grikitis, 1986) and also results in important savings in energy. Other benefits are described in Chapter 24. The criteria for selection of drying equipment and potential applications are described in Table 14.1. The relative costs of different drying methods are reported by Sapakie and Renshaw (1984) as follows: forced-air drying, 198; fluidised-bed drying, 315; drum drying, 327; continuous vacuum drying, 1840; freeze drying, 3528. Tragardh (1981) compared relative energy consumption (in kilowatt hours per kilogram of water removed) as follows: roller drying, 1.25; pneumatic drying, 1.8; spray drying, 2.5; fluidised-bed drying, 3.5.

14.2.1 Hot-air driers

14.2.1.1 Bin driers (deep-bed driers)
Bin driers are cylindrical or rectangular containers fitted with a mesh base. Hot air passes up through a bed of food at relatively low speeds (for example 0.5 m^3 s^{-1} per square metre of bin area). These driers have a high capacity and low capital and running costs. They are mainly used for 'finishing' (to 3–6% moisture content) after initial drying in other types of equipment. Bin driers improve the operating capacity of initial driers by taking the food when it is in the falling-rate period, when moisture removal is most time consuming. The deep bed of food permits variations in moisture content to be equalised and acts as a store to smooth out fluctuations in the product flow between drying stages and packaging. However, the driers may be several metres high, and it is therefore important that foods are sufficiently strong to withstand compression at the base and to retain an open structure to permit the passage of hot air through the bed.

14.2.1.2 Cabinet driers (tray driers)
These consist of an insulated cabinet fitted with shallow mesh or perforated trays, each of which contains a thin (2–6 cm deep) layer of food. Hot air is circulated through the cabinet at 0.5–5 m s^{-1} per square metre tray area. A system of ducts and baffles is used to direct air over and/or through each tray, to promote uniform air

Table 14.1 — Characteristics of driers

Type of drier	Solid	Liquid	Initial moisture content		Heat sensitive	Size of pieces			Drying rate required		Final moisture content required	
			Moderate to high	Low		Small	Intermediate to large	Mechanically strong	Moderate to fast	Slow	Moderate	Low
Bin	*			*			*	*		*	*	*
Cabinet	*		*				*		*	*	*	
Conveyor		*	*				*		*	*	*	*
Drum		*			*				*			*
Foam mat	*		*			*			*			
Fluid bed	*		*			*		*	*		*	
Kiln	*						*			*	*	
Pneumatic	*		*	*		*		*	*			*
Rotary	*	*				*		*	*			*
Spray		*	*		*	*			*		*	*
Trough	*		*		*			*	*		*	
Tunnel	*						*			*	*	
Vacuum band	*	*	*		*	*	*		*		*	*
Vacuum shelf	*	*		*	*	*			*	*	*	*
Radiant	*			*	*	*			*		*	*
Microwave or dielectric	*						*		*			*
Solar (sun)	*		*				*			*	*	

distribution. Additional heaters may be placed above or alongside the trays to increase the rate of drying. Tray driers are used for small-scale production (1–20 t·day^{-1}) or for pilot-scale work. They have low capital and maintenance costs but have relatively poor control and produce more variable product quality.

14.2.1.3 Conveyor driers (belt driers)
Continuous conveyor driers are up to 20 m long and 3 m wide. Food is dried on a mesh belt in beds 5–15 cm deep. The air flow is initially directed upwards through the bed of food and then downwards in later stages to prevent dried food from blowing out of the bed. Two- or three-stage driers (Fig. 14.4) mix and repile the partly dried

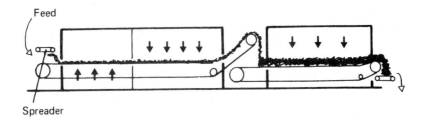

Fig. 14.4 — Two-stage conveyor drier. (Courtesy of Proctor and Schwartz Inc.)

shrunken food into deeper beds (to 15–25 cm and 250–900 cm in three-stage driers). This improves uniformity of drying and saves floor space. Foods are dried to 10–15% moisture content and then transferred to bin driers for finishing. This equipment has good control over drying conditions and high production rates. It is used for large-scale drying of foods (for example fruits and vegetables are dried in 2–3.5 h at up to 5.5 t h^{-1}). It has independently controlled drying zones and is automatically loaded and unloaded, which reduces labour costs. As a result it has largely replaced the tunnel drier (section 14.2.1.10).

A second application of conveyor driers is *foam mat drying* in which liquid foods (for example fruit juices) are formed into a stable foam by the addition of a stabiliser (Appendix B, section B.2) and aeration with nitrogen or air. The foam is spread on a perforated belt to a depth of 2–3 mm and dried rapidly in two stages by parallel and then counter-current air flows (Table 14.2). Foam drying is approximately three times faster than drying a similar thickness of liquid. The thin porous mat of dried food is ground to a free-flowing powder which has good rehydration properties. The rapid drying and low product temperatures result in a high-quality product. However a large surface area is required for high production rates, and capital costs are therefore high.

14.2.1.4 Fluidised bed driers
Metal trays with mesh or perforated bases contain a bed of particulate foods up to 15 cm deep. Hot air is blown through the bed (Fig. 14.5), causing the food to become

Table 14.2 — Advantages and limitations of parallel flow, counter-current flow, centre-exhaust and cross-flow drying

Type of air flow	Advantages	Limitations
Parallel or co-current type: food → air flow →	Rapid initial drying. Little shrinkage of food. Low bulk density. Less heat damage to food. No risk of spoilage	Low moisture content difficult to achieve as cool moist air passes over dry food
Counter-current type: Food → air flow ←	More economical use of energy. Low final moisture content as hot air passes over dry food	Food shrinkage and possible heat damage. Risk of spoilage from warm moist air meeting wet food
Centre-exhaust type: food → air flow → ↑ ←	Combined benefits of parallel and counter-current driers but less than cross-flow driers	More complex and expensive then single-direction air flow
Cross-flow type: food → air flow ↑ ↓	Flexible control of drying conditions by separately controlled heating zones, giving uniform drying and high drying rates	More complex and expensive to buy, operate and maintain

Fig. 14.5 — Fluidised-bed drying. (Courtesy of Petrie and McNaught Ltd.)

suspended and vigorously agitated (fluidised). The air thus acts as both the drying and the fluidising medium, and the maximum surface area of food is made available for drying. A sample calculation of the air speed needed for fluidisation is described in Chapter 1 (Sample problem 1.3). Driers may be batch or continuous in operation; the latter are often fitted with a vibrating base to help to move the product. Continuous 'cascade' systems, in which food is discharged under gravity from one tray to the next, employ up to six driers for high production rates (Fig. 14.6).

Fig. 14.6 — Continuous 'cascade' fluidised-bed driers. (Courtesy of Unilever Ltd.)

Fluidised-bed driers are compact and have good control over drying conditions, relatively high thermal efficiencies and high drying rates. In batch operation, products are mixed by fluidisation and this leads to uniform drying. In continuous driers, there is a greater range of moisture contents in the dried product, and bin driers are therefore used for finishing. Fluidised-bed driers are limited to small-particulate foods that are capable of being fluidised without excessive mechanical damage (for example peas, diced or sliced vegetables, grains, powders or extruded foods). These considerations also apply to fluidised-bed freeze driers and freezers (Chapters 19 and 20).

A development of the fluidised-bed drier, named the 'Torbed' drier, has potential applications for drying particulate foods. A fluidised bed of particles is made to rotate around a torus-shaped chamber, by hot air blown directly from a burner (Fig. 14.7). The drier has very high rates of heat and mass transfer and substantially reduced drying times. It is likely that some products (for example vegetable pieces) would require a period of equilibration to allow moisture redistribution before final drying. The drier operates semi-continuously under microprocessor control and is suitable for agglomeration and puff drying in addition to roasting, cooking and coating applications.

14.2.1.5   Kiln driers
These are two-storey buildings in which a drying room with a slatted floor is located above a furnace. Hot air and the products of combustion from the furnace pass through a bed of food up to 20 cm deep. These driers have been used traditionally for drying apple rings or slices in the USA, and hops or malt in Europe. There is limited control over drying conditions and drying times are relatively long. High labour costs are incurred by the need to turn the product regularly, and by manual loading and unloading. However the driers have a large capacity and are easily constructed and maintained at low cost.

14.2.1.6   Pneumatic driers
In pneumatic driers, powders or particulate foods are continuously dried in vertical or horizontal metal ducts. A cyclone separator is used to remove the dried product. The moist food (usually less than 40% moisture) is metered into the ducting and suspended in hot air. In vertical driers the air-flow is adjusted to classify the particles; lighter and smaller particles, which dry more rapidly, are carried to a cyclone more rapidly than are heavier and wetter particles which remain suspended to receive the additional drying required. For longer residence times the ducting is formed into a continuous loop (*pneumatic ring driers*) and the product is recirculated until it is adequately dried. High temperature short-time ring driers are used to expand the starch cell structure in potatoes or carrots to give a rigid, porous structure, which enhances subsequent conventional drying and rehydration rates. Calculation of air velocities needed for pneumatic drying is described in Chapter 1.

Pneumatic driers have relatively low capital costs, high drying rates and thermal efficiencies, and close control over drying conditions. They are often used after spray drying to produce foods which have a lower moisture content than normal (for example special milk or egg powders and potato granules). In some applications the simultaneous transportation and drying of the food may be a useful method of materials handling (Chapter 24).

14.2.1.7   Rotary driers
A slightly inclined rotating metal cylinder is fitted internally with flights to cause the food to cascade through a stream of hot air as it moves through the drier. Air flow may be parallel or counter-current (Table 14.2). The agitation of the food and the large area of food exposed to the air produce high drying rates and a uniformly dried product. The method is especially suitable for foods that tend to mat or stick together in belt or tray driers. However, the damage caused by impact and abrasion in the drier restrict this method to relatively few foods (for example sugar crystals and cocoa beans).

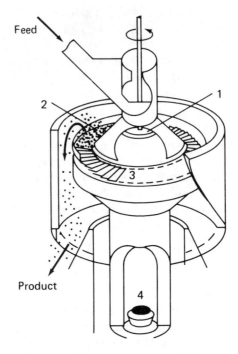

Fig. 14.7 — Torbed drier: (1) rotating disc distributor to deliver raw material evenly into processing chamber, (2) rotating bed of particles, (3) fixed blades with hot gas passing through at high velocity, (4) burner assembly. (Courtesy of Torftech Ltd.)

14.2.1.8 Spray driers

A fine dispersion of pre-concentrated food is first 'atomised' to form droplets (10–200 μm in diameter) and sprayed into a current of heated air at 150–300°C in a large drying chamber. The feed rate is controlled to produce an outlet air temperature of 90–100°C, which corresponds to a wet-bulb temperature (and product temperature) of 40–50°C. Complete and uniform atomisation is necessary for successful drying, and one of the following types of atomiser is used.

(1) *Centrifugal atomiser*. Liquid is fed to the centre of a rotating bowl (with a peripheral velocity of 90–200 m s^{-1}). Droplets, 50–60 μm in diameter, are flung from the edge of the bowl to form a uniform spray (Fig. 14.8(a)).

(2) *Pressure nozzle atomiser*. Liquid is forced at a high pressure (700–2000 kPa) through a small aperture. Droplet sizes are 180–250 μm. Grooves on the inside of the nozzle cause the spray to form into a cone shape and therefore to use the full volume of the drying chamber.

(3) *Two-fluid nozzle atomiser*. Compressed air creates turbulence which atomises the liquid (Fig. 14.8(b)). The operating pressure is lower than the pressure nozzle, but a wider range of droplet sizes is produced.

Both types of nozzle atomiser are susceptible to blockage by particulate foods, and

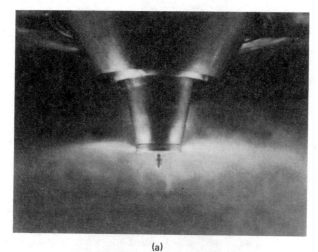

(a)

(b)

Fig. 14.8 — Atomisers: (a) centrifugal atomiser; (b) two-fluid nozzle atomiser. (After Masters (1983).)

abrasive foods gradually widen the apertures and increase the average droplet size. Studies of droplet drying, including methods for calculating changes in size, density and trajectory of the droplets are described by Charm (1978), Kerkhof and Schoeber (1974) and Masters (1972).

Rapid drying takes place (1–10 s) because of the very large surface area of the droplets. The temperature of the product remains at the wet-bulb temperature of the drying air and there is minimum heat damage to the food. Air flow may be co- or counter-current (Table 14.2). The dry powder is collected at the base of the drier and removed by a screw conveyor or a pneumatic system with a cyclone separator. There are a large number of designs of atomiser, drying chamber, air heating and powder collecting systems. The variations in design arise from the different requirements of the very large variety of food materials that are spray dried (for example milk, egg, coffee, cocoa, tea, potato, ground chicken, ice cream mix, butter, cream, yoghurt and cheese powder, coffee whitener, fruit juices, meat and yeast extracts, encapsulated flavours (Heath, 1985) and wheat and corn starch products). Detailed designs are described by Masters (1972) and Kjaergaard (1974). Spray driers may also be fitted with fluidised bed facilities to finish powders taken from the drying chamber.

Spray driers vary in size from small pilot-scale models for low-volume high-value products (for example enzymes and flavours) to large commercial models (Fig. 14.9) capable of producing 80 000 kg of dried milk per day (Byrne, 1986). The main advantages are rapid drying, large-scale continuous production, low labour costs and simple operation and maintenance. The major limitations are high capital costs and the requirement for a relatively high-feed moisture content to ensure that the food can be pumped to the atomiser. This results in higher energy costs (to remove the moisture) and higher volatile losses. Conveyor-band driers (section 14.2.1.3) and fluidised bed driers (Section 14.2.1.4) are beginning to replace spray driers as they are more compact and energy efficient (Ashworth, 1981).

The bulk density of powders depends on the size of the dried particles and on whether they are hollow or solid. This is determined by the nature of the food and the drying conditions (for example the uniformity of droplet size, temperature, solids content and degree of aeration of the feed liquid). Instant powders (section 14.3.1) are produced by either agglomeration or non-agglomeration methods. *Agglomeration* is achieved by remoistening particles in low-pressure steam in an agglomerator, and then redrying. Fluidised-bed, jet, disc, cone or belt agglomerators are described by Schubert (1980). Alternatively, 'straight-through' agglomeration is achieved directly during spray drying. A relatively moist powder is agglomerated and dried in an attached fluidised bed drier (Masters, 1972). *Non-agglomeration* methods employ a binding agent (for example lecithin) to bind particles together. This method was previously used for foods with a relatively high fat content (for example whole milk powder) but agglomeration procedures have now largely replaced this method (for example Pisecky *et al.*, 1984). Agglomeration is an example of a size enlargement operation.

14.2.1.9 Trough driers (belt-trough driers)
Small, uniform pieces of food (for example peas or diced vegetables) are dried in a mesh conveyor belt which hangs freely between rollers, to form the shape of a trough. Hot air is blown through the bed of food, and the movement of the conveyor mixes and turns it to bring new surfaces continually into contact with the drying air. The mixing action moves food away from the drying air, and this allows time for moisture to move from the interior of the pieces to the dry surface. The moisture is then rapidly evaporated when the food again contacts the hot air. The drier operates in two stages, to 50–60% moisture and then to 15–20% moisture. Foods are finished in bin driers. These driers have high drying rates (for example 55 min for diced

Fig. 14.9 — Spray drier. (Courtesy of De Melkindustrie Veghel).

vegetables, compared with 5 h in a tunnel drier), high energy efficiencies, good control and minimal heat damage to the product. However, they are not suitable for sticky foods.

14.2.1.10   Tunnel driers
Thin layers of food are dried on trays, which are stacked on trucks programmed to move semi-continuously through an insulated tunnel. Different designs use one of the types of air flow described in Table 14.2. Food is finished in bin driers. Typically a 20 m tunnel contains 12–15 trucks with a total capacity of 5000 kg of food. This ability to dry large quantities of food in a relatively short time (5-16 h) made tunnel drying widely used, especially in the USA. However, the method has now been largely superseded by conveyor drying (section 14.2.1.3) and fluidised-bed drying (section 14.2.1.4), as a result of their higher energy efficiency, reduced labour costs and better product quality.

14.2.1.11   Sun and solar drying
Sun drying (without drying equipment) is the most widely practised agricultural processing operation in the world; more than 250 000 000 t of fruits and grains are dried by solar energy per annum. In some countries, foods are simply laid out on roofs or other flat surfaces and turned regularly until dry. More sophisticated methods (solar drying) collect solar energy and heat air, which in turn is used for drying. Solar driers are classified into (Brenndorfer *et al.*, 1985)

(1) direct natural-circulation driers (a combined collector and drying chamber),
(2) direct driers with a separate collector, and
(3) indirect forced-convection driers (separate collector and drying chamber).

Both solar and sun drying are simple inexpensive technologies, in terms of both capital input and operating costs. Energy inputs and skilled labour are not required. The major disadvantages are relatively poor control over drying conditions, and lower drying rates than those found in artificial driers. This results in products which have lower quality and greater variability. In addition, drying is dependent on the weather and the time of day and requires a larger labour force than other methods.

14.2.2   Heated-surface driers
Driers in which heat is supplied to the food by conduction have two main advantages over hot-air drying.

(1) It is not necessary to heat large volumes of air before drying commences, and the thermal efficiency is therefore high.
(2) Drying may be carried out in the absence of oxygen to protect components of foods that are easily oxidised.

Typically heat consumption is 2000–3000 kJ per kilogram of water evaporated compared with 4000–10 000 kJ per kilogram of water evaporated for hot-air driers. However, foods have low thermal conductivities (Table 1.4) which become lower as the food dries. There should therefore be a thin layer of food to conduct heat rapidly, without causing heat damage. Foods may shrink during drying, lift off the hot surface and therefore introduce an additional barrier to heat transfer. Careful control is necessary over the rheological properties of the feed slurry to minimise shrinkage and to determine the thickness of the feed layer.

14.2.2.1 *Drum driers (roller driers)*
Slowly rotating hollow steel drums are heated internally by pressurised steam to 120–170°C. A thin layer of food is spread uniformly over the outer surface by dipping, by spraying, by spreading or by auxiliary feed rollers. Before the drum has completed 1 rev (within 20 s–3 min), the dried food is scraped off by a 'doctor' blade which contacts the drum surface uniformly along its length. Driers may have a single drum (Fig.14.10(a)), or double drums (Fig. 14.10(b)) or twin drums. The single

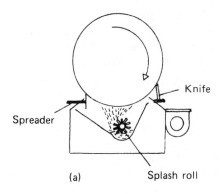

(a)

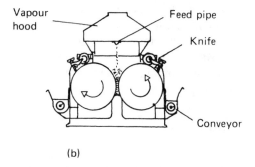

(b)

Fig. 14.10 — Drum driers: (a) single drum; (b) double drum. (Courtesy of APV Mitchell Ltd.)

drum is widely used as it has greater flexibility, a larger proportion of the drum area available for drying, easier access for maintenance and no risk of damage caused by metal objects falling between the drums.

Drum driers have high drying rates and high energy efficiencies. They are suitable for slurries in which the particles are too large for spray drying. However, the high capital cost of the machined drums, and heat damage to sensitive foods from high drum temperatures have caused a move to spray drying for many bulk dried foods. Drum drying is used to produce potato flakes, pre-cooked cereals, molasses, some dried soups and fruit purées, and whey or distillers' solubles for animal feed formulations.

Developments in drum design to improve the sensory and nutritional qualities of dried food include the use of auxiliary rolls to remove and reapply food during drying, the use of high-velocity air to increase the drying rate or the use of chilled air to cool the product. Drums may be enclosed in a vacuum chamber to dry food at lower temperatures, but the high capital cost of this system restricts its use to high-value heat-sensitive foods.

14.2.2.2 Vacuum band and vacuum shelf driers
A food slurry is spread or sprayed onto a steel belt (or 'band') which passes over two hollow drums, within a vacuum chamber at 1–70 Torr. The food is dried by the first steam-heated drum, and then by steam-heated coils or radiant heaters located over the band. The dried food is cooled by the second water-cooled drum and removed by a doctor blade. Vacuum shelf driers consist of hollow shelves in a vacuum chamber. Food is placed in thin layers on flat metal trays which are carefully made to ensure good contact with the shelves. A partial vacuum of 1–70 Torr is drawn in the chamber and steam or hot water is passed through the shelves to dry the food.

Rapid drying and limited heat damage to the food make both methods suitable for heat-sensitive foods. However, care is necessary to prevent the dried food from burning onto trays in vacuum shelf driers, and shrinkage reduces the contact between the food and heated surfaces of both types of equipment. Both have relatively high capital and operating costs and low production rates.

Vacuum band and vacuum shelf driers are used to produce puff-dried foods. *Explosion puff drying* involves partially drying food to a moderate moisture content and then sealing it into a pressure chamber. The pressure and temperature in the chamber are increased and then instantly released. The rapid loss of pressure causes the food to expand and develop a fine porous structure. This permits faster final drying and rapid rehydration. Sensory and nutritional qualities are well retained. The technique was first applied commercially to breakfast cereals and now includes a range of fruit and vegetable products.

14.3 EFFECT ON FOODS

14.3.1 Texture
Changes to the texture of solid foods are an important cause of quality deterioration. The nature and extent of pre-treatments (for example, the addition of calcium chloride to blancher water (Chapter 9), the type and extent of size reduction (Chapter 3), and peeling (Chapter 2)) each affect the texture of rehydrated fruits and vegetables. In foods that are adequately blanched, loss of texture is caused by gelatinisation of starch, crystallisation of cellulose, and localised variations in the moisture content during dehydration, which set up internal stresses. These rupture, compress and permanently distort the relatively rigid cells, to give the food a shrunken shrivelled appearance. On rehydration the product absorbs water more

slowly and does not regain the firm texture associated with the fresh material. There are substantial variations in the degree of shrinkage with different foods (Table 14.3).

Table 14.3 — Approximate ratios for drying, shrinkage and rehydration of selected vegetables

Vegetable	Drying ratio	Overall shrinkage ratio	Rehydration ratio
Cabbage	11.5	21.0	10.5
Carrots, diced	7.5	12.0	7.0
Onions, sliced	7.0	8.0	5.5
Peppers, green	17.0	22.0	8.0
Spinach	13.0	13.5	5.0
Tomato flakes	14.0	20.0	5.0

Drying is not commonly applied to meats in many countries owing to the severe changes in texture compared with other methods of preservation. These are caused by aggregation and denaturation of proteins and a loss of water-holding capacity, which leads to toughening of muscle tissue.

The rate and temperature of drying have a substantial effect on the texture of foods. In general, rapid drying and high temperatures cause greater changes than do moderate rates of drying and lower temperatures. As water is removed during dehydration, solutes move from the interior of the food to the surface. The mechanism and rate of movement are specific for each solute and depend on the type of food and the drying conditions used. Evaporation of water causes concentration of solutes at the surface. High air temperatures (particularly with fruits, fish and meats), cause complex chemical and physical changes to the surface, and the formation of a hard impermeable skin. This is termed *case hardening*. It reduces the rate of drying and produces a food with a dry surface and a moist interior. It is minimised by controlling the drying conditions to prevent excessively high moisture gradients between the interior and the surface of the food.

In powders, the *textural* characteristics are related to bulk density and the ease with which they are rehydrated. These properties are determined by the composition of the food the method of drying, and the particle size of the product. Low-fat foods (for example fruit juices, potato and coffee) are more easily formed into free-flowing powders than are whole milk or meat extracts. Powders are 'instantised' by treating individual particles so that they form free-flowing agglomerates or aggregates, in which there are relatively few points of contact (Fig. 14.11). The surface of each particle is easily wetted when the powder is rehydrated, and particles sink below the surface to disperse rapidly through the liquid. These characteristics are respectively termed *wettability*, *sinkability*, *dispersibility*, and *solubility*. For a powder to be considered 'instant', it should complete these four stages within a few seconds.

The convenience of instantised powders outweighs the additional expense of production, packaging and transport for retail products. However, many powdered foods are used as ingredients in other processes, and these are required to possess a

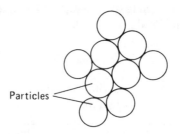

Fig. 14. 11 — Agglomerated powder.

high bulk density and a wider range of particle sizes. Small particles fill the spaces between larger ones and thus exclude air to promote a longer storage life. The characteristics of some powdered foods are described in Table 14.4.

Table 14.4 — Bulk density and moisture content of selected powdered foods

Food	Bulk density (kgm^{-3})	Moisture content (%)
Cocoa	480	3–5
Coffee (ground)	330	7
Coffee (instant)	330	2.5
Coffee creamer	470	3
Corn starch	560	12
Egg, whole	340	2–4
Milk, powdered, skimmed	640	2–4
Milk, instant, skimmed	550	2–4
Salt, granulated	960	0.2
Sugar, granulated	800	0.5
Wheat flour	450	12

Adapted from Watt and Merrill (1975) and Peleg (1983).

14.3.2 Flavour and aroma
Heat not only vaporises water during drying but also causes loss of volatile components from the food. The extent of volatile loss depends on the temperature and solids concentration of the food and on the vapour pressure of the volatiles and their solubility in water vapour. Volatiles which have a high relative volatility and diffusivity are lost at an early stage in drying. Fewer volatile components are lost at later stages. Control of drying conditions during each stage of drying minimises losses. Foods that have a high economic value due to their characteristic flavours (for

example herbs and spices) are dried at low temperatures (Mazza and LeMaguer 1980).

A second important cause of aroma loss is oxidation of pigments, vitamins and lipids during storage. The open porous structure of dried food allows access of oxygen. The rate of deterioration is determined by the storage temperature and the water activity (Chapter 1) of the food.

In dried milk the oxidation of lipids produces rancid flavours owing to the formation of secondary products including δ-lactones. Most fruits and vegetables contain only small quantities of lipid, but oxidation of unsaturated fatty acids to produce hydroperoxides, which react further by polymerisation, dehydration or oxidation to produce aldehydes, ketones and acids, causes rancid and objectionable odours. Some foods (for example carrot) may develop an odour of 'violets' produced by the oxidation of carotenes to β-ionone (Rolls and Porter 1973). These changes are reduced by vacuum or gas packing, low storage temperatures, exclusion of ultraviolet or visible light, maintenance of low moisture contents, addition of synthetic antioxidants (Appendix B, section B.2), or preservation of natural anti-oxidants.

The technical enzyme, glucose oxidase (Chapter 7), is also used to protect dried foods from oxidation. A package which is permeable to oxygen but not to moisture and which contains glucose and the enzyme is placed on the dried food inside a container. Oxygen is removed from the head space during storage. Milk powders are stored under an atmosphere of nitrogen with 10% carbon dioxide. The carbon dioxide is absorbed into the milk and creates a small partial vacuum in the head space. Air diffuses out of the dried particles and is removed by regassing after 24 h. Flavour changes, due to oxidative or hydrolytic enzymes are prevented in fruits by the use of sulphur dioxide, ascorbic acid or citric acid, by pasteurisation of milk or fruit juices and by blanching of vegetables.

Other methods which are used to retain flavours in dried foods include

(1) recovery of volatiles and their return to the product during drying,
(2) mixing recovered volatiles with flavour fixing compounds, which are then granulated and added back to the dried product (for example dried meat powders), and
(3) addition of enzymes, or activation of naturally occurring enzymes, to produce flavours from flavour precursors in the food (for example onion and garlic are dried under conditions that protect the enzymes that release characteristic flavours). Maltose is used as a carrier material when drying flavour compounds.

14.3.3 Colour

Drying changes the surface characteristics of food and hence alters the reflectivity and colour. Chemical changes to carotenoid and chlorophyll pigments are caused by heat and oxidation during drying. In general, longer drying times and higher drying temperatures produce greater pigment losses. Oxidation and residual enzyme activity cause browning during storage. This is prevented by improved blanching methods and treatment of fruits with ascorbic acid or sulphur dioxide. For moderately sulphured fruits and vegetables the rate of darkening during storage is inversely proportional to the residual sulphur dioxide content. However, sulphur dioxide bleaches anthocyanins, and residual sulphur dioxide is an important cause of colour deterioration in stored dried fruits and vegetables.

The rate of Maillard browning in stored milk and fruit products depends on the water activity of the food and the temperature of storage (Chapter 1). The rate of darkening increases markedly at high drying temperatures, when the moisture content of the product exceeds 4–5%, and at storage temperatures above 38°C (Lea, 1958).

14.3.4 Nutritive value

Large differences in reported data on the nutritive value of dried foods are due to wide variations in the preparation procedures, the drying temperature and time, and the storage conditions. In fruits and vegetables, losses during preparation usually exceed those caused by the drying operation. For example Escher and Neukom (1970) showed that losses of vitamin C during preparation of apple flakes were 8% during slicing, 62% from blanching, 10% from puréeing and 5% from drum drying.

Vitamins have different solubilities in water, and, as drying proceeds, some (for example riboflavin) become supersaturated and precipitate from solution. Losses are therefore small (Table 14.5). Others (for example ascorbic acid) are soluble until

Table 14.5 — Vitamin losses in selected dried foods

Food	Loss (%)						
	Vitamin A	Thiamin	Vitamin B$_2$	Niacin	Vitamin C	Folic acid	Biotin
Fruits[a]	6	55	0	10	56		
Fig (sun-dried)	—	48	42	37	—	—	—
Whole milk (spray dried)	—	—	—	–	15	10	10
Whole milk (drum-dried)	—	—	—	–	30	10	10
Pork		50–70					
Vegetables[b]	5	<10	<10				

[a]Fruits mean loss from fresh apple, apricot, peach and prune.
[b]Vegetables mean loss from peas, corn, cabbage and beans (drying stage only).
Adapted from Rolls (1982) and Calloway (1962).

the moisture content of the food falls to very low levels and react with solutes at higher rates as drying proceeds. Vitamin C is also sensitive to heat and oxidation. Short drying times, low temperatures, and low moisture and oxygen levels during storage, are necessary to avoid large losses. Thiamin is also heat sensitive, but other water-soluble vitamins are more stable to heat and oxidation, and losses during drying rarely exceed 5–10% (excluding blanching losses).

Oil-soluble nutrients (for example essential fatty acids and vitamins A, D, E and K) are mostly contained within the dry matter of the food and they are not therefore concentrated during drying. However, water is a solvent for heavy metal catalysts that promote oxidation of unsaturated nutrients. As water is removed, the catalysts become more reactive, and the rate of oxidation accelerates (Fig. 1.11). Fat-soluble vitamins are lost by interaction with the peroxides produced by fat oxidation. Losses during storage are reduced by low oxygen concentration and storage temperatures and by exclusion of light.

The biological value and digestibility of proteins in most foods does not change substantially. However, milk proteins are partially denatured during drum drying, and this results in a reduction in solubility of the milk powder, aggregation and loss of clotting ability. A reduction in biological value of 8–30% is reported, depending on the temperature and residence time (Fairbanks and Mitchell, 1935). Spray drying does not affect the biological value of milk proteins. At high storage temperatures and at moisture contents above approximately 5%, the biological value of milk protein is decreased by Maillard reactions between lysine and lactose. Lysine is heat sensitive and losses in whole milk range from 3–10% in spray drying and 5–40% in drum drying (Rolls and Porter, 1973). The importance of these changes to the nutritional value of foods in the diet is discussed in Chapter 1.

14.4   REHYDRATION

Rehydration is not the reverse of drying. Texture changes, solute migration and volatile losses are each irreversible. Heat reduces the degree of hydration of starch and the elasticity of cell walls and coagulates proteins to reduce their water-holding capacity. The rate and extent of rehydration may be used as an indicator of food quality; those foods that are dried under optimum conditions suffer less damage and rehydrate more rapidly and completely than poorly dried foods.

ACKNOWLEDGEMENTS

Grateful acknowledgement is made for information supplied by the following: APV Mitchell Dryers Ltd, Carlisle, Cumbria, CA5 5DU, UK; Petrie and McNaught Ltd, Rochdale, UK; Zschokke Wartmann Ltd, Stahlrain, CH-5200 Brugg, Switzerland; Proctor and Schwartz Inc., Glasgow, Scotland; Torftech Ltd, Mortimer, Reading, Berkshire, UK; Unilever, London EC4P 4BQ, UK; Chartered Institute of Building Services Engineers, 222 Balham High Road London, SW12 985, UK; De Melkindustrie Veghel.

REFERENCES

Ashworth, J. C. (1981) Developments in dehydration. *Food Manuf.* December. 25–27, 29.

Brenndorfer, B., Kennedy, L., Oswin-Bateman, C. O. and Trim, D. S. (1985) *Solar dryers*. Commonwealth Science Council, Commonwealth Secretariat, Pall Mall, London SW1Y 5HX.

Byrne, M. (1986) The £8M drier. *Food Manuf.* September. 67, 69.

Calloway, D. H. (1962) Dehydrated foods. *Nutr. Rev.* **20** 257–260.

Charm, S. E. (1978) *Fundamentals of food engineering*, 3rd edn. AVI, Westport, Connecticut. pp. 298–408.

Escher. F. and Neukom, H. (1970). Studies on drum-drying apple flakes. *Trav. Chim. Aliment. Hyg.* **61** 339–348 (in German).

Fairbanks, W. and Mitchell, H. H. (1935) The nutritive value of skim-milk powders with special reference to the sensitivity of milk proteins to heat. *J. Agric. Res.* **51** 1107–1121.

Grikitis, K. (1986) Dryer spearheads dairy initiative. *Food Process.* December. 27–28.

Hall, C. W. (1979) *Dictionary of drying*, Marcell Dekker, New York.

Heath, H. B. (1985) The flavour trap. *Food Flavour. Ingredients* **7** 21, 23, 25.

Karel, M. (1975) Dehydration of foods. In: O. R. Fennema (ed.), *Principles of food science*, Part 2, *Physical principles of food preservation*. Marcel Dekker, New York, pp. 309–357.

Kerkhof, P. J. A. M. and Schoeber, W. J. A. H. (1974) Theoretical modelling of the drying behaviour of droplets in spray driers, In: A. Spicer (ed.), *Advances in preconcentration and dehydration of foods*, Applied Science, London, pp. 349–397

Kjaergaard, O. G. (1974) Effects of latest developments on design and practice of spray drying. In: A. Spicer (ed.), *Advances in preconcentration and dehydration of foods*. Applied Science, London, pp. 321–348.

Lea, C. H. (1958) Chemical changes in the preparation and storage of dehydrated foods. In: *Proceedings of Fundamental Aspects of Thermal Dehydration of Foodstuffs*, Aberdeen, 25–27 March, 1958. Society of Chemical Industry, London, pp. 178–194.

Masters, K. (1972) *Spray drying*. Leonard Hill, London, pp. 15, 144, 160, 230, 545–586.

Masters, K. (1983) Recent developments in spray drying. In: S. Thorne (ed.), *Developments in food preservation*, Vol. 2. Applied Science, London, pp. 95–121.

Mazza, G. and LeMaguer, M. (1980) Flavour retention during dehydration of onion. In: P. Linko, Y. Malkki, J. Olkku and J.Larinkari (eds.), *Food process engineering*, Vol. 1, *Food processing systems*. Applied Science, London, pp. 399–406.

Peleg, M. (1983) Physical characteristics of food powders. In: M. Peleg and E. B. Bagley (eds.), *Physical properties of foods*. AVI, Westport, Connecticut, pp. 293–323.

Pisecky, J., Krag, J. and Sorensen, Ib. H. (1983) *Process for producing an agglomerated powdery milk product*, US Patent, No. 4,490,403.

Rolls, B. A. (1982) Effect of processing on nutritive value of food: milk and milk products. In: M. Rechcigl (ed.), *Handbook of the nutritive value of processed foods*, Vol. 1. CRC Press, Boca Raton, Florida, pp. 383–399.

Rolls, B. A. and Porter, J. W. G. (1973) Some effects of processing and storage on the nutritive value of milk and milk products. *Proc. Nutr. Soc.* **32** 9–15.

Sapakie, S. F. and Renshaw, T. A. (1984) Economics of drying and concentration of foods. In: B. M. McKenn (ed.), *Engineering and food*, Vol. 2. Elsevier Applied Science, pp. 927–938.

Schubert, H. (1980) Processing and properties of instant powdered foods. In: P. Linko, Y. Malkki, J. Olkku and J. Larinkari (eds.) *Food process engineering*, Vol. 1, *Food processing systems*. Applied Science, London, pp. 675–684.

Tragardh, C. (1981) Energy and energy analysis in some food processing industries. *Lebensm.-Wiss. Technol.* **14** 213–217.

Watt, B. K. and Merrill, A. L. (1975) *Composition of foods*, Agriculture Handbook 8. US Department of Agriculture, Washington DC.

Zagorzycki, P.E. (1983) Automatic humidity control of dryers. *Chem. Engng. Prog.* April 66–70.

15

Baking and roasting

Baking and roasting are essentially the same unit operation in that they both use heated air to alter the eating quality of foods. The terminology differs in common usage; baking is usually applied to flour based foods or fruits, and roasting to meats, nuts and vegetables. In this chapter the term *baking* is used to include both operations. A secondary purpose of baking is preservation by destruction of micro-organisms and reduction of the water activity at the surface of the food. However, the shelf life of most baked foods is short unless it is extended by refrigeration or packaging.

15.1 THEORY

In an oven, heat is supplied to the food by radiation from the oven walls, by convection from circulating air and by conduction through the tray on which the food is placed. Heat passes through the food by conduction in most cases, although convection currents are established during the initial heating of cake batters. Infrared radiation (Chapter 17) is absorbed into the food and converted to heat by interaction with molecules of the food. Air, other gases and moisture vapour in the oven transfer heat by convection. The heat is converted to conductive heat at the surface of the food and at the oven walls. A boundary film of air acts as a resistance to heat transfer into the food and to movement of water vapour from the food. The thickness of the boundary layer is determined mostly by the velocity of the air and the surface properties of the food (Chapters 1 and 14). Convection currents promote uniform heat distribution throughout the oven, and many commercial designs are fitted with fans to supplement natural convection currents and to reduce the thickness of boundary films. This increases heat transfer coefficients and improves the efficiency of energy utilisation.

Conduction of heat through the baking pan, particularly where it is in contact with the oven hearth or conveyor belt, increases the temperature difference at the base of the food and causes differences in the rate of baking. The low thermal conductivity of foods (Table 1.4) causes low rates of conductive heat transfer and is an important influence on baking time. The size of the pieces of food determines the distance that heat must travel to bake the centre of the food adequately. Methods of heat transfer and resistances to heat and mass transfer are discussed further in Chapter 1.

When a food is placed in an oven, moisture at the surface is evaporated and removed by the hot air. The low humidity of air in the oven establishes moisture vapour pressure gradients, which cause movement of moisture from the interior of the food to the surface; the extent of moisture loss is determined by the nature of the food and the rate of heating. When the rate of moisture loss exceeds the rate of movement from the interior, the zone of evaporation moves inside the food (Fig.

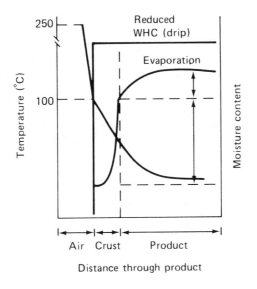

Fig. 15.1 — Changes in temperature and moisture content during baking: WHC, water-holding capacity. (Adapted from Hallstrom and Skoldebrand (1983).)

15.1), the surface dries out, its temperature rises to the temperature of the hot air (110–240°C) and a crust is formed. Because baking takes place at atmospheric pressure and moisture escapes freely from the food, the internal temperature of the food does not exceed 100°C. These changes are similar to those in hot-air drying (Chapter 14), but the more rapid heating and higher temperatures cause complex changes to the components of the food at the surface (section 15.3). These changes both enhance eating qualities and retain moisture in the bulk of the food. The types of mass and heat transfer in different parts of a food during baking are described in Table 15.1.

Equations for the calculation of heat transfer during baking are described in Chapter 1. A relevant sample problem is given in Chapter 17.

Energy consumption during baking is of the order of 450–650 kJ per kilogram of

Table 15.1 — Mass and heat transfer during baking

Zone in the food	Type of mass transfer	Type of heat transfer
Boundary layer	Vapour diffusion	Conduction, convection, radiation
Crust	Vapour diffusion	Conduction, vapour movement (convection)
Evaporation zone	Vapour diffusion, surface diffusion, capillary flow	Conduction, movement of vapour and liquid water
Interior	Capillary flow	Conduction

Adapted from Hallstrom and Skjoldebrand (1983).

food. Most of the heat is used to heat the food, to evaporate water to form the crust, to superheat water vapour (steam) that is transported through the crust and to superheat the dry crust. Commercial ovens are insulated with up to 30 cm of mineral wool, refractory tiles or similar materials, and heat losses are therefore minimised. Other energy conservation devices are described in section 15.2 and Chapter 1.

15.2 EQUIPMENT

Ovens are classified into direct- or indirect-heating types. Both types can be batch or continuous in operation (Chapter 1).

15.2.1 Direct heating ovens

In directly heated ovens, air and the products of combustion are recirculated by natural convection or by fans. The temperature in the oven is controlled automatically, by adjustment of air and fuel flow rates to the burners. Natural or town gas is commonly used, but propane, butane, fuel oil or solid fuels are also found (Chapter 1). Gas is burned in ribbon burners located above and below conveyor belts in continuous ovens, and at the base of the cabinet in batch ovens. Safety features are incorporated to extinguish the burners automatically if abnormal baking conditions arise, and pressure-relief panels are fitted to the top of the ovens to protect personnel should an explosion occur.

The advantages of direct heating ovens include:

(1) short baking times,
(2) high thermal efficiencies,
(3) good control (using the fan speed and the rate of fuel consumption) and
(4) rapid startup, as it is only necessary to heat the air in the oven.

However, care is necessary to prevent contamination of the food by undesirable products of combustion, and gas burners require regular servicing to maintain combustion efficiency. Microwave ovens (Chapter 17) are a further example of direct-heating ovens.

15.2.2 Indirect-heating ovens

Heat from burning fuel is used to heat air, or steam pipes, which are then used to heat the baking chamber. Steam tubes are either heated directly by burning fuel (Fig.

Fig. 15.2 — Batch indirectly heated oven. (Courtesy of Thomas Collins Ltd.)

15.2) or supplied with steam from a remote boiler. The steam tubes then heat air in the baking chamber. Heated air is commonly recirculated through the baking chamber and a separate heat exchanger (Fig.15.3). Alternatively, combustion gases are passed through banks of radiator tubes in the baking chamber, or fuel is burned between a double wall, and the combustion products are exhausted from the top of the oven. Electric ovens are heated by induction heating radiator plates or bars. In batch ovens, the walls and base are heated whereas, in continuous ovens, radiators are located above, alongside and below a conveyor belt.

Forced-convection hot-air systems have shorter startup times and a faster response to temperature control than do radiant ovens, because only the air is heated. Conventional heating, forced-convection heating, infrared heating and combined heating methods are compared by Malkki *et al.* (1984). Steam-heated batch ovens are also used for cooking meat products. Similar designs are fitted with

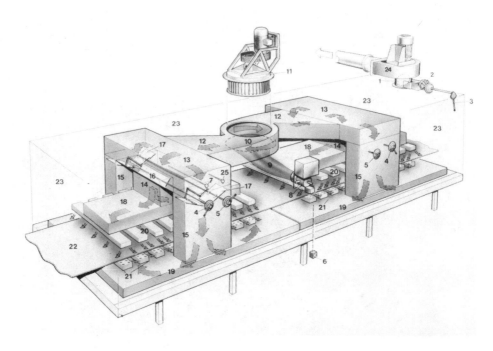

Fig. 15.3 — Continuous indirectly heated oven: (Courtesy of Spooner Industries Ltd.)

smoke generators for smoking meats, cheeses and fish. These are described in detail by Toth and Potthast (1984). The techniques used in smoking are discussed by Lee (1983).

15.2.3   Batch ovens
The advantages and limitations of batch equipment are described in Chapter 1. In the *Peel oven*, food is loaded into a baking chamber, either on trays or singly, by means of a long-handled shovel (a *peel*) which gives its name to the oven. More recent designs include the *multi-deck oven* (Fig.15.4) which is widely used for baked goods, meats and confectionery products. Some designs have a 'modular' construction to allow expansion of production by duplication of modules, without having to replace the entire plant. The main disadvantages of batch ovens are higher labour costs and lack of uniformity in baking times, caused by the delay in loading and unloading.

15.2.4   Continuous and semi-continuous ovens
Rotary-hearth ovens (Fig. 15.5(a)), *reel ovens* (Fig. 15.5(b)) and *multi-cycle tray ovens* (Fig. 15.5(c)) all circulate the food through the oven on trays, and loading and unloading take place though the same door. The operation is semi-continuous when the oven must be stopped to remove the food. The movement of food through the oven, with or without fans to circulate the air, ensures more uniform heating. *Rotary-hearth ovens* have short baking times but take up a large floor space. *Reel*

Fig. 15.4 — Multi-deck oven. (Courtesy of Werner and Pfeiderer Ltd.)

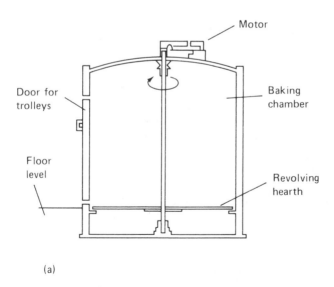

(a)

Fig. 15.5 — Ovens: (a) revolving-hearth oven (in smaller models products are placed directly onto the hearth through a narrow opening at working height); (b) reel oven (courtesy of Thomas Collins Ltd); (c) multi-cycle tray oven. (After Matz (1972).)

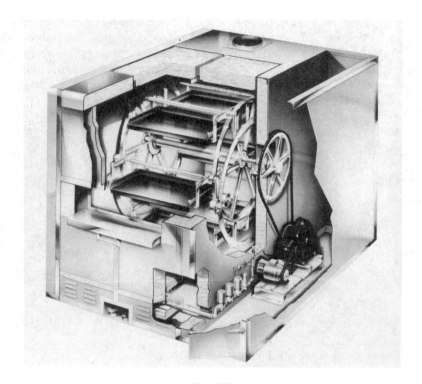

Fig. 15.5b

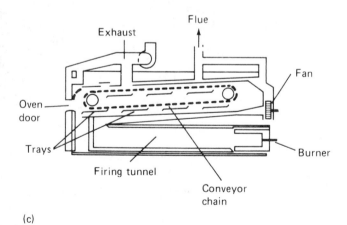

(c)

Fig. 15.5c

ovens move the product vertically through the oven and also horizontally from front to back. This permits a higher baking area for a given floor space, and more uniform temperature distribution through the oven. The disadvantages of these ovens include the absence of zones of heating, and difficulty in automating loading and unloading. In many applications they are now replaced by tray and tunnel ovens. *Tray ovens* have a similar design to tunnel ovens but have metal trays permanently fixed to a chain conveyor. Each tray holds several baking pans and is pulled through the oven in one direction, then lowered onto a second rack, returned through the oven and unloaded (Fig.15.5(c)).

Tunnel ovens (*conveyor-band* or *travelling-hearth ovens*) (Fig. 15.6) consist of a

Fig. 15.6 — Tunnel oven. (Courtesy of Werner and Pfeiderer Ltd.)

metal tunnel (up to 120 m long and 1.5 m wide) through which food is conveyed either on steel plates (in a travelling-hearth oven) or on a solid, perforated or woven metal belt in the band oven. The oven is divided into heating zones (Fig. 15.3). The temperature and humidity are independently controlled in each zone by heaters and dampers. These retain or remove moisture by adjusting the proportions of fresh and recirculated air in the oven. Vapour (and in direct-heating ovens, the products of combustion) are extracted separately from each zone. Many designs are equipped with heat recovery systems (Fig. 15.7). Microprocessor control of the belt speed,

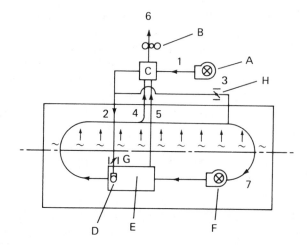

Fig. 15.7 — Heat recovery system for convection oven: A, supply air fan; B, exhaust fan; C, heat recovery heat exchanger; D, burner; E, oven chamber heat exchanger (not in direct-fired ovens); F, oven chamber air recirculating fan; G, combustion air control damper; H, zone integrity air control damper; 1, cold supply air; 2, hot combustion air; 3, hot-zone integrity air; 4, oven exhaust air plus product evaporation; 5, hot-oven heat exchanger exhaust; 6, cooled combined exhaust; 7, recirculating oven chamber air. (Courtesy of Baker Perkins Ltd.)

heater output and position of dampers automatically adjusts the baking conditions in each zone, to produce foods of a pre-determined colour or moisture content. In addition the microprocessor provides management information of production rates, energy efficiency and maintenance requirements (Chapter 24). Some ovens are fitted with programmable cycles in which temperature and time of heating, relative humidity, cooling time and air speed are independently programmed for each of 20 or more products. This allows rapid changes to baking conditions and a high degree of flexibility for different types of product.

Despite the high capital cost and large floor area, these ovens are widely used for large-scale baking. The main advantages are their high capacity, accuracy of control over baking conditions and low labour costs owing to automatic loading and unloading. In both tunnel and tray ovens, heat exchangers are fitted to the exhaust flues to remove heat from the exhaust gases and to heat fresh or recirculated air. Energy savings of 30% are achieved and startup times can be reduced by 60%.

15.3   EFFECT ON FOODS

The purpose of baking and roasting is to alter the sensory properties of foods, to improve palatability and to extend the range of tastes, aromas and textures in the diet. Baking also destroys enzymes and micro-organisms and lowers the water activity of the food to some extent (Table 1.10), thereby preserving the food.

15.3.1   Texture
Changes in texture are determined by the nature of the food (moisture content and the composition of fats, proteins and structural carbohydrates (cellulose, starches

and pectins)) and by the temperature and duration of heating. A characteristic of many baked foods is the formation of a dry crust containing the moist bulk of the food (for example meats, bread, potato or yam). Other foods (for example biscuits) are baked to a lower moisture content, and in these the changes that take place in the crust occur throughout the food.

When meat is heated, fats melt and become dispersed as oil through the food or drain out as a component of 'drip losses'. Collagen is solubilised below the surface, to form gelatin. Oils are dispersed through the channels produced in the meat. Proteins become denatured, lose their water-holding capacity and contract. This forces out additional fats and water and toughens and shrinks the food. Further increases in temperature cause destruction of micro-organisms and inactivation of enzymes. The surface dries (section 15.1), and the texture becomes crisper and harder as a porous crust is formed by coagulation, degradation and partial pyrolysis of proteins. In cereal foods, changes to the granular structure of starch, gelatinisation and dehydration produce the characteristic texture of the crust.

Rapid heating produces an impermeable crust which seals in moisture and fat and protects nutrients and flavour components from degradation. A steep moisture vapour concentration gradient is formed between the moist interior (high a_w) and hygroscopic exterior (low a_w) of the food. During storage, moisture migrates through the food. If preservative methods (for example freezing) are not used to immobilise the moisture, this migration softens the crust, lowers the eating quality and thus limits the shelf life of the food. Slower heating permits larger quantities of moisture to escape from the surface of the food before it is sealed by the crust. This results in a shallower moisture vapour concentration gradient and a drier interior in the food. In bread ovens, initial steam heating reduces dehydration of the dough surface, and the crust therefore remains elastic for longer. Ragged breaks in the dough are avoided and the dough expands more fully. The crust is smoother and glossier, and starch hydrolysis promotes Maillard browning reactions to give a better crust colour.

15.3.2 Flavour, aroma and colour

The aromas produced by baking are an important sensory characteristic of baked goods. The severe heating conditions in the surface layers of food cause Maillard browning reactions between sugars and amino acids. Details of the chemistry of the Maillard reaction and Strecker degradation are discussed by a number of workers including Mauron (1982) and Danehy (1986). The high temperatures and low moisture contents in the surface layers also cause caramelisation of sugars and oxidation of fatty acids to aldehydes, lactones, ketones, alcohols and esters. The Maillard reaction and Strecker degradation produce different aromas according to the combination of free amino acids and sugars present in a particular food. Each amino acid produces a characteristic aroma when heated with a given sugar, owing to the production of a specific aldehyde. Different aromas are produced, depending on the type of sugar and the heating conditions used (for example the amino acid proline can produce aromas of potato, mushroom or burnt egg, when heated with different sugars and at different temperatures). An abbreviated summary of the aromas produced from the most important amino acids in four foods is shown in Table 15.2.

Further heating degrades some of the volatiles produced by the above mecha-

Table 15.2 — Aromas produced by baking or roasting

Food	Predominant amino acids	Selected characteristic aromas after heating with a single sugar
Potato	Asparagine	—
	Glutamine	Caramel, butterscotch, burnt sugar
	Valine	Fruity, sweet, yeasty
	Aminobutyric acid	Caramel, maple syrup, nutty
Peanut	Alanine	Caramel, nutty, malt
	Phenylalanine	Sweet and rancid caramel, violets
	Asparagine	—
	Arginine	Bready, buttery, burnt sugar
Beef	Valine	Fruity, sweet, yeasty
	Glycine	Caramel, smoky, burnt
	Leucine	Toasted, cheesy, malt, bready
Cocoa bean	Leucine	Toasted, cheesy, malt, bready
	Alanine	Caramel, nutty, malt
	Phenylalanine	Sweet and rancid caramel, violets
Valine		Fruity, sweet, yeasty

Adapted from Adrian (1982).

nisms to produce burnt or smoky aromas. There are therefore a very large number of component aromas produced during baking. The type of aroma therefore depends on the particular combination of fats, amino acids and sugars present in the surface layers of food, the temperature and moisture content of the food throughout the heating period and the time of heating. Details of the aromatic chemicals produced during the baking of bread and roasting of peanuts, coffee, cocoa and meat are given by Adrian (1982).

The characteristic golden brown colour associated with baked foods is due to Maillard reactions, caramelisation of sugars and dextrins (either present in the food or produced by hydrolysis of starches) to furfural and hydroxymethyl furfural, carbonisation of sugars, fats and proteins.

15.3.3 Nutritional value

Some baked foods (for example bread and meat) are important components of the diet in many countries and are therefore an important source of proteins, vitamins and minerals. For example, lysine is the limiting amino acid in wheat flour and its destruction by baking is therefore nutritionally important. Other baked foods (for example nuts, biscuits, cocoa, coffee and snackfoods) are less important in the diet, and nutritional losses are therefore less significant. The effect on the diet of changes in foods due to processing is discussed in Chapter 1.

The main nutritional changes during baking occur at the surface of foods, and the ratio of surface area to volume is therefore an important factor in determining the effect on overall nutritional loss. In pan bread, only the upper surface is affected and the pan protects the bulk of the bread from substantial nutritional changes. With the exception of vitamin C, which is added to bread dough as an improver and is completely destroyed during baking, other vitamin losses are relatively small. In chemically leavened doughs the alkaline conditions release niacin which is bound to polysaccharides and polypeptides and therefore increase its concentration (Appendix A). The vitamin content of bread is also determined by the extent of fermentation which increases the amount of B vitamins (Chapter 7). In meats the size of the piece, the type of joint, the proportions of bone and fat, pre- and post-slaughter treatments and the type of animal all affect nutrient losses. Some thiamin is removed in pan drippings but, as these are usually consumed, the overall losses are smaller. Cover *et al*, (1949) studied the effect of baking temperature on vitamin losses in different meats. At 150°C the meats were well cooked and total thiamin losses were moderate. At higher temperatures the pan drippings were charred and inedible, and total losses were therefore substantially increased (Table 15.3). In biscuits, breakfast cereals and

Table 15.3 — Vitamin losses in roast meats

Vitamin	Vitamin loss (%)			
	Oven temperature, 150°C		Oven temperature, 205°C	
	Beef; internal temperature, 80°C	Pork; internal temperature, 84°C	Beef; internal temperature, 98°C	Pork; internal temperature, 98°C
Thiamin				
Meat only	39	36	53	46
Drip loss	94	83	—	—
Pantothenic acid				
Meat only	27	35	40	37
Drip loss	80	75	—	—
Niacin				
Meat only	24	31	29	33
Drip loss	84	74	—	—
Riboflavin				
Meat only	25	27	32	31
Drip loss	84	81	—	—

Adapted from Cover *et al.* (1949).

crispbread the bulk of the food is heated to a similar extent. However, these are smaller pieces which require a shorter baking time, and losses are therefore reduced. In prepared foods, which have ingredients that have been processed to stabilise them for storage, there may be additional losses in nutritional quality (for example from milling wheat, drying fruit, frozen storage of meats or fermentation and drying of cocoa and coffee beans).

Thiamin is the most important heat-labile vitamin in both cereal foods and meats, and losses are reported in Table 15.4. In cereal foods the extent of thiamin loss is

Table 15.4 — Thiamin losses during baking

Food	Thiamin loss (%)
Beef	40–60
Pork	30–40
Ham	50
Lamb	40–50
Poultry	30–45
Bread	15
Cake	23
Cake[a]	30–95
Soya bean	90

[a]Chemical leavening agent used.
Adapted from Farrer (1955).

determined by the temperature of baking and the pH of the food. Loss of thiamin in pan bread is approximately 15% (Bender, 1978) but, in cakes or biscuits that are chemically leavened by sodium bicarbonate, the losses increase to 50–95%.

During baking, the physical state of proteins and fats is altered, and starch is gelatinised and hydrolysed to dextrins and then reducing sugars. However, in each case the nutritional value is not substantially affected. The loss of amino acids and reducing sugars in Maillard browning reactions causes a small reduction in nutritive value. In particular, lysine is lost in Maillard reactions, which slightly reduces the protein quality. In bread the *protein efficiency ratio* is reduced by 23% compared with that of the original flour (Bender, 1978). The extent of loss is increased by higher temperatures, longer baking times and larger amounts of reducing sugars. The amylase activity of flour, the addition of sugar to dough, the use of fungal amylases (Chapter 7), and steam injection into ovens to gelatinise the surface starch and to improve crust colour all therefore affect the nutritive value of the proteins to some extent. In biscuits, a reduction in dough thickness from 4.9 mm to 3.8 mm, each baked at 170°C for 8 mins, produced higher losses of amino acids as follows: tryptophan, from 8% to 44%; methionine, from 15% to 48%; lysine, from 27% to 61% (Mauron *et al*, 1960). In maize, lysine loss is increased from 5% to 88% during the manufacture of breakfast cereals. This loss is corrected by fortification.

ACKNOWLEDGEMENTS

Grateful acknowledgement is made for information supplied by the following: Spooner Industries Ltd, Ilkley, West Yorkshire LS29 8JB, UK; Werner and Pfleiderer, Postfach 30 12 20, D-7000 Stuttgart 30, West Germany; Thomas Collins Ltd, Kingswood, Bristol BS15 1QH, UK; Atlas Equipment Ltd, London N17 6AZ, UK; Baker Perkins BCS Ltd, Peterborough PE3 6TA, UK.

REFERENCES

Adrian, J. (1982) The Maillard reaction. In: M. Rechcigl (ed.) *Handbook of the nutritive value of processed food,* Vol. 1. CRC Press, Boca Raton, Florida, pp. 529–608.

Bender, A. E. (1978) *Food processing and nutrition.* Academic Press, London.

Cover, S., Dilsaver, E. M., Hays, R. M., and Smith, W. H. (1949) Retention of B-vitamins after large scale cooking of meat, II, Roasting by two methods. *J. Am. Diet. Assoc.* **25** 949–954.

Danehy, J. P. (1986) Maillard reactions: non-enzymic browning in food systems with specific reference to the development of flavour. *Adv. Food Res.* **30** 77–138.

Farrer, K. T. H. (1955) The thermal destruction of vitamin B1 in foods. *Adv. Food Res.* **6** 257–311.

Hallstrom, B., and Skjoldebrand, C. (1983) Heat and mass transfer in solid foods. In: S. Thorne (ed.), *Developments in food preservation,* Vol. 2. Applied Science, London, pp. 61–94.

Lee, J., (1983) Smoked foods—past, present and future. *Food Process.* September 39–41.

Malkki, Y., Seibel, W., Skjoldebrand, C., and Rask, O. (1984). Optimization of the baking process and its influence on bread quality. In: P. Zeuthen, J. C. Cheftel, C. Eriksson, M. Jul, H. Leniger, P. Linko, G. Varela and G. Vos (eds), *Thermal processing and quality of foods.* Elsevier Applied Science, Barking, Essex, pp. 355–361.

Matz, S. A. (1972) *Bakery technology and engineering.* AVI, Westport, Connecticut.

Mauron, J., Mottu, F., and Egli, R. H. (1960) Problemes nutritionnels que pose la malnutrition protieque dans les pays en voie de developpment. *Ann. Nutr. Aliment.* **14** 135–150.

Mauron, J. (1982) Effect of processing on nutritive value of food: protein. In M. Rechcigl (ed.), *Handbook of the nutritive value of processed food,* Vol. 1. CRC Press, Boca Raton, Florida, pp. 429–472.

Toth, L., and Potthast, K., (1984) Chemical aspects of the smoking of meat and meat products. *Adv. Food Res.* **29** 87–158.

C. Heat processing using hot oils

16

Frying

Frying is a unit operation which is used to alter the eating quality of a food. A secondary consideration is the preservative effect that results from thermal destruction of micro-organisms and enzymes, and a reduction in water activity at the surface of the food (or throughout the food, if it is fried in thin slices). The shelf life of fried goods is mostly determined by the moisture content after frying. Foods that retain a moist interior (for example doughnuts, fish and poultry products which may also be breaded or battered (Chapter 21)) have a relatively short shelf life, owing to moisture and oil migration during storage. These foods are not widely produced on a commercial scale for distribution to retail stores but are important in catering applications. If necessary, these foods are preserved by chilling (Chapter 18) for a few days. Foods that are more thoroughly dried by frying (for example potato crisps (potato chips in the USA) maize and other potato snackfoods, and extruded half-products (Chapter 13)) have a shelf life of up to 12 months at ambient temperature. The quality is maintained by adequate barrier properties of packaging materials (Chapter 22) and correct storage conditions.

16.1 THEORY

When food is placed in hot oil, the surface temperature rises rapidly and water is vaporised as steam. The surface then begins to dry out in a similar way to that described during baking and roasting (Chapter 15). The plane of evaporation moves inside the food, and a crust is formed. The surface temperature of the food then rises to that of the hot oil, and the internal temperature rises more slowly towards 100°C. The rate of heat transfer is controlled by the temperature difference between the oil and the food and by the surface heat transfer coefficient. The rate of heat penetration into the food is controlled by the thermal conductivity of the food (Table 1.4). These mechanisms are described in detail in Chapter 1.

The surface crust has a porous structure, consisting of different-sized capillaries. During frying, both water and water vapour are removed from the larger capillaries first, and replaced by hot oil. Moisture moves from the surface of the food through a boundary film of oil. The thickness of the boundary layer controls the rate of heat and mass transfer (Chapter 1), and is determined by the viscosity and velocity of the oil. The water vapour pressure gradient between the moist interior of the food and the dry oil is the driving force behind moisture loss, in a similar way to hot air dehydration (Chapter 14).

The time taken for food to be completely fried depends on

(1) the type of food,
(2) the temperature of the oil,
(3) the method of frying (shallow or deep-fat frying),
(4) the thickness of the food and
(5) the required change in eating quality.

Foods that retain a moist interior are fried until the thermal centre has received sufficient heat to destroy contaminating micro-organisms and to change the organoleptic properties to the desired extent. This is particularly important for comminuted meat products or other foods that are able to support the growth of pathogenic bacteria.

The temperature used for frying is determined mostly by economic considerations and the requirements of the product. At high temperatures, processing times are reduced and production rates are therefore increased. However, high temperatures also cause accelerated deterioration of the oil to free fatty acids, which alters the viscosity, flavour and colour of the oil. This increases the frequency with which it must be changed and hence increases oil costs. A second economic loss arises from the vigorous boiling of the food at high temperatures and loss of oil by entrainment. Acrelein is a breakdown product, produced at high temperatures, which forms a blue haze above the oil and is a source of atmospheric pollution.

The temperature of frying is also determined by the product requirements. Foods in which a crust and a moist interior are required, are produced by high-temperature frying. The rapid crust formation both seals moisture into the food and restricts the rate of heat transfer to the interior. The bulk of the food therefore retains a moist texture and the flavour of the ingredients. Foods which are dried by frying are processed at a lower temperature to cause the plane of evaporation to move deeper inside the food before the crust forms. They are therefore dried before excessive changes to the surface colour or flavour occur.

There are two main methods of commercial frying which are distinguished by the method of heat transfer involved: these are shallow frying and deep-fat frying.

16.1.1 Shallow (or contact) frying

This method is most suited to foods which have a large surface-area-to-volume ratio (for example bacon slices, eggs, burgers and other types of pattie). Heat is transferred to the food mostly by conduction from the hot surface of the pan, through a thin layer of oil (Fig. 16.1). The thickness of the layer of oil varies owing to irregularities in the surface of the food. This, together with the action of bubbles of steam which lift the food off the hot surface, causes temperature variations as frying proceeds and produces the characteristic irregular browning of shallow fried foods. Shallow frying has high surface heat transfer coefficients ($200–450\,\mathrm{W\,m^{-2}\,K^{-1}}$), although as explained above this is not uniformly found across the entire surface of the food.

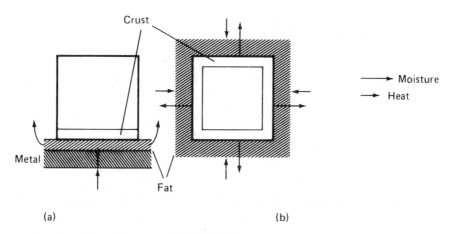

Fig. 16.1 — Heat and mass transfer in (a) shallow frying and (b) deep-fat frying.

16.1.2 Deep-fat frying

Heat transfer is a combination of convection within the hot oil and conduction to the interior of the food. All surfaces of the food receive a similar heat treatment, to produce a uniform colour and appearance (Fig. 16.1). Deep-fat frying is suitable for foods of all shapes, but irregularly shaped food tends to entrain a greater volume of oil when it is removed from the frier. Heat transfer coefficients are $250\text{--}300 \, \text{W m}^{-2} \text{K}^{-1}$ before evaporation of moisture from the surface begins but subsequently increase to $800\text{--}1000 \, \text{W m}^{-2} \text{K}^{-1}$ owing to the violent turbulence caused by steam escaping from the food. However, if the rate of evaporation is too high, a thin film of water vapour remains around the food and reduces the heat transfer coefficient (Hallstrom, 1980).

Sample problem 16.1
A deep-fat fryer tank measuring 2.8 m deep, 1 m high and 1.5 m wide, and constructed from 4 mm stainless steel, is operated for $12 \, \text{h day}^{-1}$ and 250 days year^{-1} at 200°C. Ignoring the resistance to heat transfer caused by boundary films, calculate the annual financial savings arising from reduced energy consumption if the tank is insulated with 30 mm of fibre insulation. (Additional data: the thermal conductivity of stainless steel is $21 \, \text{W m}^{-2} \, \text{K}^{-1}$, the thermal conductivity of the fibre insulation is $0.035 \, \text{W m}^{-2} \text{K}^{-1}$, the average ambient air temperature is 18°C and the energy cost is £0.01 kW h^{-1}.)

Solution to sample problem 16.1
First,

$$\text{area of uninsulated tank} = 2(1.5 \times 1 + 2.8 \times 1 + 2.8 \times 1.5)$$
$$= 17 \, \text{m}^2$$

From equations (1.14) and (1.15),

$$200 - 18 = \frac{Q}{17} \frac{0.004}{21}$$

Therefore,

$$Q = 1.625 \times 10^7 \, \text{W}$$

Now

$$\text{area of insulated tank} = 2(1.506 \times 1.06 + 2.806 \times 1.06 + 2.806 \times 1.506)$$
$$= 17.88 \, \text{m}^2$$

and

$$200 - 18 = \frac{Q}{17.88} \left(\frac{0.004}{21} + \frac{0.03}{0.035} \right)$$

Thus,

$$Q = 3797 \, W$$

The number of hours of operation per year is 3000 which equals 10.8×10^6 s. Now $1 \, \text{kWh} = 1000 \, \text{W}$ for $3600 \, \text{s} = 3.6 \times 10^6 \, \text{J}$. Therefore

$$\text{cost of energy without insulation} \frac{(1.625 \times 10^7)(10.8 \times 10^6)}{3.6 \times 10^6} \times 0.01$$
$$= £487\,500$$

and

$$\text{cost of energy with insulation} = \frac{3797(10.8 \times 10^6)}{3.6 \times 10^6} \times 0.01$$
$$= £114$$

Thus

$$\text{saving} = 487\,500 - 114$$
$$= £487\,386$$

16.2 EQUIPMENT

Shallow-frying equipment consists of a heated metal surface, covered in a thin layer of oil. Commercially, continuous deep-fat friers are more important. In batch operation the food is suspended in a bath of hot oil and retained for the required degree of frying, often assessed by changes in surface colour. Continuous deep-fat friers consist of a stainless steel mesh conveyor which is submerged in a thermostatically controlled oil tank (Fig. 16.2). They are heated by electricity, gas, fuel oil or

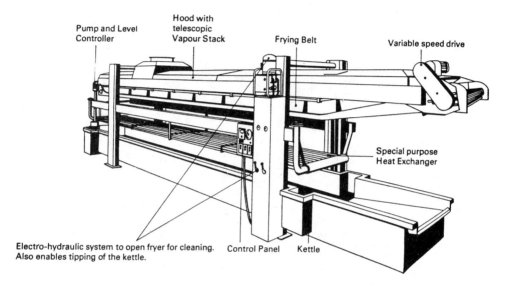

Fig. 16.2 — Continuous deep-fat frier. (Courtesy of Coat and Fry Ltd.)

steam. Food is metered into the oil by slow-moving paddles and either sinks to a submerged conveyor or, if the food floats, is held below the surface by a second conveyor (Fig. 16.3). The conveyor speed and oil temperature control the frying time. An inclined conveyor then removes the food and allows excess oil to drain back into the tank. The equipment operates automatically at production rates of up to 15 t of fried product per hour.

Oil is continuously recirculated through external heaters and filters to remove particles of food, and fresh oil is added automatically to maintain the desired level in the tank. These features extend the useful life of the oil by removing food particles that would otherwise burn and affect the flavour and colour of the product. The viscosity of the oil is important for optimum heat transfer and minimum entrainment in the food. The correct viscosity is achieved when the oil is heated until the free fatty acid content reaches 0.4%. Methyl silicone is added to prevent foaming.

Heat and oil recovery systems are used to reduce energy and oil costs. Energy saving is achieved by heat exchangers, mounted in the exhaust hood. These recover heat from escaping steam and use it to pre-heat incoming food or oil, or to heat process water. Oil recovery systems remove entrained oil from the steam and return it to the oil tank. In addition, pollution control systems prevent smoke and other

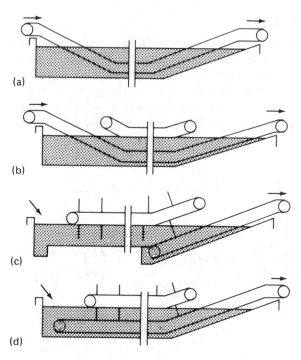

Fig. 16.3 — Different conveyor arrangements: (a) delicate non-buoyant products (for example fish sticks); (b) breadcrumb-coated products; (c) dry buoyant bulk products (for example half-product snacks); (d) dual purpose (for example nuts and snacks). (Courtesy of Coat and Fry Ltd.)

products of oil degradation from being discharged into the atmosphere, by feeding the exhaust air into the burner used to heat the oil (Fig. 16.4). Computer control of the air temperature in the heater, exhaust gas temperature, oil temperature, oil level and flow rate reduces the exhaust temperature from 245°C to 110°C to give thermal efficiencies of 80–90%.

16.3 EFFECT ON FOODS

Frying is an unusual unit operation in that the product of one food process (cooking oil) is used as the heat transfer medium. The effect of frying on foods therefore involves both the effect on the oil, which in turn influences the quality of the food, and the direct effect of heat on the fried product.

16.3.1 Effect of heat on oil

Prolonged heating of oils at the high temperatures used in frying, in the presence of moisture and oxygen released from foods, causes oxidation of the oil to a range of volatile carbonyls, hydroxy acids, keto acids and epoxy acids. These cause unpleasant flavours and darkening of the oil. Polymerisation of oil molecules in the absence of oxygen produces cyclic compounds and high-molecular-weight polymers, which

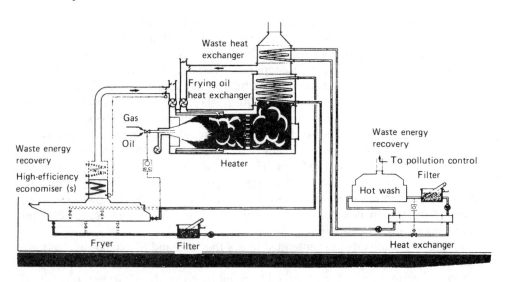

Fig. 16.4 — Heat and oil recovery system. (Courtesy of Flomech Ltd.)

increase the viscosity of the oil. This lowers the surface heat transfer coefficient during frying and increases the amount of oil entrained by the food. The potential toxicity of the products of oil decomposition and other nutritional changes are discussed by Witting and Dimick (1982) and Poling *et al.* (1960).

Oxidation of fat-soluble vitamins in the oil result in a loss of nutritive value. Retinol, carotenoids and tocopherols are each destroyed and contribute to the changes in flavour and colour of the oil. However, the preferential oxidation of tocopherols has a protective (anti-oxidant) effect on the oil. This is particularly important as most frying oils are of vegetable origin and contain a large proportion of unsaturated fats which are readily oxidised. The essential fatty acid, linoleic acid, is readily lost and therefore changes the balance of saturated and unsaturated fatty acids (Kilgore and Bailey, 1970).

16.3.2 Effect of heat on fried foods
The main purpose of frying is the development of characteristic colours, flavours and aromas in the crust of fried foods. These eating qualities are developed by a combination of Maillard reactions (described in Chapter 15) and volatile compounds absorbed from the oil. The main factors that control the changes to colour and flavour in a given food are therefore

(1) the type of oil used for frying,
(2) the age and thermal history of the oil,
(3) the temperature and time of frying,
(4) the size and surface characteristics of the food and
(5) post-frying treatments.

Each of these factors also influences the amount of oil entrained within the food. The texture of fried foods is produced by changes to proteins, fats and polymeric carbohydrates which are similar to those produced by baking (Chapter 15).

The effect of frying on the nutritive value of foods depends on the type of process used. High oil temperatures produce rapid crust formation and seal the food surface. This reduces the extent of changes to the bulk of the food, and therefore retains a high proportion of the nutrients. In addition, these foods are usually consumed shortly after frying and there are few or no losses during storage. For example a 17% loss of available lysine is reported in fried fish, although this increased to 25% when thermally damaged oil was used (Tooley, 1972). Shallow-fried liver lost 15% thiamin (Kotschevar *et al.*, 1955) and no folate (Hurdle *et al.*, 1968). Vitamin C losses in fried potatoes are reported to be lower than in boiling (Domah Aabmud *et al.*, 1974). The vitamin accumulates as dehydroascorbic acid (DAA) owing to the lower moisture content whereas, in boiling, DAA is hydrolysed to 2,3-diketogluconic acid and therefore becomes unavailable.

Frying operations that are intended to dry the food and to extend the shelf life cause substantially higher losses of nutrients, particularly fat-soluble vitamins. For example vitamin E, which is absorbed from oil by crisps during frying, is oxidised during subsequent storage. Bunnell *et al.* (1965) found 77% loss after 8 weeks at ambient temperature. Oxidation proceeds at a similar rate at low temperatures and French-fried potatoes lost 74% in a similar period under frozen storage. Heat- or oxygen-sensitive water-soluble vitamins are also destroyed by frying under these conditions. Changes to protein quality occur as a result of Maillard reactions with amino acids in the crust (Chapter 15). Losses of carbohydrates and minerals are largely unreported but are likely to be small. The fat content of the food increases owing to oil entrainment, but the nutritional significance of this is difficult to determine as it varies according to the type and thermal history of the oil, and the amount entrained in the food. The effect of changes due to processing on the nutritional value of foods is discussed further in Chapter 1.

ACKNOWLEDGEMENTS

Grateful acknowledgement is made for information supplied by the following: Atlas Equipment Ltd, London N17 6AZ, UK; Flo-Mech Ltd, Peterborough PE2 0YA, UK; Coat and Fry Ltd, Derby DE2 8JD, UK; Heat and Control Inc., San Francisco, California 94080, USA.

REFERENCES

Bunnell, R. H., Keating, J., Quaresimo, A., and Parman, G. K. (1965) Alpha-tocopherol contents of foods. *Am. J. Clin. Nutr.* **17**, 1–10.

Domah Aabmud, A. M. B., Davidek, J., and Velisek, J. (1974) Changes of L-ascorbic and L-dehydroascorbic acids during cooking and frying of potatoes. *Z. Lebensm.-Unters. Forsch.* **154** 272.

Hallstrom, B. (1980) Heat and mass transfer in industrial cooking. In: P. Linko, Y. Malkki, J. Olkku and J. Larinkari (eds), *Food process engineering*, Vol. 1, *Food processing systems*. Applied Science, London, pp. 457–465.

Hurdle, A. D. F., Barton, D., and Searles, I. H. (1968) A method for measuring folate in food and its application to a hospital diet. *Am. J. Clin. Nutr.* **21**, 1202–1207.

Kilgore, L. and Bailey, M. (1970) Degradation of linoleic acid during potato frying. *J. Am. Diet. Assoc.* **56**, 130–132.

Kotschevar, L. H., Mosso, A., and Tugwell, T. (1955) B-vitamin retention in frozen meat. *J. Am. Diet. Assoc.* **31**, 589–596.

Matz, S. A. (1972) Bakery technology and engineering. AVI, Westport, Connecticut, pp. 61–81.

Poling, C. E., Warner, W. D., Mone, P. E., and Rice, E. E. (1960) The nutritional value of fats after use in commercial deep-fat frying. *J. Nutr.* **72**, 109–120.

Tooley, P. J., (1972). The effect of deep-fat frying on the availability of fish lysine. *Nutr. Soc. Proc.* **31**, 2A.

Witting, L. A., and Dimick, P. S. (1982) Effects of processing on food lipids. In: M. Rechcigl (ed.), *Handbook of the nutritive value of processed foods*, Vol. 1, CRC Press, Boca Raton, Florida, pp. 403–428.

D. Heating by irradiated energy

17

Microwave and Infrared Radiation

Microwave and infrared (radiant) energy are two forms of electromagnetic energy (Fig. 17.1). They are both transmitted as waves, which penetrate food, and are then

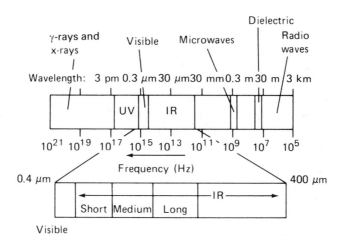

Fig. 17.1 — Electromagnetic spectrum. (Courtesy of the Electricity Council.)

converted to heat. The main differences between microwave and infrared energy are as follows.

(1) Microwaves are produced at specified specific frequency bands (2450 MHz, sometimes 896 MHz in Europe and 915 MHz in USA), whereas radiant heat is less controlled and has a wider range of frequencies.
(2) The depth of penetration into a food is directly related to frequency; the lower-

frequency microwaves therefore penetrate more deeply than radiant (infrared) energy.

(3) Microwaves induce molecular friction in water molecules to produce heat (section 17.1) whereas infrared energy is simply absorbed and converted to heat.

(4) The extent of heating by microwaves is determined in part by the moisture content of the food, whereas the extent of heating by radiant energy depends on the surface characteristics and colour of the food.

(5) The lower penetration of infrared energy means that the thermal conductivity of the food (Chapter 1) is more important in infrared heating than in microwave heating; infrared heating is limited to the surface of a food, whereas microwaves heat throughout a food.

(6) Microwaves are used to preserve foods (for example by dehydration, blanching and pasteurisation), whereas infrared radiation is mostly used to alter the eating qualities of foods by changing the surface colour, flavour and aroma.

Dielectric heating operates using a similar principle to microwave heating, but at lower frequencies (Fig. 17.1). Food is passed between capacitor plates, and high-frequency energy is applied using an alternating electrostatic field. This changes the orientation of dipoles in a similar way to microwaves. However, the thickness of the food is restricted by the distance between the capacitor plates, which is an important limitation of the method. The main applications of dielectric heating are for drying crispbread and biscuits (Anon., 1987), thawing blocks of frozen food (for example egg, meat, fish and fruit juice) and melting fats or chocolate (Jones, 1987).

The operating principles and equipment for domestic microwave and radiant heating are similar to industrial batch operations, and domestic cooking is not considered in detail here. The effects of microwave cooking on nutrient retention in domestic and catering applications are described by Klein (1982) and Lachance (1975). The use of infrared energy in analytical methods is discussed by Mohsenin (1984).

17.1 MICROWAVE HEATING

17.1.1 Theory

The molecular structure of water consists of a negatively charged oxygen atom, separated from positively charged hydrogen atoms. This forms an electric dipole. When a rapidly oscillating electric field is applied to a food, dipoles in the water reorient with each change in the field direction. The number of dipoles and the changes induced by the electric field determine the *dielectric constant* of a food (Table 17.1). This is the ratio of the capacitance of the food to the capacitance of air (or in some cases a vacuum). The various distortions and deformations to the molecular structure, caused by re-alignment of the dipoles, dissipate the applied energy as heat. There is a delay of a fraction of a microsecond before the dipoles respond to changes in the electric field, which is termed the *relaxation time*. This is influenced by the viscosity of the food and is therefore dependent on temperature. For example, when water changes state to ice, the dielectric constant falls and continues to decrease as the ice is further cooled. Ice is therefore more transparent to microwaves than water, and frozen foods that have a significant amount of moisture absorb energy more strongly as they thaw (Fig. 17.2 and section 17.1.3.2).

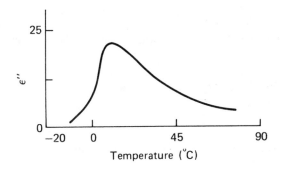

Fig. 17.2 — Variation in dielectric loss factor of water and ice. (After Lewis (1987).)

Table 17.1 — Dielectric properties of materials

Food	Temperature (°C)	Moisture content (%)	Frequency (MHz)	Dielectric constant	Loss factor
Beef	25	—	915	62	27
			2450	61	17
Pork	25	—	915	59	26
			2450	58	16
Potato	25	—	915	65	19
			2450	64	14
Carrot	25	—	915	73	20
			2450	72	15

Adapted from Mudget (1982) and Mohsenin (1984).

   When food is placed in the path of microwaves, some of the electromagnetic energy is absorbed and converted to heat. The amount of absorbed energy is determined by the *loss factor* of the material (also termed the *dielectric loss* or *loss tangent*). Foods have a high moisture content and a high loss factor; they therefore absorb energy and heat rapidly (Table 17.1). Since there is an uneven distribution of energy, heat transfer within the food also takes place by conduction (Chapter 1). Glass, papers and some polymer packaging films have a low loss factor (are transparent to microwaves) and are not therefore heated. Microwaves are reflected by metals.

The depth of penetration of microwaves is determined by the loss factor of the food and the wavelength or frequency of the microwaves:

$$x = \frac{\lambda_0}{2\pi\sqrt{(\varepsilon' \tan \delta)}} \tag{17.1}$$

where x (m) is the depth of penetration, λ (m) the wavelength in space, ε' the dielectric constant and $\tan \delta$ ($\varepsilon''/\varepsilon'$) loss tangent (or loss factor or dissipation constant).

The power absorbed by the food is found using

$$P = 55.61 + 10^{-14}fE^2\varepsilon'' \tag{17.2}$$

Where P (Wm^{-3}) is the power per unit volume, f (Hz) the frequency and E (V m^{-1}) the electrical field strength.

Greater penetration and more uniform heating is therefore obtained using longer wavelengths (896 MHz and 915 MHz), with foods that have lower loss factors, or with smaller pieces of food. However, deep penetration into food is not necessarily the main requirement and the wavelength of microwaves is chosen to suit the required application.

17.1.2 Equipment

Microwave equipment consists of a microwave generator (for example a *magnetron*), aluminium tubes named *wave guides*, and a metal chamber (for batch operation), or a tunnel fitted with a conveyor belt (Fig. 17.3). Heating chambers and tunnels are

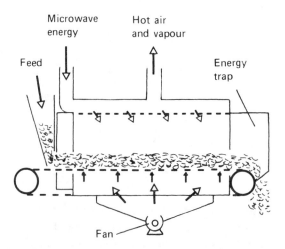

Fig. 17.3 — Continuous microwave finish drying equipment. (After Decareau (1985).)

sealed to prevent the escape of microwaves which could injure operators. The magnetron is a cylindrical diode. A ring of resonant cavities form the anode, and the cathode is a hot metal cylinder which produces free electrons and is located inside the anode ring. When a high voltage is applied, the electrons give up energy to form rapidly oscillating microwave energy, which is then directed to the waveguide by electromagnets. The waveguide reflects the energy internally and thus transfers it to the heating chamber. In batch equipment a rotating antenna (or fan) is used to distribute the energy, or the food may be rotated on a turntable. Both methods reduce *shadowing* (areas of food which are not exposed to the radiation). In continuous tunnels a different design of antennae is used to direct a beam of energy over the food as it passes on a conveyor. It is important that the power output from the magnetron is matched to the size of the heating chamber. Power outputs of continuous industrial equipment range from 30 to 120 kW. Detailed descriptions of component parts of a microwave heater are given by Copson (1975).

Microwaves selectively heat moist areas within a food. Heating is rapid and does not overheat the surface, which produces minimum heat damage and no surface browning. The equipment is small, compact, clean in operation and suited to automatic control, and there is no contamination of foods by products of combustion.

17.1.3 Applications
The attractions of microwave energy are the high rates of heating and absence of surface changes to the food. As a result, studies are reported of microwave heating of a large number of foods. These are comprehensively reviewed by Decareau (1985). The greater convenience of microwaveable foods for consumers has lead to substantial developments of products and packages that are suitable for use in domestic microwave ovens. These are reviewed by Anon. (1987b) and Anon. (1987c). Commercial microwave processing is limited by the higher costs and by the requirement to tune the magnetron to individual foods, or even to different varieties of the same food. The most important industrial applications are thawing and defrosting (or tempering), dehydration and baking. These are reviewed by Rosenberg and Bogl (1987a) and Decareau (1985). Other applications, which involve foods with higher moisture contents (for example blanching and pasteurisation) are less successful. This is due to the low depth of penetration in large pieces of food and to evaporative cooling at the surface, which results in survival of large numbers of micro-organisms. These applications are discussed briefly in this section and are reviewed by Rosenberg and Bogl (1987b). Accelerated freeze drying by microwaves has been extensively investigated (Copson, 1975), but the process remains expensive and is not widely used (Chapter 20).

17.1.3.1 Dehydration and baking
The main disadvantages of hot-air drying are

(1) low rates of heat transfer, caused by the low thermal conductivity of dry foods (Table 1.4),
(2) damage to sensory characteristics and nutritional properties caused by long drying times and overheating at the surface,
(3) oxidation of pigments and vitamins by hot air and
(4) case hardening (Chapter 14).

Microwaves generate heat within the food to vaporise moisture and to overcome the barrier to heat transfer caused by the low thermal conductivity. This therefore prevents damage to the surface, improves moisture transfer during the later stages of drying and eliminates case hardening. Microwaves are mostly used to finish partly dried foods, where the radiation selectively heats moist areas while leaving dry areas unaffected. It is not necessary to heat large volumes of air, and oxidation by atmospheric oxygen is minimised. However, the higher cost of microwaves and the smaller scale of operation, compared with traditional methods of dehydration, restrict microwave drying to finishing operations of partly dried or low-moisture foods.

For example, pasta drying times are reduced from 8 h to 90 min by microwave drying, bacterial counts are 15 times lower, there is a reduction in energy consumption of 20–25%, and there is no case hardening (Decareau, 1985). Microwave drying under reduced pressure is faster because of the higher temperature gradient. In grain drying, it is cheaper, more energy efficient and quieter than conventional methods and does not cause dust pollution. The lower drying temperature improves grain germination rates.

In conventional freeze drying, the low rate of heat transfer to the sublimation front limits the rate of drying (Chapter 20). Microwave freeze drying overcomes this problem because heat is only supplied to the ice front. However, careful control over drying conditions is necessary to prevent localised melting of the ice. Any water produced in the drying food heats rapidly, owing to the higher loss factor, and causes a chain reaction, leading to widespread melting and an end to sublimation.

The efficiency of *baking* is improved by microwave finishing, for thin products (for example biscuits and crispbread). Conventional ovens operate effectively when products have relatively high moisture contents, but the thermal conductivity falls as baking proceeds, and considerable time is necessary to bake the centre of the product adequately without excessive changes to the surface colour. Microwave heaters are located at the exit to tunnel ovens (Chapter 15) to reduce the moisture content and to complete the baking without further changes in colour. This reduces baking times by up to 30% (Jones, 1987) and hence increases the throughput of the ovens.

17.1.3.2 Thawing and defrosting

During conventional thawing of frozen foods (Chapter 19), the lower thermal conductivity of water, compared with ice, reduces the rate of heat transfer. Microwaves rapidly thaw small portions of food, but difficulties arise with large (25 kg) blocks of frozen food used in industrial processes. Water has a higher loss factor than ice and, as a result, heats rapidly once the ice melts. In the large blocks, thawing does not take place uniformly, and some portions of the food may cook while others remain frozen. This is overcome to some extent by reducing the microwave power and extending the thawing period or by using pulsed microwaves to allow time for temperature equilibration.

A more common application is to defrost foods (that is to raise the temperature from −20°C to −3°C). Here there is a limited phase change and problems of overheating occur to a lesser extent. This procedure is widely used for meat products, which are more easily sliced, boned or ground at a temperature just below the freezing point, and for butter and other edible fats. Production rates range from 1–4 t of meat per hour or 1.5–6 t of butter per hour in equipment which has power outputs of 32–120 kW. The advantages include

(1) faster processing (for example meat blocks are defrosted in 10 min instead of several days in a cold room),
(2) less storage space required,
(3) no drip loss, which improves product yields and reduces nutritional losses (Chapter 19),
(4) lower labour requirements,
(5) more hygienic defrosting because products are defrosted in the storage boxes and
(6) better control over defrosting conditions and hence improved product quality.

17.1.3.3 Other applications

Compared with conventional cooking, microwave *rendering* of fats improves the colour, reduces fines by 95% and costs by 30% and does not cause unpleasant odours (Decareau, 1985). Microwave *frying* is not successful when deep baths of oil are used, because the oil cools and does not adequately seal the surface of the food. The problem is overcome by using shallow trays in which the food is rapidly heated by microwaves. The smaller volume of oil can be held at the required temperature and frying times are substantially reduced. The smaller volume of oil (smaller oil-to-product ratio) reduces the load on oil filters, and energy is used more efficiently. The turnover of oil is rapid as it is removed on the product, and there is less deterioration in oil quality (Copson, 1975).

Doughnuts are cooked without oil using microwaves, which reduces processing times by 20% and increases product yield by 25% (Schiffman *et al.*, 1972). Microwave frying of potato crisps was one of the first commercial applications. Frying alters the colour of potatoes by Maillard browing, but potatoes which have a reducing sugar concentration greater than 0.2% darken excessively when fried to the required moisture content. They are therefore conditioned at 12–18°C for several weeks, to convert reducing sugars back to starch. This is expensive in terms of capital equipment, product holdup, losses through sprouting and weight loss. These costs are eliminated by removing residual moisture by microwave drying, after the potatoes have been fried to the required colour. However, the technique did not prove to be economically viable in commercial production in the USA. The reasons for this are discussed by a number of researchers, including O'Meary (1973).

Blanching by microwaves has been extensively investigated, but at present the additional costs compared with steam blanching have prevented its use for low-cost vegetables. Microwave blanching of products that are more difficult to blanch by conventional methods is under development but may be limited by the high capital investment and the short harvest season. Studies of combined steam and microwave blanching are reported to reduce blanching time (Huxsoll *et al.*, 1970).

Pasteurisation of packed peeled potatoes by microwaves raises the temperature to 85°C. They are then cooled to give an essentially raw product with a shelf life of 6 weeks at 8°C. Alternatively, heating is allowed to continue by conduction, to produce a partly cooked product. Details of a procedure for the pasteurisation of fruit juices, to inactivate pectinesterase, are reported by Copson (1975).

Sterilisation by microwaves is achieved in plastic laminated pouches in the Multi-therm process. The pouches, which are transparent to microwaves, are formed and filled from a continuous reel of film (Chapter 23) but are not separated. This produces a chain of pouches that passes through a continuous hydrostat system, similar to a small hydrostatic steam steriliser (Chapter 11). In this case the product is submerged in a medium that has a higher dielectric constant than the product, and heating is by microwaves instead of steam. In a system described by Stenstrom (1972, 1973), the product passes through seven liquid baths, heated at up to 90°C, and the final sterilising temperature reaches more than 130°C, before cooling to 10°C. The process is not yet used commercially.

17.1.4 Effect on foods
Microwaves have no direct effect on micro-organisms, in contrast with ionising radiation (Chapter 8), and any changes are caused by heat. In pasteurisation and blanching applications, the high rates of heat transfer for a specified level of microbial or enzyme destruction would be expected to result in reduced losses of heat-sensitive nutrients. The reported data indicate that this is so for many foods (for example there is no loss of carotene in microwave-blanched carrots, compared with 28% loss by steam blanching and 45% loss by water blanching (von Loesecke, 1942)). However, the results for some foods are highly variable and, for these, microwave heating offers no nutritional advantage over steaming. Details of changes to foods during each of these unit operations are given in the relevant chapters.

17.2 INFRARED RADIATION

17.2.1 Theory
Infrared energy is electromagnetic radiation (Fig.17.1) which is emitted by hot objects. The radiation gives up its energy to heat materials when it is absorbed. The rate of heat transfer depends on

(1) the surface temperatures of the heating and receiving materials,
(2) the surface properties of the two materials and
(3) the shapes of the emitting and receiving bodies.

The amount of heat emitted from a *perfect radiator* (termed a *black body*) is calculated using the Stefan–Boltzmann equation

$$Q = \sigma A T^4 \qquad\qquad (17.3)$$

Where Q (J s^{-1}) is the rate of heat emission, $s = 5.7 \times 10^{-8}$(J s^{-1} m^{-2} K^{-4}) the Stefan–Boltzmann constant, A (m^2) the surface area and T (K = °C + 273) the absolute temperature. This equation is also used for a *perfect absorber* of radiation, again known as a *black body*.

However, radiant heaters are not prefect radiators and foods are not perfect absorbers, although they do emit and absorb a constant fraction of the theoretical maximum. To take account of this, the concept of *grey bodies* is used, and the Stefan–Boltzmann equation is modified to

$$Q = \varepsilon\sigma A T^4 \tag{17.4}$$

Where ε is the emissivity of the grey body expressed as a number from 0 to 1 (Table 17.2). Emissivity varies with the temperature of the grey body, and the wavelength of the radiation emitted.

Table 17.2 — Approximate emissivities of materials in food processing

Material	Emissivity
Burnt toast	1.00
Dough	0.85
Water	0.955
Ice	0.97
Lean beef	0.74
Beef fat	0.78
White paper	0.9
Painted metal or wood	0.9
Unpolished metal	0.7–0.25
Polished metal	<0.05

From Earle (1983) and Lewis (1987).

The amount of radiation absorbed by a grey body is termed the *absorptivity* α and is numerically equal to the emissivity. Radiation which is not absorbed is reflected and this is expressed as the *reflectivity* $1-\alpha$. The amount of absorbed energy, and hence the degree of heating, varies from zero to complete absorption. This is determined by the components of the food, which absorb radiation to different extents, and the wavelength of the radiated energy. The wavelength of infrared radiation is determined by the temperature of the source. Higher temperatures produce shorter wavelengths and greater depth of penetration. The net rate of heat transfer to a food therefore equals the rate of absorption minus the rate of emission:

$$Q = \varepsilon\sigma A(T_1^4 - T_2^4) \tag{17.5}$$

Where T_1 (K) is the temperature of emitter and T_2 (K) the temperature of absorber.

Sample problem 17.1
An 8 kW batch oven has a hearth area of 4 m² and operates at 210°C. It is loaded with two batches of bread dough in baking tins; 150 loaves on the first batch and 120 loaves on the second batch. The surface of each loaf measures 12 cm × 20 cm. Assuming that the emissivity of dough is 0.85, that the dough bakes at 100°C, and that 90% of the heat is transmitted in the form of radiant energy, calculate the efficiency of energy use (as the percentage of the supplied radiant energy which is absorbed by the food) for each batch.

Solution to sample problem 17.1
In the first batch,

$$\text{area of dough} = 150(0.2 \times 0.12)$$
$$= 3.6 \text{ m}^2$$

From equation (17.5)

$$Q = 3.6 \times 0.85 \, (5.73 \times 10^{-8}) \, (483^4 - 373^4)$$
$$= 6145.6 \text{ W}$$

In the second batch,

$$\text{area of dough} = 120(0.2 \times 0.12)$$
$$= 2.88 \text{ m}^2$$

and

$$Q = 2.88 \times 0.85 \, (5.73 \times 10^{-8}) \, (483^4 - 373^4)$$
$$= 4916 \text{ W}$$

Thus, for the first batch,

$$\text{efficiency} = \frac{6145.6}{8 \times 0.9}$$
$$= 85\%$$

and, for the second batch,

$$\text{efficiency} = \frac{4916}{8 \times 0.9}$$
$$= 68\%$$

17.2.2 Equipment

Types of radiant heaters include flat or tubular metal heaters, ceramic heaters, and quartz or halogen tubes fitted with electric filaments (Table 17.3).

The main commercial application of radiant energy is in drying low-moisture foods (for example breadcrumbs, cocoa, flours, grains, malt, pasta products and tea). Products pass through a tunnel, beneath banks of radiant heaters, on a conveyor (Ginzberg, 1969). In addition, solar energy consists of approximately 48% infrared energy and is an important drying method in some countries (Chapter 14). Radiant energy is also used in vacuum band driers and cabinet driers (Chapter 14)

Table 17.3 — Infrared emitter characteristics

Type of emitter	Maximum running temperature (°C)	Maximum intensity (kW m^{-2})	Maximum process temperature (°C)	Radiant heat (%)	Convection heat (%)	Heating–cooling time (s)	Expected life
Short wavelength							
Heat lamp	2200	10	300	75	25	1	5000 h
IR gun	2300	2	1600	98	2	1	—
Quartz tube	2200	80	600	80	20	1	5000 h
Medium wavelength							
Quartz tube	950	60	500	55	45	30	Years
Long wavelength							
Element	800	40	500	50	50	<120	Years
Ceramic	700	40	400	50	50	<120	Years

From Anon. (1981).

and accelerated freeze driers (Chapter 20). It is not, however, widely used as a single source of energy for drying solid pieces of food because of the limited depth of penetration. Radiant heating is used in baking or roasting ovens (Chapter 15) and is also used to heat shrink packaging film (Chapter 23).

17.2.3 Effect on foods

The rapid surface heating of foods seals in moisture and flavour or aroma compounds. Changes to surface components of foods are similar to those that occur during baking and are described in Chapter 15.

ACKNOWLEDGEMENTS

Grateful acknowledgement is made for information supplied by the following: APV Parafreeze Ltd, Thetford, Norfolk, UK; Raytheon Co., Waltham, Massachusetts 02154, USA; Petrie and McNaught Ltd, Rochdale, Lancashire Ol16 5NX, UK; The National Committee for Electroheat, 30 Millbank, London SW1P 4RD, UK.

REFERENCES

Anon. (1981) *The application of infra-red heating to industrial processes*. British National Committee for Electroheat, 30 Millbank, London SW1P 4RD.

Anon. (1987) Radio frequency energy boosts biscuit baking. *Food Process* May, 45–46.

Anon. (1987b) Microwavable foods — industry's response to consumer demands for convenience. *Food Technol. (USA)* June 52–62.

Anon. (1987c) Ingredients and packages for microwaveable foods. *Food Technol. (USA)* June 100, 102, 104.

Copson, D. A. (1975) *Microwave heating*. AVI, Westport, Connecticut, pp. 262–285.

Decareau, R. V. (1985) *Microwaves in the food processing industry*. Academic Press, Orlando, Florida.

Earle, R. L. (1983) *Unit operations in food processing*, 2nd edn. Pergamon Press, Oxford, pp. 46–63.

Ginsberg, A. S. (1969) *Applications of infra-red irradiation in food processing*. Leonard Hill, London.

Huxsoll, C. C., Dietrich, W. C., and Morgan, A. I. (1970) Comparison of microwave and steam or water blanching of corn on the cob. *Food Technol.* **24** 84–87.

Jeppson, M. R. (1968) *Apparatus and procedure for microwave treatment*. US Patent, No. 3,365,562, 23 January.

Jones, P. L. (1987) Dielectric heating in food processing. In: *Food technology international, Europe*. A. Turner (Ed.), Sterling, London, pp. 57, 59–60.

Klein, B. P. (1982) Effect of processing on nutritive value of food: microwave cooking. In: M. Rechcigl (ed.), *Handbook of the nutritive value of processed food*, Vol. 1. CRC Press, Boca Raton, Florida, pp. 209–236.

Lachance, P. A. (1975) Effects of preparation and service of food on nutrients. In: R. S. Harris and E. Karmas (eds.) *Nutritional evaluation of food processing*, 2nd edn. AVI, Westport, Connecticut, pp. 463–528.

Lewis, M. J. (1987) *Physical properties of foods and food processing systems*. Ellis Horwood, Chichester, West Sussex; VCH, Weinheim, pp. 277–287.

Mohsenin, N. N. (1984) *Electromagnetic radiation properties of foods and agricultural products*. Gordon and Breach, New York.

Mudget, R. E. (1982) Electrical properties of foods in microwave processing. *Food Technol.* **36** 109–115.

O'Meary, J. P. (1973) Progress report on microwave drying. *Proceedings of the First International production and Technical Division Meeting on Potato Chips, Las Vegas, Nevada, 30 January, 3 February* 1966, pp. 55–59.

Rosenberg, U., and Bogl, W. (1987a) Microwave thawing, drying and baking in the food industry. *Food Technol. (USA)* June 85–91.

Rosenberg, U., and Bogl, W. (1987b) Microwave pasteurization, sterilization and pest control in the food industry. *Food Technol. (USA)* June 92–99.

Schiffman, R. F., Stein, E. W., and Kaufmann, H. B. (1972) Application of microwave energy to doughnut production. *Food Technol.* **25** 718–722.

Stenstrom, L. A. (1972) *Method and apparatus for sterilisation of heat sensitive products by electromagentic radiation*, Swedish Patent Appl., No. 352 230.

Stenstrom. L. A. (1973) *Method for heating a product unit in an electromagnetic field of the lowest microwave frequency*, Swedish Patent Appl., No. 355 479.

von Loesecke, H. W. (1942) Vegetable preparation and processing. *West. Canner Packer* **34** 35–38.

Part IV
Processing by the removal of heat

A reduction in the temperature of a food retards all changes that take place during storage. In general, the longer the storage period, the lower the temperature that is required. Although low temperatures inhibit changes and therefore stabilise a food, the products are not sterilised and careful control over preparation procedures (Chapter 2) is therefore necessary. The absence of substantial heat treatment in the unit operations described in this section, together with adequate control over enzymic and microbiological changes, results in only small changes to the nutritional and sensory characteristics of foods and resulting high quality products.

18

Chilling and controlled-atmosphere storage

Chilling is the unit operation in which the temperature of a food is reduced to between $-1°C$ and $8°C$. It is used to reduce the rate of biochemical and microbiological changes, and to extend the shelf life of fresh and processed foods. It causes minimal changes to sensory characteristics and nutritional properties of foods and, as a result, chilled foods are perceived by consumers as being 'healthy' and 'fresh'. Chilling is often used in combination with other unit operations (for example fermentation (Chapter 7), irradiation (Chapter 8) or pasteurisation (Chapter 10)) to extend the shelf life of mildly processed foods.

The successful supply of chilled foods to the consumer is heavily dependent on sophisticated distribution systems which involve chill stores, refrigerated transport and chilled retail display cabinets. In particular, low-acid chilled foods, which are susceptible to contamination by pathogenic bacteria (for example fresh and pre-cooked meats, pizzas and unbaked dough) must be prepared and packaged under strictly controlled hygienic conditions.

Foods are grouped into three categories according to the storage temperature range as follows (Hendley, 1985):

(1) $-1°C$ to $+1°C$ (fresh fish, meats, sausages and ground meats, smoked meats and fish);
(2) $0°C$ to $+5°C$ (pasteurised canned meat, milk, cream, yoghurt, prepared salads, sandwiches, baked goods, pasta, pizzas, unbaked dough and pastry);
(3) $0°C$ to $+8°C$ (fully cooked meats and fish pies, cooked or uncooked cured meats, butter, margarine, hard cheese and soft fruits).

Not all foods can be chilled; for example tropical, subtropical and some temperate fruits suffer from chilling injury at $3–10°C$ above their freezing point.

There is a greater preservative effect when chilling is combined with control of the composition of the storage atmosphere than that found using either unit operation alone. A reduction in oxygen concentration and/or increase in carbon dioxide concentration of the storage atmosphere reduce the rate of respiration of fresh fruits and vegetables and also inhibit microbial and insect growth. The atmospheric composition is changed using three methods:

(1) *controlled-atmosphere storage* (CAS) where the concentrations of oxygen, carbon dioxide and sometimes ethene (ethylene) are monitored and regulated;
(2) *modified-atmosphere storage* (MAS) in which the gas composition in a sealed store is allowed to change by normal respiratory activity of the food, but little control is exercised;
(3) *modified-atmosphere packaging* (MAP) (or gas flushing) in which the composition of gases in a package of known permeability is altered after the food is filled, but before the package is sealed.

In commercial operation, CAS and MAS are at present limited to use with apples and small quantities of pears and cabbage. MAP is used for some fresh foods and a number of mildly processed foods (including sandwiches, cheese and cooked meats) and is gaining in popularity as new applications are developed.

18.1 CHILLING

18.1.1 Theory
A reduction in temperature below the minimum necessary for microbial growth extends the generation time of the micro-organism and in effect prevents or retards reproduction. There are three broad categories of micro-organism, based on the temperature range for growth:

(1) thermophilic (35–55°C);
(2) mesophilic (10–40°C);
(3) psychrophilic (− 5–15°C).

Chilling prevents the growth of thermophilic and many mesophilic micro-organisms. A number of psychrophilic micro-organisms cause food spoilage, but there are no psychrophilic pathogens. Chilling to temperatures below 5–7°C therefore retards microbial spoilage and prevents the growth of pathogens. The rate of biochemical changes by either micro-organisms or naturally occurring enzymes changes logarithmically with temperature (Chapter 1). Chilling therefore reduces the rate of enzymic and microbiological change and retards respiration of fresh foods. The factors that control the shelf life of fresh crops in chill storage include

(1) the type of food and variety or cultivar,
(2) the part of the crop selected (the fastest growing parts have the highest metabolic rates and the shortest storage lives (Table 18.1)),
(3) the condition of the food at harvest (for example the presence of mechanical damage or microbial contamination, and the degree of maturity),
(3) the temperature of distribution and retail display,
(4) the relative humidity of the storage atmosphere, which influences dehydration losses.

Table 18.1 — Botanical function related to respiration rate and storage life for selected products

Product	Relative respiration rate	Botanical function	Typical storage life (weeks at 2°C)
Asparagus	40	Actively	
Mushrooms	21	growing	0.2–0.5
Artichokes	17	shoots	
Spinach	13	Aerial	
Lettuce	11	parts of	1–2
Cabbage	6	plants	
Carrots	5	Storage	
Turnips	4	roots	5–20
Beetroots	3		
Potatoes	2	Specialised	
Garlic	2	storage	25–50
Onions	1	organs	

From Alvarez and Thorne (1981).

The shelf life of processed chilled foods is determined by

(1) the type of food,
(2) the degree of microbial destruction or enzyme inactivation achieved by the process,
(3) control of hygiene during processing and packaging,
(4) the barrier properties of the package and
(5) temperatures during distribution and storage.

The rate of respiration of fresh fruits is not necessarily constant at a constant storage temperature. Fruits which undergo 'climacteric' ripening show a short but abrupt increase in the rate of respiration (Fig. 18.1) which occurs near to the point of optimum ripeness. Climacteric fruits include apple, apricot, avocado, banana, mango, peach, pear, plum and tomato. Non-climacteric fruits include cherry, cucumber, fig, grape, grapefruit, lemon, pineapple and strawberry. Vegetables respire in a similar way to non-climacteric fruits. Undesirable changes to some fruits and vegetables occur when the temperature is reduced below a specific optimum for the individual fruit. This is termed *chilling injury* and results in various physiological changes (for example internal or external browning, failure to ripen and skin blemishes). It is found for example in apples (less than 2–3°C), avocados (less than 4–13°C), bananas (less than 12–13°C), lemons (less than 14°C), mangoes (less than 10–13°C), melons, pineapples and tomatoes (each less than 7–10°C). Further details are given by Duckworth (1966). Undesirable changes due to incorrect relative humidity are described by van den Berg and Lentz (1974).

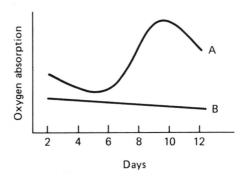

Fig. 18.1 — Changes in respiration of climacteric (curve A) and non-climacteric (curve B) fruits.

In animal tissues, aerobic respiration rapidly declines when the supply of oxygenated blood is stopped at slaughter. Anaerobic respiration of glycogen to lactic acid then causes the pH of the meat to fall, and the onset of rigor mortis, in which the muscle tissue becomes firm and inextensible. Cooling during anaerobic respiration is necessary to produce the required texture and colour of meat and to reduce bacterial contamination. Undesirable changes, caused by cooling meat before rigor mortis has occurred, are termed *cold shortening*. Details of post mortem changes to meat are given by Laurie (1985).

Details of correct storage conditions for specific products are listed by (Anon., 1979), and procedures for the correct handling of chilled foods are described by (Anon., 1982).

To chill fresh foods it is necessary to remove both *sensible heat* (also known as *field heat*) and heat generated by respiratory activity. The production of respiratory heat is given by

$$C_6H_{12}O_6 + 6O_2 \rightarrow 6CO_2 + 6H_2O + 2.835 \times 10^6 \, J \, kmol^{-1} \, C_6H_{12}O_6$$

at 20°C and atmospheric pressure. Differences in respiratory activity of selected fruits and vegetables are shown in Table 18.2.

The size of refrigeration plant and the processing time required to chill a crop are calculated using unsteady-state heat transfer methods (Chapter 1). The calculations are simpler when processed foods are chilled as respiratory activity does not occur. A number of assumptions are made to simplify calculations further; for example the initial temperature of a food is constant and uniform throughout the food, and the temperature of the cooling medium, respiratory activity and all thermal properties of the food are constant during cooling. Detailed derivations of theoretical considerations and examples of calculations of heat load and chilling rate are described by van Beek and Meffert (1981).

Table 18.2 — Heat produced by respiration in selected foods

Food	Heat ($W t^{-1}$) of respiration for the following storage temperatures		
	0°C	10°C	15.5°C
Apples	10–12	41–61	58–87
Bananas	—	65–116	—
Beans	73–82	—	440–580
Carrots	46	93	—
Celery	21	58–81	—
Oranges	9–12	35–40	68
Lettuce	150	—	620
Pears	8–20	23–63	—
Potatoes	—	20–30	—
Strawberries	36–52	145–280	510
Tomatoes	57–75	—	78

Adapted from Leniger and Beverloo (1975) and Lewis (1987).

Sample problem 18.1
Freshly harvested berries measuring 2 cm in diameter are chilled from 18°C to 7°C in a chiller at − 2°C, with a surface heat transfer coefficient of $16\,W\,m^{-2}\,K^{-1}$. They are then loaded in 250 kg batches into containers and held for 12 h in a cold store operating at − 2°C, prior to further processing. The cold store holds an average of 2.5 t of food and measures 3 m high by 10 m × 10 m. The walls and roof are insulated with 300 mm of polyurethane foam, and the floor is constructed from 450 mm of concrete. The ambient air temperature averages 12°C and the soil temperature 9°C. An operator spends an average of 45 min day^{-1} moving the containers in the store and switches on four 100 W lights when in the store. Each container weighs 50 kg. Calculate the time required to cool the berries in the chiller and determine whether a 5 kW refrigeration plant would be suitable for the cold store. (Additional data: the thermal conductivity of the berries is $0.127\,W\,m^{-1}\,K^{-1}$, the thermal conductivity of the insulation is $0.026\,W\,m^{-1}\,K^{-1}$, the thermal conductivity of the concrete is $0.87\,W\,m^{-1}\,K^{-1}$ (Table 1.4), the specific heat of the berries is $3778\,J\,kg^{-1}\,K^{-1}$, the specific heat of the container is $480\,J\,kg^{-1}\,K^{-1}$, the density of berries is $1050\,kg\,m^{-3}$, the heat produced by the operator is 240 W, and the average heat of respiration of berries is $0.275\,J\,kg^{-1}\,s^{-1}$.)

Solution to sample problem 18.1
To calculate the time required to cool the berries, from equation (1.18) for unsteady-state heat transfer (Bi = $h\delta/k$) for berries,

$$Bi = \frac{16 \times 0.01}{0.127}$$

$$= 1.26$$

$$\frac{1}{Bi} = 0.79$$

From equation (1.19) for cooling,

$$\frac{\theta_h - \theta_f}{\theta_h - \theta_i} = \frac{7 - (-2)}{18 - (-2)}$$

$$= 0.45$$

From Fig. 1.6 for a sphere, Fo = 0.38. From equation (1.20),

$$0.38 = \frac{k}{c\rho} \frac{t}{\delta^2}$$

Therefore,

$$t = \frac{0.38 \times 3778 \times 1050(0.01)^2}{0.127}$$

$$\text{time of cooling} = 1187\,\text{s}$$

$$= 19.8\,\text{min}$$

To determine whether the refrigeration plant is suitable as a cold store, assume that the berries enter the store at chill temperature.

$$\frac{\text{total}}{\text{heat load}} = \frac{\text{heat of respiration}}{} + \frac{\text{sensible heat of containers}}{} + \frac{\text{heat evolved by operators and lights}}{} + \frac{\text{heat loss through roof and walls}}{} + \frac{\text{heat loss through floor}}{}$$

Now

$$\text{heat of respiration} = 2500 \times 0.275$$

$$= 687.5\,\text{W}$$

Assuming that the containers have the same temperature change as the berries and the number of containers is 2500/250 = 10,

$$\text{heat removed from containers} = \frac{10 \times 50 \times 480(18 - 7)}{12 \times 3600}$$

$$= 61\,\text{W}$$

Next

$$\text{heat evolved by operators and lights} = \frac{(240 + 4 \times 100)(45 \times 60)}{24 \times 3600}$$

$$= 20\,\text{W}$$

From equation (1.5), for an area of $60 + 60 + 100 = 220\,\text{m}^2$

$$\text{heat loss through roof and walls} = \frac{0.026 \times 220[12 - (-2)]}{0.3} = 267\,\text{W}$$

Finally,

$$\begin{array}{l}\text{heat loss through floor} \\ \text{(of area 100m}^2\text{)}\end{array} = \frac{0.87 \times 100[9 - (-2)]}{0.45} = 2127\,\text{W}$$

Therefore the total heat load is the sum of the heat loads $687.5\,\text{W} + 61\,\text{W} + 20\,\text{W} + 2394\,\text{W} = 3162.5\,\text{W} = 3.2\,\text{kW}$.

Thus a $5\,\text{kW}$ refrigeration plant is suitable.

18.1.2   Equipment
Chilling equipment is classified by the method used to remove heat into

(1) mechanical refrigerators and
(2) cryogenic systems.

Batch or continuous operation is possible with both types of equipment, but all should lower the temperature of the product as quickly as possible through the critical warm zone (50–10°C) where maximum growth of micro-organisms occurs.

18.1.2.1   Mechanical refrigerators
Mechanical refrigerators have four basic elements: an evaporator, a compressor, a condenser and an expansion valve (Fig. 18.2). Components of refrigerators are frequently constructed from copper as the low thermal conductivity (Table 1.4) allows high rates of heat transfer and high thermal efficiencies. A refrigerant (Table 18.3) circulates between the four elements of the refrigerator, changing state from liquid to gas, and back to liquid as follows. In the evaporator the liquid refrigerant evaporates under reduced pressure, and in doing so absorbs latent heat of vaporisa-

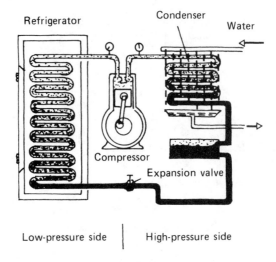

Fig. 18.2 — Mechanical (compression–expansion) refrigerator. (After Patchen (1971).)

Table 18.3 — Properties of some common refrigerants.

Refrigerant		Boiling point (°C) at 100 kPa	Latent heat (kJ kg^{-1})	Toxicity	Flammability	Vapour density (kg m^{-3})	Oil solubility
Number	Formula						
11	CCl_3F	23.8	194.2	Low	Low	1.31	Complete
12	CCl_2F_2	− 29.8	163.54	Low	Low	10.97	Complete
21	$CHCl_2F$	− 44.5	254.2	Low	Low	1.76	Complete
22	$CHClF_2$	− 40.8	220.94	Low	Low	12.81	Partial
717	NH_3	− 33.3	1328.48	High	High	1.965	<1%
744	CO_2	− 78.5 (sublimes)	352	Low	Low	60.23	<1%

tion and cools the freezing medium. This is the most important part of the refrigerator; the remaining equipment is used to recycle the refrigerant. Refrigerant vapour passes from the evaporator to the compressor where the pressure is increased. The vapour then passes to the condenser where the high pressure is maintained and the vapour is condensed. The liquid passes through the expansion valve where the pressure is reduced to restart the refrigeration cycle.

The important properties of refrigerants are as follows:

(1) a low boiling point and high latent heat of vaporisation;
(2) a dense vapour to reduce the size of the compressor;
(3) low toxicity;
(4) non flammable;

(5) low miscibility with oil in the compressor;
(6) low cost.

Ammonia has excellent heat transfer properties and is not miscible with oil. It is toxic and flammable, however, and causes corrosion of copper pipes. Carbon dioxide is non-flammable and non-toxic, making it safer for use for example on refrigerated ships but considerably higher operating pressures are required. Halogen refrigerants are all non-toxic and non-flammable. They possess good heat transfer properties and have lower costs than other refrigerants. They are therefore widely used despite their miscibility with oil.

The chilling medium in mechanically cooled chillers may be air, water or metal surfaces. Air chillers (for example *blast chillers*) use forced convection to circulate air, to reduce the thickness of boundary films (Chapter 1) and thus to increase the rate of heat transfer. Air-blast chillers are also used in refrigerated vehicles. However, food should be adequately chilled when loaded onto the vehicle, as the refrigeration plant is only designed to hold food at the required temperature and cannot provide additional cooling of incompletely chilled food. Computerised planning of vehicle loads and transport routes is used by some companies to reduce distribution times and therefore to improve product quality and reduce transport costs (Hendley, 1985; Byrne, 1986a).

Retail chill cabinets use chilled air which circulates by natural convection. Forced convection is not usually necessary because the equipment holds pre-chilled food, and the heat load is therefore small. The cost of chill storage is high, and some stores have a centralised plant to produce refrigerant for all cabinets. The heat generated by the condenser (Fig. 18.2) can be used for in-store heating. Computer control of multiple cabinets detects excessive rises in temperature and warns of any requirement for emergency repairs or planned maintenance (Cambell-Platt, 1987). Other energy-saving devices include night blinds or glass doors on the front of cabinets to trap cold air. Causes of loss of efficiency in refrigeration equipment are described by Perry and Gluckman (1983).

Foods with a large surface area (for example lettuce) are washed and *vacuum cooled*. The food is placed in a large vacuum chamber and the pressure is reduced to approximately 0.5 kPa. Cooling takes place as moisture evaporates from the surface (a reduction of 5°C for each reduction of 1% in moisture content). Direct immersion in chilled water (*hydrocooling*) is used to remove field heat from fruit and vegetables. Recirculated chilled water is used in *plate heat exchangers* (Chapter 10) to cool liquid foods. Liquid and semi-solid foods (for example butter and margarine (Chapter 4)) are cooled by contact with refrigerated, or water-chilled metal surfaces in the *scraped-surface heat exchanger* (also Chapters 11, 12 and 19).

18.1.2.2 Cryogenic chilling

A *cryogen* is a refrigerant that changes phase by absorbing latent heat to cool the food (Fig. 18.3). Cryogenic chillers use solid carbon dioxide, liquid carbon dioxide or liquid nitrogen. Solid carbon dioxide removes latent heat of sublimation ($352 \, kJ \, kg^{-1}$ at $-78°C$), and liquid cryogens remove latent heat of vaporisation ($358 \, kJ \, kg^{-1}$ at $-196°C$ for liquid nitrogen; liquid carbon dioxide has a similar latent heat to the solid). The gas also absorbs sensible heat as it warms from $-78°C \, (CO_2)$

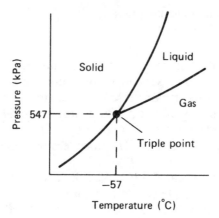

Fig. 18.3 — Phase diagram for carbon dioxide.

or $-196°C$ (liquid nitrogen) to give a total refrigerant effect of 565 kJ kg^{-1} and 690 kJ kg^{-1} respectively. Further details are given in Chapter 19.

The advantages of carbon dioxide include

(1) a higher boiling and sublimation point than nitrogen, and therefore a less severe effect on the food,
(2) most of enthalpy (heat capacity) in carbon dioxide arises from the conversion of solid or liquid to gas.

The gas itself contains only 13% of enthalpy from liquid carbon dioxide and 15% from the solid. This compares with 52% in nitrogen gas (that is, approximately half of the refrigerant effect of liquid nitrogen arises from sensible heat absorbed by the gas). Carbon dioxide does not therefore require gas handling equipment to extract most of the heat capacity, whereas liquid nitrogen does. The main limitation of carbon dioxide is its toxicity. A maximum safe limit for operators is 0.5% by volume, and additional costs may be incurred for air extraction systems. Liquid nitrogen has advantages over carbon dioxide in freezing applications (Chapter 19).

Liquid carbon dioxide is injected into air to produce fine particles of solid carbon dioxide, which rapidly sublime to gas. Solid carbon dioxide 'snow' is larger particles which are deposited into trays or cartons of food. They produce rapid cooling without dehydration, and a small excess of snow continues the cooling during transportation. If the product is despatched immediately in insulated vehicles, this type of chilling is able to replace on-site cold stores and thus saves space and labour costs.

Other applications of cryogenic cooling include sausage manufacture, where carbon dioxide snow removes the heat generated during size reduction and mixing. In *cryogenic grinding*, the cryogen reduces dust levels, avoids the possibility of dust explosions and improves the throughput of mills. In the production of multi-layer chilled foods (for example trifle and other desserts) the first layer of product is filled and the surface is hardened with carbon dioxide. The next layer can then be added immediately, without waiting for first layer to set, and thus permit continuous and more rapid processing.

18.1.3 Cook–chill systems
Individual foods (for example roast meats) or complete meals (termed *second-generation products*) are produced by *cook–chill* or *cook–pasteurise–chill* processes (Byrne, 1986b) . They are used in institutional catering to replace *warm holding* (where food is kept hot for long periods before consumption). This reduces losses in nutritional and eating quality and is less expensive. In retail stores the sales of cooked–chilled ready meals are increasing owing to their convenience, mild process-ing and healthy image.

Initial preparation of cooked–chilled foods is as normal. The food is then portioned and chilled to 3°C within 30 min of cooking. Chilling should be completed within 90 min and the food should be stored at 0–3°C to control the growth of spoilage micro-organisms. Foods have a shelf life of up to 5 days. In the cook–pasteurise–chill system, hot food is filled into a flexible container, a partial vacuum is formed to remove oxygen and the pack is heat sealed. It is then pasteurised to a minimum temperature of 80°C for 10 min at the thermal centre, followed by immediate cooling to 3°C. Foods have a shelf life of 2–3 weeks (Hill, 1987).

18.1.4 Effect on foods
Chilling causes little or no reduction in the nutritional properties of food. Deteriora-tive changes to fresh foods during storage are retarded by the reduction in tempera-ture. The temperature, relative humidity and expected storage times for a variety of fruits and vegetables are described by Farrel (1976) and Duckworth (1966). The effect of a reduction in temperature on micro-organisms is described in most microbiological texts (for example Frazer and Westhoff, 1978). The most significant effect of chilling on the sensory characteristics of processed foods is hardening due to solidification of fats and oils. Physiological damage of some tropical fruits due to chilling is described in section 18.1.1. In cook–chill systems, nutritional losses are reported by Bognar (1980) as follows: there are insignificant losses of thiamine, riboflavin and retinol, but vitamin C losses are 3.3–16% day^{-1} at 2°C. The large variation is due to differences in the chilling time, storage temperature, oxidation (the amount of food surface exposed to air) and reheating conditions. Vitamin C losses in cook–pasteurise–chill procedures are lower than cooked–chilled foods (for example spinach lost 66% within 3 days at 2–3°C after cooking–chilling compared with 26% loss within 7 days at 2–4°C after cooking–pasteurising–chilling.

18.2 CONTROLLED- AND MODIFIED-ATMOSPHERE STORAGE
The normal composition of air is 78% nitrogen and 21% oxygen, with the balance made up of carbon dioxide and other gases. By artificially increasing the proportion of carbon dioxide and/or reducing the proportion of oxygen, the rate of respiration of fresh foods is reduced and shelf life is extended. However, close control over the degree of modification is necessary to prevent physiological disorders in the living tissues and secondary spoilage by anaerobic micro-organisms. Carbon dioxide has

anti-microbial properties but, although this is widely reported, the mechanism is not fully understood. The effect is likely to be due to the toxicity of carbon dioxide but, as it is an end product of respiratory pathways, it is unlikely to have direct effect on the rate of respiration of foods.

Two types of atmosphere are used commercially:

(1) modification of oxygen and carbon dioxide levels to give a total concentration which is the same as oxygen in normal air (21%) and
(2) reduction in the total concentration of carbon dioxide and oxygen to 4–5%.

The first method is used for both MAS and CAS, whereas the second is used only for CAS.

18.2.1 Controlled-atmosphere storage

CAS is useful for crops that ripen after harvest, or deteriorate quickly, even at optimum storage temperatures. The gas composition is carefully monitored, and a proportion of the store atmosphere is recirculated through scrubbers, which contain calcium hydroxide or activated carbon, to control the carbon dioxide concentration. In modern stores, microcomputers monitor gas composition and control air vents and gas scrubbers, to maintain a pre-determined atmosphere. Controlled-atmosphere stores have a higher relative humidity (90–95%) than normal cold stores and therefore retain the crispness of fresh foods and reduce weight losses. The effects of CAS continue after the food is returned to air. Details of the atmospheric composition required for different products, building construction, equipment and operating conditions are described by Ryall and Lipton (1979).

The main limitations of CAS are as follows.

(1) The low levels of oxygen, or high levels of carbon dioxide needed to inhibit bacteria or fungi, are toxic to many foods.
(2) CAS conditions may lead to an increase in the concentration of ethylene in the atmosphere and accelerate ripening and the formation of physiological defects.
(3) The imbalance in gas composition may change the biochemical activity of tissues, leading to the development of off-odours and off-flavours, a reduction in characteristic flavours, or anaerobic respiration.
(4) Most fruits and vegetables have a critical tolerance to low oxygen and high carbon dioxide concentrations (Table 18.4), but this varies according to the conditions under which crop is grown, the maturity at harvest and the storage conditions employed.
(5) Cultivars of the same species respond differently to a given gas composition, and growers who regularly change cultivars are unwilling to risk losses due to incorrect CAS conditions.

Table 18.4 — Maximum levels of carbon dioxide and minimum levels of oxygen for storage of selected fruits and vegetables

Food	CO_2 (%)	O_2 (%)
Apple[a] (Golden Delicious)	2	2
Asparagus (5°C)	10	10
Avocado	5	3
Banana	5	—
Broccoli	15	1
Cabbage	5	2
Carrot	4	3
Cauliflower	5	2
Citrus fruits	—	5
Cucumber	10	3
Lettuce	1	2
Onion	10	1
Pea	7	5
Pear (Bartlett)	5	2
Potato	10	10
Spinach	20	—
Strawberry	20	2
Sweetcorn	20	—
Tomato	2	3

From Anon. (1979) and Ryall and Pentzer (1982).

[a] Dewey (1983) describes gas compositions for other varieties of UK apples.

(5) Economic viability may be unfavourable owing to competition from other producing areas which have different harvest seasons, and higher costs of CAS over a longer storage period (twice that of cold storage).

18.2.2 Modified-atmosphere storage

In MAS the store is made airtight, and the atmosphere is changed by respiratory activity of fresh foods. Oxygen concentrations as low as 0%, and carbon dioxide concentrations of 20% or higher are produced. This is used in for example grain storage, where high carbon dioxide concentrations destroy insects and mould growth. The required atmospheric composition is maintained by venting air or removing excess carbon dioxide through scrubbers. Alternatively, individual gases may be added from pressurised cylinders. The main disadvantages of MAS are economic; crops other than apples (and to a lesser extent cabbage and pears) have insufficient sales to justify the investment. Short season crops, which increase in price out of season, justify the additional costs of MAS or CAS, but the plant cannot be used throughout the year for such products. Plant utilisation cannot be increased by storing crops together, because of the different requirements for gas composition, and the risk of odour transfer.

Storage in a partial vacuum reduces the oxygen concentration by the same proportion as the reduction in air pressure (that is, if the pressure is reduced by a factor of 10, then the oxygen concentration is reduced by the same factor). The main advantages are the continuous removal of ethylene and other volatiles from the atmosphere and precise control of air pressure ($\pm 0.1\%$). However, the method is not commonly used owing to the higher costs.

18.2.3 Modified-atmosphere packaging

Food is packaged in film which has the required permeability to moisture, oxygen, nitrogen and carbon dioxide. Air is removed from the pack and replaced with a controlled mixture of gases, and the package is heat sealed. Continuous production uses horizontal form–fill–seal equipment (Chapter 23), to allow space around food for the gas. In batch equipment, pre-formed bags are filled, evacuated, gas flushed and heat sealed in a programmed sequence. Changes in gas composition during storage depend on

(1) the respiration rate of fresh foods, and hence the temperature of storage,
(2) the permeability of the packaging material to water vapour and gases,
(3) the external relative humidity, which affects the permeability of some films, and
(4) the surface area of the pack in relation to the amount of food it contains.

Details of types of film and their permeability to moisture and gases are given in Chapter 22.

18.3 EFFECT ON FOODS

A large number of studies of the effect of MAP on the microbiology of foods are reported; for example meat poultry and fish (Finne, 1982, Christopher et al., 1980), baked goods (Knorr and Tomlins, 1985; Ooraikul, 1982). Examples of commercially produced MAP foods include fresh meats, fish, fruit and vegetables, baked goods and cheese. For example the shelf life of fresh red meat is extended from 3 days to 7 days at 0–2°C by packaging in 20% carbon dioxide–80% oxygen or 20% carbon dioxide–69% oxygen–11% nitrogen. In both atmospheres the oxygen concentration is sufficient to inhibit anaerobic bacteria, and to retain the red colour of oxymyoglobin. The rate of oxidative rancidity is also reduced. Pork, poultry and cooked meats have no oxygen requirement to maintain the colour, and a higher carbon dioxide concentration (90%) is possible to extend the shelf life to 11 days.

Carbon dioxide is absorbed into fish tissue, which lowers the pH and increases drip losses. In addition the reduction in gas pressure causes the pack to collapse. These effects are prevented when 30% oxygen and 30% nitrogen are used as filler gases. In fresh fruits and vegetables, a concentration of 10–15% carbon dioxide is required to control decay. Some crops can tolerate this level (for example strawberries and spinach) but most cannot (Table 18.4) and MAP is unsuitable. A high carbon dioxide concentration prevents mould growth in cakes and increases the shelf life to 3–6 months. Other bakery products (for example hamburger buns) have the shelf life increased from 2 days to 3–4 weeks (Guise 1983).

ACKNOWLEDGEMENTS

Grateful acknowledgement is made for information supplied by the following: Distillers Co. Ltd, Reigate, Surrey RH29QE, UK, Liquid Carbonic, Chicago, Illinois 80603, USA.

REFERENCES

Alvarez, J. S., and Thorne, S. (1981) The effect of temperature on the deterioration of stored agricultural produce. In: S. Thorne (ed.), *Developments in food preservation*, Vol. 1, Applied Science, London, pp. 215–237.

Anon. (1979) *Recommendations for chilled storage of perishable produce*. International Institute for Refrigeration, Paris.

Anon. (1982) *Guidelines for the handling of chilled foods*. Institute of Food Science and Technology, 20 Queensberry Place, London.

Bognar, A. (1980) Nutritive value of chilled meals. In: G. Glew (ed.), *Advances in catering technology*. Applied Science, London, pp. 387–408.

Byrne, M. (1986a) The chill chain. *Food Manuf.* January 28–29.

Byrne, M. (1986b) Chilled food is hot property. *Food Manuf.* March 57–58.

Cambell-Platt, G. (1987). Recent developments in chilling and freezing. In: A. Turner (ed.), *Food Technology International, Europe*. Sterling, London, pp. 63–66.

Christopher, F. M., Carpenter, Z. L., Dill, C. W., Smith, G. C., and Vanderzant, C. (1980) Microbiology of beef, pork and lamb stored in vacuum or modified gas atmospheres, *J. Food Protect.* **43** 259.

Dewey, D. H. (1983). Controlled atmosphere storage of fruits and vegetables. In: S. Thorne (ed.) *Developments in food preservation*, Vol. 2, Applied Science, London, pp. 1–24.

Duckworth, R. B. (1966) *Fruits and vegetables*. Pergamon Press, Oxford.

Farrel, A. W. (1976) Cooling and refrigeration. In: A. W. Farrall (ed.) *Food engineering systems*, AVI, Westport, Connecticut, pp. 91–117.

Finne, G. (1982) Modified and controlled atmosphere storage of muscle foods. *Food Technol.* **36** 128–133.

Frazer, W. C., and Westhoff, D. C. (1978). *Food microbiology*, 3rd edn. McGraw-Hill, New York.

Guise, B. (1983). Controlled atmosphere packaging. *Food Process* **52** 29–33.

Hendley, B. (1985) Markets for chilled foods. *Food Process.* February 25–28.

Hill, M. A. (1987). The effect of refrigeration on the quality of some prepared foods. In: S. Thorne, (ed.) *Developments in food preservation*. Vol. 4. Elsevier Applied Science, Barking, Essex, pp. 123–152.

Knorr D., and Tomlins, R. I. (1985) Effect of carbon dioxide modified atmosphere on the compressibility of stored baked goods. *J. Food Sci.* **50** 1172–1176.

Laurie, R. A. (1985) *Meat science*, 4th edn. Pergamon Press, Oxford, pp. 112–134

Leniger, H. A., and Beverloo, W. A. (1975) *Food process engineering*. D. Reidel, Dordrecht, pp. 346–353.

Lewis, M. J. (1987) *Physical properties of foods and food processing systems*. Ellis Horwood, Chichester, West Sussex; VCH, Weinheim, pp. 319–323.

Ooraikul, B. (1982) Gas packing for bakery products. *Can. Inst. Food Sci. Technol.* **15** 313.

Patchen, G. O. (1971). *Storage for apples and pears*, Marketing Research Report, No. 24. US Department of Agriculture, Washington, DC.

Perry, E. J., and Gluckman, R. (1983) A cold front in energy costs. *Food Process.* May 29–32.

Ryall, A. L., and Lipton, W. J. (1979). *Handling, transportation and storage of fruits and vegetables*, Vol. 1. AVI, Westport, Connecticut.

Ryall, A. L., and Pentzer W. T. (1982). Controlled atmosphere storage of apples and pears. In: *Handling, transportation and storage of fruits and vegetables*, Vol. 2, 2nd edn. AVI, Westport, Connecticut, pp. 375–402.

van Beek, G., and Meffert, H. F. Th. (1981) Cooling of horticultural produce with heat and mass transfer by diffusion. In: S. Thorne (ed.) *Developments in food preservation*, Vol. 1. Applied Science, London, pp. 39–92.

van den Berg, L., and Lentz, C. P. (1974) Effect of relative humidity on decay and other quality factors during long term storage of fresh vegetables. In: *ASHRAE Symposium, Semi-annual Meeting, Chicago*, 1973. American Society of Heating Refrigerating and Air-conditioning Engineers, Atlanta, Georgia, pp. 12–18.

19

Freezing

Freezing is the unit operation in which the temperature of a food is reduced below the freezing point, and a proportion of the water undergoes a change in state to form ice crystals. The immobilisation of water to ice and the resulting concentration of dissolved solutes in unfrozen water lower the water activity of the food (Chapter 1). Preservation is achieved by a combination of low temperatures, reduced water activity and, in some foods, pre-treatment by blanching. There are only small changes in nutritional or sensory qualities when correct freezing and storage procedures are followed.

The major groups of commercially frozen foods are as follows:

(1) fruits (strawberries, raspberries, blackcurrants) either whole or puréed, or as juice concentrates;
(2) vegetables (peas, green beans, sweetcorn, spinach, sprouts and potatoes);
(3) fish fillets and seafoods (cod, plaice, shrimps and crab meat) including fish fingers, fish cakes or prepared dishes with an accompanying sauce;
(4) meats (beef, lamb, poultry) as carcasses, boxed joints or cubes, and meat products (sausages, beefburgers, reformed steaks);
(5) baked goods (bread, cakes, fruit and meat pies);
(6) prepared foods (pizzas, desserts, ice cream, complete meals and cook–freeze dishes).

Rapid increases in sales of frozen foods in recent years are closely associated with increased ownership of domestic freezers and microwave ovens.

19.1 THEORY

During freezing, sensible heat is first removed to lower the temperature of a food to the freezing point. In fresh foods, heat produced by respiration is also removed (Chapter 18). This is termed the *heat load*, and is important in determining the correct size of freezing equipment. Latent heat of crystallisation is then removed and ice crystals are formed. The latent heat of other components of the food (for example fats) must also be removed before they solidify. However, most foods contain a large proportion of water (Table 19.1), and these other components require a relatively

Table 19.1 — Water contents and freezing points of selected foods

Food	Water content (%)	Freezing point (°C)
Vegetables	78–92	−0.8 to −2.8
Fruits	87–95	−0.9 to −2.7
Meat	55–70	−1.7 to −2.2
Fish	65–81	−0.6 to −2.0
Milk	87	−0.5
Egg	74	−0.5

small amount of heat for crystallisation. Water has a high specific heat $(4200\,\mathrm{J\,kg^{-1}\,K^{-1}})$ and a high latent heat of fusion $(335\,\mathrm{kJ\,kg^{-1}})$. A substantial amount of energy is therefore needed to freeze foods. This is supplied as electrical energy, which is used to compress gases (refrigerants) in mechanical freezing equipment (Chapter 18) or to compress and cool cryogens (section 19.2.4).

If the temperature is monitored at the thermal centre of a food (the point that cools most slowly) as heat is removed, a characteristic curve is obtained (Fig. 19.1).

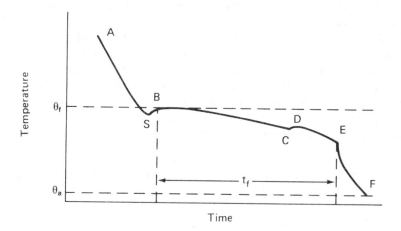

Fig. 19.1 — Time–temperature data during freezing.

The six portions of the curve are as follows.

AS   The food is cooled to below its freezing point θ_f which, with the exception of pure water, is always below 0°C (Table 19.1). At point S the water remains liquid, although the temperature is below the freezing point. This phenomenon is known as supercooling and may be as much as 10°C below the freezing point.

SB   The temperature rises rapidly to the freezing point as ice crystals begin to form and latent heat of crystallisation is released.

BC   Heat is removed from the food at the same rate as before. Latent heat is removed and ice forms, but the temperature remains almost constant. The freezing point is depressed by the increase in solute concentration in the unfrozen liquor, and the temperature therefore falls slightly. It is during this stage that the major part of the ice is formed (Fig. 19.2).

CD   One of the solutes becomes supersaturated and crystallises out. The latent heat of crystallisation is released and the temperature rises to the eutectic temperature for that solute (section 19.1.2).

DE   Crystallisation of water and solutes continues. The total time t_f taken (the freezing plateau) is determined by the rate at which heat is removed.

EF   The temperature of the ice–water mixture falls to the temperature of the freezer. A proportion of the water remains unfrozen at the temperatures used in commercial freezing; the amount depends on the type and composition of the food and the temperature of storage (for example at a storage temperature of -20°C the percentage of ice is 88% in lamb, 91% in fish and 93% in egg albumin).

19.1.1   Ice crystal formation

The freezing point of a food is the temperature at which a minute crystal of ice exists in equilibrium with the surrounding water. However, before an ice crystal can form, a nucleus of water molecules must be present. Nucleation therefore precedes ice crystal formation. There are two types of nucleation: homogeneous nucleation (the chance orientation and combination of water molecules), and heterogeneous nucleation (the formation of a nucleus around suspended particles or at a cell wall). Heterogeneous nucleation is more likely to occur in foods and takes place during supercooling (Fig. 19.1).

The length of the supercooling period depends on the type of food and the rate at which heat is removed. High rates of heat transfer therefore produce large numbers of nuclei. Water molecules migrate to existing nuclei in preference to forming new nuclei. Fast freezing therefore produces a large number of small ice crystals. However, large differences in crystal size are found in different types of food and even in similar foods which have received different pre-freezing treatments. The rate of ice crystal growth is controlled by the rate of heat transfer for the majority of the freezing plateau. The rate of mass transfer (of water molecules moving to the growing crystal and of solutes moving away from the crystal) does not control the rate of crystal growth except towards the end of the freezing period when solutes become more concentrated. The time taken for the temperature of a food to pass through the *critical zone* (Fig. 19.2) therefore determines both the number and the size of ice crystals.

19.1.2   Solute concentration

The increase in solute concentration during freezing causes changes in the pH, viscosity and redox potential of the unfrozen liquor. As the temperature falls,

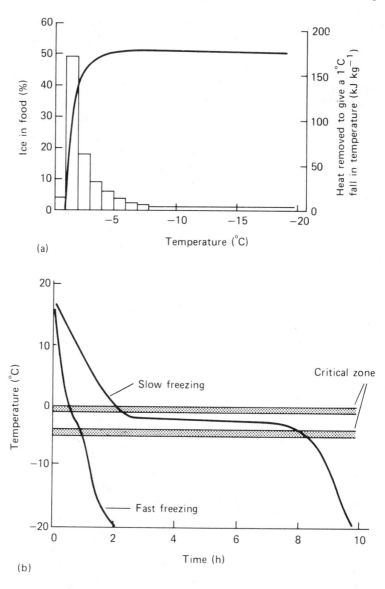

(a)

(b)

Fig. 19.2 — Freezing: (a) ice formation at different freezing temperatures; (b) temperature changes of food through the critical zone. (After Leniger and Beverloo (1975).)

individual solutes reach saturation point and crystallise out. The temperature at which a crystal of an individual solute exists in equilibrium with the unfrozen liquor and ice is its *eutectic temperature* (for example for glucose this is −5°C, for sucrose −14°C, for sodium chloride −21.13°C and for calcium chloride −55°C). However, it is difficult to identify individual eutectic temperatures in the complex mixture of solutes in foods, and the term *final eutectic temperature* is used. This is the lowest eutectic temperature of the solutes in a food (for example for ice-cream this is −55°C, for meat −50 to −60°C and for bread −70°C (Fennema, 1975a)). Maximum ice crystal formation is not possible until this temperature is reached. Commercial foods are not frozen to such low temperatures and unfrozen water is therefore always present.

19.1.3 Volume changes
The volume of ice is 9% greater than that of pure water, and an expansion of foods after freezing would therefore be expected. However, the degree of expansion varies considerably owing to the following factors:

(1) moisture content (higher moisture contents produce greater changes in volume);
(2) cell arrangement (plant materials have intercellular air spaces which absorb internal increases in volume without large changes in their overall size (for example whole strawberries increase in volume by 3.0% whereas coarsely ground strawberries increase by 8.2% when both are frozen to −20°C (Leniger and Beverloo, 1975)));
(3) the concentrations of solutes (high concentrations reduce the freezing point and do not freeze—or expand—at commercial freezing temperatures) and
(4) the freezer temperature (this determines the amount of unfrozen water and hence the degree of expansion. Crystallised components, including ice, fats and solutes, contract when they are cooled and this reduces the volume of the food).

19.1.4 Calculation of freezing time
During freezing, heat is conducted from the interior of a food to the surface and is removed by the freezing medium. The factors which influence the rate of heat transfer are

(1) the thermal conductivity of the food,
(2) the area of food available for heat transfer,
(3) the distance that the heat must travel through the food,
(4) the temperature difference between the food and the freezing medium,
(5) the insulating effect of the boundary film of air surrounding the food (Chapter 1).

If packaging is present, this is an additional barrier to heat flow (Fig. 19.3).

It is difficult to define the freezing time precisely but two approaches are taken. The *effective freezing time* is the time required to lower the temperature of a food from an initial value to a pre-determined final temperature at the thermal centre. The *nominal freezing time* is the time between the surface of the food reaching 0°C and the thermal centre reaching 10°C below the temperature of the first ice formation. The effective freezing time measures the time that food spends in a freezer and is used to calculate the throughput of a manufacturing process, whereas the nominal freezing time is used to estimate product damage as it takes no account of the initial conditions or the different rates of cooling at different points on the surface of the food.

The calculation of freezing time is complicated for the following reasons:

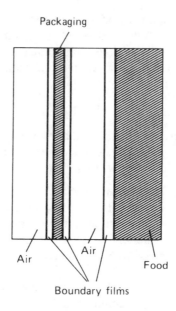

Fig. 19.3 — Barriers to heat flow.

(1) differences in the initial temperature of the food;
(2) differences in size and shape of individual pieces of food;
(3) differences in the freezing point and the rate of ice crystal formation within different regions of a piece of food;
(4) changes in density, thermal conductivity, specific heat and thermal diffusivity with a reduction in temperature of the food.

Removal of latent heat complicates the unsteady-state heat transfer calculations (Chapter 1), and a complete mathematical solution of freezing rate is not possible. For most practical purposes an approximate solution based on formulae developed by Plank is adequate (equation (19.1)). This involves the following assumptions.

(1) Freezing starts with all water in the food unfrozen but at its freezing point, and loss of sensible heat is ignored.
(2) Heat transfer takes place sufficiently slowly for steady-state conditions to operate.
(3) The freezing front maintains a similar shape to that of the food (for example in a rectangular block the freezing front remains rectangular).
(4) There is a single freezing point.
(5) The density of the food does not change.
(6) The thermal conductivity and specific heat of the food are constant when unfrozen and then change to a different constant value when the food is frozen.

The freezing time for cubes of food is calculated using

$$t_f = \frac{\lambda \rho}{\theta_f - \theta_a}\left[\frac{L}{6}\left(\frac{1}{h} + \frac{x}{k_1}\right) + \frac{L^2}{24k_2}\right] \tag{19.1}$$

where t_f (s) is the freezing time, L (m) the length of cube, h ($W\,m^{-2}\,K^{-1}$) the surface heat transfer coefficient, θ_f (°C) the freezing point of food, θ_a (°C) the temperature of freezing medium, λ ($J\,kg^{-1}$) the latent heat of crystallisation, ρ ($kg\,m^{-3}$) the density of food, x (m) the thickness of packaging, k_1 ($W\,m^{-1}\,K^{-1}$) the thermal conductivity of packaging and k_2 ($W\,m^{-1}\,K^{-1}$ the thermal conductivity of frozen zone; 6 and 24 are factors. Other shapes require different factors (which represent the shortest distance from the centre to the surface of the food); these are 2 and 8 for a slab, 4 and 16 for a cylinder, and 6 and 24 for a sphere. Derivation of the equation is described by Earle (1983).

Equation (19.1) may be rearranged to find the heat transfer coefficient as follows:

$$h = \frac{L}{6}\left[\frac{t_f(\theta_f - \theta_a)}{\lambda \rho} - \frac{Lx}{6k_1} - \frac{L^2}{24k_2}\right] \tag{19.2}$$

Other equations produced by different research workers are described by Jackson and Lamb (1981). The many assumptions made using these equations lead to a small underestimation of freezing time when compared with experimental data. More complex formulae which give closer approximations have been described by a number of workers including Cleland and Earle (1982).

Sample problem 19.1
Five-centimetre potato cubes are individually quick frozen (IQF) in a blast freezer operating at $-40°C$ and with a surface heat transfer coefficient of $30\,W\,m^{-2}\,K^{-1}$ (Table 19.3). If the freezing point of the potato is measured as $-1.0°C$ and the density is $1180\,kg\,m^{-3}$, calculate the expected freezing time for each cube. If the cubes are then packed into a cardboard carton measuring $20\,cm \times 10\,cm \times 10\,cm$, calculate the freezing time. Also calculate the freezing time for IQF freezing of 2.5 cm cubes. (Additional data: the thickness of the card is 1.5 mm, the thermal conductivity of the card is $0.07\,W\,m^{-1}\,K^{-1}$, the thermal conductivity of potato is $2.5\,W\,m^{-1}\,K^{-1}$ (Table 1.4) and the latent heat of crystallisation $2.74 \times 10^5\,J\,kg^{-1}$).

Solution to sample problem 19.1
To calculate the expected freezing time of each cube, from equation (19.1), for an unwrapped cube,

$$t_f = \frac{(2.74 \times 10^5)1180}{-1-(-40)}\left[\frac{0.05}{6}\left(\frac{1}{30} + 0\right) + \frac{0.05^2}{24 \times 2.5}\right] = 2648\,s\ = 44\ \text{min}$$

To calculate the freezing time for cubes packed together to form a slab 10 cm thick,

$$t_f = \frac{(2.74 \times 10^5)1180}{-1-(-40)}\left[\frac{0.1}{2}\left(\frac{1}{30}+\frac{0.0015)}{0.07}\right)+\frac{0.1^2}{8 \times 2.5}\right] = 26\,700\,s$$
$$\approx 7.4\,h$$

To calculate the freezing time for IQF freezing of 2.5 cm cubes,

$$t_f = \frac{(2.74 \times 10^5)1180}{-1-(-40)}\left[\frac{0.025}{6}\left(\frac{1}{30}+0\right)+\frac{0.025^2}{24 \times 25}\right] = 1226\,s$$
$$\approx 20\,min$$

IQF foods freeze more rapidly, enable packaged foods to be partly used and then refrozen, and permit better portion control. However, the low bulk density and high void space causes greater risk of dehydration and freezer burn (section 19.3.2.1).

19.2 FREEZING EQUIPMENT

Freezers are broadly categorised into

(1) mechanical refrigerators, which evaporate and compress a refrigerant in a continuous cycle (Chapter 18) and
(2) cryogenic freezers.

Mechanical freezers use cooled air, cooled liquid or cooled surfaces to remove heat from foods. Cryogenic freezers use carbon dioxide, liquid nitrogen or liquid Freon directly in contact with the food.

The selection of freezing equipment should take the following factors into consideration:

(1) rate of freezing required;
(2) size, shape and packaging requirements of the food;
(3) batch or continuous operation, depending on the scale of production and the number of product types.

An alternative classification, based on the rate of movement of the ice front is
(1) *slow freezers* and *sharp freezers* ($0.2\,cm\,h^{-1}$) including still-air freezers and cold stores,
(2) *quick freezers* (0.5–$3\,cm\,h^{-1}$) including air-blast and plate freezers,
(3) *rapid freezers* (5–$10\,cm\,h^{-1}$) including fluidised-bed freezing and

(4) *ultrarapid freezers* (10–100 cm h^{-1}), that is cryogenic freezers.

All freezers are insulated with expanded polystyrene, polyurethane or other materials which have low thermal conductivity (Table 1.4).

19.2.1 Cooled air freezers
19.2.1.1 Chest freezers
Food is frozen in stationary (natural-circulation) air at between − 20°C and − 30°C. Chest freezers are not used for commercial freezing owing to low freezing rates (3–72 h), which result in poor process economics and loss of product quality (section 19.3). Cold stores can be regarded as large chest freezers. They are used to freeze carcass meat, for frozen storage of foods frozen by other methods, and as hardening rooms for ice cream. Air is usually circulated by fans to improve the uniformity of temperature distribution, but heat transfer coefficients are low (Table 19.3).

19.2.1.2 Blast freezers
Air is recirculated over food at between − 30°C and − 40°C at a velocity of 1.5–6.0 m s^{-1}. The high air velocity reduces the thickness of boundary films surrounding the food (Chapter 1) and thus increases the surface heat transfer coefficient (Table 19.3). In batch equipment, food is stacked on trays in rooms or cabinets. Continuous equipment consists of trolleys stacked with trays of food or of conveyor belts which carry the food through an insulated tunnel. The trolleys should be fully loaded to prevent air from bypassing the food through spaces between the trays. Multipass tunnels have a number of belts, and products fall from one to another. This breaks up any clumps of food and allows control over the product depth (for example a 25–50 mm bed is initially frozen for 5–10 min and then repiled to 100–125 mm on a second belt). The smaller surface-area-to-volume ratio of these freezers permits a 30% saving in energy from reduced heat penetration and 20% less floor space.

Air flow is either parallel or perpendicular to the food and is ducted to pass evenly over all food pieces. Blast freezing is relatively economical and highly flexible in that foods of different shapes and sizes can be frozen. The equipment is compact and has a relatively low capital cost and a high throughput (200–1500 kg h^{-1}). However, the large volumes of recycled air can cause freezer burn and oxidative changes to unpackaged or IQF foods. Moisture from the food is transferred to the air and builds up as ice on the refrigeration coils, and this necessitates frequent defrosting.

19.2.1.3 Belt freezers (spiral freezers)
These are modified air-blast freezers in which a continuous flexible mesh belt is formed into spiral tiers. Food is carried up through a refrigerated chamber on the belt. In some designs each tier rests on the vertical sides of the tier beneath (Fig. 19.4) and the belt is therefore 'self-stacking'. This eliminates the need for support rails and improves the capacity by up to 50% for a given stack height. Cold air or sprays of liquid nitrogen (section 19.2.4) are directed down through the belt stack (countercurrent flow) to reduce weight losses due to evaporation of moisture. Spiral freezers require relatively small floor-space and have high capacity (for example a 50–75 cm belt in a 32-tier spiral processes up to 3000 kg h^{-1}). Other advantages include

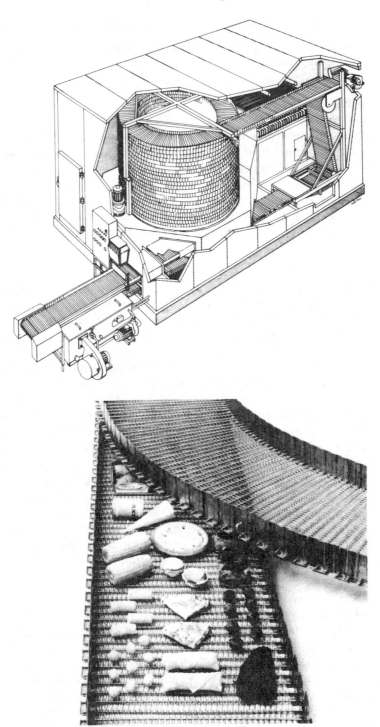

Fig. 19.4 — Spiral freezer, self-stacking belt. (Courtesy of Frigoscandia Ltd.)

automatic loading and unloading, low maintenance costs and flexibility for different products. They are used for a wide range of foods including pizzas, cakes, pies, ice cream, whole fish and chicken portions.

19.2.1.4 Fluidised-bed freezers

These are a modified blast freezers in which air at between $-25°C$ and $-35°C$ is passed at a high velocity ($2–5\,m\,s^{-1}$) through a 2–13 cm bed of food, contained on a perforated tray or conveyor belt. In some designs there are two stages; after initial rapid freezing to produce an ice glaze on the surface of the food, freezing is completed on a second belt in beds 10–15 cm deep. The formation of a glaze is useful for fruit pieces and other products that have a tendency to clump together. The shape and size of the pieces of food determine the thickness of the fluidised bed and the air velocity needed for fluidisation. A sample calculation of air velocity is shown in Chapter 1. Food comes into greater contact with the air than in blast freezers, and all surfaces are frozen simultaneously and uniformly. This produces higher heat transfer coefficients, shorter freezing times (Table 19.3), higher production rates ($10\,000\,kg\,h^{-1}$) and less dehydration of unpackaged food than blast freezing. The equipment therefore needs less frequent defrosting. However, the method is restricted to particulate foods (for example peas, sweetcorn kernels, shrimps, strawberries or French fried potatoes). Similar equipment, named *through-flow freezers*, in which air passes through a bed of food but fluidisation is not achieved, is suitable for larger pieces of food (for example fish fillets). Both types of equipment are compact, have a high capacity and are highly suited to the production of IQF foods.

19.2.2 Cooled liquid freezers
19.2.2.1 Immersion freezers

Packaged food is passed through a bath of refrigerated propylene glycol, brine, glycerol or calcium chloride solution on a submerged mesh conveyor. In contrast with cryogenic freezing (section 19.2.3), the liquid remains fluid throughout the freezing operation and a change of state does not occur. The method has high rates of heat transfer (Table 19.3) and capital costs are relatively low. It is used commercially for concentrated orange juice in laminated card–polyethylene cans, and to pre-freeze film-wrapped poultry before blast freezing.

19.2.3 Cooled-surface freezers
19.2.3.1 Plate freezers

Plate freezers consist of a vertical or horizontal series of hollow plates, through which refrigerant is pumped at $-40°C$ (Fig. 19.5). They may be batch, semi-continuous or continuous in operation. Flat, relatively thin foods (for example filleted fish, fish fingers or beefburgers) are placed in single layers between the plates and a slight pressure is applied by moving the plates together. This improves the contact between surfaces of the food and the plates and thereby increases the rate of heat transfer. If packaged food is frozen in this way, the pressure prevents the larger surfaces of the packs from bulging. Production rates range from $90–2700\,kg\,h^{-1}$ in batch equipment. Advantages of this type of equipment include good economy and space utilisation, relatively low operating costs compared with other methods, little

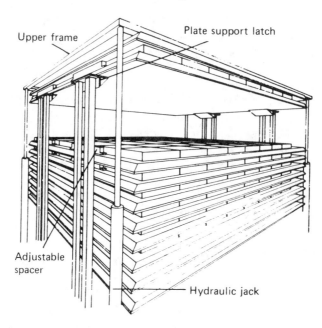

Upper frame

Plate support latch

Adjustable spacer

Hydraulic jack

Fig. 19.5 — Plate freezer. (Courtesy of Frigoscandia Ltd.)

dehydration of the product and therefore minimum defrosting and high rates of heat transfer (Table 19.3). The main disadvantages are the relatively high capital costs, and restrictions on the shape of foods to those that are flat and relatively thin.

19.2.3.2 Scraped-surface freezers
Scraped-surface freezers are used for liquid or semi-solid foods (for example ice cream). They are similar in design to equipment used for evaporation (Fig. 12.8) and heat sterilisation (Chapter 11) but are refrigerated with ammonia, brine or a fluorocarbon refrigerant (Table 18.3). In ice cream manufacture, the rotor scrapes frozen food from the wall of the freezer and incorporates air (Chapter 3). The temperature is reduced to between $-4°C$ and $-7°C$ when the forzen aerated mixture is pumped into containers and freezing is completed in a hardening room (section 19.2.1.1).

19.2.4 Cryogenic freezers
Freezers of this type are characterised by a change of state in the refrigerant (or cryogen) as heat is absorbed from the freezing food. The cryogen is in intimate contact with the food and rapidly removes energy from the food to provide its latent heat of vaporisation or sublimation, to produce high heat transfer coefficients and rapid freezing. The two most common refrigerants are liquid nitrogen and solid or liquid carbon dioxide.

Dichlorodifluoromethane (refrigerant 12 or Freon 12) is also used to a lesser extent and is claimed to be the only refrigerant that is almost fully recoverable (Table 19.2) and is thus more economical (Astrom and Lascelles, 1976). It produces less

Table 19.2 — Properties of food cryogens

	Liquid nitrogen	Carbon dioxide	Freon 12
Density (kg m $^{-3}$)	784	464	1485
Specific heat (liquid) (kJ kg $^{-1}$ K $^{-1}$)	1.04	2.26	0.984
Latent heat (kJ kg $^{-1}$)	358	352	297
Total usable refrigeration effect (kJ kg $^{-1}$)	690	565	297
Boiling point (°C)	-196	-78.5 (sublimation)	-29.8
Thermal conductivity (W m $^{-1}$ K $^{-1}$)	0.29	0.19	0.095
Consumption per 100 kg of product frozen (kg)	100–300	120–375	1–3

From: Graham (1984).
*Low consumption of Freon because it is recovered and re-used.

heat shock than other cryogens and is particularly useful for sticky heat-sensitive foods (for example tomato slices and meat paste). Production rates are 500–9000 kg h $^{-1}$. The main limitation is the risk of excessive cryogen residues in foods and a limit of 300 mg kg $^{-1}$ is a legislative requirement in many countries.

Both liquid-nitrogen and carbon dioxide refrigerants are colourless, odourless and inert. When liquid nitrogen is sprayed onto food, 48% of the total freezing capacity (enthalpy) is taken up by the latent heat of vaporisation needed to form the gas (Table 19.2). The remaining 52% of the enthalpy is available in the cold gas, and gas is therefore recirculated to achieve optimum use of the freezing capacity. Carbon dioxide has a lower enthalpy than liquid nitrogen (Table 19.2) but the lower boiling point produces a less severe thermal shock. Most of the freezing capacity (85%) is available from the subliming solid. Liquid carbon dioxide is therefore sprayed onto food to form a fine snow which sublimes on contact, and gas is not recirculated. Carbon dioxide is a bacteriostat but is also toxic, and gas should be vented from the factory to avoid injury to operators (also Chapter 18). Carbon dioxide consumption is higher than liquid-nitrogen consumption, but storage losses are lower and gas recovery systems are sometimes used to improve the economics. The choice of refrigerant is largely determined by its cost and the nature of the product. Liquid nitrogen is widely used in the UK, whereas carbon dioxide is more popular in the USA and Europe where production costs are lower.

In liquid-nitrogen freezers, packaged or unpackaged food travels on a perforated belt through a tunnel (Fig. 19.6), where it is cooled by gaseous nitrogen and then frozen by liquid-nitrogen sprays. Tne temperature is allowed to equilibrate at the

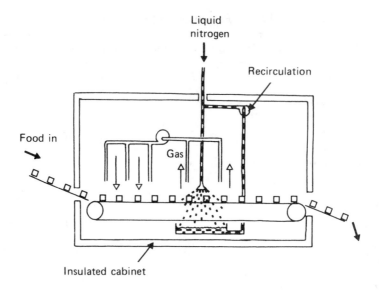

Fig. 19.6 — Liquid-nitrogen freezer.

required storage temperature (between $-18°C$ and $-20°C$) before the food is removed from the freezer. Production rates are $45–1350\,kg\,h^{-1}$. Gaseous nitrogen reduces the thermal shock to the food, and the recirculation fans produce higher rates of heat transfer than would be achieved by stationary gas. The temperature and belt speed are controlled by microprocessors to maintain the product at a pre-set exit temperature, regardless of the heat load of incoming food. The equipment therefore has the same efficiency at or below its rated capacity. This results in greater flexibility and economy than mechanical systems, which have a fixed rate of heat extraction. Other advantages include

(1) simple continuous equipment with relatively low capital costs (approximately 30% of the capital cost of mechanical systems),
(2) smaller weight losses from dehydration of the product (0.5% compared with 1.0–8.0% in mechanical air-blast systems),
(3) rapid freezing (Table 19.3) which results in smaller changes to the sensory and nutritional characteristics of the product,
(4) the exclusion of oxygen during freezing,
(5) rapid startup and no defrost time and
(6) low power consumption (Leeson, 1987).

The main disadvantage is the relatively high cost of refrigerant (nitrogen consumption is shown in Table 19.2).

Liquid nitrogen is also used in spiral freezers (section 19.2.1.3) instead of vapour recompression refrigerators. The advantages include higher rates of freezing, and smaller units for the same production rates because heat exchanger coils are not used. Other applications include rigidification of meat for high-speed slicing, and surface hardening of ice cream prior to chocolate coating.

Table 19.3 — A comparison of freezing methods

Method of freezing	Typical film heat transfer coefficients $(W\,m^{-2}\;K^{-1})$	Typical freezing times for specified foods to $-18°C$ (min)	Food
Still air	6–9	180–4320	Meat carcass
Blast (5 m s^{-1})	25–30	15–20	Unpackaged peas
Blast (3 m s^{-1})	18	—	
Spiral belt	25	12–19	Hamburgers, fish fingers
Fluidised bed	90–140	3–4 15	Unpacked peas Fish fingers
Plate	100	75 25	25 kg blocks of fish 1 kg carton vegetables
Scraped surface	—	0.3–0.5	Ice cream (layer approximately 1 mm thick)
Immersion (Freon)	500	10–15 — 0.5 4–5	170 g card cans of orange juice Peas Beefburgers, fish fingers
Cryogenic (liquid nitrogen)	1500	1.5 0.9 2–5 0.5–6	454 g of bread 454 g of cake Hamburgers, seafood Fruits and vegetables

Adapted from Earle (1983), Olsson and Bengtsson (1972), Desrosier and Desrosier (1978), Leeson (1987) and Holdsworth (1987).

Immersion of foods in liquid nitrogen produces no loss in product weight but causes a high thermal shock. This is acceptable in some products (for example raspberries, shrimps and diced meat), but in many foods the internal stresses created by the extremely high rate of freezing cause the food to crack or split. The rapid freezing permits high production rates of IQF foods using small equipment (for example a 1.5 m long bath of liquid nitrogen freezes 1 t of small-particulate food per hour).

19.3 CHANGES IN FOODS

19.3.1 Effect of freezing

The main effect of freezing on food quality is damage caused to cells by ice crystal growth. Freezing causes negligible changes to pigments, flavours or nutritionally important components, although these may be lost in preparation procedures or deteriorate later during frozen storage (section 19.3.2). Food emulsions (Chapter 3) can be destabilised by freezing, and proteins are sometimes precipitated from solution. These changes prevent the widespread use of frozen milk. In baked goods a high proportion of amylopectin is needed in the starch to prevent retrogradation and staling during slow freezing and frozen storage.

There are important differences in resistance to freezing damage between animal and plant tissues. Meats have a more flexible fibrous structure which separates during freezing instead of breaking, and the texture is not seriously damaged. In fruits and vegetables, the more rigid cell structure may be damaged by ice crystals. The extent of damage depends on the size of the crystals and hence on the rate of heat transfer (section 19.1.1). However, differences in the variety and quality of raw materials and the degree of control over pre-freezing treatments both have a substantially greater effect on food quality than changes caused by correctly operated freezing, frozen storage and thawing procedures (see also Chapter 2).

The influence of freezing rate on plant tissues is shown in Fig. 19.7. During slow freezing (section 19.2), ice crystals grow in intercellular spaces and deform and rupture adjacent cell walls. Ice crystals have a lower water vapour pressure than regions within the cells, and water therefore moves from the cells to the growing crystals. Cells become dehydrated and permanently damaged by the increased solute concentration. On thawing, cells do not regain their original shape and turgidity. The food is softened and cellular material leaks out from ruptured cells (*drip loss*). In fast freezing, smaller ice crystals form within both cells and intercellular spaces. There is little physical damage to cells, and water vapour pressure gradients are not formed; hence there is minimal dehydration of the cells. The texture of the food is thus retained to a greater extent (Fig. 19.7(b)). However, very high freezing rates may cause stresses within some foods that result in splitting or cracking of the tissues. These changes are discussed by Spiess (1980).

19.3.2 Effects of frozen storage

In general, the lower the temperature of frozen storage, the lower is the rate of microbiological and biochemical changes. However, freezing and frozen storage do not inactivate enzymes and have a variable effect on micro-organisms. Relatively high storage temperatures (between $-4°C$ and $-10°C$) have a greater lethal effect on micro-organisms than do lower temperatures (between $-15°C$ and $-30°C$). Different types of micro-organism also vary in their resistance to low temperatures; vegetative cells of yeasts, moulds and gram-negative bacteria (for example coliforms and *Salmonella* species) are most easily destroyed; gram-positive bacteria (for example *Staphylococcus aureus* and *Enterococci*) and mould spores are more resistant, and bacterial spores (especially *Bacillus* species and *Clostridium* species such as *Clostridium botulinum*) are virtually unaffected by low temperatures. The majority of vegetables are therefore blanched to inactivate enzymes and to reduce the numbers of contaminating micro-organisms (Chapter 9). In fruits, enzyme

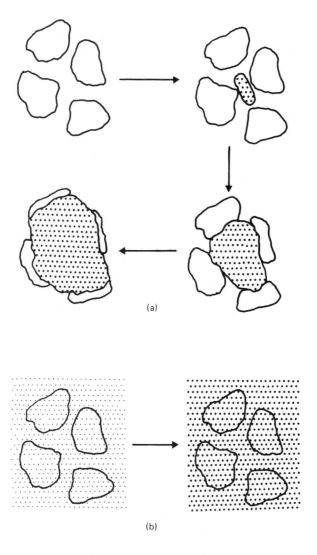

Fig. 19.7 — Effect of freezing on plant tissues: (a) slow freezing; (b) fast freezing. (After Meryman (1963).)

activity is controlled by the exclusion of oxygen, acidification or treatment with sulphur dioxide.

At normal frozen storage temperatures ($-18°C$), there is a slow loss of quality owing to both chemical changes and, in some foods, enzymic activity. These changes are accelerated by the high concentration of solutes surrounding the ice crystals, the reduction in water activity (to 0.82 at $-20°C$ in aqueous foods) and by changes in pH and redox potential. The effects of storage temperature on food quality are shown in Fig. 19.8. If enzymes are not inactivated, the disruption of cell membranes by ice crystals allows them to react with concentrated solutes.

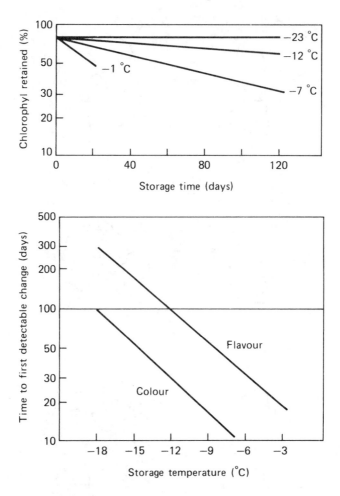

Fig. 19.8 — Effect of storage temperature on sensory characteristics. (After Jul (1984).)

The main changes to frozen foods during storage are as follows.

(1) *Degradation of pigments*. Chlorophyll is slowly degraded to brown pheophytin even in blanched vegetables. In fruits, changes in pH due to precipitation of salts in concentrated solutions change the colour of anthocyanins (Chapter 1).

(2) *Loss of vitamins*. Water-soluble vitamins (for example vitamin C and pantothenic acid) are lost at subfreezing temperatures (Table 19.4). Vitamin C losses are highly temperature dependent; a 10°C increase in temperature causes a sixfold to twentyfold increase in the rate of vitamin C degradation in vegetables and a thirtyfold to seventyfold increase in fruits (Fennema, 1975b). Losses of other vitamins are mainly due to drip losses, particularly in meat and fish (if the drip loss is not consumed).

(3) *Residual enzyme activity*. In vegetables which are inadequately blanched or in fruits, the most important loss of quality is due to polyphenoloxidase activity

Table 19.4 — Vitamin losses during frozen storage

Product	Loss (%) at -18 °C during storage for 12 months						
	Vitamin C	Vitamin B_1	Vitamin B_2	Niacin	Vitamin B_6	Pantoth-enic acid	Carotene
Beans (green)	52	0–32	0	0	0–21	53	0–23
Peas	11	0–16	0–8	0–8	7	29	0–4
Beef steaks[a]		8	9	0	24	22	—
Pork chops[a]		+–18	0–37	+–5	0–8	18	—
Fruits[b]							
Mean	18	29	17	16	—	—	37
Range	0–50	0–66	0–67	0–33	—	—	0–78

+ , apparent increase.
[a]Storage for 6 months.
[b]Mean results from apples, apricots, blueberries, cherries, orange juice concentrate (rediluted), peaches, raspberries and strawberries; storage time not given.
Adapted from Burger (1982) and Fennema (1975b).

which causes browning, and lipoxygenase activity which produces off-flavours and off-odours from lipids. Proteolytic and lipolytic activity in meats may alter the texture and flavour over long storage periods.

(4) *Oxidation of lipids*. This reaction takes place slowly at -18°C and causes off-odours and off-flavours.

These changes are discussed in detail by Fennema (1975a, 1982). The effect of these changes on the nutritive value of foods in the diet is discussed in Chapter 1.

19.3.2.1 Recrystallisation
Physical changes to ice crystals (for example changes in shape, size or orientation of ice crystals) are collectively known as recrystallisation and are an important cause of quality loss in some foods. There are three types of recrystallisation in foods as follows.

(1) *Isomass recrystallisation*. This is a change in surface shape or internal structure, usually resulting in a lower surface-area-to-volume ratio.
(2) *Accretive recrystallisation*. Two adjacent ice crystals join together to form a larger crystal and cause an overall reduction in the number of crystals in the food.
(3) *Migratory recrystallisation*. This is an increase in the average size and a reduction in the average number of crystals, caused by the growth of larger crystals at the expense of smaller crystals (Fig. 19.9).

Migratory recrystallisation is the most important in most foods and is largely caused by fluctuations in the storage temperature. When heat is allowed to enter a freezer

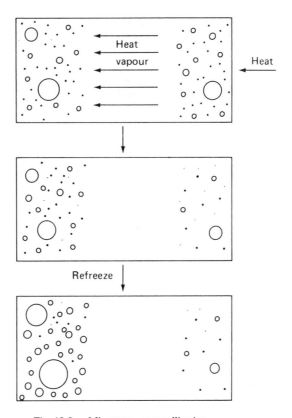

Fig. 19.9 — Migratory recrystallisation.

(for example, by opening a door and allowing warm air to enter), the surface of the food nearest to the source of heat warms slightly. This causes ice crystals to melt partially; the larger crystals become smaller and the smallest (less than $2\,\mu$m) disappear. The melting crystals increase the water vapour pressure, and moisture then moves to regions of lower vapour pressure. This causes areas of the food nearest to the source of heat to become dehydrated. When the temperature falls again, water vapour does not form new nuclei but joins onto existing ice crystals, thereby increasing their size. There is therefore a loss of quality similar to that observed in slow freezing.

Cold stores have a low humidity because moisture is removed from the air by the refrigeration coils (see psychrometrics in Chapter 14). Moisture leaves the food to the storage atmosphere and produces areas of visible damage known as *freezer burn*. Such areas have a lighter colour due to microscopic cavities, previously occupied by ice crystals, which alter the wavelength of reflected light. Freezer burn is a particular problem in foods that have a large surface-area-to-volume ratio (for example IQF foods) but is minimised by packaging in moistureproof materials (Chapter 22). The causes of dehydration during freezing and frozen storage are discussed in detail by Norwig and Thompson (1984).

Temperature fluctuations are minimised by

(1) control of storage temperature (± 1.5°C),
(2) automatic doors and airtight curtains for loading refrigerated trucks (Guilfoy, 1957),
(3) rapid movement of foods between stores and
(4) correct stock rotation and control.

These techniques, and technical improvements in handling, storage and display equipment, have substantially improved the quality of frozen foods (Jul, 1984).

The quality of frozen foods is assessed at each stage of manufacture, storage and distribution using the concept of *high-quality life* (HQL). This is defined as the time that a food may be stored before 70–80% of taste panellists detect a definite quality change. It is therefore the period that food remains essentially the same as when it was frozen. This should not be confused with storage life or consumer acceptability, as foods are acceptable for three to six times longer than the HQL. Examples of HQL for four vegetables, stored at different temperatures, are shown in Table 19.5. The

Table 19.5 — HQL of retail packs of vegetables stored at different temperatures

Vegetable	HQL (days)		
	− 18 °C	− 12 °C	− 7 °C
Green beans	296	94	30
Cauliflower	291	61	13
Peas	305	90	27
Spinach	187	57	23

Source: Guadagni (1968).

logarithm of HQL is related to storage temperature and is analogous to the decimal reduction time in heat processing (Chapter 1). Fluctuating temperatures have a cumulative effect on food quality and the proportion of HQL lost can be found by integrating losses over time. This concept is useful in identifying the points when loss of quality occurs (Fig. 19.10).

The time–temperature tolerance and product–processing–packaging concepts are used to monitor and control the effects of temperature fluctuations on frozen food quality during production, distribution and storage (Olsson, 1984; Bogh-Sorensen, 1984). Coloured indicators are used

(1) to show the temperature of food (for example, liquid crystal coatings which change colour with storage temperature),
(2) to indicate temperature abuse (for example wax melts and releases a coloured dye when an unacceptable increase in temperature occurs) or
(3) to integrate the time–temperature combination that a food has received after packaging and to give an indication of the remaining shelf life (Fig. 19.11).

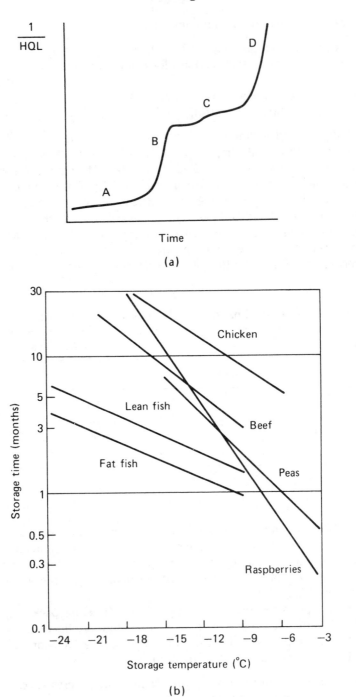

Fig. 19.10 — (a) Change in HQL during storage and distribution: (A) manufacturers cold storage, (B) distribution to retail stores, (C) retail display cabinets, (D) transport and storage by consumer. (b) Relationship of time and temperature of storage to HQL of frozen foods. (Adapted from Burger (1982) and Fennema (1975a).)

An example of a time–temperature integrator, based on an enzymic reaction which changes the colour of a pH indicator, is described by Blixt (1984).

19.3.3   Thawing

When food is thawed in air or water, surface ice melts to form a layer of water. Water has a lower thermal conductivity and a lower thermal diffusivity than ice (Chapter 1). The surface layer of water therefore reduces the rate at which heat is conducted to the frozen interior. This insulating effect increases as the layer of thawed food grows thicker. (In contrast, during freezing, the increase in thickness of ice causes heat transfer to accelerate.) Thawing is therefore a substantially longer process than freezing when temperature differences and other conditions are similar.

In Fig. 19.12, the initial rapid rise in temperature (AB) is due to the absence of a significant layer of water around the food. There is then a long period when the temperature of the food is near to that of melting ice (BC). Cellular damage, caused by slow freezing or recrystallisation, releases cell constituents to form drip losses. This causes loss of water-soluble nutrients (for example beef loses 12% thiamine, 10% riboflavin, 14% niacin, 32% pyridoxine and 8% folic acid (Pearson *et al.*, 1951) and fruits lose 30% of the vitamin C).

In addition, drip losses form substrates for enzyme and microbial activity. Microbial contamination of foods, caused by inadequate cleaning or blanching (Chapters 2 and 9), has a pronounced effect during this period. In the home, food is often thawed using a small temperature difference (for example 25–40°C, compared with 50–80°C for commercial freezing). This further extends the thawing period and increases the risk of contamination by spoilage and pathogenic micro-organisms. Commercially, foods are often thawed to just below the freezing point, to retain a firm texture for subsequent processing (*tempering*, see Chapter 17).

Some foods are cooked immediately and are therefore heated rapidly to a temperature which is sufficient to destroy micro-organisms. Others (for example ice cream, cream, frozen cakes and gateaux) are not cooked and should therefore be consumed within a short time of thawing. Details of changes to foods during thawing are described by Fennema (1975a). When food is thawed by microwave or dielectric heaters (Chapter 17), heat is generated within the food, and the changes described above do not take place.

19.3.3.1   Equipment for thawing

Commercially, foods are thawed in a vacuum chamber by condensing steam, at low temperatures by warm water (approximately 20°C) or by moist air which is recirculated over the food. Dielectric or microwave heating (Chapter 17) is also used for thawing food. The main considerations in thawing are

(1) to avoid overheating,
(2) to minimise thawing times and
(3) to avoid excessive dehydration of the food.

Details of the types and method of operation of thawing equipment are described by Jason (1981).

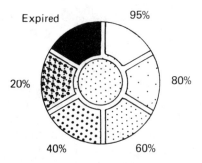

Fig. 19.11 — Time–temperature integrator. (After Fields and Prusik (1983).)

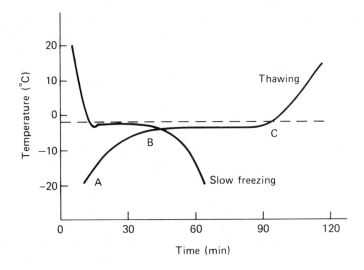

Fig. 19.12 — Temperature changes during thawing. (After Fennema and Powrie (1964).)

ACKNOWLEDGEMENTS

Grateful acknowledgement is made for information supplied by the following: APV Jackstone Ltd, Thetford, Norfolk IP24 3RP, UK; Frigoscandia Contracting Ltd, Hoddesdon, Hertfordshire EN11 8TT, UK; BOC Ltd, London SW19 3UF, UK; The Distillers Co. Ltd, Reigate, Surrey RH2 9QE, UK.

REFERENCES

Astrom, S., and Lascelles, A. (1976). Freon opens the way to new processing techniques. *Food. Process. Ind.* April 19.

Blixt, K. (1984) The I-point TTM—a versatile biochemical time-temperature integrator. In: P. Zeuthen, J. C. Cheftel, C. Eriksson, M. Lul, H. Leniger, P. Linko, G. Varela and G. Vos (eds), *Thermal processing and quality of foods*. Elsevier Applied Science, Barking, Essex, pp. 789–791.

Bogh-Sorensen, L. (1984) The TTT–PPP concept. In: P. Zeuthen, J. C. Cheftel, C. Eriksson, M. Lul, H. Leniger, P. Linko, G. Varela and G. Vos (eds), *Thermal processing and quality of foods*. Elsevier Applied Science, Barking, Essex, pp. 511–521.

Burger, I. H. (1982) Effect of processing on nutritive value of food: meat and meat products. In: M. Rechcigl (ed.), *Handbook of the nutritive value of processed food*, Vol. 1, CRC Press, Boca Raton, Florida, pp. 323–336.

Cleland, A. C., and Earle, R. L. (1982) *Int. J. Refrig.* **5** 134.

Desrosier, W., and Desrosier, N. (1978) *Technology of food preservation*, 4th edn. AVI, Westport, Connecticut, pp. 110–151.

Earle, R. L. (1983) *Unit operations in food processing*, 2nd edn. Oxford University Press, Oxford, pp. 78–84.

Fennema, O. R. (1975a) Freezing preservation. In: O. R. Fennema (ed.), *Principles of Food Science*, Part 2, *Physical principles of food preservation*. Marcel Dekker, New York, pp. 173–215.

Fennema, O. (1975b) Effects of freeze-preservation on nutrients. In: R. S. Harris and E. Karmas (eds) *Nutritional evaluation of food processing* AVI, Westport, Connecticut, pp. 244–288.

Fennema, O. (1982) Effect of processing on nutritive value of food: freezing. In: M. Rechcigl (ed.), *Handbook of the nutritive value of processed food*, Vol. 1. CRC Press, Boca Raton, Florida, pp. 31–44.

Fennema, O., and Powrie, W.D. (1964) *Adv. Food Res.* **13**, 219.

Fields, S. C., and Prusik, T. (1983) Time–temperature monitoring using solid-state chemical indicators 16*th International Congress of Refrigeration, Paris*, 1983.

Graham, J. (1984) *Planning and engineering data*, 3; *Fish freezing*, FAO Fisheries Circular, No 771. FAO, Rome.

Guadagni, D. G. (1968) In: J. Hawthorn and E. J. Rolfe (eds), *Low temperature biology of foodstuffs*. Pergamon Press, Oxford, pp. 399–412.

Guilfoy, R. F. (1957) A new cold curtain for refrigerated trucks. *Agric. Mark.* **2** 7.

Holdsworth, S. D. (1987) Physical and engineering aspects of food freezing. In: S. Thorne (ed.) *Developments in food preservation*, Vol. 4, Elsevier Applied Science, Barking, Essex, pp. 153–204.

Jackson, A. T., and Lamb, J. (1981) *Calculations in food and chemical engineering*. Macmillan, London, pp. 50–64.

Jason, A. C. (1981) *Thawing frozen fish*, Torry Advisory Note, No 25. Torry Research Station, PO Box 31, Aberdeen AB9 8DG.

Jul, M. (1984) *The quality of frozen foods*. Academic Press, London, pp. 44–80, 156–251.

Leeson, R. (1987) *Applications of liquid nitrogen in individual quick freezing and chilling*. BOC (UK) Ltd, London SW19 3UF.

Leniger, H. A., and Beverloo, W. A. (1975) *Food process engineering*. D. Reidel, Dordrecht, pp. 351–398.

Meryman, H. T. (1963) *Food Process* **22** 81.

Norwig, J. F., and Thompson, D. R. (1984) Review of dehydration during freezing. *Trans. ASAE* 1619–1624.

Olson, R. L., (1968) Objective tests for frozen food quality. In: J. Hawthorn and E. J. Rolfe (eds), *Low temperature biology of foodstuffs*. Pergamon Press, Oxford, pp. 381–397.

Olsson, P. (1984) TT-integrators—some experiments in the freezer chain. In: P. Zeuthen, J. C. Cheftel, C. Eriksson, M. Lul, H. Leniger, P. Linko, G. Varela and G. Vos (eds), *Thermal processing and quality of foods*. Elsevier Applied Science, Barking, Essex, pp. 782–788.

Olsson, P. and Bengtsson, N. (1972) *Time–temperature conditions in the freezer chain*, Report, No. 30 SIK. Swedish Food Institute, Gothenburg.

Pearson, A. M., Burnside, J. E., Edwards, H. M., Glassock, R. R., Cunha, T. J., and Novak, A. F. (1951) Vitamin losses in drip obtained upon defrosting frozen meat. *Food Res.* **16** 85–87.

Spiess, W. E. L. (1980) Impact of freezing rates on product quality of deep-frozen foods. In: P. Linko, Y. Mallki, J. Olkku and J. Larinkari (eds) *Food process engineering*. Applied Science, London, pp. 689–694.

20

Freeze drying and freeze concentration

The advantages of dried and concentrated foods compared to other methods of preservation are described in Chapters 14 and 12. The heat used to dry foods or concentrate liquids by boiling removes water and therefore preserves the food by a reduction in water activity (Chapter 1). However, the heat also causes a loss of sensory and nutritional qualities. In freeze drying and freeze concentration a similar preservative effect is achieved by reduction in water activity without heating the food, and nutritional and sensory qualities are consequently better retained. However, both operations are slower than conventional dehydration or evaporation. Energy costs for refrigeration are high and, in freeze drying, the production of a partial vacuum is an additional expense. This, together with a relatively high capital investment, results in high production costs for freeze-dried and freeze-concentrated foods. Freeze drying is the more important operation commercially and is used to dry expensive foods which have delicate aromas or textures (for example coffee, mushrooms, herbs and spices, fruit juices, meat, seafoods, vegetables and complete meals for military rations or expeditions). In addition, microbial cultures for use in food processing (Chapter 7) are freeze dried for long-term storage prior to inoculum generation. Products that are concentrated by freeze concentration include fruit juices, vinegar and pickle liquors. Freeze concentration is also used to pre-concentrate coffee extract prior to freeze drying and to increase the alcohol content of wine.

20.1 FREEZE DRYING (LYOPHILISATION)

The main differences between freeze drying and conventional hot air drying are shown in Table 20.1.

20.1.1 Theory

The first stage of freeze drying is to freeze the food in conventional freezing equipment. The type of equipment used depends on the nature of the food. Small pieces of food are frozen rapidly to produce small ice crystals and to reduce damage to the cell structure of the food (Chapter 19). In liquid foods, slow freezing is used to

Table 20.1 — Difference between conventional drying and freeze drying

Conventional drying	Freeze drying
Successful for easily dried foods (vegetables and grains)	Successful for most foods but limited to those that are difficult to dry by other methods
Meat generally unsatisfactory	Successful with cooked and raw meats
Temperature range 37–93°C	Temperatures below freezing point
Atmospheric pressures	Reduced pressures (27–133 Pa)
Evaporation of water from surface of food	Sublimation of water from ice front
Movement of solutes and sometimes case hardening	Minimal solute movement
Stresses in solid foods cause structural damage and shrinkage	Minimal structural changes or shrinkage
Slow, incomplete rehydration	Rapid complete rehydration
Solid or porous dried particles often having a higher density than the original food	Porous dried particles having a lower density than original food
Odour and flavour frequently abnormal	Odour and flavour usually normal
Colour frequently darker	Colour usually normal
Reduced nutritional value	Nutrients largely retained
Costs generally low	Costs generally high, up to four times those of conventional drying

form an ice crystal lattice, which provides channels for the movement of water vapour.

If the water vapour pressure of a food is held below 4.58 Torr (610.5 Pa) and the water is frozen, when the food is heated the solid ice sublimes directly to vapour without melting (Fig. 20.1). Water vapour is continuously removed from food by keeping the pressure in the freeze drier cabinet below the vapour pressure at the surface of the ice, removing vapour with a vacuum pump and condensing it on refrigeration coils. As drying proceeds a *sublimation front* moves into the food (Fig 20.2). The latent heat of sublimation is either conducted through the food to the sublimation front or produced in the food by microwaves (section 20.1.1.1). Water

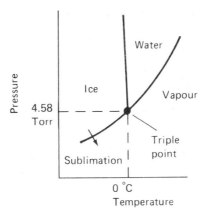

Fig. 20.1 — Phase diagram for water showing sublimation of ice.

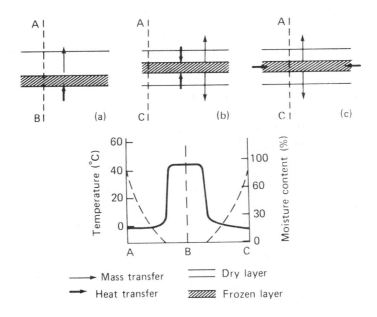

Fig. 20.2 — Heat and moisture transfer during freeze drying: (a) heat transfer through the frozen layer; (b) heat transfer from hot surfaces or radiant heaters through the dry layer; (c) heat generated in the ice by microwaves. The graphs show changes in temperature (---) and moisture content (—) along the line A → B → C through each sample.

vapour travels out of the food through channels formed by the sublimed ice and is removed. Foods are dried in two stages; first by sublimation to approximately 15% moisture content (wet-weight basis), and then by evaporative drying (desorption) of unfrozen water to 2% moisture content (wet-weight basis). Desorption is achieved by raising the temperature in the drier to near ambient temperature whilst retaining the low pressure.

In some liquid foods (for example fruit juices and concentrated coffee extract), the formation of a glassy vitreous state on freezing causes difficulties in vapour transfer. Either the liquid is therefore frozen as a foam (vacuum puff freeze drying), or the juice is dried together with the pulp. Both methods produce channels through the food for the vapour to escape. In a third method, frozen juice is ground to produce granules, which both dry faster and allow better control over the particle size of the dried food.

The rate of drying depends mostly on the resistance of the food to heat transfer and to a lesser extent on the resistances to vapour flow (mass transfer) from the sublimation front.

20.1.1.1   Rate of heat transfer
There are three methods of transferring heat to the sublimation front.

(1) *Heat transfer through the frozen layer* (Fig. 20.2(a)). The rate of heat transfer depends on the thickness and thermal conductivity of the ice layer. As drying proceeds, the thickness of the ice is reduced and the rate of heat transfer increases. The surface temperature is limited to avoid melting the ice.

(2) *Heat transfer through the dried layer* (Fig. 20.2(b)). The rate of heat transfer to the sublimation front depends on the thickness and area of the food, the thermal conductivity of the dry layer and the temperature difference between the surface of the food and ice front. At a constant cabinet pressure the temperature of the ice front remains constant. These factors are discussed in detail in Chapter 1 and related in equation (1.5). The dried layer of food has a very low thermal conductivity (similar to insulation materials (Table 1.4)) and therefore offers a high resistance to heat flow. As drying proceeds, this layer becomes thicker and the resistance increases. As in other unit operations, a reduction in the size or thickness of food and an increase in the temperature difference increase the rate of heat transfer. However, in freeze drying, the surface temperature is limited to 40–65°C, to avoid denaturation of proteins and other chemical changes that would reduce the quality of the food.

(3) *Heating by microwaves* (Fig. 20.2(c)). Heat is generated at the ice front, and the rate of heat transfer is not influenced by the thermal conductivity of ice or dry food, or the thickness of the dry layer. However, microwave heating is less easily controlled (Chapter 17).

20.1.1.2   Rate of mass transfer
When heat reaches the sublimation front, it raises the temperature and the water vapour pressure of the ice. Vapour then moves through the dried food to a region of low vapour pressure in the drying chamber. 1 g of ice forms 2 m^3 of vapour at 67 Pa and, in commercial freeze drying, it is therefore necessary to remove several hundred cubic metres of vapour per second through the pores in the dry food. The factors that control the water vapour pressure gradient are

(1) the pressure in the drying chamber,

(2) the temperature of the vapour condenser, both of which should be as low as economically possible, and

(3) the temperature of ice at the sublimation front, which should be as high as possible, without melting.

In practice, the lowest economical chamber pressure is approximately 13 Pa and the lowest condenser temperature is approximately − 35°C.

Theoretically the temperature of the ice could be raised to just below the freezing point. However, above a certain *critical temperature* (Table 20.2) the concentrated

Table 20.2 — Collapse temperatures for selected foods in freeze drying

Food	Collapse temperature (°C)
25% coffee extract	− 20
22% apple juice	− 41.5
16% grape juice	− 46

From Bellows and King (1972).

solutes in the food are sufficiently mobile to flow under the forces operating within the food structure. When this occurs, there is an instantaneous irreversible collapse of the food structure, which restricts the rate of vapour transfer and effectively ends the drying operation. In practice, there is therefore a maximum ice temperature, a minimum condenser temperature and a minimum chamber pressure, and these control the rate of mass transfer.

The moisture content falls from the initial high level in the frozen zone to a lower level in the dried layer (Fig. 20.2), which depends on the water vapour pressure in the cabinet. When heat is transferred through the dry layer, the relationship between the pressure in the cabinet and the pressure at the ice surface is

$$P_i = P_s + \frac{k_d}{b\lambda_s} (\theta_s - \theta_i) \tag{20.1}$$

where P_i (Pa) is the partial pressure of water at the sublimation front, P_s (Pa) the partial pressure of water at the surface, k_d (W m^{-1} K^{-1}) the thermal conductivity of the dry layer, b (kg s^{-1} m^{-1}) the permeability of the dry layer, λ_s (J kg^{-1}) the latent heat of sublimation, θ_s (°C) the surface temperature and θ_i (°C) the temperature at the sublimation front (°C). The factors that control the drying time are related by (Karel, 1974).

$$t_d = \frac{x^2 \rho (M_1 - M_2)\lambda_s}{8 \, k_d \, (\theta_s - \theta_i)} \tag{20.2}$$

where t_d (s) is the drying time, x (m) the thickness of food, ρ (kg m^{-3}) the bulk density of dry food, M_1 the initial moisture content and M_2 the final moisture content in dry layer.

Sample problem 20.1
Food with an initial moisture content of 400% (dry-weight basis) is poured into 1 cm layers in a tray placed in a freeze drier operating at 40 Pa. It is to be dried to 8% moisture (dry-weight basis) at a maximum surface temperature of 55°C. Assuming that the pressure at the ice front remains constant at 78 Pa, calculate the drying time. (Additional data: the dried food has a thermal conductivity of 0.03 W m^{-1}K^{-1}, a density of 470 kg m^{-3}, a permeability of 2.4 x 10^{-8} kg s^{-1} m^{-1}, and the latent heat of sublimation is 2.95 x 10^3 kJ kg^{-1}.

From equation (20.1),

$$78 = 40 + \frac{0.03}{2.4 \times 10^{-8} \times 2.95 \times 10^6} (55 - \theta_i)$$

$$78 = 40 + 0.42(55 - \theta_i)$$

Therefore,

$$\theta_i = -35.7°C$$

From equation (20.2)

$$t_d = \frac{(0.005)^2 \, 470(4 - 0.08)2.95 \times 10^6}{8 \times 0.03[55 - (-35.7)]}$$

$$= 6238.5 \text{ s}$$

$$\approx 1.7 \text{ h}$$

20.1.2 Equipment
Freeze driers consist of a vacuum chamber which contains trays to hold the food during drying, and heaters to supply latent heat of sublimation. Refrigeration coils (Chapter 18) are used to condense the vapours. They are fitted with automatic defrosting devices to keep the maximum area of coils free of ice for vapour condensation. This is necessary because the major part of the energy input is used in refrigeration of the condensers, and the economics of freeze drying are therefore determined by the efficiency of the condenser:

$$\text{efficiency} = \frac{\text{temperature of sublimation}}{\text{refrigerant temperature in the condenser}} \qquad (20.3)$$

Vacuum pumps remove non condensible vapours.

Different types of drier are characterised by the method used to supply heat to the surface of the food. Conduction and radiation types are used commercially. Microwave freeze drying is under development (convection heating is not important in the partial vacuum of the freeze drier cabinet). Both batch and continuous versions are found for each type of drier; the advantages and limitations of batch and continuous operation are described in Chapter 1. In batch drying, the product is sealed into the drying chamber, the heater temperature is maintained at 100–120°C for initial drying and then gradually reduced over a drying period of 6–8 hours. The precise drying conditions are determined for individual foods, but the surface temperature of the food does not exceed 60°C. In continuous freeze drying, trays of food enter and leave the drier through vacuum locks. A stack of trays, interspersed by heater plates (Fig. 20.3) is moved on guide rails through heating zones in a long vacuum chamber.

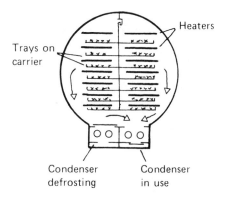

Fig. 20.3 — Continuous freeze drier. (After Rolfgaard (1987).)

Heater temperatures and product residence times in each zone are pre-programmed for individual foods, and microprocessors are used to monitor and control process time, temperature and pressure in the chamber, and the temperature at the product surface (also Chapter 24). Details of drying equipment are given by Lorentzen (1981).

20.1.2.1 Contact freeze driers
Food is placed onto ribbed trays which rest on heater plates (Fig. 20.4(a)). This type of equipment dries more slowly than other designs because heat is transferred, by conduction, to one side of the food. There is uneven contact between the frozen food and the heated surface, which reduces the rate of heat transfer. There is also a pressure drop through the food which results in differences between the drying rates of the top and bottom layers. The vapour velocity is of the order of 3 m s^{-1} and fine particles of product may be carried over in the vapour and lost. However, contact freeze driers have higher capacity than other types.

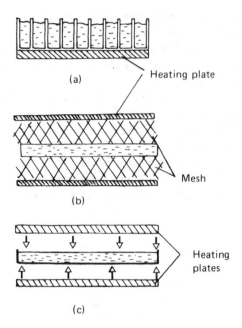

Fig. 20.4 — Freeze-drying methods: (a) conduction through ribbed tray; (b) expanded mesh for accelerated freeze drying; (c) radiant heating of flat trays. (After Rolfgaard (1987).)

20.1.2.2 Accelerated freeze driers

In this equipment, food is held between two layers of expanded metal mesh and subjected to a slight pressure on both sides (Fig. 20.4(b)). Heat is transferred more rapidly into food by the mesh than by solid plates, and vapour escapes more easily from the surface of the food. Both mechanisms cause a reduction in drying times compared with contact methods.

20.1.2.3 Radiation freeze driers

Infrared radiation from radiant heaters (Chapter 17) is used to heat shallow layers of food on flat trays (Fig. 20.4(c)). Heating is more uniform than in conduction types, because surface irregularities on the food have a smaller effect on the rate of heat transfer. There is no pressure drop through the food and constant drying conditions are therefore created. Vapour movement is approximately 1m s^{-1} and there is little risk of product carryover. Close contact between the food and heaters is not necessary and flat trays are used, which are cheaper and easier to clean.

20.1.2.4 Microwave and dielectric freeze driers

Microwave and dielectric heaters have potential use in freeze drying but are not yet used on a commercial scale. Microwave freeze drying is difficult to control because water has a higher loss factor than ice and any local melting of the ice causes 'runaway' overheating in a chain reaction (Chapter 17).

A modification of freeze drying is named *reversible freeze-dried compression*. Food is freeze dried to remove 90% of the moisture and it is then compressed into bars using a pressure of 69 000 kPa. The residual moisture keeps the food elastic during compression, and the food is then vacuum dried. When packaged in inert gas these foods are reported to have a shelf life of 5 years. They are used in military rations (for example a 0.3 kg meal consisting of separate bars of pepperoni, stew, granola dessert and an orange drink). The bars reconstitute rapidly, during which time the compressed food 'groans, rumbles, quivers and eventually assumes its normal shape and size' (Unger, 1982).

20.1.3 Effect on foods

Freeze-dried foods have a very high retention of sensory and nutritional qualities and a shelf life of longer than 12 months when correctly packaged. Volatile aroma compounds are not present in the pure water of ice crystals. They are not therefore entrained in the water vapour produced by sublimation and are trapped in the food matrix. As a result, aroma retention of 80–100% is possible. Theories of volatile retention are discussed in detail by Karel (1975).

The texture of freeze-dried foods is well maintained; there is little shrinkage and no case hardening (Chapter 14). The open porous structure (Fig. 20.5 and Fig. 20.6)

Dry solids

Ice

Fig. 20.5 — Porous structure of freeze-dried food.

allows rapid and full rehydration, but it is fragile and requires protection from mechanical damage. There are only minor changes to proteins, starches or other carbohydrates. However, the open porous structure of the food may allow oxygen to enter and cause oxidative deterioration of lipids. Food is therefore packaged in an inert gas (Chapter 18). Changes in thiamine and ascorbic acid content during freeze drying are moderate and there are negligible losses of other vitamins (Table 20.3). However, losses due to preparation procedures (Chapter 2) may substantially affect the final nutritional quality of a food. The importance of these changes to the nutritional value of the diet are discussed in Chapter 1.

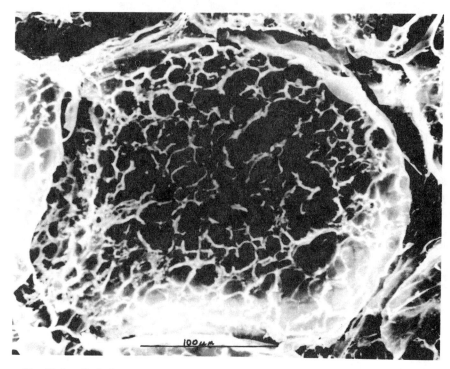

Fig. 20.6 — Boiled potato—freeze dried and fractured showing cell filled with starch gel.
Porous nature of starch gel is caused by freeze drying as also is the cell wall separation.
(Courtesy of IFR)

Table 20.3 — Vitamin losses during freeze drying

Food	Loss (%)						
	Vitamin C	Vitamin A	Thiamin	Riboflavin	Folic acid	Niacin	Pantothenic acid
Beans (green)	26–60	0–24	—	0	—	10	—
Peas	8–30	5	0	—	—	0	10
Orange juice	3	3–5	—	—	—	—	—
Beef	—	—	2	0	+	0	13
Pork	—	—	<10	0	—	0	56

+ , apparent increase.
Adapted from Flink (1982).

20.2 FREEZE CONCENTRATION

Freeze concentration of liquid foods involves the fractional crystallisation of water to
ice and subsequent removal of the ice. This is achieved by freezing, followed by
mechanical separation techniques (Chapter 5) or washing columns. Freeze concentration comes closest to the ideal of selectively removing water from a food without

alteration of other components. In particular, the low temperatures used in the process cause a high retention of volatile aroma compounds. However, the process has high refrigeration costs, high capital costs for equipment required to handle the frozen solids, high operating costs and low production rates, compared with concentration by boiling (Chapter 12). The degree of concentration achieved is higher than in membrane processes (Chapter 6), but lower than concentration by boiling. As a result of these limitations, freeze concentration is only used for high-value juices or extracts (Thijssen, 1982).

20.2.1   Theory

The factors that control the rate of nucleation and ice crystal growth are described in Chapter 19. In freeze concentration it is desirable for ice crystals to grow as large as is economically possible, to reduce the amount of concentrated liquor entrained with the crystals. This is achieved in a *paddle crystalliser* (section 20.2.2) by stirring a thick slurry of ice crystals and allowing the large crystals to grow at the expense of smaller ones (Muller, 1967). Details of the effect of solute concentration and supercooling on the rate of nucleation and crystal growth are described by Thijssen (1974). Calculations of the degree of solute concentration obtained by a given reduction in the freezing point of a solution are used to produce *freezing point curves* for different products (Fig. 20.6).

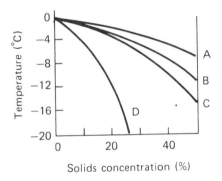

Fig. 20.6 — Freezing point curves: curve A, coffee extract; curve B, apple juice; curve C, blackcurrant juice; curve D, wine. (After Kessler (1986).)

The efficiency of crystal separation from the concentrated liquor is determined by the degree of clumping of the crystals, and amount of liquor entrained. Efficiency of separation is calculated using

$$\eta_{sep} = x_{mix} \frac{x_l - x_i}{x_l - x_j} \qquad (20.4)$$

where: η_{sep} (%) is the efficiency of separation, x_{mix} the weight fraction of ice in the frozen mixture before separation, x_1 the weight fraction of solids in liquor after freezing, x_i the weight fraction of solids in ice after separation and x_j the weight fraction of juice before freezing.

Separation efficiencies of 50% for centrifuging, 71% for vacuum filtration, 89–95% for filter pressing and 99.5% for wash columns (section 20.2.2) are reported (Mellor, 1978).

20.2.2 Equipment

The basic components of a freeze concentration unit are shown in Fig 20.7. These are

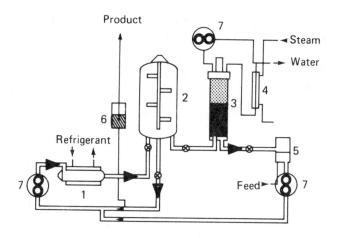

Fig. 20.7 — Freeze concentration plant: 1, scraped-surface heat exchanger; 2, mixing vessel; 3, wash column; 4, melting device; 5, storage tank; 6, expansion vessel; 7, pump. (After Kessler (1986).)

(1) a direct freezing system (for example solid carbon dioxide) or indirect equipment (for example a scraped surface heat exchanger) to freeze the liquid food,
(2) a mixing vessel to allow the ice crystals to grow and
(3) a separator to remove the crystals from the concentrated solution.

Details of scraped surface heat exchangers are given in Chapters 11, 12 and 19. The mixing vessel typically contains a slowly rotating paddle agitator (Chapter 4). Separation is achieved by centrifugation, filtration, filter pressing or wash columns. Wash columns operate by feeding the ice–concentrate slurry into the bottom of a vertical enclosed cylinder. The majority of the concentrate drains through the crystals and is removed. The ice crystals are melted by a heater at the top of the column and some of the melt water drains through the bed of ice crystals to remove entrained concentrate (Fig. 20.8). Detailed descriptions of wash columns are given by Mellor (1978).

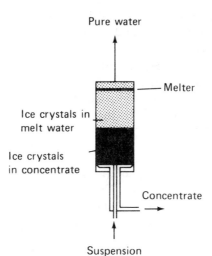

Fig. 20.8 — Wash column. (After Thijssen (1974).)

Concentration takes place in either single-stage or, more commonly, multi-stage equipment. Multi-stage concentrators have lower energy consumption and higher production rates. Improvements in techniques for generating large ice crystals and more efficient washing have increased the maximum obtainable concentration to 45% solids (Kessler, 1986). The energy consumption and the degree of concentration achieved by freeze concentration, in comparison with other methods of concentration, are shown in Table 20.4.

ACKNOWLEDGEMENTS

Grateful acknowledgement is made for information supplied by the AFRC Institute of Food Research, Colney Lane, Norwich, UK.

REFERENCES

Bellows, R. J., and King, C. J. (1972) Freeze drying of aqueous solutions: maximum allowable operating temperatures. *Cryobiology*, **9**, 559.

Flink, J. M. (1982) Effect of processing on nutritive value of food: freeze-drying. In: M. Rechcigl (ed.), *Handbook of the nutritive value of processed food*, Vol.1, CRC Press, Boca Raton, Florida, pp. 45–62.

Karel, M. (1974) Fundamentals of dehydration processes. In: A. Spicer (ed.), *Advances in preconcentration and dehydration*. Applied Science, London, pp. 45–94.

Karel, M. (1975) Dehydration of foods. In: O. R. Fennema (ed.), *Principles of food science*, Part 2, *Physical principles of food preservation*. Marcel Dekker, New York, pp. 359–395.

Table 20.4 — A comparison of energy efficiency and degree of concentration in different methods of concentration

	Steam equivalent (cost per kilogram of water removed divided by equivalent cost of steam)	Maximum concentration possible (%)
Ultrafiltration	0.001	28
Reverse osmosis	0.028	30
Freeze concentration	0.090–0.386	40
Evaporation:		
Triple effect without aroma recovery	0.370	80
Triple effect with aroma recovery	0.510	80

From Thijssen, (1974).

Kessler, H. G. (1986) Energy aspects of food preconcentration. In: D. MacCarthy (ed.) *Concentration and drying of foods*. Elsevier Applied Science, Barking, Essex, pp. 147–163.

Lorentzen, J. (1981) Freeze drying: the process, equipment and products. In:S. Thorne (ed.), *Developments in food preservation*, Vol.1, Applied Science, London, pp. 153–175.

Mellor, J. D. (1978) *Fundamentals of freeze-drying*. Academic Press, London, pp. 257–288.

Muller, J. G. (1967) Freeze concentration of food liquids: theory, practice and economics. *Food Technol.* **21**, 49–52, 54–56, 58, 60, 61.

Rolfgaard, J. (1987) Freeze drying: processing, costs and applications. In: A. Turner (ed.), *Food technology international Europe*. Sterling, London, pp. 47–49.

Thijssen, H. A. C. (1974) Freeze concentration. In: A. Spicer (ed.), *Advances in preconcentration and dehydration*. Applied Science, London.

Thijssen, H. A. C. (1982) Freeze concentration of liquid foods, freeze concentration of fruit juices. *Food Technol.* **3** (5).

Unger, H. G. A. (1982) Revolution in freeze drying. *Food Process Ind.* April 20.

Part V
Post-processing operations

The unit operations described in preceding chapters alter the sensory characteristics of foods and/or permit an extension of the shelf life. An ancillary method of improving the eating quality of some foods is to coat the food with breadcrumbs, batter or sweet coatings (Chapter 21). The retention of food quality during subsequent storage depends to a large extent on the selection of suitable packaging materials and maintenance of correct storage conditions. In this section, packaging materials are described in detail in Chapter 22 and the associated filling and sealing machines are described in Chapter 23.

Unit operations are linked to form a process (see Introduction). The flow of materials and energy through each process is controlled to ensure production of the correct-quality food at the lowest cost. This is frequently accomplished automatically. Details of the techniques used for control of materials and processing conditions are described in Chapter 24, and examples of the way in which unit operations are linked together to process raw materials are described in Chapter 25.

21

Coating or enrobing

Coating with batter, breadcrumbs, chocolate and other compound coatings is used to improve the eating quality of the food and to increase variety. In some cases, coatings provide a barrier to the movement of moisture and gases or protect against mechanical damage. Coatings of salt, flavouring or colouring (for example on snackfoods), or sugar (on biscuits) increase variety and improve the eating quality. Coating operations have a minimal effect on the nutritional quality of foods (except in terms of the ingredients added to food in the coatings).

21.1 COATING MATERIALS

Chocolate or compound coatings (in which cocoa solids and hardened vegetable oils are used to replace cocoa butter) are used to enrobe confectionery, ice cream and baked goods. The principal ingredients in a coating are fat and sugar. Corn syrup, flavourings, fat-soluble colourings and emulsifiers are also added to achieve the desired properties. Fat is *tempered* (that is it is melted at approximately 43°C and then cooled with constant stirring to 29°C to form nuclei for fat crystal growth). It is then reheated to 31–32°C to melt unstable crystals and held at that temperature during production. Subsequent cooling then produces only stable fat crystals and avoids the development of *bloom* (a thin layer of fat at the surface of the coating which causes dullness or white specks). Corn syrup and starch are used to reduce the sweetness and cost of coatings. The particle size of the starch has an important effect on the texture and is closely controlled.

The thickness of a coating is determined in part by the viscosity of the material. This is controlled by the fat content (more fat produces a lower viscosity), and the type and amount of emulsifier and anti-oxidant used (Appendix B). The ratios of sugar, starch and fat are carefully controlled to achieve the required flow characteristics for application of the coating and the desired mouthfeel and taste in the final product.

21.2   ENROBING EQUIPMENT

Food passes on a stainless steel wire conveyor, beneath a single or double curtain of hot liquid coating (Fig. 21.1). The coating is applied

(1) by passing it through a slit in the base of a vessel,
(2) over the edge of the vessel or
(3) by coating rollers.

A pan beneath the conveyor collects the excess coating and recirculates it through a heater to the enrobing curtain. If bottom coating is required, a bottom roller passes the coating material through the wire conveyor. Excess coating is removed by air blowers, shakers licking rolls and anti-tailer rollers. This also gives a clean edge to the product. Discs, rollers or wires may be used to decorate the surface of the coating.

The coating is then cooled by recirculated air in a cooling tunnel. Temperature zones are used to cool the product rapidly but prevent overcooling which would produce surface bloom. The thickness of the coating is determined by the temperature of both the food and the coating, by the viscosity of the coating, by the speed of the air in air blowers and by the rate of cooling. Coated foods are held at 22°C for 48 h to allow fat crystallisation to continue. Latent heat of crystallisation is removed from the product to prevent fat crystals from remelting (Matz, 1972).

21.3   BATTERING AND BREADING

Batters are a suspension of flour in water to which various concentrations of sugar, salt, thickening, flavourings and colourings are added to achieve the required characteristics. They are applied for example to fish, poultry and potato products. A single layer of viscous batter (termed Tempura) is used for products that are not subsequently breaded. It is applied by passing the product through a bath of batter between two submerged mesh conveyors. A thinner adhesive batter is used to coat products prior to breading. This is applied either by submerging the product or by passing it through one or more curtains of batter in similar equipment to enrobers (section 21.2). Both types of equipment are fitted with fans to remove excess batter and to control the thickness of the coating. Products are then frozen (Chapter 19) or fried and chilled (Chapters 16 and 18).

Breadcrumbs are supplied in specified particle sizes and are flavoured or coloured if required. All are fragile and require delicate handling. Pneumatic conveyors (Chapter 24) are often used. Food products pass from a battering machine to the breadcrumb applicator. They are deposited onto a moving bed of breadcrumbs which coats the base. They then pass through a curtain of breadcrumbs to coat the upper surface. The crumbs are gently pressed into the batter by rollers, and excess crumbs are removed by air blowers. Similar designs of applicator are used to coat confectionery and baked goods with sugar, nuts or dried fruit pieces.

21.4   SEASONING

A hopper fitted with a mesh base is located over a conveyor. The mesh screen is changeable for different types of seasoning, flavourings or salt. Foods pass through a

(a)

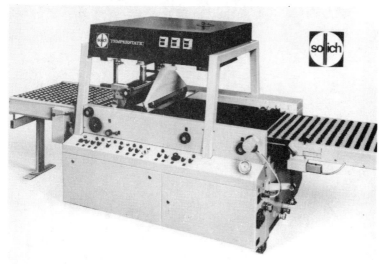

(b)

Fig. 21.1 — (a),(b) Enrober. (Courtesy of Sollich Ltd and Robinson's of Derby Ltd.)

curtain of seasoning and then to a rotating stainless steel drum which is slightly inclined from the horizontal. The drum is fitted internally with angled flights or ribs to tumble the food gently and to coat all surfaces with seasoning. The angle and speed of rotation are adjusted to control the product throughput. A similar design is used for spraying products with oil or liquid flavourings. In other designs, flavours are blown directly into the drum by compressed air, or salt is blown through the product by compressed air in an enclosed chamber. Fluidised beds and Torbed equipment (Chapter 14) are also used as flavour applicators.

ACKNOWLEDGEMENTS

Grateful acknowledgement is made for information supplied by the following: Coat and Fry Ltd, Derby DE2 8JD, UK; Allen Machinery Systems, Stourbridge, West Midlands DY9 7NB, UK; Baker Perkins Ltd, Peterborough PE3 6TA, UK; Torftech Ltd, Mortimer, Reading, Berkshire RG7 3PG, UK; Interfood Ltd, Hemel Hempstead, Hertfordshire HP2 7DU, UK; Robinson's of Derby, Derby DE2 6JL, UK; Sollich GmbH and Co. KG, D-4902 Bad Salzuflen, West Germany; Sandvik Jahn, Huntingdon PE18 7EW, UK; Neilsen Ltd, c/o Robinson's of Derby Ltd., Derby DE2 6JL, UK.

REFERENCE

Matz, S. A. (1972) *Bakery technology and engineering*. AVI, Westport, Connecticut, pp. 237–257.

22

Packaging

Packaging is an integral part of food processing. It performs two main functions: to advertise foods at the point of sale, and to protect foods to a pre-determined degree for the expected shelf life. The main factors that cause deterioration of foods during storage are:

(1) mechanical forces (impact, vibration, compression or abrasion),
(2) climatic influences that cause physical or chemical changes (UV light, moisture vapour, oxygen, temperature changes),
(3) contamination (by micro-organisms, insects or soils) and
(4) pilferage, tampering or adulteration.

In addition the package should not influence the product (for example by migration of toxic compounds, by reactions between the pack and the food or by selection of harmful micro-organisms in the packaged food). Other requirements of packaging are smooth efficient and economical operation on the production line, resistance to breakage (for example fractures, tears or dents caused by filling and closing equipment, loading/unloading or transportation) and minimum total cost.

The main marketing considerations are:

(1) the brand image and style of presentation required for the food,
(2) flexibility to change the size and design of the containers and
(3) compatibility with the method of handling distribution, and the requirements of the retailer.

In summary, the package should be aesthetically pleasing, have a functional size and shape, retain the food in a convenient form, possibly act as a dispenser and be suitable for easy disposal or re-use. The package design should also meet any legislative requirements concerning labelling of foods.

22.1 THEORY

Packaging provides a barrier between the food and the environment. It controls light transmission, the transfer of heat, moisture and gases, and movement of micro-organisms or insects.

22.1.1 Light

Light transmission is required in packages that are intended to display the contents but is restricted when foods are susceptible to deterioration by light (for example by oxidation of lipids, destruction of riboflavin and loss of colour). The amount of light absorbed by a package is found using

$$I_a = I_i T_p \frac{1 - R_f}{1 - R_f R_p} \tag{22.1}$$

where: I_a (Cd) is the intensity of light absorbed by the food, I_i (Cd) the intensity of incident light, T_p the fractional transmission by packaging material, R_p the fraction reflected by packaging material and R_f the fraction reflected by the food.

The fraction of light transmitted by a packaging material is found using the Beer–Lambert law

$$I_t = I_i e^{-kx} \tag{22.2}$$

where: I_t (Cd)is the intensity of light transmitted by packaging, k the characteristic absorbance of packaging material and x (m) the thickness of packaging material.

The amount of light that is absorbed or transmitted varies with the packaging material and with the wavelength of incident light. Some materials (for example low-density polyethylene) transmit both visible and ultraviolet light to a similar extent, whereas others (for example polyvinylidene chloride) transmit visible light but absorb ultraviolet light. Pigments are incorporated into glass containers or polymer films, or they are printed (section 22.2.7) to reduce light transmission to sensitive products.

22.1.2 Heat

The insulating effect of a package is determined by its thermal conductivity (Chapter 1) and its reflectivity. Materials which have a low thermal conductivity (for example paperboard (section 22.2.5), polystyrene or polyurethane) reduce conductive heat transfer, and reflective materials (for example aluminium foil (section 22.2.2.4)) reflect radiant heat.

22.1.3 Moisture and gases

The rates of moisture and oxygen transfer are the main factors that control the shelf life of dehydrated foods and those that contain appreciable quantities of lipids or other oxygen-sensitive components (section 22.3). Transfer of moisture, oxygen and carbon dioxide through packaging materials is critically important in determining the shelf life and quality of chilled fresh foods and of foods packaged in modified atmospheres (Chapter 18). The importance of oxygen concentration on the nutritional and sensory qualities of other foods is described in preceding chapters. The effect of water activity on shelf life is described in Chapter 1.

Assuming that a packaging material has no defects (for example pinholes in can seams or flexible films) and that there is no interaction between the film and the gas or vapour, the mass transfer rate m ($cm^3 m^{-2}$ per 24 h) of gas or vapour through a packaging material is found using

$$m = \frac{bAt\,\Delta P}{x} \qquad (22.3)$$

where b is the permeability of the material, A (m^2) the area of material, t (h) the time, ΔP (Pa) the difference in pressure or concentration between the two sides of the material and x (m) the thickness of the material.

Permeability is related to both the film and the gas or vapour and is not therefore a property of the film (for example the permeability of cellulose, nylon and poly(vinyl alcohol)) changes with humidity variation, owing to interaction of water with the film). The thickness, chemical composition, structure and orientation of molecules in a packaging material influence the barrier properties. These factors are discussed further by Pascat (1986) and Jasse (1986). Plasticisers and pigments loosen the film structure and increase permeability. Permeability is also related exponentially to temperature and it is therefore necessary to quote both the temperature and relative humidity of the atmosphere in which permeability measurements are made (Table 22.1). The rate of gas or moisture transfer is found using

$$m = \frac{b\,\Delta P}{x} \qquad (22.4)$$

22.1.4 Micro-organisms
Intact packaging materials are a barrier to micro-organisms, but seals are a potential source of contamination (packs that are folded, stapled or twist-wrapped are not truly sealed). The main causes of microbial contamination of adequately processed foods are

(1) contaminated air or water drawn through pinholes in hermetically sealed containers as the head space vacuum forms (Chapter 11),
(2) contamination of heat seals by product (Chapter 23),
(3) poorly aligned lids or caps and
(4) damage to the packaging material (tears, creases).

The effect of differences in permeability of packaging materials on the growth of micro-organisms in food is discussed by Bureau (1986).

22.1.5 Mechanical strength
The ability of packages to protect foods from mechanical damage is measured by

(1) the tensile strength,
(2) Young's modulus,
(3) the tensile elongation,
(4) the yield strength (Fig. 22.1) and

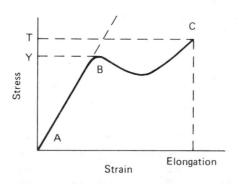

Fig. 22.1 — Stress–strain curve for flexible packaging: T, tensile strength; Y, yield strength; slope of curve AB = Young's Modulus; C, breaking point. (After Briston (1980).)

(5) the impact strength (force required to penetrate the material).

Each of these factors is influenced by the temperature of the material and the length of time that the force is applied (Briston and Katan, 1974a). The molecular structure of polymer films is aligned in different ways depending on the type of film and method of manufacture. Each of these properties is therefore measured in both the axial (or machine) direction and the lateral (or transverse) direction of the film. Orientation of molecules in one direction (uniaxial) or in both directions (biaxial) improves the mechanical properties of some films (for example polyethylene, polypropylene, polyethylene terephthalate and polystyrene (section 22.2.4.1)). Experimental studies are described by Jasse (1986) and examples of the tensile strength of selected films are given in Table 22.1.

22.2 TYPES OF PACKAGING MATERIAL

There are two main groups of packaging materials:

(1) shipping containers which contain and protect the contents during transport and distribution (including wooden, metal or fibreboard cases, crates, barrels, drums and sacks);
(2) retail containers (or *consumer units*) which protect and advertise the food in convenient quantities for retail sale and home storage (for example metal cans, glass bottles, jars, rigid and semi-rigid plastic tubs, collapsible tubes, paperboard cartons, and flexible plastic bags, sachets and overwraps).

22.2.1 Textiles and wood

Textile containers have poor gas and moisture barrier properties; they are not suited to high-speed filling and have a poorer appearance than plastics. They are therefore restricted to shipping containers. Woven jute sacks, which are chemically treated to prevent rotting and to reduce their flammability, are non-slip, have a high tear resistance, low extensibility and good durability. They are used to transport a wide variety of bulk foods including grain, flour, sugar and salt. Wooden shipping containers have traditionally been used for a wide range of solid and liquid foods including fruits, vegetables, tea and beer. Wood offers good mechanical protection, good stacking characteristics and a high weight-to-strength ratio. However, polypropylene and polyethylene containers have a lower cost and have largely replaced wood in many applications. The use of wood continues for some wines and spirits because the transfer of flavour compounds from the wooden barrels improves the quality of the product. Wooden tea chests are produced more cheaply than other containers in tea-producing countries and these are still widely used.

22.2.2 Metal

Metal cans have a number of advantages over other types of container, including the following.

(1) They provide total protection of the contents,
(2) They are convenient for ambient storage and presentation.
(3) They are tamperproof.

However, the high cost of metal and relatively high manufacturing costs make cans expensive. They are heavier than other materials, except glass, and therefore incur higher transport costs.

22.2.2.1 Three-piece cans

Three-piece 'sanitary' cans consisting of a can body and two end pieces, are used to seal heat-sterilised foods hermetically (Chapter 11) and also for powders, syrups and cooking oils which are not heat treated. They are made from steel which is electrolytically coated on both sides with a thin layer of tin ($2.8-11.2 \, \mathrm{g \, m^{-2}}$ or $0.1-0.3$ mm thick). Methods of manufacture are described in detail by Malin (1980) and summarised in Fig. 22.2. Changes in materials and manufacturing technology have reduced the cost of cans as in the following examples.

(1) Steel is made thinner by additional rolling in a *double-reduction process*. Beading (corrugations in the metal) around the can body maintains the can strength.
(2) Different thicknesses of tin are applied on each side of the steel (differential coating).
(3) Welded side seams, made by forge welding or 'lost-wire' welding, have a better appearance and greater integrity than the traditional soldered seams.
(4) Side seams are bonded by thermoplastic polyamide (nylon) adhesives.
(5) The tin coating is replaced by a chromium–chromium dioxide surface (tin-free

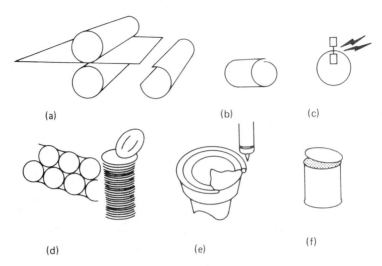

(a)   (b)   (c)

(d)   (e)   (f)

Fig. 22.2 — Manufacture of three-piece electrically welded cans: (a) tinplate rolled into cylinders; (b) edges overlapped; (c) edges welded and seam lacquered; (d) base stamped out; (e) rims curled and sealing compound injected; (f) base seamed onto body. (Courtesy of Metal Box plc.)

steel), which has better compatability with the product. However, external corrosion may occur if it is not protected by a lacquer.

These developments are described in detail by Malin (1980). Methods of filling and sealing cans are described in Chapter 23.

22.2.2.2 *Two-piece cans*

Two-piece aluminium cans are made by the *draw-and-wall-iron* (DWI) process or *draw-and-redraw* (DRD) *process*. The DWI process produces thinner walls than the DRD process does and is used to produce aluminium cans for carbonated beverages where the gas pressure supports the container. DRD cans are able to withstand the head-space vacua required in heat sterilisation (Chapter 11). Steel and tin-free steel are also used, but they are heavier and more difficult to form. In the DWI process the ironing stage destroys the resistance of the tin coating on steel cans, and both internal and external lacquers are necessary to prevent corrosion of the metal or contamination of the product. The advantages of two-piece cans include greater integrity, more uniform lacquer coverage, savings in metal and greater consumer appeal.

In the DWI process a disc-shaped blank is cut and formed (drawn) into a cup. This is forced through a number of annular rings (wall ironed), to reduce the thickness of the wall metal and to increase the can height to the required extent (Fig. 22.3). The process permits good control over the wall thickness and therefore saves metal. Modifications to the basic two-piece design include

(1) a reduced diameter at the neck of the can which improves the appearance and the stacking efficiency and saves metal,

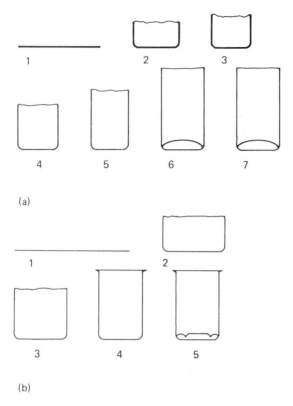

Fig. 22.3 — Two-piece can manufacture. (a) DWI cans: 1, body blank; 2+3, drawn and redrawn cups; 4–6, three stages of wall ironing and base formation; 7, finished can trimmed to the required height. (b) DRD cans: 1, body blank; 2, drawn cup; 3+4, stages in redrawn cups; 5, finished trimmed can with profiled base. (After Malin (1980).)

(2) ring-pull tabs or full-aperture easy-open ends for greater convenience,
(3) computer-aided print design and abrasion-resistant inks allow the blank to be printed before the can is formed. The ink is then stretched with the metal during the DWI process, to produce the required design on the finished can.

The DRD process is similar to the initial stages of the DWI process but, instead of ironing to reduce the wall thickness, metal is moved from the base of the container to the wall by reducing the diameter of the container (Fig. 22.3).

Lacquers are applied internally to prevent interactions between the metal and the product. The type of lacquer depends on the type of metal used and the type of food packed. Expoxy phenolic or vinyl-based lacquers are commonly used.

22.2.2.3 *Aerosol cans*
Aerosol cans are two- or three-piece cans fitted with an aerosol valve. The propellant gas is either mixed with the product or kept separate by a plastic bag or a piston

device. Nitrous oxide propellant is used for ultrahigh-temperature sterilised cream (Woollen, 1984), but other gases (for example argon, nitrogen and carbon dioxide) are approved for use with foods. Other food applications include oil sprays for baking pans and cheese spreads.

22.2.2.4 Aluminium foil

This is produced by a *cold reduction* process in which pure aluminium (purity, greater than 99.4%) is passed through rollers to reduce the thickness to less than 0.152 mm and annealed to give dead-folding properties. The advantages of foil include a good appearance, dead-folding, the ability to reflect radiant energy and an excellent barrier to moisture and gases. Foil (more than 0.015 mm thick) is totally impermeable to moisture, gases, light and micro-organisms. It is widely used for wraps (0.009 mm), bottle caps (0.05 mm) and trays for frozen and ready meals (0.05–0.1 mm). Foil trays are coated with vinyl epoxy compounds to make them suitable for microwave heating without damage to the magnetron (Chapter 17). Foil is also used as the barrier material in laminated films (section 22.2.4.3), and aluminium is used to 'metallise' flexible films (section 22.2.4.2).

22.2.3 Glass

Glass jars and bottles are made by heating a mixture of sand (73%), sodium oxide (13%) and calcium oxide (12%) with a proportion of broken glass (15–30% of total weight). The molten glass is shaped in a mould by the *blow-and-blow process* or the *press-and-blow process* (Fig. 22.4). The glass is then annealed at 540–570°C to

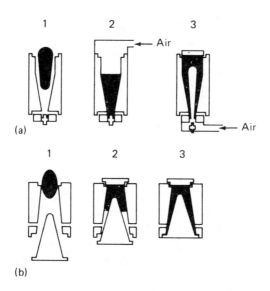

Fig. 22.4 — Glass-blowing techniques. (a) Blow-and-blow process: 1, gob drops into parison mould; 2, settle blow to form finish; 3, counter-blow to complete parison. (b) Press-and-blow process: 1, gob drops into parison mould; 2, plunger presses parison; 3, parison completed. (After Osborne (1980).)

remove stresses and cooled under carefully controlled conditions to prevent distortion or fracturing. Details of manufacturing techniques are given by Osborne (1980).

Glass containers have the following advantages.

(1) They are impervious to moisture, gases, odours and micro-organisms.
(2) They are inert and do not react with or migrate into food products.
(3) They have filling speeds comparable with those of cans.
(4) They are suitable for heat processing when hermetically sealed.
(5) They are transparent to microwaves.
(6) They are re-useable and recyclable.
(7) They are resealable.
(8) They are transparent to display the contents.
(9) They can be moulded into a variety of shapes and colours.
(10) They are perceived by the customer to add value to the product.
(11) They are rigid, to allow stacking without container damage.

The disadvantages of glass include

(1) higher weight which incurs higher transport costs than other types of packaging,
(2) lower resistance than other materials to fractures, scratches and thermal shock,
(3) more variable dimensions than other containers and
(4) potentially serious hazards from glass splinters or fragments in foods.

Developments in glass-making technology, including reductions in wall thickness (*light-weighting*) and computer design of containers, are described by Lomax (1987).

22.2.4 Flexible films
Flexible packaging describes any type of material that is not rigid, but the term *flexible film* is usually reserved for non-fibrous materials which are less than 0.25 mm thick. In general, flexible films have the following properties.

(1) Their cost is relatively low.
(2) They have good barrier properties against moisture and gases.
(3) They are heat sealable to prevent leakage of contents.
(4) They are suitable for high-speed filling (Chapter 23).
(5) They have wet and dry strength.
(6) They are suitable for printing.
(7) They are easy to handle and convenient for the manufacturer, retailer and consumer.
(8) They add little weight to the product.
(9) They fit closely to the shape of the food, thereby wasting little space during storage and distribution.

Ranges of mechanical, optical, thermal and barrier properties are produced for each type of polymer by variation in film thickness and in the type and thickness of coatings. Plasticisers are added to soften the film and to make it more flexible for use in cold climates or for frozen foods. Pigment is used to avoid the need for large areas of printing. Films may be used singly, coated with polymer or metal or in multi-layered laminates or coextrusions. There are thus a large number of possible combinations of polymer and treatment, to meet the varied requirements of foods. Details of chemical structure of films and additives are given by Briston and Katan (1974a).

22.2.4.1 Single films
Most polymer films are made by *extrusion*, in which pellets of the polymer are melted and extruded under pressure as a sheet or tube. Other methods are *callandering* (where the polymer is passed through heated rollers until the required thickness is achieved) and *casting* (in which the extruded polymer is cooled on chilled rollers). The most important types of film for food packaging are described below and selected properties are shown in Table 22.1.

22.2.4.1.1 Cellulose
Films are produced by mixing sulphite paper pulp (Section 22.2.5) with sulphur dioxide and carbon disulphide to form *viscose*. This is then extruded onto an acid–salt bath to form cellulose hydrate. Glycerol is added as a softener and the film is dried on heated rollers. Higher quantities of softener and longer residence times in the acid–salt bath produce more flexible and more permeable films. Plain cellulose is a glossy transparent film which is odourless, tasteless and biodegradable (within approximately 100 days). It is tough and puncture resistant, although it tears easily. It has low-slip and dead-folding properties and is unaffected by static buildup, which make it suitable for twist-wrapping. However, it is not heat sealable (Chapter 23), and the dimensions and permeability of the film vary with changes in humidity. It is used for foods that do not require a complete moisture or gas barrier.

22.2.4.1.2 Polypropylene
Oriented polypropylene is a clear glossy film with good optical properties and a high tensile strength and puncture resistance. It has moderate permeability to moisture, gases and odours, which is not affected by changes in humidity. It is thermoplastic and therefore stretches, although less than polyethylene, and has low friction, which minimises static buildup and makes it suitable for high-speed filling equipment (Chapter 23). Biaxially oriented polypropylene has similar properties to oriented polypropylene but is much stronger.

22.2.4.1.3 Polyester
Polyethylene terephthalate is a very strong transparent glossy film which has good moisture and gas barrier properties. It is flexible at temperatures from $-70°C$ to $135°C$ and undergoes little shrinkage with variations in temperature or humidity. It is more commonly used in semi-rigid containers (section 22.2.4.5).

22.2.4.1.4 Polyethylene
Low-density polyethylene is heat sealable, chemically inert, odour free and shrinks when heated. It is a good moisture barrier but has a relatively high gas permeability, sensitivity to oils and poor odour resistance. It is less expensive than

most films and is therefore widely used, including applications in shrink- or stretch-wrapping (Chapter 23). Low-slip properties are introduced for safe stacking, or conversely high-slip properties permit easy movement of wrapped packs into an outer container. Stretch-wrapping uses thinner low-density polyethylene than shrink-wrapping does (25–38 μm compared with 45–75 μm), or linear low-density polyethylene (17–24 μm). Linear low-density polyethylene has a highly linear arrangement of molecules and the distribution of molecular weights is smaller than for low-density polyethylene. It therefore has greater strength and a higher restraining force. The cling properties of both films are biased on one side, to maximise adhesion between layers of the film but to minimise adhesion to adjacent packages.

High-density polyethylene is stronger, thicker, less flexible and more brittle than low-density polyethylene and has lower permeability to gases and moisture. It has a higher softening temperature (121°C) and can therefore be heat sterilised. Sacks made from 0.03–0.15 mm high-density polyethylene have a high tear strength, tensile strength, penetration resistance and seal strength. They are waterproof and chemically resistant and are used instead of multi-wall paper sacks (section 22.2.5). A foamed high-density polyethylene film is thicker and stiffer than conventional film and has dead-folding properties (Anon, 1980). It can be perforated with up to 80 holes cm^{-1} for use with fresh foods or bakery products. When unperforated, it is used for edible fats. Both types are suitable for shrink-wrapping.

22.2.4.1.5 Polyvinylidene chloride
Uncoated polyvinylidene chloride film has very good moisture, odour and gas barrier properties. It is fat resistant and does not melt in contact with hot fats, making it suitable for 'freezer-to-oven' foods. Polyvinylidene chloride is also used as a coating for films and bottles to improve the barrier properties.

22.2.4.1.6 Other films
Polystyrene is a brittle clear sparkling film which has high gas permeability. It may be oriented to improve the barrier properties. *Rubber hydrochloride* is similar to polyvinyl chloride but becomes brittle in ultraviolet light and at low temperatures and is penetrated by some oils. *Polyvinyl chloride–vinylidene chloride* copolymer is very strong and is therefore used in thin films. It has very low gas and water vapour permeabilies and is heat shrinkable and heat sealable. However, it has a brown tint which limits its use in some applications. *Nylon* has good mechanical properties in a wide temperature range (from −60°C to 200°C). However, the films are expensive to produce, they require high temperatures to form a heat seal, and the permeability changes at different storage humidities. *Ethylene vinyl acetate* is low-density polyethylene, polymerised with vinyl acetate. It has high mechanical strength, and flexibility at low temperatures. Ethylene vinyl acetate which contains less than 5% vinyl acetate, is used for deep-freeze applications. Films with 6–10% vinyl acetate are used in bag-in-box applications and milk pouches, and above 10% vinyl acetate the material is used as a hot-melt adhesive. *High-nitrile resins* are acrylonitrile–methyl acrylate and acrylonitrile–styrene copolymers. They are moulded by each of the methods described in section 22.2.4.5 to form containers which have very good barrier properties. They are used for processed meat, cheese, margarine and peanut butter (Briston, 1987).

Table 22.1 — Selected properties of packaging films

Film	Thickness (μm)	Yield (m² kg⁻¹)	Moisture vapour transmission rate (ml m⁻² per 24 h)		Oxygen transmission rate (ml m⁻² per 24 h)		Barrier
			38°C 90% RH	23°C 85% RH	23°C 85% RH	25°C 0% RH	25°C 45% RH
Cellulose							
Uncoated	21–40	30–18	1500–800	400–275	25–20		10–8
Nitrocellulose coated	22–24	31–29	12–8	1.8	15–9	10–8	8–6
Polyvinylidene chloride coated	19–42	36–17	7–4	1.7		7–5.5	7–5
Metallised, polyvinylidene chloride coated	21–42	31–17	5–4	0.8		3	3–2
Vinyl chloride coated			400–320	80–70			9
Polyethylene							
Low density	25–200	43–5	19–14	3000	120		8000
Stretch-wrap	17–38						
Shrink-wrap	25–200	43–11					
High density	350–1000		6.4				2000–500
Polypropylene							
Oriented	20–30	24	7–5	1.4–1.0	2200–1100		2000–1600
Biaxially oriented	20–40	55–27	7–3	1.2–0.6	1500		
Polyvinylidene chloride coated	18–34	53–30	8–4	1.4–0.6	6–10	13–6	
MG	20–40	55–27	7–4	1.4–0.6	2200–1100	2300–900	
Metallised	20–30	55–36	1.3	0.3–0.2	300–80	300	
Polyester							
Plain	12–23	59–31	40–20	8			110–53
850	12–30	60–24	40–17				120–48
Metallised			2.0–0.8				1.5–0.5
Polyvinylidene chloride coated and metallised			1.3–0.3				0.1
Polyvinylidene chloride	10–50	35–17	4–1	1.7	17–7		2

RH, relative humidity; TP, transparent.
[a] Will not heat seal.

properties				Mechanical properties		Optical properties		
Nitrogen transmission rate (ml m⁻² per 24 h)		Carbon dioxide transmission rate (ml m⁻² per 24 h)		Tensile strength machine direction	Tensile strength transverse direction	Total light transmission	Gloss	Sealing temperature
25°C 0% RH	30°C 0% RH	25°C 0% RH	25°C 45% RH	(MN m⁻²)	(MN m⁻²)	(%)	(%)	(°C)
	28	40–30		33		TP	110	a
		30–20		35		TP	130	90–130
		15		32–60		TP	150	100–130
		20–15		28–60		0	130	90–130
		30		120–130		TP		100–160
	19		40000	16–7				121–170
			8000–7000	61–24				135–170
285		3250		145–200	0.4–0.6		75–85	145
				118–260			80–85	117–124
		30–20				TP		
650–270		7000–3000		210	0.3–0.4	TP	75–85	120–145
85		900		215	0.5–0.6	0.5–3.1		120–145
25–7			500–150			87		100–200
25–10			500–200			88		100–200
1.8	0.0094	20		120–130		90	95–113	100–160

22.2.4.2 Coated films

Films are coated with other polymers or aluminium to improve the barrier properties or to impart heat sealability. For example nitrocellulose is coated on one side of cellulose film to provide a moisture barrier but to retain oxygen permeability. A nitrocellulose coating on both sides of the film improves the barrier to oxygen, moisture and odours and enables the film to be heat sealed when broad seals are used. A polyvinylidene chloride coating is applied to cellulose, using either an aqueous dispersion (MXXT/A cellulose) or an organic solvent (MXXT/S cellulose). In each case the film becomes heat sealable and the barrier properties are improved (Table 22.1). A coating of vinyl chloride or vinyl acetate gives a stiffer film which has intermediate permeability. Sleeves of this material are tough, stretchable and permeable to air, smoke and moisture. They are used for example for packaging meats before smoking and cooking.

A thin coating of aluminium (termed *metallisation*) produces a very good barrier to oils, gases, moisture, odours and light. Metallised film is less expensive and more flexible than foil laminates which have similar barrier properties, and it is therefore suitable for high-speed filling on form–fill–seal equipment (Chapter 23) (Guise, 1984). Cellulose, polypropylene or polyester are metallised by depositing vaporised aluminium onto the surface of a film under vacuum. The degree of metallisation is expressed in optical density units, up to a maximum of 4 units. Metallised polyester has higher barrier properties than metallised polypropylene, but polypropylene is finding more widespread use as it it is currently less expensive (Guise, 1987).

22.2.4.3 Laminated films

Lamination of two or more films improves the appearance, barrier properties or mechanical strength of a package. The most versatile method is *adhesive laminating* (or dry bonding). An adhesive is applied to the surface of one film and dried. The two films are then pressure bonded by passing between rollers (Fig. 22.5). Two-part urethane adhesives, consisting of a polyester or polyether resin with an isocyanate cross-linking agent, are widely used. Not all polymer films can be successfully laminated. The two films should have similar characteristics, and the film tension, adhesive application and drying conditions should be accurately controlled to prevent the laminate from blocking (not unwinding smoothly), curling (edges of the roll curl up) or delaminating (separation of the layers). Commonly used laminates are described in Table 22.2.

22.2.4.4 Coextruded films

This is the simultaneous extrusion of two or more layers of different polymers. Coextruded films have three main advantages over other types of film.

(1) They have very high barrier properties, similar to multi-layer laminates but produced at a lower cost.
(2) They are thinner than laminates and closer to monolayer films and are therefore easier to use on forming and filling equipment and
(3) The layers do not separate.

The copolymers used in coextruded films should have similar chemical structures,

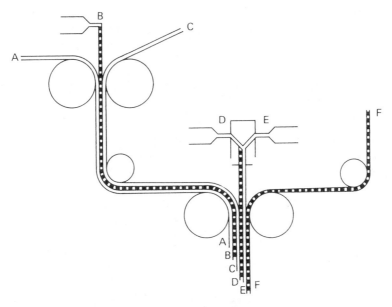

Fig. 22.5 — Methods of forming multi-web laminates: A–F, six layer laminate; A,C,F, reelstock; B,D,E, extrusion die. (After Goddard (1980).)

flow characteristics and viscosities when melted, to achieve strong adhesion. There are three main groups of polymers:

(1) olefins (low-density and high-density polyethylene, and polypropylene);
(2) styrenes (polystyrene and acrylonitrile–butadiene–styrene);
(3) polyvinyl chloride polymers.

All members of each group adhere to each other, as does acrylonitrile–butadiene–styrene with polyvinyl chloride, but other combinations must be bonded with ethylene vinyl acetate. There are two main methods of producing coextrusions: blown films and flat-sheet coextrusion.

Blown-film coextrusions are thinner than flat-sheet types and are suitable for high-speed form–fill–seal and pouch or sachet equipment (Chapter 23). Typically a three-layer coextrusion has an outside presentation layer, which has a high gloss and printability, a middle bulk layer which provides stiffness, strength and split resistance, and an inner layer which is suitable for heat sealing. These films have good barrier properties and are at present more cost effective than wax-coated paper or laminates. They are used for example for confectionery, snackfoods, cereals and dry mixes. A five-layer coextrusion is used to replace metallised polyester for bag-in-box applications.

Flat-sheet coextrusions (75–3000 μm thick) are formed into pots, tubs or trays (Table 22.3).

Table 22.2 — Selected laminated films used for food packaging

Type of laminate	Typical food application
Polyvinylidene chloride-coated polypropylene–polyvinylidene chloride-coated polypropylene–	Crisps, snackfoods, confectionery, ice cream, biscuits, chocolate confectionery
Polyvinylidene chloride-coated polypropylene–polyethylene	Bakery products, cheese, confectionery, dried fruit, frozen vegetables
Polypropylene–ethylene vinyl acetate	Modified-atmosphere-packaged (Chapter 18) bacon, cheese, cooked meats
Biaxially oriented polypropylene–nylon–polyethylene	Retort pouches
Cellulose–polyethylene–cellulose	Pies, crusty bread, bacon, coffee, cooked meats, cheese
Cellulose acetate–paper–foil–polyethylene	Dried soups
Metallised polyester–polyethylene	Coffee, dried milk, bag-in-box packaging, potato flakes, frozen foods, modified-atmosphere-packaged (Chapter 18) foods
Polyethylene terephthalate aluminium–polypropylene	Retort pouches
Polyethylene–nylon	Vacuum packs for bulk fresh meat, cheese
Polyethylene–aluminium–paper	Dried soup, dried vegetables, chocolate
Nylon–polyvinylidene chloride-polyethylene–aluminium–polyethylene	Bag-in-box packaging
Nylon–medium-density ethylene–butene copolymer	Boil-in-bag packaging

The type of laminate reads from the outside to the inside of the package. All examples of polyethylene are low-density polyethylene.

22.2.4.5 *Rigid and semi-rigid containers*
Trays, bottles and jars are made from single or coextruded polymers. The main advantages, compared with glass and metal, are as follows.

(1) They have a greater corrosion resistance.

Table 22.3 — Selected applications of flat-sheet coextrustions

Type of coextrusion	Properties	Applications
High-impact polystyrene–polyethylene terephthalate		Margarine, butter
Polystyrene–polystyrene–polyvinylidene chloride–polystyrene	Ultraviolet and odour barrier	Juices, meats, milk products
Polystyrene–polystyrene–polyvinylidene chloride–polyethylene	Ultraviolet and odour barrier	Butter, cheese, margarine, coffee, mayonnaise, sauce
Polypropylene–saran–polypropylene	Retortable trays	Sterilised foods
Polystyrene–ethylene vinyl acetate–polyethylene	Modified-atmosphere packs	Meats, fruits

(2) They have a lower weight, resulting in savings of up to 40% in transport and distribution costs.

(3) They are produced at a lower temperature (300°C) than glass (800°C) and therefore lower energy costs are incurred.

(4) They are precisely moulded into convenient flexible shapes.

(5) They are tough, unbreakable and easy to seal.

(6) They are produced at relatively low cost.

However, they are not re-usable, have a lower heat resistance and are less rigid than glass or metal.

There are six methods of manufacture.

(1) *Thermoforming*. Here the film is softened over a mould, and a vacuum and/or pressure is applied (Fig. 22.6(a)). More complex systems, which prevent the sheet from thinning at the edges, are described by Briston (1980, 1987). Thermoforming is also used for forming–filling–sealing (Chapter 23). These containers are thin walled and possess relatively poor mechanical properties (for example trays or punnets for chocolates, eggs or soft fruit, and cups or tubs for dairy products, margarine, dried foods or ice cream).

(2) *Blow moulding* is similar to glass making (section 22.2.3) and is used in either a single- or two-stage process for producing bottles, jars or pots (for cooking oil, vinegar and beverages).

(3) *Injection moulding*. Grains of polymer are mixed and heated by a screw in a moulding machine and injected under a high pressure into a cool mould. This method is used for wide-mouthed containers (for example tubs and jars) and for lids.

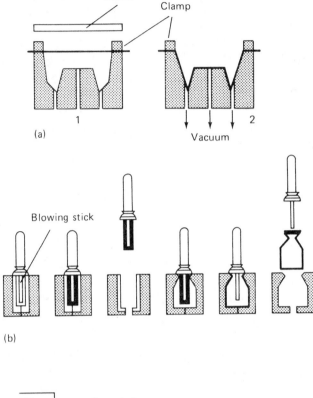

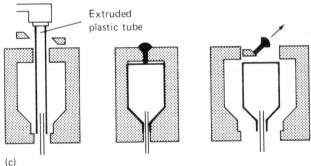

Fig. 22.6 — Manufacture of rigid containers: (a) thermoforming; (b) injection blow moulding; (c) extrusion blow moulding. (After Briston (1987).)

(4) *Injection blow moulding* (Fig. 22.6(b)). Polymer is injection moulded around a blowing stick and, while molten, this is transferred to a blowing mould. Compressed air is then used to form the final shape of the container.

(5) *Extrusion blow moulding* (Fig.22. 6(c)). A continuously extruded tube of softened polymer is trapped between two halves of a mould and inflated by

compressed air to the shape of the mould. Careful control is needed to ensure uniform thickness in the container wall.

(6) *Stretch blow moulding*. A *pre-form* (or *parison*) is injection or extrusion moulded. It is reheated to produce biaxial orientation of the molecules and finally stretch blown. This produces a glass clear container which has a high impact resistance, high tensile strength, good barrier properties to moisture and gases and stability over a wide temperature range.

Injection-blow-moulded polyethylene terephthalate bottles are widely used for carbonated beverages. Polyvinyl chloride bottles are made by extrusion stretch blow moulding or injection stretch blow moulding. Polyvinyl chloride has lower strength than polyethylene terephthalate and therefore cannot withstand the pressure of carbonation. Polyvinyl chloride has low gas permeability and is therefore used for edible oils, fruit juices, squashes and concentrates. A five-layer polypropylene coextrusion, in which ethylene–vinyl alcohol copolymer is a central barrier material, is used for tomato ketchup or barbecue sauce containers to give a shelf life of 18 months. They are shatterproof, oxygen and moisture resistant, squeezable and suitable for hot filling. High-density polyethylene containers include bottles for vinegar, drums for salt and bulk fruit juices (Briston, 1987).

Multi-chamber polyethylene terephthalate trays have a hygienic smooth white finish. They are fat and grease resistant, heat sealable and of a light-weight nature. They are used for example for frozen or chilled ready meals (Chapters 18 and 19), where the cover is left on during either microwave or conventional cooking and then peeled off to give an attractive table dish. A coextruded five-layer sheet of polypropylene or polycarbonate, with polyvinylidene chloride or ethylene-vinyl alcohol barrier layers, is used to form heat-sterilisable trays and pots, by a process of injection moulding, blow moulding or thermoforming (Briston, 1980). *Plastic cans* are made from similar material which is thermoformed or injection blow moulded to form the can body. They are sealed using easy-open aluminium ends and processed on existing canning lines with considerably reduced noise levels (Louis, 1986; Darrington, 1986).

22.2.5 Paper and board
Paper pulp is produced from wood chips by acid or alkaline hydrolysis. The pulp is suspended in water and beaten with rotating impellers and knives to split the cellulose fibres longitudinally. The fibres are then refined and passed through heated rollers to reduce the moisture content, and then through finishing rollers to give the final surface properties to the paper. Alkaline hydrolysis produces *sulphate pulp* and acid hydrolysis produces *sulphite pulp*.

Sulphate pulp is used to make *kraft paper*. This is a strong paper which is used for 25–50 kg multi-wall sacks for powders, flour, sugar, fruits and vegetables. *Vegetable parchment*, is produced from sulphate pulp which is passed through a bath of sulphuric acid. It has a surface that is more intact than kraft paper and therefore has greater oil resistance and wet strength properties. Both types of paper protect foods from dust and soils. They have negligible moisture or gas barrier properties and are not heat sealable.

Sulphite paper is lighter and weaker than sulphate papers. It is used for grocery bags and sweet wrappers, as an inner liner for biscuits and in laminations (section 22.2.4.3). *Greaseproof paper* is made from sulphite pulp in which the fibres are more thoroughly beaten to produce a closer structure. It is resistant to oils and fats, but this property is lost when the paper becomes wet. It is widely used for wrapping fish, meat and dairy products. *Glassine* is a greaseproof sulphite paper which is given a high gloss finish by the finishing rollers. It is more resistant to water when dry but loses the resistance once it becomes wet. *Tissue paper* is a soft non-resilient paper used for example to protect fruits against dust and bruising.

Many papers are treated with wax by

(1) coating,
(2) dry waxing (in which wax penetrates the paper while hot) or
(3) wax sizing (in which the wax is added during the preparation of the pulp).

Wax provides a moisture barrier and allows the paper to be heat sealed. However, a simple wax coating is easily damaged by folding or by abrasive foods. This is overcome by laminating the wax between layers of paper and/or polyethylene. Waxed papers are used for bread wrappers and inner liners for cereal cartons.

Boards are made in a similar way to paper but are thicker to protect foods from mechanical damage. The main characteristics of board are thickness, stiffness, the ability to crease without cracking, the degree of whiteness, surface properties and suitability for printing. *White board* is suitable for contact with food and is often coated with polyethylene, polyvinyl chloride or wax for heat sealability. It is used for ice cream, chocolate and frozen food cartons. *Chipboard* is made from recycled paper and is not used in contact with foods (for example the outer cartons for tea and cereals). It is often lined with white board to improve the appearace and strength. *Duplex board* has two layers, produced from virgin pulp. The liner is produced from bleached woodpulp and the outer is unbleached. Other types include paperboard (0.3–1.0 mm), boxboard (1.00–3.00 mm) and moulded paperboard trays (for example egg cartons).

22.2.5.1 Laminated paperboard cartons
Low-density polyethylene–paper–low-density polyethylene–aluminium–surlyn–low-density polyethylene is used for packaging aseptically sterilised foods (Chapter 11). There are two systems. In one the material is supplied as individual pre-formed collapsed sleeves with the side seam formed by the manufacturer (Fig. 22.7). The cartons are erected at the filling line, filled and sealed (Chapter 23). In this system the top seal is formed above the food. A head space allows the product to be mixed by shaking, and there is less spillage on opening. In the second system, the laminate is supplied as a roll and formed into cartons on form–fill–seal equipment (Chapter 23). The advantages of this system include a lower space required for storage of packaging material and easier handling. Both types of carton have the following advantages.

(1) They are unbreakable.
(2) There is no additional labelling or capping needed.

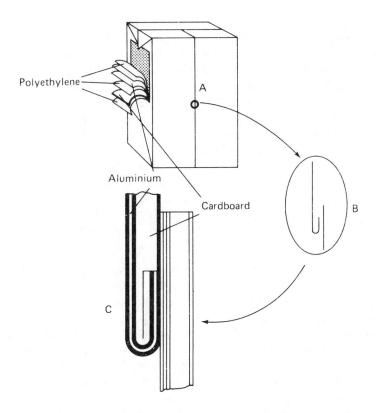

Fig. 22.7 — Construction of laminated paperboard carton for aseptic foods: A, side seam; B, folded to prevent leakage of contents into laminate; C, laminate chamfered to prevent seam bulging. (Courtesy of Bowater PKL (UK) Ltd.)

(3) They incurr lower energy costs in manufacture and give a substantial saving in weight compared with cans and glass.
(4) They are easier to open and dispose of than cans.
(5) They save on shelf space and bold graphics give a 'billboard effect' on display shelves.

Fibreboard (more than 0.11 mm thick) is either solid or corrugated. The solid type has an outer kraft layer and an inner bleached board. It is able to resist compression and to a lesser extent impact. Small fibreboard cylinders with plastic or metal caps are used for confectionery and spice tubs. Larger drums are used as a cheaper alternative to metal drums for powders and other dry foods and, when lined with polyethylene, for fats. They should be stored in a dry atmosphere to retain their strength.

Corrugated board has an outer and inner lining of kraft paper with a central corrugating (or fluting) material. It is made by softening the fluting material with steam and passing it over corrugating rollers. The liners are then applied to each side using a suitable adhesive (Fig. 22.8). The board is formed into 'cut-outs' which are then assembled into cases at the filling line. Corrugated board resists impact abrasion and compression damage and is therefore used for shipping containers. Smaller more numerous corrugations (for example 164 flutes m^{-1}, with a flute height of 2.7 mm) give rigidity, whereas larger corrugations (for example 127 flutes m^{-1}, and a flute height of 3.4 mm) or double and triple walls give resistance to impact (cushioning).

A high storage humidity may cause delamination of the corrugated material. This is prevented by lining with polyethylene, which also reduces moisture migration and tainting (for example for chilled bulk meat (Anon., 1982)). Alternatively the liner may be a laminate of greaseproof paper, coated with microcrystalline wax and polyethylene (for fresh fruit and vegetables, dairy products, meat and frozen food). Twin-ply fluting, with a strengthening agent between the layers, has the same stacking strength but half the weight of solid board, and a space saving of 30% compared with double-corrugated boards of comparable strength.

22.2.6 Combined packaging systems

Cartons are frequently used to contain multiple packs of food in flexible film. These in turn are shrink-wrapped or placed in corrugated board shipping containers. Bag-in-box packaging consist of a laminated film bag, fitted with an integral tap, and contained within a solid or corrugated fibreboard case. The bag collapses evenly as liquid is withdrawn which prevents the product from becoming trapped in the folds of the bag and prevents oxidation of the product by air. It is a convenient light-weight secure container for liquid foods (for example wine, fruit juice, edible oils, syrups and milk). The design allows savings in mass and space compared with glass (for example a saving in mass from 5.13 kg to 3.24 kg and a saving in volume from 0.011 m^3 to 0.004 m^3 for containers of 3 l size compared with glass.

22.2.7 Printing

Printing inks for films and papers consist of a dye which is dispersed in a blend of solvents, and a resin which forms a varnish. The ink may also contain extenders, plasticisers and slip agents. Solvents must be carefully removed after application of the ink to prevent odour contamination of the product and blocking of the film during use. Other considerations include the cost of the ink and compatability with the film, which is needed to achieve a high bond strength.

There are three processes used to print films and papers.

(1) *Flexographic printing*, in up to six colours, is high speed and suitable for lines or blocks of colour. A fast-drying ink is applied to the film by a flexible rubber plate with raised characters. The plate is pressed against an inked roller to cover the raised portions in ink and then against the film or paper (Fig. 22.9(a)).

(2) *Photogravure printing* is able to produce high-quality detail and realistic pictures but is more expensive than flexographic printing. It uses an engraved chromium-plated roller with the printing surfaces recessed in the metal. Ink is applied to the roller and the excess is wiped from all but the recesses. The remaining ink is then transferred to the packaging material (Fig. 22.9(b)).

(3) *Offset lithography* is based on the incompatibility of grease and water. A greasy

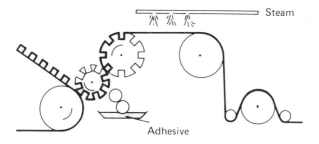

Fig. 22.8 — Corrugated board manufacture.

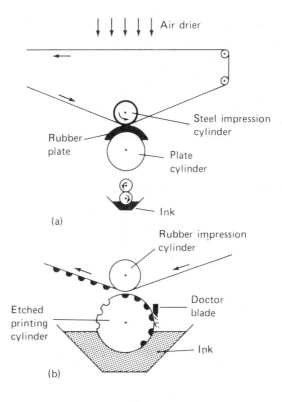

Fig. 22.9 — Printing: (a) flexographic printing; (b) rotogravure printing. (After Briston (1980).)

ink is repelled by moistened parts of a printing plate but remains on compatible parts which carry the design. This method produces a print of similar quality to that of rotogravure and is suitable for papers that are too rough for rotogravure printing.

Printing may be on the inside of the film (reverse printing) which has the advantage of producing a high gloss finish. However, the ink should have negligible odour to prevent contamination of the product. Surface printing avoids the risk of contact between the ink and product, but the ink must have a high gloss and be scuff resistant to prevent it from rubbing off during handling. The ink may also be located between two layers of a laminate. This is achieved by reverse printing onto one film and then laminating the two films. Alternatively the ink is overcoated with polyvinylidene chloride latex, which gives a surface gloss, protects the print and contributes to the barrier properties of the film.

22.2.7.1 Bar codes
Bar codes are printed on retail packs for laser reading at supermarket checkouts. They allow faster stock-taking and reordering, avoid individual price labelling of packs and produce itemised bills. Information from bar code tills is collated to produce product sales reports, and information on competitor sales and the results of promotion and marketing strategies. Corrugated board shipping containers are also bar coded, but at present this is not possible with shrink-wrapping (Osborne, 1986). Markings are also required on containers to show the 'sell-by' date in many countries. A manufacturer's code is printed onto containers to identify the factory, the production line and the shift during which the product was made. The use of laser printers, which are capable of 3000 marks min^{-1}, is described by Campey (1987).

22.3 REQUIREMENTS OF FOODS
The shelf life of packaged foods is controlled by the *properties of the food*, (including water activity, pH, susceptibility to enzymic or microbiological deterioration, mechanism of spoilage, and the requirement for or sensitivity to oxygen, light, carbon dioxide and moisture) and the barrier properties of the package (Section 22.1). A summary of the packaging requirements of selected food groups is shown in Table 22.4.

Moisture loss or uptake is one of the most important factors that controls the shelf life of foods. There is a microclimate within a package, which is determined by the vapour pressure of moisture in the food at the temperature of storage (Chapter 1). In some foods a change in moisture content leads to microbiological or enzymic spoilage, whereas in others this causes drying out or softening of the food. The effect of changes in moisture content is shown by the water sorption isotherm of the food and depends on the water vapour transmission rate of the package. Control of moisture exchange is also necessary to prevent condensation on the inside of packages, and resulting mould growth (for example in fresh vegetables and bread), and to prevent freezer burn in frozen foods (Chapter 19).

Some foods (for example fatty foods and freeze-dried foods) are susceptible to oxidation, and it is therefore necessary to use a package with low oxygen permeability. This also reduces losses of vitamin C in other foods (for example fruit and vegetable products). In contrast, fresh foods require oxygen for respiration (Chapter 18), and a permeable or perforated package is used.

Packaging should retain desirable odours (for example in coffee or snackfoods)

Table 22.4 — Packaging requirements of selected foods

Food	Moisture Loss	Moisture Uptake	Oxygen uptake	Light	Heat	Micro-organisms	Mechanical damage	Odour Loss	Odour Pickup	Oil resistance	Reseal-ability
Frozen foods											
Fish	*		*					*	*	*	
Vegetables	*		*						*		
Pastry	*		*						*		
Chilled											
Fresh foods											
Fruit	*		*a	*		*	*	*			
Vegetables	*		*a	*		*	*	*			
Meat	*		*b		*	*	*		*	*	
Cooked or cured meats	*								*		
Dairy products											
Milk			*	*	*	*			*		
Butter			*	*	*	*			*	*	
Cheese	*		*	*	*	*	*		*	*	
Whole meals	*			*		*	*		*		
Dried foods											
Air dried											
Hygroscopic		*	*				*	*			
Non-hygroscopic		*	*				*	*			
Freeze dried		*	*				*	*			
Snackfoods		*	*				*	*	*	*	*
Concentrates			*	*					*		
Squashes	*		*	*		*		*			*
Baked foods											
Bread	*	*	*	*		*	*		*		
Pies	*	*	*	*	*	*	*		*	*	
Cakes	*	*	*	*			*		*	*	
Biscuits		*	*	*			*		*	*	
Sugar confectionery and preserves											
Chocolate		*	*	*	*		*		*	*	
Hard-boiled sweets		*		*							
Jams											
Carbonated beverages	*		*	*				*			*
Sterilised foods	*		*	*		*					*
Pasteurised foods	*		*		*				*	*	*

a For respiration.
b For preservation of colour of red meat.
Adapted from Goddard (1986).

or prevent odour pickup (for example by powders or fatty foods). There should also be negligible odour pickup from the plasticisers, printing inks, adhesives or solvents used in the manufacture of the packaging material.

Most foods deteriorate more rapidly at higher temperatures, and storage conditions are therefore controlled to minimise temperature fluctuations. Heat-resistant packaging is required to retain the heat in hot foods that have a short shelf life (for example take-away foods), to prevent heating of other foods (for example chocolate confectionery) that are not stored at low temperatures and to prevent freezer burn. Some packages are required to withstand processing conditions (for example hot filling or heat sterilisation (Chapter 11)).

Packaging protects food from mechanical damage, caused by transportation or handling (for example impact, vibration and compression damage). Compression damage during storage may arise owing to overstacking. Metals, wood or fibreboard shipping cases prevent mechanical damage, and products are held tightly within retail containers by moulded trays or fin seals (Chapter 23) to prevent movement. Groups of retail containers are similarly immobilised by shrink- or stretch-wrapping.

22.3.1   Interaction of package and food
The toxicological effects of interactions between food and packaging materials and also the effect of such interactions on the shelf life and sensory quality of the food are extremely complex. The main aspects that are being intensively studied are

(1) lacquers and coatings for metal containers to prevent interaction of food acids, sulphur compounds and other components with steel, tin or aluminium,
(2) the migration of plasticisers, pigments, metal ions and other components of plastic packaging into foods,
(3) the migration of oils from foods into plastics, and
(4) the interaction of the package and food under different processing conditions.

Research on these aspects is reviewed by Heidelbaugh and Karel (1982), Karel and Heidelbaugh (1975) and Anon. (1971). International legislation on food packaging is reviewed by Andrews (1980) and Briston and Katan (1974b)

ACKNOWLEDGEMENTS

Grateful acknowledgement is made for information supplied by the following: Rose Forgrove Ltd, Seacroft, Leeds LS14 2AN, UK; Bowater PKL Ltd, Houghton-le-Spring, Tyne and Wear, DH4 6JN, UK; British Sidac, Wigton, Cumbria, UK; BCL Shorko Films, Swindon, Wiltshire, SN2 2QF, UK; Tetra-Pak (UK), Kingston on Thames, Surrey KT1 1LF, UK; Bonar Cooke Cartons Ltd, Manchester M16 0NP, UK; Thames Case Ltd, Purfleet, Essex RM16 1RD, UK; H. Erben Ltd, Ipswich IP7 6AS, UK; Reed Corrugated Cases Uxbridge, Middlesex. UB8 2JP, UK; J. Gosheron and Co. Ltd, Isleworth, Middlesex. TW7 4DT, UK; BCL Plastic Films, Bridgewater, Somerset TA6 3UA, UK; Beatson Clark plc, Rotherham, South

Yorkshire S60 2AA, UK; Star Aluminium plc, Bridgnorth, Shropshire WV15 6AW, UK; ICI plc, Welwyn Garden City, Hertfordshire AL7 1HD, UK; Metal Box plc, Reading, Berkshire, UK.

REFERENCES

Andrews, M. A. (1980) International legislation. In: S. J. Palling (ed.), *Developments in food packaging,* Vol. 1. Applied Science, London, pp 157–184.

Anon. (1971) *Food packaging and health: migration and legislation. Proceedings of Conference.* Institute of Packaging, London.

Anon. (1980) *New foamed HDPE wrapping material from BXL.* BXL Ltd, London.

Anon. (1982) Packaging breakthrough for bulk meat delivery. *Food Process. Ind.* October 46.

Briston, J. H. (1980) Rigid plastics packaging. In: S. J. Palling (ed.), *Developments in food packaging,* Vol. 1. Applied Science, London, pp. 27–53.

Briston, J. H. (1987) Rigid plastics containers and food packaging. In: A. Turner, (ed.), *Food technology international, Europe.* Sterling, London, pp. 283, 285–287.

Briston, J. H., and Katan, L. L. (1974a) *Plastics in contact with food.* Food Trade Press, London, pp. 5–20.

Briston, J. H., and Katan, L. L. (1974b) *Plastics in contact with food.* Food Trade Press, London, pp. 251–328.

Bureau, G. (1986) Microbiological consequences of mass transfer. In: M. Mathlouthi (ed.), *Food packaging and preservation*, Elsevier Applied Science, Barking, Essex, pp. 93–114.

Campey, D. R. (1987) The application of laser marking. In: A. Turner (ed.), *Food technology international, Europe,* Sterling, London, pp. 303–304.

Darrington, H. A. (1980) In: S. J. Palling (ed.) Developments in food packaging, Vol. 1. Applied Science, London.

Goddard, K. (1980) In: S. J. Palling (ed.), *Developments in food packaging*, Vol. 1. Applied Science, London, pp. 55–79.

Guise, B. (1984) Metallised films for food. *Food Process* **53** 31–34.

Guise, B. (1987) Spotlight on sachet packaging. *Food Process* **56** 35–37.

Heidelbaugh, N. D., and Karel, M. (1982) Function of food packaging in the preservation of nutrients. In: M. Rechcigl (ed.), *Handbook of the nutritive value of foods*, Vol. 1. CRC Press, Boca Raton, Florida, pp. 265–273.

Jasse, B. (1986) Orientation and properties of some polymers used in the foodstuffs packaging industry. In: M. Mathlouthi (ed.), *Food packaging and preservation.* Elsevier Applied Science, Barking, Essex, pp. 283–324.

Karel, M., and Heidelbaugh, N. D. (1975) Effects of packaging on nutrients. In: R. S. Harris and E. Karmas (eds), *Nutritional evaluation of food processing.* AVI, Westport, Connecticut, pp. 412–462.

Lomax, J. J. S. (1987) Glass manufacture and the technological challenge. In: A. Turner (ed.), *Food Technology International, Europe.* Sterling, London. pp. 298, 299, 301, 302.

Louis, P. J. (1986) Packaging trends in food. *World Packag. News* **34**, April (Bulletin of World Packaging Organisation, 42 avenue de Versailles, 75016 Paris, France).

Malin, J. D. (1980) Metal containers and closures. In: S. J. Palling (ed.), *Developments in food packaging,* Vol. 1. Applied Science, London, pp. 1–26.

Osborne, D. G. (1980) Glass. In: S. J. Palling (ed.), *Developments in food packaging,* Vol. 1. Applied Science, London, pp. 81–115.

Osborne, A. (1986) Cracking codes of communication, *Food Process.* January 29–31.

Pascat, B. (1986) Study of some factors affecting permeability. In: M. Mathlouthi (ed.), *Food packaging and preservation.* Elsevier Applied Science, Barking, Essex, pp. 7–24.

Woollen, A. (1984) La crème de la can. *Food Process.* **53** 33–35.

23

Filling and sealing of containers

Accurate filling of containers is important to ensure compliance with legislation (for example the 'average weight' legislation in the EEC (Mayo, 1979)), and to prevent 'giveaway' by overfilling. The composition of some foods (for example meat products and canned mixed vegetables) is also subject to legislation in some countries, and accurate filling of multiple ingredients is therefore necessary.

The maintenance of food quality for the required shelf life depends largely on adequate sealing of containers. Seals are the weakest part of a container and also suffer more frequent faults during production (for example food trapped in a seal, incorrect sealing temperatures or seamer settings). In this chapter the techniques used to fill and seal rigid and flexible containers are described. By themselves these operations have no effect on the quality or shelf life of foods, but incorrect filling or sealing has a substantial effect on foods during subsequent storage. Details of deterioration of foods during storage is included in preceding chapters, and interactions of packaging and foods are summarised in Chapter 22.

23.1 RIGID AND SEMI-RIGID CONTAINERS

'Commercially clean' metal and glass containers are supplied as palletised batches, which are wrapped in shrink or stretch film (section 23.1.3) to prevent contamination. They are depalletised and inverted over steam or water sprays. They remain inverted until filling to prevent recontamination. Wide-mouthed plastic pots or tubs are fitted one inside another in stacks, contained in boxes or shrink film. They are cleaned by moist hot air. If they are to be filled with aseptically sterilised food (Chapter 11), they are sterilised with hydrogen peroxide. Laminated paperboard cartons are supplied either as a continuous reel or as partly formed flat containers. Both are sterilised with hydrogen peroxide.

23.1.1 Filling
The selection of an appropriate filling machine depends on the nature of the product and the production rate required. Gravity, pressure and vacuum fillers are described

by Osborne (1980). Volumetric fillers (for example a piston filler (Fig. 23.1)) are commonly used for liquids, pastes, powders and particulate foods. The filling heads are either in line (Fig. 23.2) or in a 'carousel' (or rotary) arrangement (Fig. 23.3). Fillers should accurately fill the container ($\pm1\%$ of the filled volume) without spillage and without contamination of the seal. They should also have a 'no container–no fill' device and be easily changed to accommodate different container sizes. Except for very low production rates or for difficult products (for example bean sprouts), fillers operate automatically, often with microprocessor control, to achieve the required filling speeds (for example up to 1000 cans per minute using rotary fillers).

Hermetically sealed containers are not filled completely. A head space is needed above the food to form a partial vacuum. This reduces pressure changes inside the container during processing and reduces oxidative deterioration of the product during storage (also Chapter 11). Glass containers and cans should have a head space of 6–10% of the container volume at normal sealing temperatures. Care is necessary when filling solid foods or pastes, to prevent air from becoming trapped in the product, which would reduce the head space vacuum. Viscous sauces or gravies are therefore added before solid pieces of food. This is less important with dilute brines or syrups, as air is able to escape before sealing. The functions of these added liquids of food are as follows:

(1) to improve the rate of heat transfer into solid pieces of food,
(2) to displace air from the container,
(3) to improve flavour and acceptability,
(4) to act as a medium for adding colours or flavours.

The proportions of solid and liquid components in a container are also subject to legislation or trade standards in many countries.

23.1.2 Sealing
23.1.2.1 Rigid and semi-rigid containers
The requirements of closures for glass containers are described by Osborne (1980) and developments in tamper-evident closures are described in section 23.2. Glass containers are sealed by one of the following types of seal.

(1) *Pressure seals*. These are used mostly for carbonated beverages and include cork or injection-moulded polyethylene stoppers, crown caps (pressed tinplate, lined with cork or polyvinyl chloride) or aluminium roll-on screw caps.
(2) *Normal seals*. These are used for example for pasteurised milk or wine bottles. Examples include cork stoppers fitted with tinned lead or aluminium capsules, and aluminium foil caps.
(3) *Vacuum seals*. These include *Omnia* and *twist-off* lids (Fig. 23.4) and *lever-off* or *pry off* types. They are used for example for preserves or paste jars.

Can lids are sealed by a *double seam*. In a seaming machine the 'first operation roller' rolls the cover hook around the body hook (Fig. 23.5(a)) and the 'second operation roller' then tightens the two hooks to produce the double seam (Fig. 23.5(b)). A thermoplastic sealing compound melts during heat processing and fills the spaces in the seam, to provide an additional barrier to contaminants. The can

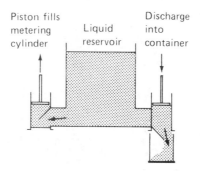

Fig. 23.1 — Piston filler.)

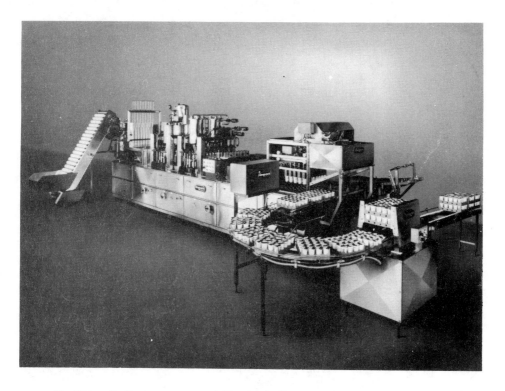

Fig. 23.2 — 'In-line' arrangement of filling heads. (Courtesy of Ampack–Ammann Co.)

seam is the weakest point of the can and the seam dimensions are routinely examined by quality control staff to ensure that they comply with specifications (Table 23.1).

Fig. 23.3 — 'Carousel' filler. (Courtesy of Peter Holland Machinery Ltd.)

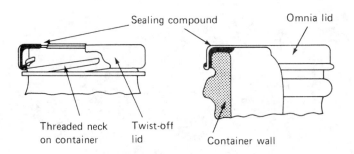

Fig. 23.4 — Lids for glass containers: (a) twist-off type; (b) Omnia type. (After Hersom and Hulland (1980).)

Free space is calculated using

$$\text{Free space} = \text{seam thickness} - [2(t_b) + 3(t_e)] \tag{23.1}$$

$$\text{and Percent Body Hook Butting} = [x - 1.1t_e/L - 1.1(2t_e + t_b)] \times 100 \tag{23.2}$$

$$\text{Actual overlap} = y + x + 1.1t_e - L \tag{23.3}$$

where x (mm) is the body hook length, y (mm) the cover hook length, t_e (mm) the thickness of the can end, t_b (mm) the template thickness of the can body, L (mm) the seam length and c the internal seam length (mm).

Different types of easy-open end are fitted to cans, depending on the type of

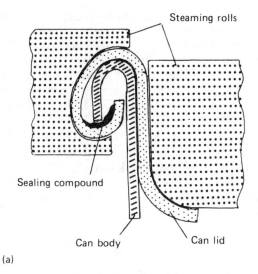

(a)

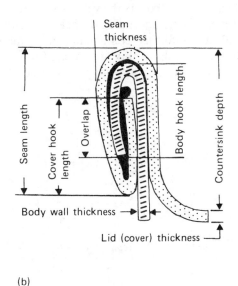

(b)

Fig. 23.5 — Can seam formation: (a) first operation; (b) double seam. (After Hersom and Hulland (1980).)

product. Ring pull closures are used for beverages, and many designs retain the ring pull within the can after opening, to reduce litter problems. Full-aperture ring pull closures are used for example for meat products and nuts. Both types are produced by scoring the metal lid and coating it with an internal lacquer. A metallised peelable plastic strip is used to close cans of non-carbonated non-pasteurised beverages (Malin, 1980). In aerosol cans, a pre-sterilised top is seamed on, and a pre-sterilised

Table 23.1 — Seam specifications for selected cylindrical cans

Type of can	Dimensions (mm)		Dimensions of seam (mm)		
	Diameter	Height	Length	Thickness	Hooks*
A1	65.3	101.6	2.97–3.17	1.40–1.45	1.90–2.16
A2	87.3	115.3	2.97–3.17	1.47–1.52	1.90–2.16
A21/2	103.2	115.3	2.97–3.17	1.52–1.57	1.90–2.16
A10	157.2	177.8	3.10–3.30	1.65–1.70	2.03–2.29
Actual overlap > 1.143 mm, % Body Hook Butting > 70%					

*Range of lengths for cover and body hooks.

Adapted from Lock (1969).

valve is fitted. The can is then dosed with gas and pressure checked. A cap is fitted onto the valve and finally an overcap covers the valve assembly.

Rigid and semi-rigid plastic pots and tubs are sealed by either clip-on lids or thermoplastic films. Small thermoformed containers (for example individual portions for ultrahigh-temperature sterilised milk or jam) are formed–filled–sealed in a single machine (Fig. 23.6) at up to 50 000 containers per hour (Guise, 1985). A

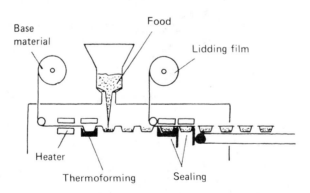

Fig. 23.6 — Forming–filling–sealing of individual portion pots. (After Briston and Katan (1974).)

similar concept is used to produce and fill plastic bottles (Fig. 23.7). Rigid laminated paperboard cartons have thermoplastic film on the inside. In one system a continuous roll of material is aseptically formed-filled-sealed (section 23.1.2.2.2) whereas, in a second system, pre-formed cartons are erected, filled and sealed in an aseptic filler (Fig. 23.8). In the second system the paperboard can be heavier than form–fill

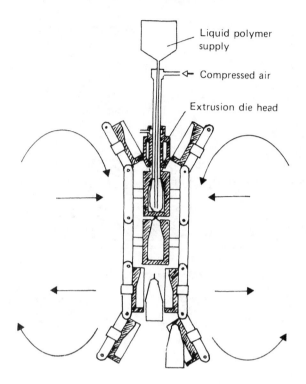

Liquid polymer supply

Compressed air

Extrusion die head

Fig. 23.7 — Forming–filling–sealing of plastic bottles; Bottlepack 4000 machine. (After Briston (1987).)

systems, because it does not require the flexibility needed for the forming machine. As a result the carton is more rigid and particulate foods may be filled without contamination of the seam.

23.1.2.2 Flexible containers

Thermoplastic materials or coatings become fluid when heated and resolidify on cooling. A heat sealer heats the surfaces of two films (webs) until the interface disappears and then applies pressure to fuse the films. The strength of the seal is determined by the temperature, pressure and time of sealing. The seal is weak until cool and should not therefore be stressed during cooling. Three common types of seal are as follows:

(1) bead seals (Fig. 23.9(a));
(2) lap seals (Fig. 23.9(b));
(3) fin seals (Fig. 23.9(c)).

The bead seal is a narrow weld at the end of the pack. In a lap seal, opposite surfaces are sealed, and both should therefore be thermoplastic. In a fin seal, the same surface of a sheet is sealed and only one side of the film need be thermoplastic. Fin seals protrude from the pack and no pressure is exerted on the food during sealing. They are therefore suitable for fragile foods (for example biscuits).

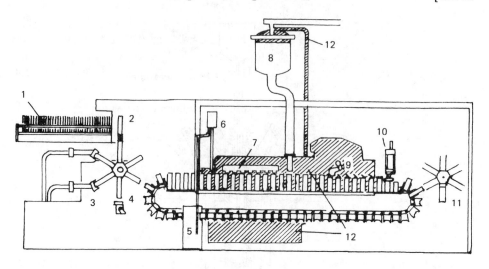

Fig. 23.8 — Aseptic filler: (1) carton sleeve magazine, (2) sleeve feed and opening, (3) bottom forming in hot sterile air, (4) bottom sealing, (5) hydrogen peroxide reservoir, (6) hydrogen peroxide vapour spraying to sterilse package, (7) hot sterile air drying zone to remove hydrogen peroxide, (8) product reservoir and filler, (9) ultrasonic top sealer, (10) top forming, (11) pack ejector, (12) sterile zone. (Courtesy of Bowater PKL (UK) Ltd.)

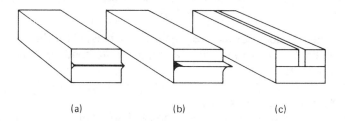

     (a)   (b)   (c)

Fig. 23.9 — Seals: (a) bead seal; (b) lap seal; (c) fin seal.

23.1.2.2.1 Types of sealer.

(1) *Hot-wire sealer*. A metal wire is heated to red heat simultaneously to form a bead seal and to cut the film.

(2) *Hot-bar sealer* (or jaw sealer). The two webs are held in place between heated jaws until the seal is formed.

(3) *Impulse sealer*. Film is clamped between two cold jaws, which each have a metal ribbon down the centre. The films are heated and fused, but the jaws remain in place until the seal cools and sets, to prevent shrinkage or wrinkling. Both types of sealer conduct heat through the film and therefore risk causing heat damage to the film.

(4) *Rotary sealers* are used for higher filling speeds. The centres of metal belts are heated by stationary shoes. The mouth of a package passes between the belts, and the two films are welded together. The edges of the belts support the unsoftened film. The seal then passes through cooling belts which clamp it until the seal sets.

(5) *High-frequency sealer*. An alternating electric field (1–50 MHz) induces molecular vibration in the film and thus heats and seals it. The film should have a high loss factor (Chapter 17) to ensure that the temperature is raised sufficiently by a relatively low voltage.

(6) *Ultrasonic sealer*. High-frequency vibrations (20 kHz) are transmitted through the film and dissipate as localised heat at the clamped surfaces.

(7) *Cold seals* (adhesive seals) are used to package heat sensitive products (for example chocolate, chocolate-coated biscuits or ice cream).

23.1.2.2.2   Form–fill–seal equipment

In *vertical form–fill–seal* (transwrap) equipment, a web of film is pulled intermittently over a forming shoulder by the vertical movement of the sealing jaws. A fin seal is formed at the side. The bottom is sealed by jaw sealers and the product is filled. The second seal then closes the top of the package and also forms the next bottom seal (Fig. 23.10a). This type of equipment is suitable for powders and

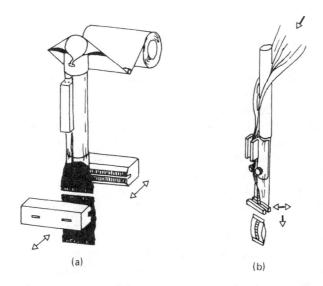

(a)   (b)

Fig. 23.10 — (a) Vertical form–fill–seal (transwrap) (after Briston (1980)); (b) flow pack. (Courtesy of Rose Forgrove Ltd.)

granular products, but liquids may contaminate the seal. Filling speeds are 30–90 min^{-1}. Films should have good slip characteristics and resistance to creasing or cracking, in order to pass over the filling tube, and a high melt strength to support the product on the hot seal.

In *flow pack* (flow wrap) equipment either a vertical or a horizontal tube of film is formed. The vertical system differs from the transwrap design in two ways. First a forming shoulder is not used and the film is therefore less stressed; secondly, the action is continuous and not intermittent. The side seam is formed by heaters and crimp rollers, which pull the tube tightly around the product, make a fin seal and lay it flat against the pack (Fig. 23.10b). In a horizontal system, products are pushed into

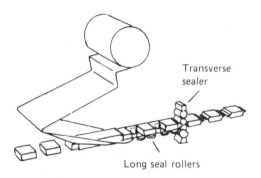

Transverse
sealer

Long seal rollers

Fig. 23.11 — Horizontal pillowpack. (After Guise (1987b).)

the tube of film as it is being formed (Fig. 23.11). In both types, the transverse seals are made by rotary sealers, which also separate the packs. Filling speeds are up to $400 \, \text{min}^{-1}$. Films should be thin and have a high melt strength, to produce a strong seal in the short heating time available (Briston and Katan, 1974).

A modification of this equipment is used to fill laminated cartons aseptically. A web of material is sterilised in a bath of hydrogen peroxide and formed into a vertical tube. An internal heater vaporises remaining hydrogen peroxide. The tube is then filled, sealed through the product, shaped into a carton and top sealed. The 'ears' on the base of the carton are folded flat and sealed into place.

In *sachet pack* machines, either horizontal or vertical packs are formed from single or double sheets of film. Horizontal single-web machines fold the film over a triangular shoulder and then form two side seams. The sachets are then separated, opened by a jet of compressed air, filled and heat sealed across the top (Fig. 23.12). The vertical single-web machine is similar to the transwrap machine. Horizontal machines have a smaller distance for the product to fall into the package and are therefore more suitable for sticky foods. Vertical machines have lower cost and take up less floor space.

On two-reel machines, one web forms the front and the second forms the back of the pack. Two blanks are cut from a roll of film, brought together and sealed on three sides. The package is filled and the final seal is made. Sachet machines are widely used for powders or granules (for example coffee, salt and sweeteners), liquids (for example cream) and sauces (for example ketchup and salad cream). Filling speeds are $70–1000 \, \text{min}^{-1}$, depending on the size of the sachet and the type of product.

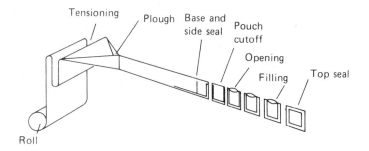

Fig. 23.12 — Forming–filling–sealing of sachets. (Courtesy of Engelmann and Buckham Machinery Ltd.)

Sachets are automatically cartoned, and the cartoning machine is therefore an integral part of sachet production (Guise, 1987a, and 1987b).

Bag-in-box packaging is filled by first removing air by vacuum. The bag is filled through the tap hole at up to 600 bags h^{-1}, the tap is then sterilised and refitted, and the bag is placed into the outer carton. Recent developments include the ability to hot-fill the bags and their use with aseptically sterilised foods (Chapter 11) which have a shelf life of 18 months.

23.1.3 Shrink-wrapping and stretch-wrapping

Low-density polyethylene is biaxially oriented to produce a range of films that shrink in two directions (Chapter 22). The shrink ratios are measured in both the machine direction (MD) and the transverse direction (TD). Films are *preferentially balanced* (shrink ratios are MD = 50%, TD = 20%), *fully balanced* (MD = 50%, TD = 50%) or *low balanced* (MD = 10%, TD = 10%). In general a small amount of shrinkage is required to tighten a loosely wrapped package, but contoured packages require a higher shrink ratio. The size of film required to shrink-wrap a sleeve-wrapped package is calculated using

$$\text{width} = A + \tfrac{3}{4}C$$

$$(23.4)$$

$$\text{length} = 2(B + C) + 10\% \text{ shrink allowance}$$

where A is the width of the package, B the length of the package and C the height of the package.

The total mass of film used equals the width (m) multiplied by the length (m) divided by the yield (a measure of film density) (m^2 kg^{-1}). The size of film required to shrink-wrap an overwrap package using centre-fold film is found using

$$\begin{aligned}
\text{width} &= (B + C) + 10\% \text{ shrink allowance} \\
\text{length} &= (A + C) + 10\% \text{ shrink allowance}
\end{aligned} \qquad (23.5)$$

The total mass of film used equals twice the width (m) multiplied by the length (m) divided by the yield ($m^2 kg^{-1}$).

The film is shrunk by passing through a hot-air tunnel or beneath radiant heaters. Alternatively a heat storage gun fires an intermittent pulse of hot air to shrink the film when a package passes beneath. This reduces energy consumption by 70%.

In stretch-wrapping, low-density polyethylene, polyvinyl chloride or linear low-density polyethylene (Chapter 22) is wrapped under tension around collated packages. The main advantages over shrink-wrapping include lower energy use than in shrink tunnels (1.5–6 kW compared with 20–30 kW), and lower film use. In shrink-wrapping, 5–10% extra film is used to allow for shrinkage, whereas stretch film is elongated by 2–5%. Together this gives a 10–15% saving in film.

23.2 TAMPER-EVIDENT PACKAGING

The habit of some consumers of *grazing* (opening packs, tasting the food, and returning it to the shelves) and a number of cases of deliberate poisoning of packaged foods have caused food manufacturers to modify package designs. Although total protection is not possible, tamper-evident packaging delays entry into the package and indicates whether tampering has occurred (Box, 1986).

Some existing packages are tamper resistant (for example metal cans and aerosols, cartons, packs from form–fill–seal machines and shrink-wrapped packs). The main problems occur with bottles and jars because they need to be reclosable. There are five options to make these packs tamper evident:

(1) heat-shrinkable polyvinyl chloride sleeves for bottle necks;
(2) foil or membrane seals for wide-mouthed containers;
(3) rings or bridges to join a hinged cap to a lower section on bottles (the container cannot be opened without breaking the bridge or removing the ring);
(4) roll-on pilfer-proof caps for bottles or jars (during rolling, a tamper-evident ring in the cap locks onto a special bead in the neck to produce a seal which breaks on opening and drops slightly);
(5) a safety button in press-on twist off closures for heat sterilised jars (a concave section, formed in the lid by the head space vacuum, becomes convex when opened).

ACKNOWLEDGEMENTS

Grateful acknowledgement is made for information supplied by the following: ICI Petrochemicals and Plastics Division, Stockton on Tees, Cleveland TS18 3RD, UK; Ampack Ammann GmbH and Co. KG, D-8901 Konigsbrunn, West Germany; Rose Forgrove Ltd, Seacroft, Leeds LS14 2AN, UK; Engelmann and Buckham Machinery Ltd, Alton, Hampshire, UK; Ben Nevis Packaging Ltd, Trowbridge, Wiltshire BA14 8AB, UK; Ilapak Ltd, Hayes, Middlesex UB3 3BN, UK; Peter Holland Machinery Ltd, Stamford, Lincolnshire, UK; Bowater PKL Ltd, Houghton-le-Spring, Tyne and Wear DH4 6JN, UK.

REFERENCES

Box, E. C. (1986) Rest assured with contents secure. *Food Process*. June 33–34.

Brennan, J. G., Butters, J. R., Cowell, N. D., and Lilly, A. E. V. (1976) *Food engineering operations*, 2nd edn. Applied Science, London.

Briston, J. H. (1980) Rigid plastics packaging. In: S. J. Palling (ed.), *Developments in food packaging*, Vol. 1. Applied Science, London, pp. 27–53.

Briston, J. H. (1987) Rigid plastics containers and food packaging. In: A. Turner (ed.), *Food technology international, Europe*. Sterling, London, pp. 283,285–287.

Briston, J. H., and Katan, L. L. (1974) *Plastics in contact with food*. Food Trade Press, London, pp. 331–348.

Guise, B. (1985) Shrinking to style, *Food Process*, **54** 23–27.

Guise, B. (1987a) Spotlight on sachet packaging. *Food Process*. **56** 35–37.

Guise, B. (1987b) Filling an industry need. *Food Process*, July 31–33.

Hersom, A. C., and Hulland, E.D. (1980) *Canned foods*, 7th edn. Churchill Livingstone, London, pp. 67–102, 342–356.

Lock, A. (1969) *Practical canning*, 3rd edn. Food Trade Press, London, pp. 26–40.

Malin, J. D. (1980) Metal containers and closures. In: S. J. Palling (ed.), *Developments in food packaging*, Vol. 1. Applied Science, London, pp. 1–26.

Mayo, G. (1979) New rules for Europe. *Food Manuf*. September 49, 51.

Osborne, D. G. (1980) Glass. In: S. J. Palling (ed.), *Developments in food packaging* Vol. 1. Applied Science, London, pp. 81–115.

24

Materials handling and process control

The correct control of materials and processing conditions is essential to optimise product quality and to minimise production costs. Improvements in the efficiency of materials handling and the development of small powerful computers have lead to substantial improvements in production efficiencies in recent years. Both types of improvement are used at all stages in a manufacturing process, from ordering of raw materials, through processing, packaging and warehouse storage, to distribution and presentation to the consumer. Individual processing machines are routinely fitted with sophisticated microprocessors, to monitor and control processing conditions, product quality and energy consumption. In this chapter, the principles of materials handling, control and automation and selected examples of equipment are described. Other examples of specific uses of microprocessors with processing equipment are described in preceding chapters that deal with individual unit operations.

24.1 MATERIALS HANDLING

Efficient materials handling is the organised movement of materials in the correct quantities, to and from the correct place, accomplished with a minimum of time, labour, wastage and expenditure and with maximum safety. Some advantages of correct materials handling are summarised in Table 24.1.

The important techniques identified in Table 24.1 are

(1) a systems approach to planning a handling scheme,
(2) the use of bulk handling, and
(3) automation (discussed in section 24.2).

24.1.1 Systems approach to materials handling

When establishing methods of materials handling, a systems approach covering raw materials, materials in process and finished products is needed, in order to optimise flow rates in the correct sequence throughout the production process and to avoid bottlenecks or shortages. Additionally the flow of foods through a factory should be

Table 24.1 — Advantages of correct materials-handling techniques and methods of achieving efficiency in materials handling

Advantages	Methods of achieving efficiency
Savings in storage and operating space	Do not move materials unless necessary; minimise all movements
Better stock control	Handle materials in bulk
Improved working conditions	Package or group materials together for easier handling
Improved product quality	
Lower risk of accidents	Use of continuous handling techniques
Reduced processing time	
Lower costs of production	Automate where possible
Improved product quality	Use a systems approach to optimise flow of materials
Less wastage of materials and operator time	Use all layers of a building's height
	Use adaptable equipment suitable for different applications
	Use gravity where possible

as simple as possible to reduce costs, to avoid confusion which could lead to the contamination of processed foods by raw foods, to improve working conditions and to attain the other benefits described in Table 24.1. Examples of correctly and incorrectly designed factory layouts are shown in Figs 24.1(a) and (b). The design and construction of food plant are described by Ingram (1979). Important questions to be asked when designing a materials handling system are listed by Farrall (1979) for different areas of a food factory, and Sidebottom (1985) describes advances in the control of materials handling in processing and warehousing.

24.1.2   Unit loads
Packages which are grouped into larger loads require less handling when products are moved through storage and distribution networks. Wooden pallets (13 cm high) are commonly used to move the unitised load of cases or sacks by fork-lift or stacker trucks. A development of this method uses fibreboard slipsheets to reduce the volume occupied by pallets in vehicles and warehouses (Spreen and Ellis, 1983). Products are secured onto the pallet or slipsheet by shrink-film or stretch-film (Chapter 23).

24.1.3   Continuous handling
Continuous handling equipment is an essential component of continuous processes but also improves the efficiency of batch processing. The most important types of

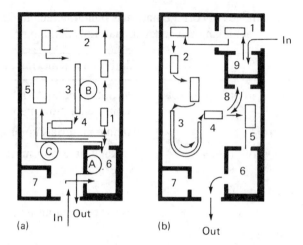

Fig. 24.1 — Two designs of a factory floor plan for seafood processing (a) incorrectly designed and (b) correctly designed: 1, cleaning; 2, peeling and preparation; 3, inspection; 4, packaging; 5, freezing; 6, cold store; 7, office; 8, overflow cold store; 9, raw material cold store. Note the following faults in the design (a): A, raw material, partly processed product and finished product in same cold store; B, adjacent inspection of prepared food and washing of raw material; C, confused and excessive materials handling.

materials-handling equipment used in food processing are conveyor belts and elevators. Other types of equipment are described by Brennan *et al.* (1976) and are summarised in Table 24.2.

24.1.3.1 *Conveyors*
Conveyors are widely used in all food processing industries for the movement of solid materials, both within unit operations and between operations (Table 24.2). There are a large number of conveyor designs, produced to meet specific applications. Common types include the following.

(1) *Belt conveyor.* This is an endless belt which is held under tension between two rollers, one of which is driven. The belts may be stainless steel mesh or wire, synthetic rubber, or a composite of canvass, steel and polyurethane or polyester. They are described in detail by Brown (1983). Flat belts are used to carry packed foods, and trough-shaped belts are used for bulk materials. Belts may be inclined up to 45°, if they are fitted with cross slats to prevent the product from slipping. Metal or wooden slatted conveyors are used instead of belts for greater load bearing and a reduced risk of damage to the conveyor.
(2) *Roller conveyor* and *skate wheel conveyor.* Free-running (unpowered) rollers or wheels are either horizontal, to allow packed foods to be pushed along, or slightly inclined for transport under gravity. Rollers are heavier and stronger than wheels and therefore able to carry heavier loads. However, they are more difficult to start and stop, and more difficult to use around corners. Steeper inclines produce greater acceleration of packages, and a fall of approximately 10 cm in 3 m is sufficient for most purposes. Powered conveyors are used horizontally, or at a maximum inclination of 10–12°.

Table 24.2 — Applications of materials-handling equipment

	Conveyors	Elevators	Cranes and hoists	Trucks	Pneumatic equipment	Water flumes
Direction						
Vertical up		*	*		*	
Vertical down		*	*		*	
Incline up	*	*			*	
Incline down	*	*			*	*
Horizontal	*			*	*	
Frequency						
Continuous	*	*			*	*
Intermittent			*	*		
Location served						
Point	*	*			*	*
Path	*				*	*
Limited area			*			
Unlimited area				*		
Height						
Overhead	*	*	*		*	
Working height	*			*	*	*
Floor level	*		*	*		*
Underfloor	*				*	*
Materials						
Packed	*	*	*	*		
Bulk	*	*	*	*	*	
Solid	*	*	*	*	*	*
Liquid				*	*	*
Service						
Permanent	*	*	*		*	*
Temporary			*	*		

From Brennan *et al*. (1976).

(3) *Chain conveyor*. This is used to move churns, barrels, crates and similar bulk containers by placing them directly over a driven chain, with protruding lugs, located at floor level. A similar monorail conveyor is used for moving meat carcasses on an overhead track.

(4) *Screw conveyor*. This consists of a rotating helical screw inside a metal trough. It is used to move bulk foods (for example flour and sugar) and small-particulate foods (for example peas or grains). The main advantages are the uniform, easily controlled discharge, the compact cross-section (without a return conveyor) and total enclosure to protect the product and to prevent contamination. They may be horizontal or vertically inclined but are generally limited to a maximum length of 6 m as, above this, high friction forces result in excessive power consumption. The use of screw conveyors is described in detail by Bates (undated).

(5) *Vibratory conveyors*. These impart a vertical movement to food, to raise it a few millimetres off the conveyor, and a forward movement, to move the food along the conveyor (Fig. 24.2). The amplitude of vibration is adjusted to control the speed and direction of movement. This precise control makes vibratory conveyors useful as feed mechanisms for processing equipment. They are also useful

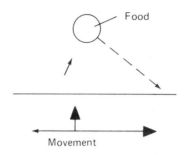

Fig. 24.2 — Action of vibrating conveyor.

for moving sticky foods (for example minced meat) or friable foods (for example snackfoods).

(6) *Flight conveyors*. Here, bulk material (for example grain or flour) is dragged through an enclosed channel by an endless chain fitted with hooks or flights. Chain speeds are low (6–10 m min−1) and the inclination is limited to 30°, above which the material slips back.

24.1.3.2 Elevators
Four of the commonest types of elevator are as follows (Table 24.2).

(1) *Bucket elevators* consist of metal or plastic buckets fixed between two endless chains. They have a high capacity for free-flowing powders and particulate foods. The shape and spacing of the buckets, the method of discharge and the speed of the conveyor ($15–100$ m min^{-1}) control the flow rate of materials.
(2) *Magnetic elevators* are used for conveying cans within canneries. They have a positive action in being able to hold the cans in place and are thus able to to invert empty cans for cleaning and operate at high speeds with minimal noise.
(3) *Flight elevators* are essentially inclined flight conveyors. They have flexibility in use for a wide range of free-flowing bulk foods, high capacity and good space utilisation.
(4) *Pneumatic elevators*. Powders or small-particulate foods are suspended in air which is recirculated at $1000–1700$ m min^{-1} inside a system of pipes. The air velocity is critical; if it is too low, the solids settle out whereas, if it is too high, there is abrasion damage to the pipe surfaces. The calculation of air velocity needed to achieve transport is described in Chapter 1. Similar equipment is used to classify foods (Chapter 2) and to dry foods (Chapter 14). A buildup of static electricity is prevented by control over the moisture content of the food and earthing the equipment. This is necessary when conveying powders to minimise the risk of dust explosions. This type of equipment has a smooth operation and cannot be overloaded. It has few moving parts, low maintenance costs and only requires a supply of compressed air at 700 kPa.

24.2 PROCESS CONTROL AND AUTOMATION

Process control improves product uniformity and production efficiency and reduces processing costs. The important elements of process control are as follows:

(1) detailed production planning and supervision;
(2) scheduling of materials and resources;
(3) tracking the flow of product through the process;
(4) management of orders, recipes and batches;
(5) evaluation of process and product data.

Control systems used in food processing can be viewed as having up to four layers of control as follows:

(1) local equipment controllers which are an integral part of the process plant;
(2) a process computer (a centralised computer or distributed on-line controllers), which monitors and controls the process in specified zones,
(3) a supervisory computer, which monitors processing data and presents summaries of information for management decision making,
(4) a management link, to accept and feed management data from the supervisory computer (Sidebottom, 1986).

In this section the first two levels of control are described. Aspects of the use of computers in management are discussed by Hamilton (1985), Sidebottom (1986) and Marien (1987), and the stages used for the implementation of a control system are described by Kirk (1987).

24.2.1 Sensors
The pre-requisites for automatic control of a process are sensors, which measure process variables, and an 'interface' between the sensors and the process controller. Parameters commonly measured by sensors are classified into

(1) primary measurements (for example temperature, weight and pressure),
(2) comparative measurements, obtained from comparison of primary measurements (for example specific gravity),
(3) inferred measurements, where the value of an easily measured variable is assumed to be proportional to a phenomenon that is difficult to measure (for example texture measurement) and
(4) calculated measurements, found using qualitative and quantitative data from analytical instruments (for example biomass in a fermenter).

Sensors used in food processing are shown in Table 24.3.
Solid-state electronic sensors have largely replaced mechanical sensors. They have greater reliability, greater accuracy and precision, and faster response times. Advances in sensors are described in detail by Paschold (1980). Developments in biological sensors are described by Kress-Rogers (1985). However, simple electronic sensors do not measure more complex, and to consumers more important, quality characteristics (for example colour, texture, surface appearance and shape), and this is becoming an important application of microprocessor control. The power of small computers enables large amounts of information about a food to be stored, measured

Table 24.3 — Parameters measured by sensors in food processing

Parameter	Sensor	Applications
Weight	Strain gauge, load cell	Accurate measurement of tank contents, checkweighers
Temperature	Thermocouples resistance thermometers	Heat processing, refrigeration
Pressure or vacuum	Bourdon gauge	Evaporation
Flow rate	Mechanical flowmeters, magnetic vortex meter, turbine meter	Most processes
pH	Electrometric	
Refractometric solids	Refractometer	Sugar processing, preserves
Humidity	Hygrometer, capacitance	Drying, freezing, chill storage
Level	Capacitance, mechanical float, nucleonic	Automatic filling of tanks and process vessels in most processes
Valve position	Proximity switch	Most processes
Pump and motor speeds	Tachometer	Most processes
Turbidity	Absorbance meter	Fermentations, sugar processing
Conductivity	Capacitance gauge	Strength of cleaning solutions

From Hamilton (1985) and Paschold (1980).

and compared with specifications which are entered into the computer memory. Examples of this type of control for colour sorting and shape sorting are described in Chapter 2.

The important advantage of microprocessors is the ability to analyse data from sensors rapidly and to use the results of the analysis directly in automatic control of the process. The reduction in cost of electronic components in recent years has provided the stimulus for the widespread use of process controllers.

24.2.2 Controllers

Sensors measure process variables and pass the information to a controller, where it is compared with a set point. If the input deviates from the set point (termed the *error*), the controller alters an actuator (for example a motor, solenoid or valve) to correct the deviation. In *closed-loop control*, there is a continuous flow of information around the loop. Sensors produce information which is used to produce changes to the processing conditions via the actuator, which in turn further alters the actuator (for example Fig. 24.3). A single loop involves one control algorithm (section 24.2.2.1) and one actuator for the measurement, and maintenance at a set point of one process variable. A common example of closed-loop control is *feedback control* (Fig. 24.3). Other types include *sequence control*, in which the completion of one operation signals the controller to start the next, with or without a time delay, and *feedforward control*, in which process conditions are monitored and compared

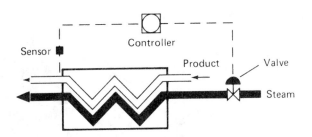

Fig. 24.3 — Feedback control. (Courtesy of APV Ltd.)

with a model system which anticipates process performance; if the operating conditions deviate from the model, they are altered via actuators. Automated processes consist of many individual loops and some more complex ones. The design, action and applications of controllers are described by Green (1984) and Fell (1987). Other examples of automatic control are described in preceding chapters.

24.2.2.1 Programmable logic controllers
Programmable logic controllers (PLCs) are based on microcomputers, which have a fixed program stored in two modes in a read only memory. The first (teach) mode allows instructions to be programmed into the memory by an operator, via a random access memory keyboard. In the second (run) mode the program is executed automatically in response to data received from sensors. This is possible with the use of software building blocks termed *algorithms*. These construct control sequences for a particular application and allow the operator to program the system. Each algorithm carries out a specific function, and the operator simply defines the series of algorithms, and the data on which they are to operate to control the process, in response to a series of questions displayed on a screen.

A display monitor provides information on the progress of the control, and a printed record gives a summary of the processing conditions used. If a process parameter exceeds a pre-set limit, a warning is activated to attract the attention of the operator. Alternatively the program may automatically correct the deviation from specification. PLCs are highly reliable, relatively low cost and easy to install and use. An important advantage is the ease and speed with which they can be reprogrammed by factory staff who do not possess sophisticated computing experience. This allows great flexibility in being able to modify process conditions or change product formulations.

A second important function of PLCs is to collect and process data to show the performance of the process plant (for example length and causes of stoppages, and energy consumption) and to prepare summary reports. Factory engineers can then design more effective maintenance programmes and locate faults more quickly. Summaries of processing costs and production line efficiencies are used by production staff to improve materials-handling and scheduling procedures and hence to improve the efficiency of production. Sales managers use this information to control stocks of products and raw materials and to compare actual production levels with targets. Selected applications of automatic control are described in the following sections, and an example is shown in Fig. 24.4.

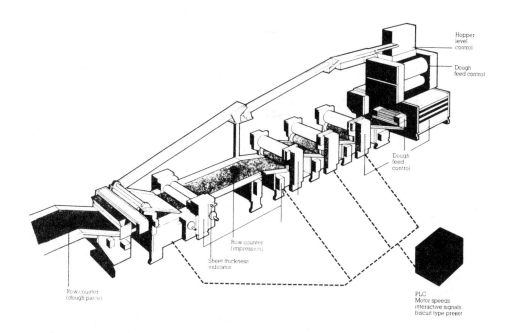

Fig. 24.4 — PLC control of biscuit manufacture. (Courtesy of Baker Perkins Ltd.)

24.2.2.2 Automatic control of product formulation

The increase in the range of products required by consumers causes manufacturers to produce smaller batches, with more frequent changes to processing conditions and product formulations. This is complex and time consuming if performed manually but is well suited to automatic control by PLCs. The equipment (termed a *batcher*) has a microprocessor which stores information about the types and weights of ingredients for all products made on the production line (for example one system stores up to 200 recipes and 30 different mix cycles (Kimber, 1983)). Each formulation is assigned a number and, when a number is entered by the operator, the microprocessor controls the flow of ingredients from storage silos, through automatic weighers, to mixing vessels. This type of control is widely used in the production of baked goods, snackfoods and ice cream.

A similar system is used for the automatic control of flow blending, to adjust the strength of beer to a pre-set specification. Beer from the fermentation tanks, which has a higher strength than that required in a particular product, is mixed with deaerated water to the correct proportions. The operator enters the specific gravity of the beer, the specific gravity of the diluent and the required specific gravity of the product. The microcomputer then calculates the required ratio of the two fluid streams and adjusts one until the measured ratio meets the specification. It also controls liquid flow rates and initiates an alarm if there is a discrepancy between incoming and outgoing flows.

A second application is concerned with raw materials that have a variable composition but are used to produce a final product in which the composition is subject to legislation or trade standards. A computer is used to determine the least cost formulation needed to produce the required specification from different combinations of raw material. For example in meat products, the quality of the product and the profitability of production are determined by accurate proportioning of meat ingredients, the fat content of the meat and accurate proportioning of non-meat ingredients. Data on the composition of the raw materials are fed into the computer. It simulates possible formulations and selects the one that has the lowest cost. Automatic control of the formulation produces the exact lean-to-fat ratio and the exact meat-to-non-meat ratio required in the product, whatever the composition of the batch of raw meat (Shields, 1981; Newman, 1986). This system is also used in buying departments to assess the implications of purchasing particular raw materials and hence to determine the overall financial savings from a given set of purchases.

24.2.2.3 Weighing

The fill weights of packaged foods are subject to legislative control in many countries. In addition a manufacturer does not wish to give product away consistently by overfilling containers and a consumer expects to receive the stated quantity when purchasing a food. Automatic checkweighers are therefore routinely used after food is packaged. These are described in detail by Spencer (1983). A checkweigher is programmed with the target weight for all products produced on a particular production line. It weighs each package as it passes on a conveyor belt and continuously updates the mean weight and standard deviation of the pack weights. If the average weight falls below a pre-set level, a warning is given to operators or to the process computer, and the checkweigher automatically rejects any individual packages that are substantially underweight or empty. A printed summary of the statistical information, including the number of packages that fell outside tolerance limits, for the total production of an individual product or during a shift, is prepared for the factory records (Slade, 1983).

24.2.2.4 Automated processes

Computer systems exist to control each stage of a process from initial ordering of supplies to distribution of finished goods. Advances that have taken place in automatic warehouse control (Anon., 1983) include computer-controlled stacker trucks and computer management of the loads and journeys of distribution vehicles. In newly constructed factories, such control systems are included in the plant design (for example Perry et al., 1983). The advantages of automation are summarised as follows:

(1) more frequent checks of critical control points and a reduction in sampling errors or bias;
(2) improved product quality due to accurate formulation and repeatability of machine performance;
(3) improved productivity and savings in materials and energy;
(4) rapid diagnosis of plant faults and automatic preparation of plant performance records;
(5) a reduction in hazards to operators;

(6) a reduction in labour costs.

The main disadvantage is the social effects of a reduction in the availability of employment.

In a fully automated milk processing plant, each piece of equipment is controlled by its own instrumentation to maintain pre-set temperatures, pressures or flow rates automatically. Each process area has a *mimic panel* to indicate continuously the status of instruments and process variables. Closed-circuit television cameras view the plant and relay the information to monitors located in a central control room. A computer checks the positions of valves and the measured fluid levels, pressures, flow rates, densities and temperatures in the processing equipment, at a rate of for example 998 inputs every 7 s. When a fault occurs, the computer sounds an alarm and produces a printout of the equipment, its location and the nature of the fault, for the operators in the control room. The computer also prints detailed production data and the status of stocks at any time. Larger systems are able to control 2600 plant actuators and monitor 5000 inputs at a rate of 2000 per second. A modern plant is described by Anon. (1987). Many other examples of computer control are reported including those given by Bimbelet (1986), Perry *et al.* (1983) (refrigeration), Green (1984) (temperature and relative humidity in stores) and Anon. (1986) (computer aided design of packages).

ACKNOWLEDGEMENTS

Grateful acknowledgement is made for information supplied by the following: Mettler Instrument Corporation, Hightstown, New Jersey 08520, USA; CAP Industry Ltd, Reading, UK; Ferranti Computer Systems, Simonsway, Wythenshawe, Manchester M22 5LA, UK; APV International Ltd, PO Box 4, Crawley, West Sussex RH10 2QB, UK; Baker Perkins Ltd, Peterborough PE3 6TA, UK; Alfa Laval Ltd, Brentford, Middlesex TW8 9BT, UK.

REFERENCES

Anon. (1983) Computerised warehouse control. *Food Process*. September p. 10.
Anon. (1986) Breaking new ground in computer aided design. *Food Process*. April p. 4.
Anon. (1987) A fresh approach. *Food Process*. November 26, 27.
Bates, L. (undated) *Interfacing hoppers with screw conveyors*. Ajax Equipment Ltd, Bolton, Lancashire.
Bimbelet, J. J. (1986) Automation comes to the food industries. *Food Eur*. May–June, 17–18.
Brennan, J. G., Butters, J. R., Cowell, N. W. and Lilly, A. E. V. (1976) *Food engineering operations*. Applied Science, London, pp. 467–498.
Brown, L. (1983) Belting up. *Food Process*. April 43–46.
Farrall, A. W. (1979) *Food engineering systems*, Vol. 2, *Utilities*. AVI, Westport, Connecticut, pp. 474–517.

Fell, J. (1987) High tech help for temperature control. *Food Manuf.* August, 20–21, 23.

Green, D. A. (1984) The use of microprocessor for control and instrumentation in the food industry. In: B. M. McKenna (ed.), *Engineering and Food*, Vol. 2, Elsevier Applied Science, Barking, Essexz, pp. 757–772.

Hamilton, B. (1985) The sensor scene. *Food Manuf.* September 39, 41–42.

Ingram, A. (1979) Food plant design and construction. In: A. W. Farrall (ed.) *Food engineering systems*, Vol. 2. AVI, Westport, Connecticut, pp. 339–371.

Kimber, A. (1983) Ferranti's souper system. *Food Manuf.* November 59, 61.

Kirk, P. (1987) Bringing control to food and drink processes. In: A. Turner (ed.) *Food technology international*, *Europe* Sterling, London, pp. 77, 79–80.

Kress-Rogers, E. (1985) Seeking sensor improvements. *Food Process.* September 37–39.

Marien, M. (1987) Planning for automation success in the food industry. *Food Eur.* May–June 13–15, 17–19.

Newman, D. (1986) Programmed solutions to meat formulations. *Food Process.* August 25–26.

Paschold, H. (1980) Sensors — the prerequisite for automation in the food industry. *Chem. Ind.* **21** 485–491.

Perry, M. H., Perry, T. C., Murray, B. and Swientek, R. J. (1983) Programmable controllers automate new dairy plant. *Food Process.* October 62–64.

Shields, B. (1981) Automatic control of meat product recipes. *Food Process. Ind.* July 31–34.

Sidebottom, B. (1985) Coordinating material flows. *Food Process.* December 29–32.

Sidebottom, B. (1986) Controlling automation. *Food Process.* December 15–18.

Slade, E. (1983) Modularity and microprocessors. *Food Process.* January 19–23.

Spencer, D. J. (1983) Food processing under control. *Food Process.* July 37–40.

Spreen, F. W. and Ellis, R. F. (1983). Unitized loads on slipsheets save $2-million in freight costs. *Food Process.* (*USA*) October 150–152.

25

Processing examples

The unit operations described in preceding chapters are linked together to form the integrated processes necessary for food production. In this chapter, examples of processes for the production of foods found on the two following typical breakfast menus are given in (Figs 25.1 and 25.2).

Menu 1 Orange juice
          Coffee
          Buttered toast and marmalade
          Yoghurt
          Cereal and milk

Menu 2 Tea
          Bacon
          Fried egg
          Baked beans and
          Tomatoes

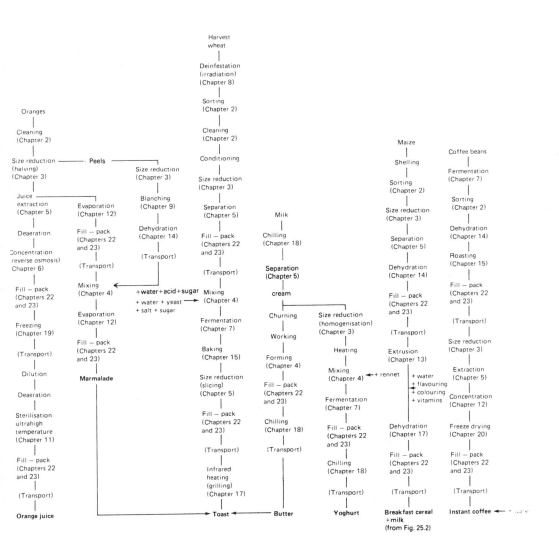

Fig. 25.1 — Components of Menu 1.

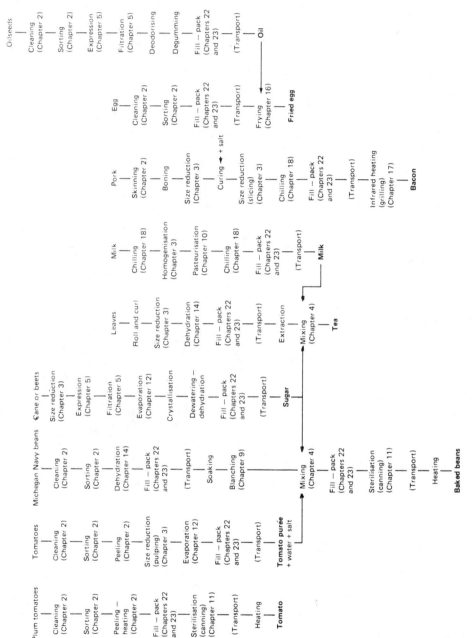

Fig. 25.2 — Components of Menu 2.

Appendices

Appendix A

Vitamins in Foods

Vitamin	Nature and properties
Vitamin A	Present in animal foods as retinol, and in plant foods mostly as all-*trans* β-carotenes. The chemical structure includes double bonds which are susceptible to oxidation. Attacked by peroxides and free radicals formed from lipid oxidation. Losses promoted by traces of copper and iron which catalyse the oxidation. Negligible losses due to leaching. Heat converts part of the *trans* isomer to neo-β-carotene-U which has lower potency
Thiamin (Vitamin B$_1$)	Present in animal and plant tissues either as free thiamin or bound to pyrophosphate or protein. Destroyed by sulphur dioxide (in sulphited fruits and vegetables), potassium bromate flour improver and thiaminase. Polyphenoloxidase catalyses thiamin destruction by phenols in plant tissues. Substantial losses due to leaching (Chapter 9) and drip losses (Chapters 15 and 19)
Riboflavin (Vitamin B$_2$)	Occurs as free form in milk but mostly bound with phosphate in other foods. Destroyed by alkaline conditions, light and excessive heat. Stable to air and acids
Niacin	Occurs as nicotinamide (as nicotinamide adenine dinucleotide and nicotinamide adenine dinucleotide phosphate) and as nicotinic acid. Bound to polysaccharides and peptides and therefore not available in many cereals unless liberated by heat or alkaline conditions (for example by baking powder (Chapter 15)). The amino acid tryptophan is converted to niacin in the body (niacin equivalent is free niacin plus one sixtieth of the tryptophan). Generally stable

Folic acid	Occurs in various forms, expressed as pteroylglutamic equivalents, with various numbers of glutamate residues and methyl or formyl groupings. Richest sources are dark green leaves, liver and kidney. More difficult to assay than other vitamins. Possibly one of the few causes of deficiency disease in industrialised countries, especially in pregnant women, pre-term infants and the elderly
Pyridoxine (Vitamin B_6)	Occurs in three forms: pyridoxine, pyridoxal and pyridoxamine. The first two are found in plants and the last two in animal tissues. Most is in a free form in milk but is otherwise bound. Difficult to assay and may be deficient in some diets. Lost by reaction with sulphydryl groups of proteins and amino acids when heated or during storage.
Cyanocobalamin (Vitamin B_{12})	Small losses due to interaction with vitamin C and sulphydryl compounds in the presence of oxygen in milk. Generally stable.
Ascorbic acid (Vitamin C)	Occurs as both ascorbic acid and dehydroascorbic acid. The latter is very heat labile, with or without the presence of oxygen. Very soluble and readily lost by leaching and in drip losses. Destroyed by a number of plant enzymes, including ascorbic acid oxidase, peroxidase, cytochrome oxidase and phenolase. Copper and iron catalyse oxidation in air, but sulphur dioxide protects against oxidation. Most labile of the vitamins and substantial losses in most food processing. Vitamin C retention sometimes used as an indicator of the severity of processing. Also used as an anti-oxidant and stabiliser (Appendix D), as a flour improver and in cured meats
Vitamin D	Occurs in foods as cholecalciferol (D_3) and produced in the skin under the influence of UV light. The synthetic type, ergocalciferol (D_2) is added to some milk products, baby foods and margarine. The vitamin is stable under all normal processing and storage conditions
Vitamin E	Occurs as eight compounds: four tocopherols and four tocotrienols, each of which has a different potency. Activity usually expressed as α-tocopherol equivalents. Naturally occurring anti-oxidant but is lost relatively slowly. Generally stable during processing, except frying (Chapter 16) in which it is destroyed by peroxides

Appendix B

EEC Permitted Food Additives

In the following tables the E numbers are generally recognised by the EEC as safe additives. Those without the prefix E are, at the time of writing, proposals and need not necessarily be adopted.

B.1 PERMITTED COLOURS

Colour	Alternative name(s)	E number
Curcumin		E100
Riboflavin	Lactoflavin	E101
Riboflavin-5′-phosphate		101(a)
Tartrazine		E102
Quinoline yellow		E104
Yellow 2G		107
Sunset yellow FCF	Orange yellow S	E110
Cochineal	Carminic acid	E120
Carmoisine	Azorubine	E122
Amaranth		E123
Ponceau 4R	Cochineal red A	E124
Erythrosine BS		E127
Red 2G		128
Patent blue V		E131
Indigo carmine	Indigotine	E132
Brilliant blue FCF		133
Chlorophyll		E140
Copper complexes of chlorophyll and chlorophyllins		E141
Green S	Acid brilliant green BS	E142
Caramel		E150
Black PN	Brilliant black PN	E151

Carbon black	Vegetable carbon	E153
Brown FK		154
Brown Ht	Chocolate brown HT	155
Carotene α, β or γ		E160(a)
Annatto, bixin, norbixin		E160(b)
Capsanthin	Capsorubin	E160(c)
Lycopene		E160(d)
β-apo-8'-carotenal (C_{30})		E160(e)
Ethyl ester of		
β-apo-8'-carotenoic acid (C_{30})		E160(f)
Flavoxanthin		E161(a)
Lutein		E161(b)
Cryptoxanthin		E161(c)
Rubixanthin		E161(d)
Violaxanthin		E161(e)
Rhodoxanthin		E161(f)
Canthaxanthin		E161(g)
Beetroot red	Betanin	E162
Anthocyanins		E163
Titanium dioxide		E171
Iron oxides and hydroxides		E172
Aluminium		E173
Silver		E174
Gold		E175
Pigment rubine	Lithol rubine BK	E180

B.2 PERMITTED STABILISERS

Emulsifier–stabiliser	Alternative name	E number
Alginic acid		E400
Sodium alginate		E401
Potassium alginate		E402
Ammonium alginate		E403
Calcium alginate		E404
Propane-1,2-diol alginate	Propylene glycol alginate	E405
Agar		E406
Carrageenan		E407
Locust bean gum	Carob gum	E410
Guar gum		E412
Tragacanth		E413
Gum arabic	Acacia	E414
Xanthan gum		E415
Karaya gum		416
Sorbitol	Sorbitol syrup	E420

Mannitol		E421
Glycerol		E422
Polyoxyethylene (8) stearate		430
Polyoxyethylene (40) stearate		431
Polyoxyethylene (20) sorbitan monolaurate	Polysorbate 20	432
Polyexyethylene (20) sorbitan mono-oleate	Polysorbate 80	433
Polyoxyethylene (20) sorbitan monopalmitate	Polysorbate 40	434
Polyoxyethylene (20) sorbitan monostearate	Polysorbate 60	435
Polyoxyethylene (20) sorbitan tristearate	Polysorbate 65	436
Pectin		E440(a)
Amidated pectin		E440(b)
Ammonium phosphatides		442
*Di*sodium dihydrogen diphosphate		
*Tri*sodium diphosphate		E450(a)
*Tetra*sodium diphosphate		
*Tetra*potassium diphosphate		
*Penta*sodium triphosphate		E450(b)
*Penta*potasium triphosphate		
Sodium polyphosphates		E450(c)
Potassium polyphosphates		
Microcrystalline cellulose	α-cellulose, Powdered cellulose	E460
Methylcellulose		E461
Hydroxypropylcellulose		E463
Hydroxypropylmethylcellulose		E464
Ethylmethylcellulose		E465
Carboxymethylcellulose, sodium salt (CMC)		E466
Sodium, potassium and calcium salts of fatty acids		E470
Mono- and di-glycerides of fatty acids		E471
Acetic acid esters of mono- and di-glycerides of fatty acids		E472(a)
Lactic esters of mono- and di-glycerides of fatty acids	Lactoglycerides	E472(b)
Citric acid esters of mono- and dl-glycerides of fatty acids	Citroglycerides	E472(c)
Mono- and di-acetyltartaric acid esters of mono- and di-glycerides of fatty acids		E472(e)
Sucrose esters of fatty acids		E473
Sucroglycerides		E474
Polyglycerol esters of fatty acids		E475

Polyglycerol esters of polycondensed fatty acids of castor oil	Polyglycerol polyricinoleate	476
Propane-1,2-diol esters of fatty acids		E477
Lactylated fatty acid esters of glycerol and propane-1,2-diol		478
Sodium stearoyl-2-lactylate		E481
Calcium stearoyl-2-lactylate		E482
Stearoyl tartrate		E483
Sorbitan monostearate		491
Sorbitan tristearate		492
Sorbitan monolaurate		493
Sorbitan mon-eleate		494
Sorbitan monopalmitate		495

B.3 PERMITTED ACIDS, BASES AND SALTS

	Alternative name(s)	E number
Sodium bicarbonate	Bicarbonate of soda	500
Potassium carbonate and potassium hydrogen carbonate		501
Ammonium carbonate and ammonium hydrogen carbonate		503
Magnesium carbonate		504
Hydrochloric acid		507
Potassium chloride		508
Calcium chloride		509
Ammonium chloride		510
Sulphuric acid		513
Sodium sulphate		514
Potassium sulphate		515
Calcium sulphate		516
Magnesium sulphate		518
Sodium hydroxide		524
Potassium hydroxide		525
Calcium hydroxide		526
Ammonium hydroxide		527
Magnesium hydroxide		528
Calcium oxide		529
Magnesium oxide		530
Sodium ferrocyanide	Sodium hexacyanoferrate (II)	535
Potassium ferrocyanide	Potassium hexacyanoferrate (II)	537
Dicalcium diphosphate		540
Sodium aluminium phosphate		541
Edible bone phosphate		542

Calcium polyphosphates		544
Ammonium polyphosphates		545
Silicon dioxide	Silica	551
Calcium silicate		552
Magnesium silicate synthetic	Magnesium trisilicate	553(a)
Talc		553(b)
Aluminium sodium silicate		554
Aluminium calcium silicate		556
Bentonite		558
Kaolin		559
Stearic acid		570
Magnesium stearate		572
D-Glucono-1,5-lactone	Glucono δ-lactone	575
Sodium gluconate		576
Potassium gluconate		577
Calcium gluconate		578

B.4 PERMITTED FLAVOUR ENHANCERS

	Alternative name(s)	E number
L-Glutamic acid		620
Sodium hydrogen L-glutamate	*Mono*Sodium glutamate (MSG)	621
Potassium hydrogen L-glutamate	*Mono*Potassium glutamate	622
Calcium dihydrogen di-L-glutamate	Calcium glutamate	623
Guanosine 5'-(disodium phosphate)	Sodium guanylate	627
Inosine 5'-(disodium phosphate)	Sodium inosinate	631
Sodium 5'-ribonucleotide		635
Maltol		636
Ethyl maltol		637

B.5 PERMITTED PROCESSING AIDS

	Alternative name(s)	E number
Dimethylpolysiloxane		900
Beeswax		901
Carnauba wax		903
Shellac		904
Mineral hydrocarbons		905
Refined microcrystalline wax		907
L-Cysteine hydrochloride		920
Potassium bromate		924
Chlorine		925

Chlorine dioxide		926
Azodicarbonamide	Azoformamide	927

B.6 SELECTED PERMITTED PRESERVATIVES AND ANTIOXIDANTS

Preservative	E number
Sorbic acid	E200
Sodium, potassium, calcium sorbate	E201–203
Benzoic acid	E210
Sodium, potassium benzoate	E212–213
Hydroxybenzoates	E214–219
Sulphur dioxide	E220
Sodium sulphite, bisulphite, metabisulphite	E221–223
Diphenyl	E230
Nisin	234
Potassium and sodium nitrite	E249–250
Sodium and potassium nitrate	E251–252
Acetic acid	E260
Potassium, sodium hydrogen, sodium, calcium acetate	E261–263
Lactic acid	E270
Propianic acid	E280
Sodium, calcium, potassium propionate	E281–283
Carbon dioxide	E290
Malic acid	E296

Antioxidant	E number
Ascorbic acid	E300
Sodium and calcium ascorbate	E301–302
α-, γ-, δ-tocopherol	E307–309
Propyl-, octyl-, dodecyl gallate	E310–312
Butylated hydroxyanisole (BHA)	320
Butylated hydroxytoluene (BHT)	321
Lecithins	E322
Sodium, potassium, calcium lactate	E325–327
Citric acid	E330
Sodium, potasium, calcium citrate	E331–333
Tartaric acid	E334
Sodium, potassium, potassium sodium tartrate	E335–337
Phosphoric acid	E338
Sodium, potassium, calcium salts of phosphoric acid	E339–341
Sodium, postassium, calcium malate	350–352
Tartaric acid	353
Succinic acid	363
Nicotinic acid	375
Ammonium citrate, ammonium Perric citrate	380–381
Calcium disodium EBTA	385

Appendix C

Units and Dimensions

All physical properties are measured by a quantitative numerical value and a qualitative definition in terms of its dimensions. For example, in Table 1.4, the thermal conductivity of frozen beef is 1.3 W m^{-1} K^{-1}; 1.3 is the quantitative value and W m^{-1} K^{-1} is the qualitative definition. There are three main fundamental dimensions: mass (M), length (L) and time (T). Temperature (θ) is also accepted as a fourth dimension. Other properties are described by these four dimensions: for example density = mass/unit volume and has the dimensions ML^{-3}. Other examples are shown in Table C.1.

Table C.1 — Units and dimensions

Quantity	Unit name	Unit	Dimension
Mass	Kilogram	kg	M
Length, diameter	Metre	m	L
Time	Second	s	T
Temperature	Kelvin	K	θ
Derived units with a special name			
Force	Newton (N)	kg m s^{-2}	MLT^{-2}
Pressure	Pascal (Pa)	N m^{-2}	ML^{-1}T^{-2}
Energy	Joule (J)	N m	ML^{2}T^{-2}
Power	Watt (W)	J s^{-1}	ML^{2}T^{-3}
Frequency	Hertz (Hz)	Hz	T^{-1}
Absorbed dose of ionising radiation	Gray (Gy)	J kg^{-1}	L^{2}T^{-2}
Derived units without a special name			
Area		m^2	L^2
Volume		m^3	L^3
Density		kg m^{-3}	ML^{-3}
Specific gravity		None	None

Quantity	Unit	Dimension
Dynamic viscosity	$N\,s\,m^{-2}$	$ML^{-1}T^{-1}$
Kinematic viscosity	$m^2\,s^{-1}$	L^2T^{-1}
Enthalpy	$J\,kg^{-1}$	L^2T^{-2}
Specific heat	$J\,kg^{-1}\,K^{-1}$ (or °C)	$LT^{-2}\theta^{-1}$
Thermal conductivity	$W\,m^{-1}\,K^{-1}$ (or $W\,m^{-1}\,°C^{-1}$)	$MLT^{-3}\,\theta^{-1}$
Heat transfer coefficient	$W\,m^{-2}\,K^{-1}$ (or $W\,m^{-2}\,°C^{-1}$)	$MT^{-2}\theta^{-1}$
Velocity	$m\,s^{-1}$	LT^{-1}
Acceleration	$m\,s^{-2}$	LT^{-2}
Momentum	$kg\,m\,s^{-1}$	MLT^{-1}

Some combinations of physical properties produce ratios in which the dimensions cancel out. These are termed *dimensionless groups*. For example, the Reynolds number (Chapter 1) = (density × velocity of a liquid × diameter of the pipe)/ viscosity of the liquid. From table C.1 the dimensions are as follows:

$$\frac{L \times LT^{-1} \times ML^{-3}}{ML^{-1}T^{-1}}$$

The dimensions cancel and the Reynolds number is therefore dimensionless.

In the SI system, there are seven basic units of measurement:

(1) length (metres (m));
(2) mass (kilograms (kg));
(3) time (seconds (s));
(4) electric current (amperes (A));
(5) thermodynamic temperature (kelvins (K));
(6) luminous intensity (candela (Cd));
(7) amount of substance (mole).

In practice, degrees Celsius (°C) is often used in food processing instead of degrees kelvin (K). Other units are derived from these. Some have a special name, but most are expressed in basic units, as shown in Table C.1. Multiples of these units use the prefixes given in Table C.2.

Table C.2 — Prefixes in common use before units.

Prefix	Symbol	Multiple	Prefix	Symbol	Multiple
atto	a	10^{-18}	decca	da	10^1
femto	f	10^{-15}	hecto	h	10^2
pico	p	10^{-12}	kilo	k	10^3
nano	n	10^{-9}	mega	M	10^6
micro	μ	10^{-6}	giga	G	10^9
milli	m	10^{-3}	tera	T	10^{12}
centi	c	10^{-2}	peta	P	10^{15}
deci	d	10^{-1}	exa	E	10^{18}

A selection of conversion factors from imperial units to SI units is shown in Table C.3.

Table C.3 — Conversion factors.

Quantity	British (Imperial) system	SI
Length	1 ft	0.3048 m
Time	1 h	3.6 ks
Area	1 ft^2	0.09290 m^2
Volume	1 ft^3	0.02832 m^3
Mass	1 lb	0.4536 kg
Density	1 lb ft^{-3}	16.019 kg m^{-3}
Force	1 lbf	4.4482 N
Energy	1 Btu	1055.1 J
	1 cal	4.1868 J
Pressure	1 lbf in^{-2}	6894.8 Pa
	1 atm	1.0133×10^5 Pa
	1 torr	133.32 Pa
Power	1 Btu h^{-1}	0.29307 W
	1 hp	745.70 W
Velocity	1 ft s^{-1}	0.3048 m s^{-1}
Dynamic viscosity	1 P (poise)	0.1 N s m^{-2}
Kinematic viscosity	1 St (stokes)	10^{-4} m^2 s^{-1}
Specific heat	1 Btu lb^{-1} °F^{-1}	4.1868 kJ kg^{-1} K^{-1}
Thermal conductivity	1 Btu h^{-1} ft^{-1} °F^{-1}	1.7303 W m^{-1} K^{-1}
Heat transfer coefficient	1 Btu h^{-1} ft^{-2} °F^{-1}	5.6783 W m^{-2} K^{-1}
Mass transfer coefficient	1 lb ft^{-2} s^{-1}	1.3563 g m^{-2} s^{-1}
Temperature	°F	$\dfrac{5}{9}$ °C

Appendix D

Temperatures of Saturated Steam

The temperature of saturated steam at gauge pressures from 1 kPa to 199 kPa (from 0 lbf in^{-2} to 29 lbf in^{-2}) are given in Table D.1.

Table D.1 — Temperatures of saturated steam.

Temperature (°C)	Pressure (lbf in^{-2})	Pressure (kPa × 100)	Temperature (°C)	Pressure (lbf in^{-2})	Pressure (kPa × 100)
100.0	0	1.0	121.0	15	103.4
101.9	1	6.9	122.0	16	110.3
103.6	2	13.8	123.0	17	117.2
105.3	3	20.7	124.1	18	124.1
106.9	4	27.6	125.0	19	131.0
108.4	5	34.5	126.0	20	137.9
109.8	6	41.4	126.9	21	144.8
111.3	7	48.3	127.9	22	151.7
112.6	8	55.2	128.7	23	158.6
113.9	9	62.1	129.6	24	165.5
115.2	10	68.9	130.4	25	172.4
116.4	11	75.8	131.2	26	179.3
117.6	12	82.7	132.1	27	186.2
118.8	13	89.6	133.0	28	193.1
119.9	14	96.5	133.6	29	199.9

Appendix E

Sizes of Some Common UK Round Cans

The sizes of some round cans common in the UK are given in Table E.1, using the accepted notation (for example 201 means $2\frac{1}{16}$ in).

Table E.1 — Sizes of round cans

	Dimension							
	Diameter				Height			
Trade name	(mm)	Size	(in)	(mm)	Size	(in)		Capacity (ml)
Baby food	54	202	$2\frac{2}{16}$	71	213	$2\frac{53}{64}$		128
5 oz	68	211	$2\frac{11}{16}$	154	202	$2\frac{1}{8}$		156
6 oz evap	68	211	$2\frac{11}{16}$	59	205	$2\frac{5}{16}$		173
U8 handy	76	300	3	62	207	$2\frac{7}{16}$		224
Picnic	68	211	$2\frac{11}{16}$	78	301	$3\frac{1}{16}$		236
A1	68	211	$2\frac{11}{16}$	102	400	4		315
UT/tall	76	300	3	114	408	$4\frac{17}{32}$		446
1 lb flat	103	401	$4\frac{1}{16}$	119	212	$2\frac{3}{4}$		469
A2	87	307	$3\frac{7}{16}$	114	408	$4\frac{1}{2}$		574
$A2\frac{1}{2}$	103	401	$4\frac{1}{16}$	119	411	$4\frac{11}{16}$		843
A6	157	603	$6\frac{3}{16}$	152	600	6		2627
A10	157	603	$6\frac{3}{16}$	178	700	7		3096

Appendix F

Latent Heat of Vaporisation of Water

The latent heat of vaporisation of water is given in Table F.1.

Table F.1 — Latent heat of vaporisation of water

Temperature (°C)	Latent heat (J kg^{-1})
0	2.494×10^6
20	2.448×10^6
40	2.402×10^6
60	2.357×10^6
80	2.309×10^6
100	2.258×10^6

Index